Data Analysis with IBM SPSS Statistics

Implementing data modeling, descriptive statistics and ANOVA

Kenneth Stehlik-Barry

Anthony J. Babinec

Packt>

BIRMINGHAM - MUMBAI

Data Analysis with IBM SPSS Statistics

Copyright © 2017 Packt Publishing

All rights reserved. No part of this book may be reproduced, stored in a retrieval system, or transmitted in any form or by any means, without the prior written permission of the publisher, except in the case of brief quotations embedded in critical articles or reviews.

Every effort has been made in the preparation of this book to ensure the accuracy of the information presented. However, the information contained in this book is sold without warranty, either express or implied. Neither the authors, nor Packt Publishing, and its dealers and distributors will be held liable for any damages caused or alleged to be caused directly or indirectly by this book.

Packt Publishing has endeavored to provide trademark information about all of the companies and products mentioned in this book by the appropriate use of capitals. However, Packt Publishing cannot guarantee the accuracy of this information.

First published: September 2017

Production reference: 1190917

Published by Packt Publishing Ltd.
Livery Place
35 Livery Street
Birmingham
B3 2PB, UK.
ISBN 978-1-78728-381-7

www.packtpub.com

Credits

Authors
Kenneth Stehlik-Barry
Anthony J. Babinec

Reviewers
James Mott
James Sugrue

Commissioning Editor
Amey Varangaonkar

Acquisition Editor
Tushar Gupta

Content Development Editor
Tejas Limkar

Technical Editor
Dharmendra Yadav

Copy Editor
Manisha Sinha

Project Coordinator
Manthan Patel

Proofreader
Safis Editing

Indexer
Tejal Daruwale Soni

Graphics
Tania Dutta

Production Coordinator
Deepika Naik

About the Authors

Kenneth Stehlik-Barry, PhD, joined SPSS as Manager of Training in 1980 after using SPSS for his own research for several years. Working with others at SPSS, including Anthony Babinec, he developed a series of courses related to the use of SPSS and taught these courses to numerous SPSS users. He also managed the technical support and statistics groups at SPSS. Along with Norman Nie, the founder of SPSS and Jane Junn, a political scientist, he co-authored Education and Democratic Citizenship. Dr. Stehlik-Barry has used SPSS extensively to analyze data from SPSS and IBM customers to discover valuable patterns that can be used to address pertinent business issues. He received his PhD in Political Science from Northwestern University and currently teaches in the Masters of Science in Predictive Analytics program there.

Anthony J. Babinec joined SPSS as a statistician in 1978 after assisting Norman Nie, SPSS founder, in a research methods class at the University of Chicago. Anthony developed SPSS courses and trained many SPSS users. He also wrote many examples found in SPSS documentation and worked in technical support. Anthony led a business development effort to find products implementing then-emerging new technologies such as CHAID decision trees and neural networks and helped SPSS customers successfully apply them. Anthony uses SPSS in consulting engagements and teaches IBM customers how to use its advanced features. He received his BA and MA in sociology with a specialization in advanced statistics from the University of Chicago and teaches classes at the Institute for Statistics Education. He is on the Board of Directors of the Chicago Chapter of the American Statistical Association, where he has served in different positions including President.

Acknowledgement

A book such as this is always a collaboration that extends beyond the authors. We owe a depth of gratitude to many and we would like to begin by thanking our family members, Janis, Cassiopeia, Leila, and Thea Stehlik-Barry, Tony's wife Terri M. Long, and their children Gina and Anthony. Authoring a book inevitably takes time away from family and the patience of our spouses and children is much appreciated. We would also like to thank our late parents, Leo and Patricia Barry and Anthony and Dorothy Babinec. They fostered our love of learning and supported our scholastic pursuits during our youth.

We would also like to acknowledge the late Norman Nie, a founder of SPSS and highly regarded social scientist. Norman was an empirical researcher and SPSS was his tool as well as his creation. His use of SPSS for his own analysis led to many valuable additions to the software. Ken coauthored Education and Democratic Citizenship with Norman and Jane Junn. Tony was a teaching assistant and research assistant with Norman at the University of Chicago. Norman was a colleague, mentor, and a valued friend and is greatly missed.

The team at Packt was enormously helpful in bringing this book to fruition. Tejas Limkar, our most frequent contact person, brought enthusiasm and encouragement to the project and kept things on track. Tushar Gupta was instrumental in launching the book initially, and Dharmendra Yadav drove the final push to get it completed. We also thank those at Packt that worked behind the scenes to deal with the graphics, editing, proofing and productions tasks.

Finally, we would like thank Colin Shearer, our IBM/SPSS colleague who put us in touch with Tushar at Packt initially and our two reviewers, James Mott and James Sugrue. They are long term colleagues of the authors and have a very deep knowledge of SPSS Statistics. Their feedback helped to make this a better book. We also thank our many colleagues at SPSS Inc., who collectively over the years built SPSS Statistics into the great product it has become.

Kenneth Stehlik-Barry

Anthony J. Babinec

About the Reviewers

James Mott, Ph.D, is a senior education consultant with extensive experience in teaching statistical analysis, modeling, Data Mining and Predictive Analytics. He has over 30 years of experience using SPSS products in his own research including IBM SPSS Statistics, IBM SPSS Modeler, and IBM SPSS Amos. He has also been actively teaching these products to IBM/SPSS customers for over 30 years. In addition, he is an experienced historian with expertise in the research and teaching of 20th Century United States Political history and Quantitative Methods.

Specialties: Data Mining, Quantitative Methods, Statistical Analysis, Teaching and Consulting.

James Sugrue has been selling and supporting SPSS Statistics since 1982. He is currently the president of Channel Group Inc. Channel Group Inc. began in 1996 as the holding company for the SPSS Inc. operations in Argentina, Chile, Paraguay, Uruguay, Bolivia, and Mexico. In 1998, they acquired the Quantime Inc. (Quantum, Quanvert, and so on) operations in Latin America. They later became the regional overlay team for the SPSS Market Research product line (Dimensions, Data Collection) for all of Latin America and the Caribbean.

www.PacktPub.com

For support files and downloads related to your book, please visit www.PacktPub.com. Did you know that Packt offers eBook versions of every book published, with PDF and ePub files available? You can upgrade to the eBook version at www.PacktPub.com and as a print book customer, you are entitled to a discount on the eBook copy. Get in touch with us at service@packtpub.com for more details. At www.PacktPub.com, you can also read a collection of free technical articles, sign up for a range of free newsletters and receive exclusive discounts and offers on Packt books and eBooks.

Mapt

https://www.packtpub.com/mapt

Get the most in-demand software skills with Mapt. Mapt gives you full access to all Packt books and video courses, as well as industry-leading tools to help you plan your personal development and advance your career.

Why subscribe?

- Fully searchable across every book published by Packt
- Copy and paste, print, and bookmark content
- On demand and accessible via a web browser

Customer Feedback

Thanks for purchasing this Packt book. At Packt, quality is at the heart of our editorial process. To help us improve, please leave us an honest review on this book's Amazon page at https://www.amazon.com/dp/178728381X.

If you'd like to join our team of regular reviewers, you can email us at customerreviews@packtpub.com. We award our regular reviewers with free eBooks and videos in exchange for their valuable feedback. Help us be relentless in improving our products!

Table of Contents

Preface — 1
Chapter 1: Installing and Configuring SPSS — 7
    The SPSS installation utility — 8
        Installing Python for the scripting — 9
    Licensing SPSS — 11
        Confirming the options available — 14
    Launching and using SPSS — 15
    Setting parameters within the SPSS software — 16
    Executing a basic SPSS session — 17
    Summary — 21
Chapter 2: Accessing and Organizing Data — 23
    Accessing and organizing data overview — 24
    Reading Excel files — 25
    Reading delimited text data files — 28
    Saving IBM SPSS Statistics files — 30
    Reading IBM SPSS Statistics files — 32
    Demo - first look at the data - frequencies — 33
    Variable properties — 34
        Variable properties - name — 36
        Variable properties - type — 37
        Variable properties - width — 37
        Variable properties - decimals — 37
        Variable properties - label — 38
        Variable properties - values — 38
        Variable properties - missing — 39
        Variable properties - columns — 40
        Variable properties - align — 40
        Variable properties - measure — 40
        Variable properties - role — 41
        Demo - adding variable properties to the Variable View — 41
        Demo - adding variable properties via syntax — 42
        Demo - defining variable properties — 44
    Summary — 47

Chapter 3: Statistics for Individual Data Elements — 49
- Getting the sample data — 49
- Descriptive statistics for numeric fields — 50
  - Controlling the descriptives display order — 54
  - Frequency distributions — 55
- Discovering coding issues using frequencies — 57
  - Using frequencies to verify missing data patterns — 59
- Explore procedure — 60
  - Stem and leaf plot — 62
  - Boxplot — 63
  - Using explore to check subgroup patterns — 64
- Summary — 68

Chapter 4: Dealing with Missing Data and Outliers — 71
- Outliers — 72
  - Frequencies for histogram and percentile values — 72
  - Descriptives for standardized scores — 75
  - The Examine procedure for extreme values and boxplot — 76
  - Detecting multivariate outliers — 80
- Missing data — 84
  - Missing values in Frequencies — 85
  - Missing values in Descriptives — 86
  - Missing value patterns — 87
  - Replacing missing values — 90
- Summary — 92

Chapter 5: Visually Exploring the Data — 93
- Graphs available in SPSS procedures — 94
  - Obtaining bar charts with frequencies — 94
  - Obtaining a histogram with frequencies — 99
  - Creating graphs using chart builder — 103
  - Building a scatterplot — 103
  - Create a boxplot using chart builder — 108
- Summary — 111

Chapter 6: Sampling, Subsetting, and Weighting — 113
- Select cases dialog box — 113
  - Select cases - If condition is satisfied — 115
    - Example — 117
    - If condition is satisfied combined with Filter — 117
    - If condition is satisfied combined with Copy — 121

[ ]

If condition is satisfied combined with Delete unselected cases	122
The Temporary command	123
Select cases based on time or case range	124
Using the filter variable	126
Selecting a random sample of cases	126
Split File	129
Weighting	132
Summary	134

Chapter 7: Creating New Data Elements — 135

Transforming fields in SPSS	136
The RECODE command	137
Creating a dummy variable using RECODE	137
Using RECODE to rescale a field	141
Respondent's income using the midpoint of a selected category	142
The COMPUTE command	143
The IF command	146
The DO IF/ELSE IF command	148
General points regarding SPSS transformation commands	151
Summary	152

Chapter 8: Adding and Matching Files — 153

SPSS Statistics commands to merge files	154
Example of one-to-many merge - Northwind database	155
Customer table	156
Orders table	158
The Customer-Orders relationship	159
SPSS code for a one-to-many merge	160
Alternate SPSS code	162
One-to-one merge - two data subsets from GSS2016	163
Example of combining cases using ADD FILES	166
Summary	170

Chapter 9: Aggregating and Restructuring Data — 171

Using aggregation to add fields to a file	172
Using aggregated variables to create new fields	176
Aggregating up one level	178
Preparing the data for aggregation	182
Second level aggregation	185
Preparing aggregated data for further use	185
Matching the aggregated file back to find specific records	188

[ ]

Restructuring rows to columns	190
Patient test data example	192
Performing calculations following data restructuring	198
Summary	198

Chapter 10: Crosstabulation Patterns for Categorical Data — 201

Percentages in crosstabs	201
Testing differences in column proportions	205
Crosstab pivot table editing	209
Adding a layer variable	214
Adding a second layer	217
Using a Chi-square test with crosstabs	222
Expected counts	223
Context sensitive help	225
Ordinal measures of association	226
Interval with nominal association measure	228
Nominal measures of association	230
Summary	233

Chapter 11: Comparing Means and ANOVA — 235

SPSS procedures for comparing Means	236
The Means procedure	236
Adding a second variable	239
Test of linearity example	241
Testing the strength of the nonlinear relationship	244
Single sample t-test	246
The independent samples t-test	249
Homogeneity of variance test	250
Comparing subsets	251
Paired t-test	252
Paired t-test split by gender	254
One-way analysis of variance	257
Brown-Forsythe and Welch statistics	259
Planned comparisons	260
Post hoc comparisons	264
The ANOVA procedure	269
Summary	271

Chapter 12: Correlations — 273

Pearson correlations	275
Testing for significance	278
Mean differences versus correlations	279
Listwise versus pairwise missing values	280

Comparing pairwise and listwise correlation matrices	281
Pivoting table editing to enhance correlation matrices	282
Creating a very trimmed matrix	286
Visualizing correlations with scatterplots	287
Rank order correlations	289
Partial correlations	291
Adding a second control variable	294
Summary	295

Chapter 13: Linear Regression — 297

Assumptions of the classical linear regression model	298
Example - motor trend car data	299
Exploring associations between the target and predictors	300
Fitting and interpreting a simple regression model	304
Residual analysis for the simple regression model	309
Saving and interpreting casewise diagnostics	313
Multiple regression - Model-building strategies	317
Summary	323

Chapter 14: Principal Components and Factor Analysis — 325

Choosing between principal components analysis and factor analysis	326
PCA example - violent crimes	328
Simple descriptive analysis	329
SPSS code - principal components analysis	331
Assessing factorability of the data	332
Principal components analysis of the crime variables	336
Principal component analysis – two-component solution	340
Factor analysis - abilities	345
The reduced correlation matrix and its eigenvalues	347
Factor analysis code	351
Factor analysis results	352
Summary	359

Chapter 15: Clustering — 361

Overview of cluster analysis	362
Overview of SPSS Statistics cluster analysis procedures	363
Hierarchical cluster analysis example	365
Descriptive analysis	366
Cluster analysis - first attempt	366
Cluster analysis with four clusters	371
K-means cluster analysis example	378

[ ]

Descriptive analysis	379
K-means cluster analysis of the Old Faithful data	383
Further cluster profiling	387
Other analyses to try	388
Twostep cluster analysis example	389
Summary	400

Chapter 16: Discriminant Analysis — 401

Descriptive discriminant analysis	402
Predictive discriminant analysis	403
Assumptions underlying discriminant analysis	403
Example data	404
Statistical and graphical summary of the data	405
Discriminant analysis setup - key decisions	406
Priors	407
Pooled or separate	407
Dimensionality	407
Syntax for the wine example	408
Examining the results	409
Scoring new observations	422
Summary	424

Index — 425

Preface

SPSS Statistics is a software package used for logical batched and non-batched statistical analysis. Analytical tools such as SPSS can readily provide even a novice user with an overwhelming amount of information and a broad range of options to analyze patterns in the data. This book will have a comprehensive coverage of IBM's premier statistics and data analysis tool--IBM SPSS Statistics. It is designed for business professionals who wish to analyze their data. By the end of this book, you will have a firm understanding of the various statistical analysis techniques offered by SPSS Statistics, and be able to master its use for data analysis with ease.

What this book covers

Chapter 1, *Installing and Configuring SPSS*, covers the initial installation of SPSS and the configuration of the system for use on the user's machine.

Chapter 2, *Accessing and Organizing Data*, covers the process of opening various types of data files (Excel, CSV, and SPSS) in SPSS and performing some simple tasks, such as labeling data elements. It demonstrates how to save new versions of the data that incorporate the changes so that they are available for subsequent use.

Chapter 3, *Statistics for Individual Data Elements*, is about the tools in SPSS that are available for obtaining descriptive statistics for each field in a data file.

Chapter 4, *Dealing with Missing Data and Outliers*, focuses on assessing data quality with respect to missing information and extreme values. It also deals with the techniques that can be used to address these problems.

Chapter 5, *Visually Exploring the Data*, discusses topics such as histograms, bar charts, box and whisker plots, and scatter plots.

Chapter 6, *Sampling, Subsetting and Weighting*, describes the options available in SPSS for taking samples from a dataset, creating subgroups with the data, and assigning weights to individual rows.

Chapter 7, *Creating New Data Elements*, discusses when it is useful to define new data elements to support analysis objectives and the process involved in building these elements in SPSS.

Preface

Chapter 8, *Adding and Matching Files*, describes the process of combining multiple data files to create a single file for use in an analysis. Both appending multiple files and merging files to add information are addressed.

Chapter 9, *Aggregating and Restructuring Data*, is about two topics--changing the unit of analysis via aggregation, and restructuring the data from wide to long or long to wide to facilitate analysis.

Chapter 10, *Crosstabulation Patterns for Categorical Data*, covers descriptive and inferential analysis of categorical data in two-way and multi-way contingency tables.

Chapter 11, *Comparing Means and ANOVA*, is about descriptive and inferential analysis involving the mean of a variable across groups.

Chapter 12, *Correlations*, discusses descriptive and inferential analysis of associations involving numeric variables via the use of the Pearson correlation coefficient and some analogs.

Chapter 13, *Linear Regression*, covers using linear regression to develop predictions of numeric target variables.

Chapter 14, *Principal Components and Factor Analysis*, is about the use of principal components analysis and factor analysis to understand patterns among the variables.

Chapter 15, *Clustering*, covers methods to find groups in the data through analyzing the data rows.

Chapter 16, *Discriminant Analysis*, discusses using discriminant analysis to develop classifications involving categorical target variables.

What you need for this book

You will need: IBM SPSS Statistics 24 (or higher).

Here are the download links to the software:

- Trial
  https://www.ibm.com/analytics/us/en/technology/spss/spss-trials.html
- Info on subscription:
  https://www-01.ibm.com/software/analytics/subscriptionandsupport/spss.html

- Info on hardware specs:
  https://www.ibm.com/software/reports/compatibility/clarity-reports/report/html/osForProduct

You will also need Windows 10 or recent versions.

IBM SPSS Statistics is available via trial download. However, the trial period is something in the order of 14 days, which is probably too short.

IBM SPSS Statistics is available via annual single-user license and various other licenses, and relatively recently, via a subscription.

Price lists and terms probably vary by country.

IBM SPSS Statistics is packaged as Base plus optional modules. We made an effort to only use only elements of SPSS Base.

Detailed installation steps (software-wise) in theIBM SPSS Statistics installation documentation can be found
at http://www-01.ibm.com/support/docview.wss?uid=swg24041224.

Who this book is for

This book is designed for analysts and researchers who need to work with data to discover meaningful patterns but do not have the time (or inclination) to become programmers. We assume a foundational understanding of statistics such as one would learn in a basic course or two on statistical techniques and methods.

Conventions

In this book, you will find a number of text styles that distinguish between different kinds of information. Here are some examples of these styles and an explanation of their meaning. Code words in text, database table names, folder names, filenames, file extensions, pathnames, dummy URLs, user input, and Twitter handles are shown as follows: "we will focus on the `Extreme Values` table and the boxplot."

Preface

A block of code is set as follows:

```
FREQUENCIES VARIABLES=Price
  /FORMAT=NOTABLE
  /PERCENTILES=1.0 5.0 10.0 25.0 50.0 75.0 90.0 95.0 99.0
  /STATISTICS=MINIMUM MAXIMUM
  /HISTOGRAM
  /ORDER=ANALYSIS.
```

Any command-line input or output is written as follows:

```
RECODE quality (1 thru 3=0) (4 thru 5=1) INTO qualsatpos.
VARIABLE LABELS qualsatpos 'Satisfied with Quality.
```

New terms and **important words** are shown in bold. Words that you see on the screen, for example, in menus or dialog boxes, appear in the text like this: "In order to download new modules, we will go to **Files** | **Settings** | **Project Name** | **Project Interpreter**."

> Warnings or important notes appear like this.

> Tips and tricks appear like this.

Reader feedback

Feedback from our readers is always welcome. Let us know what you think about this book-what you liked or disliked. Reader feedback is important for us as it helps us develop titles that you will really get the most out of. To send us general feedback, simply email feedback@packtpub.com, and mention the book's title in the subject of your message. If there is a topic that you have expertise in and you are interested in either writing or contributing to a book, see our author guide at www.packtpub.com/authors.

Customer support

Now that you are the proud owner of a Packt book, we have a number of things to help you to get the most from your purchase.

Downloading the example code

You can download the example code files for this book from your account at `http://www.packtpub.com`. If you purchased this book elsewhere, you can visit `http://www.packtpub.com/support` and register to have the files emailed directly to you. You can download the code files by following these steps:

1. Log in or register to our website using your email address and password.
2. Hover the mouse pointer on the **SUPPORT** tab at the top.
3. Click on **Code Downloads & Errata**.
4. Enter the name of the book in the **Search** box.
5. Select the book for which you're looking to download the code files.
6. Choose from the drop-down menu where you purchased this book from.
7. Click on **Code Download**.

Once the file is downloaded, please make sure that you unzip or extract the folder using the latest version of:

- WinRAR / 7-Zip for Windows
- Zipeg / iZip / UnRarX for Mac
- 7-Zip / PeaZip for Linux

The code bundle for the book is also hosted on GitHub at `https://github.com/PacktPublishing/Data-Analysis-with-IBM-SPSS-Statistics`. We also have other code bundles from our rich catalog of books and videos available at `https://github.com/PacktPublishing/`. Check them out!

[5]

Errata

Although we have taken every care to ensure the accuracy of our content, mistakes do happen. If you find a mistake in one of our books-maybe a mistake in the text or the code- we would be grateful if you could report this to us. By doing so, you can save other readers from frustration and help us improve subsequent versions of this book. If you find any errata, please report them by visiting http://www.packtpub.com/submit-errata, selecting your book, clicking on the **Errata Submission Form** link, and entering the details of your errata. Once your errata are verified, your submission will be accepted and the errata will be uploaded to our website or added to any list of existing errata under the Errata section of that title. To view the previously submitted errata, go to https://www.packtpub.com/books/content/support and enter the name of the book in the search field. The required information will appear under the **Errata** section.

Piracy

Piracy of copyrighted material on the internet is an ongoing problem across all media. At Packt, we take the protection of our copyright and licenses very seriously. If you come across any illegal copies of our works in any form on the internet, please provide us with the location address or website name immediately so that we can pursue a remedy. Please contact us at copyright@packtpub.com with a link to the suspected pirated material. We appreciate your help in protecting our authors and our ability to bring you valuable content.

Questions

If you have a problem with any aspect of this book, you can contact us at questions@packtpub.com, and we will do our best to address the problem.

1
Installing and Configuring SPSS

If the SPSS Statistics package is not already available for you to use, you will need to start by installing the software. This section establishes the foundation to use this tool for data analysis. Even if the software is available on your computer, you will want to become familiar with setting up the environment properly in order to make the analyzing process efficient and effective.

It is also a good idea to run a basic SPSS job to verify that everything is working as it should and to see the resources that are provided by way of tutorials and sample datasets.

Before you can use IBM SPSS Statistics for data analysis, you will need to install and configure the software. Typically, an analyst or researcher will use their desktop/laptop to analyze the data and this is where the SPSS software will be installed.

> When you purchase the software, or obtain it through your organization, you will receive an executable with a name such as `SPSS_Statistics_24_win_64.exe`. The 64 in this file name indicates that the 64-bit version of the software was selected and version 24 of SPSS is being installed.

Running this `.exe` file will launch the installation process but prior to this, there are some things to consider. During the installation process, you will be asked where you want the files associated with SPSS to be stored. Most often, users will put the software in the same location that they use for other applications on their machine. This is usually the `C:Program Files` folder.

Installing and Configuring SPSS

Topics that will be covered in this chapter include the following:

- Running the SPSS installation utility
- Setting parameters during the installation process
- Licensing the SPSS software
- Setting parameters within the SPSS software
- Executing a basic SPSS session

The SPSS installation utility

To begin the installation, double-click on the installation `.exe` file that you downloaded. You should see a screen similar to the one shown in the following screenshot:

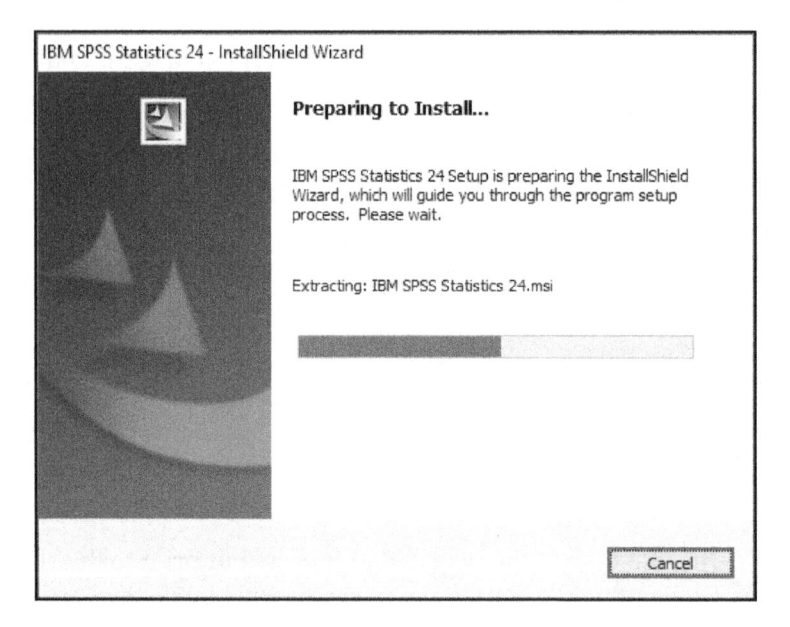

Once the extraction is finished, two license-related screens will appear. Click on **Next** on the first screen and, after accepting the license terms (read through them first if you want), click on **Next** again on the second screen to continue with the installation.

Installing and Configuring SPSS

Installing Python for the scripting

SPSS includes a scripting language that can be used to automate various processes within the software. While the scripting language will not be covered in this section, you may find it useful down the road.

The scripting is done via the Python language, and part of the installation process involves installing Python. The next three screens deal with installing Python and agreeing to the associated license terms. We recommend that you include Python as part of your basic software installation for SPSS. The following screenshot shows the initial screen where you indicate that the Python component is to be included in the installation:

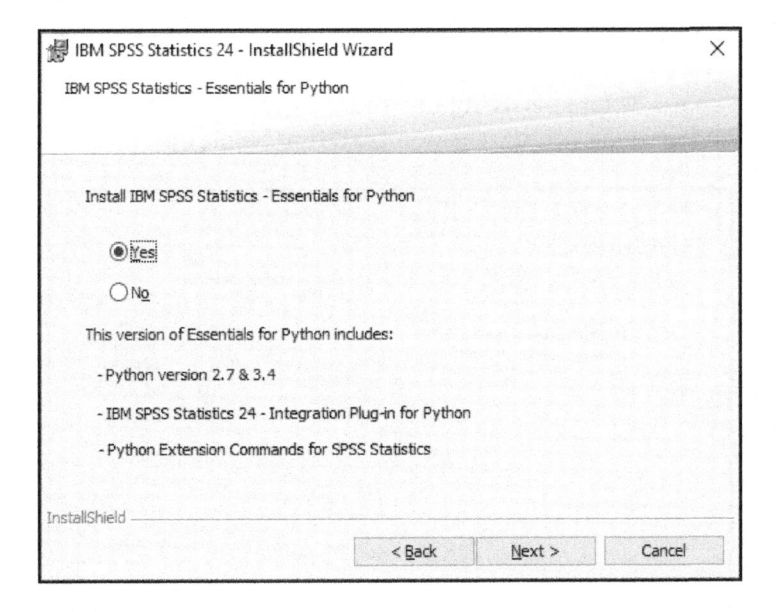

On the two following screens, accept the license terms for Python and click on **Next** to proceed.

[9]

Installing and Configuring SPSS

As part of the installation, you will be asked where to put the files associated with the SPSS software. By default, they will be placed in the `C:\Program Files\IBM\SPSS\Statistics\24` folder, where `24` refers to the version of the SPSS software that you are installing. You can change the location for these files using the **Browse** button but unless you have a compelling reason to do so, we recommend using the setting shown in the image after the paragraph.

> **TIP**: If you are concerned about having sufficient disk space on the `C:` drive, you can use the **Available Space** button to see how much free disk space is available.

Depending on the options you have licensed (SPSS consists of a base package along with options such as Advanced Statistics, Decision Trees, Forecasting, and so on), you may need up to 2 GB of disk space. After specifying the folder to use for the SPSS files, click on **Next** and, on the following screen, click on **Install** to begin the process:

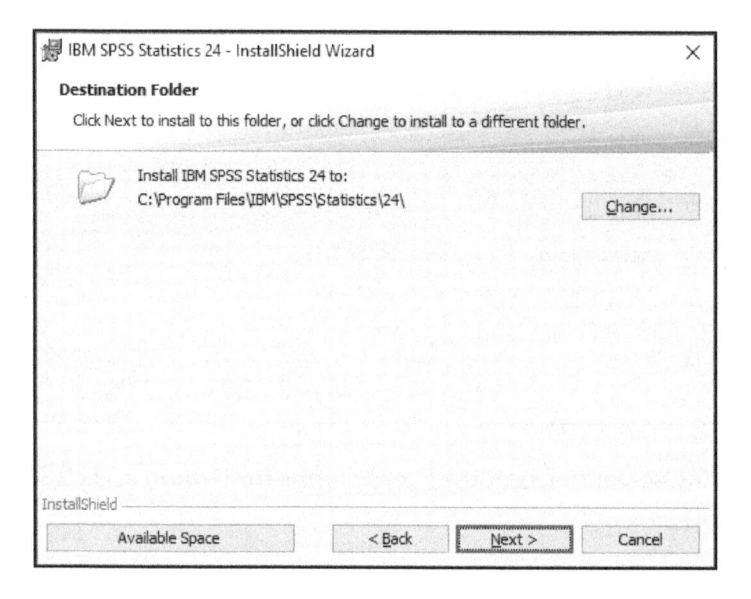

[10]

Installing and Configuring SPSS

The process of copying the files to the folder and performing the installation may take a couple of minutes. A screen displays the progress of the file copying step. Installing the Python component for use within SPSS results in a screen as shown in the following screenshot. There are no buttons associated with this screen, only a display of the files being compiled:

Licensing SPSS

When the screen titled **InstallShield Wizard Completed** appears, you can click on **Finish** to launch SPSS and perform the final step. SPSS uses an activation code to license the product after purchase. You should have obtained this code when you downloaded the software initially. It is typically a 20-character code with a mix of numbers and letters.

Installing and Configuring SPSS

On the screen shown in the following screenshot, click on **License Product** to initiate the authorization of the software:

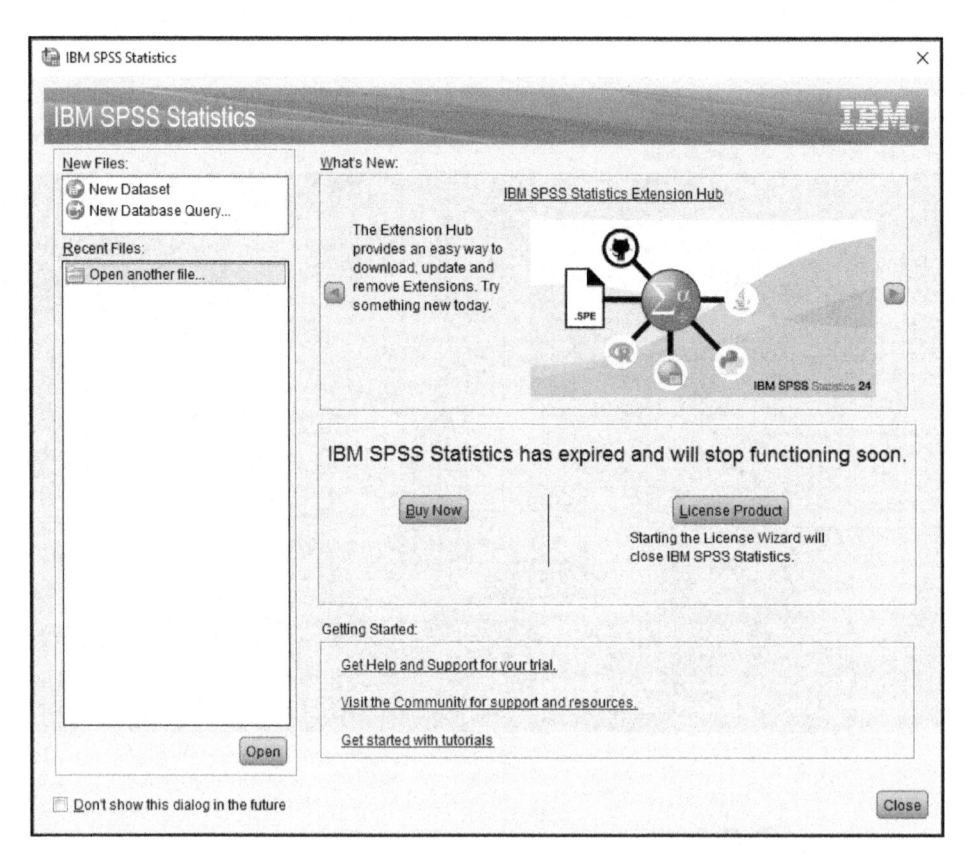

![IBM SPSS Statistics license screen showing New Files, Recent Files, What's New with Extension Hub information, a notice that "IBM SPSS Statistics has expired and will stop functioning soon" with Buy Now and License Product buttons, and Getting Started links.]

> **TIP**
> The SPSS home screen shown in the preceding screenshot contains several useful links that you may want to explore, such as the **Get started with tutorials** link at the bottom. If you no longer want to see this screen each time you launch SPSS, check the box at the lower left.

[12]

Use the **Next** button to proceed through this screen and the two following screens. The authorized user license choice on the last screen is the right choice, unless your organization has provided you with information for a concurrent user setup. If this is the case, change the setting to that option before proceeding.

The following screenshot shows the screen where you will enter your authorization code to activate the software via the Internet. While you can enter the code manually, it is easier to use copy/paste to ensure the characters are entered correctly.

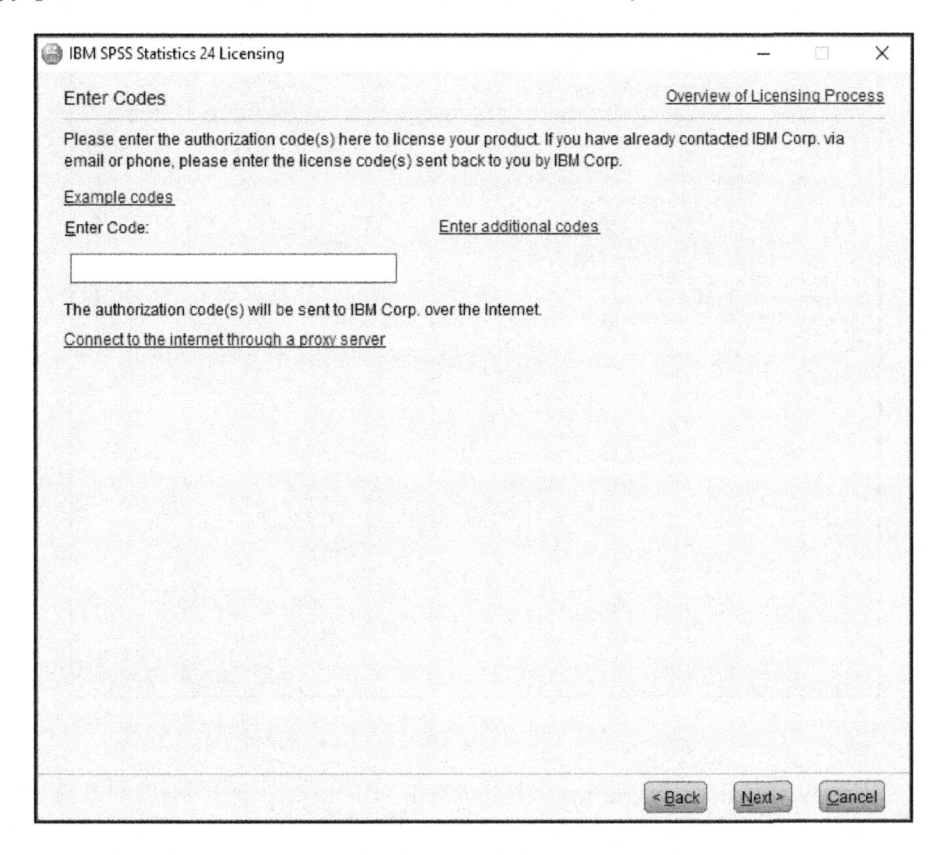

Installing and Configuring SPSS

Confirming the options available

The authorization code unlocks SPSS Statistics base along with any options that you are entitled to use. If your purchase included the **Forecasting** option, for example, there would be a **Forecasting** choice on the **Analyze** menu within the SPSS software. Some of the options included in the activation code used in this example are shown in the following screenshot:

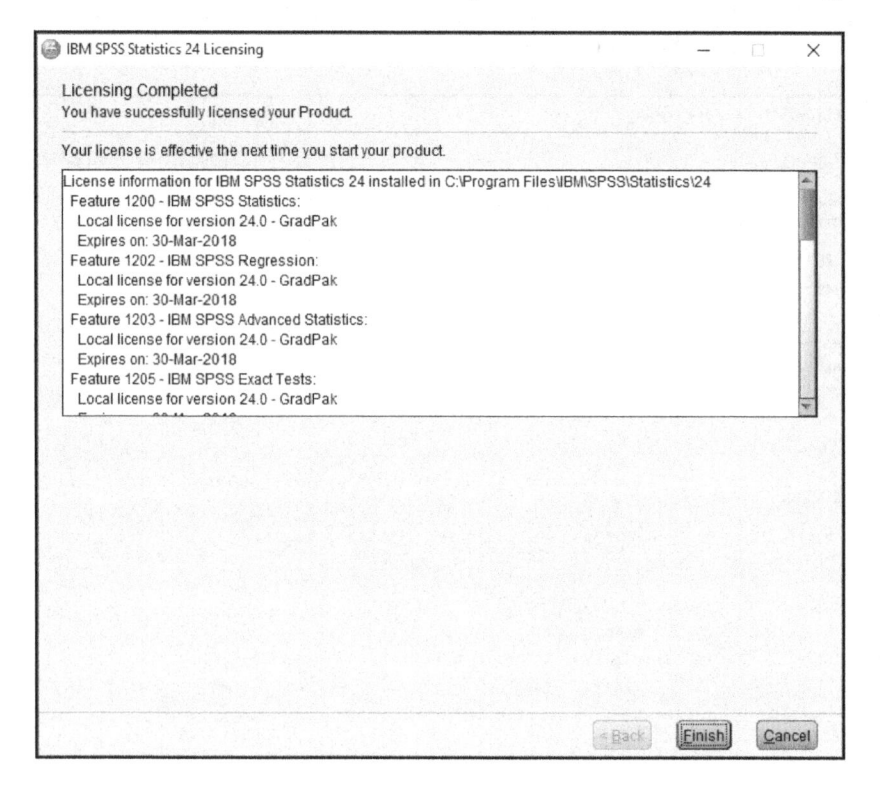

Scroll through the license information to see which options are included in your SPSS license.

> **TIP**
> In the installation example shown here, the user purchased the Grad Pack version of SPSS, which includes a specific set of options along with the base portion of the software. The expiration date for the license just entered is displayed as well.

[14]

Installing and Configuring SPSS

Launching and using SPSS

After reviewing the options that you have available, click on **Finish** to exit the installation process. Launch SPSS Statistics by going to the main Windows menu and finding it under **Recently added** in the upper left of the screen. The first screenshot shown under the licensing SPSS section is displayed initially. The tutorials included with SPSS can be accessed via the link on this screen, but they are also available via the **Help** menu within SPSS. Close this dialog box and the **SPSS Data Editor** window will be displayed.

The **Data Editor** window resembles a spreadsheet in terms of the layout, with the columns representing fields and the rows representing cases. As no data file has been loaded at this point, the window will have no content in the cells. Go to the **Edit** menu and select **Options** at the very bottom, as shown in the following screenshot:

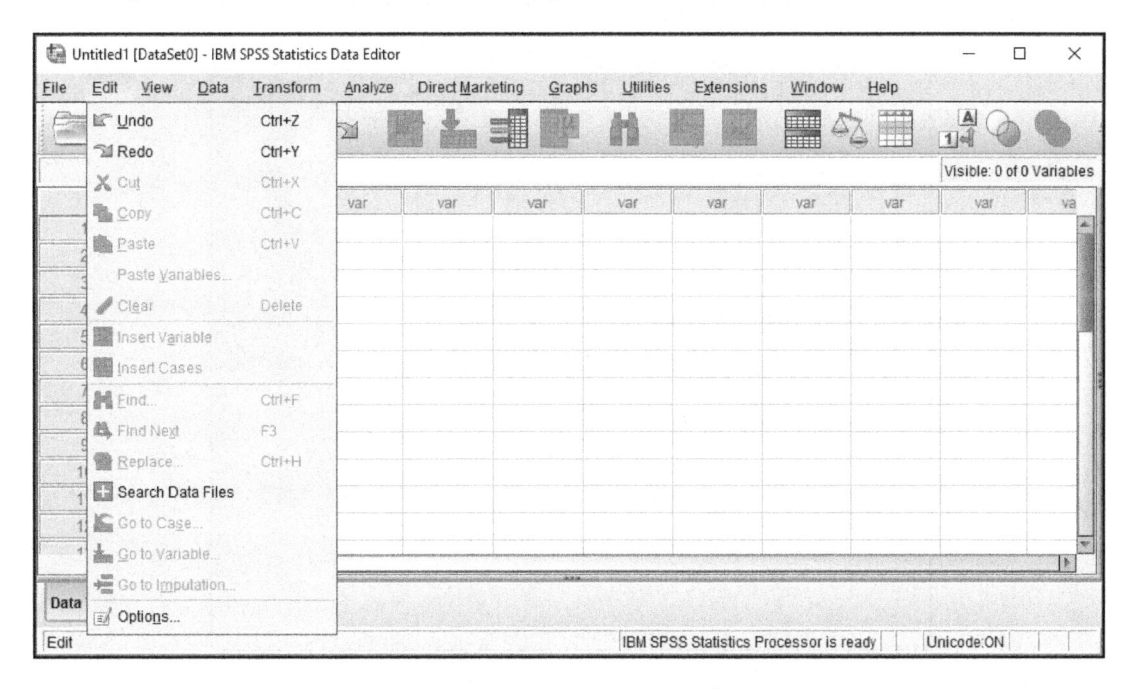

[15]

Installing and Configuring SPSS

Setting parameters within the SPSS software

The **General** tab, which is where some of the basic settings can be changed, is displayed. It is likely that you will not need to change any of these specifications initially, but at some point, you may want to alter these default settings. Click on the **File Locations** tab to display the dialog box in the following screenshot. Again, there is typically no need to change the settings initially, but be aware that SPSS creates temporary files during a session that are deleted when you exit the software.

If you are working with large volumes of data, you may need to direct these files to a location with more space, such as a network drive or an external device connected to your machine:

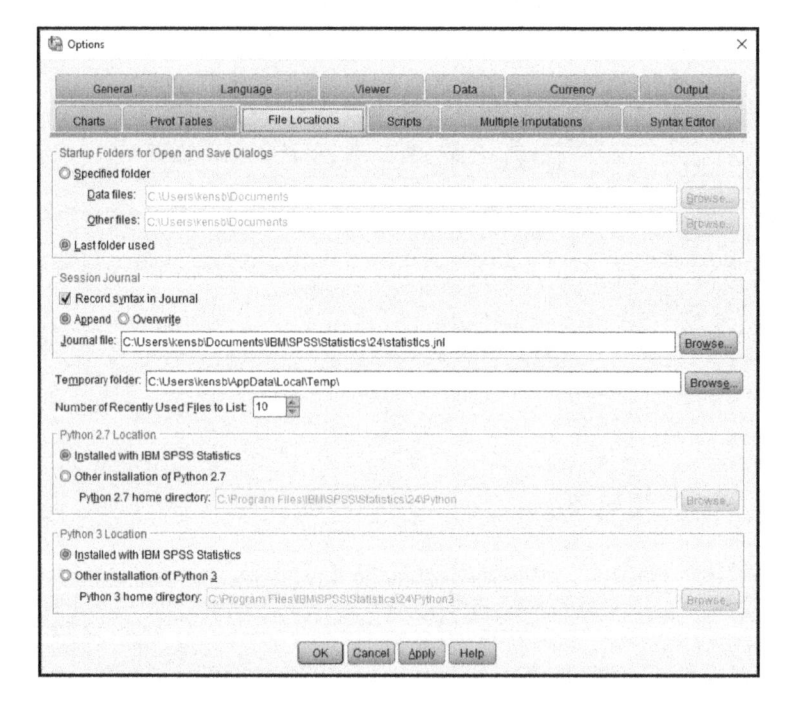

SPSS maintains a `Journal` file, which logs all the commands created as you move through various dialog boxes and make selections. This file provides an audit trail of sorts that can be quite useful. The file is set up to be appended and it is recommended that you keep this setting in place. As only the commands are logged in this file, it does not become very large, even over many months of using SPSS.

[16]

Executing a basic SPSS session

Click on **OK** to return to the **Data Editor** window. To confirm that the software is ready for use, go to the **File** menu and select **Open Data**. Navigate to the location where SPSS Statistics was installed, and down through the folders to the `SamplesEnglish` subfolder. The path shown here is typically where the sample SPSS data files that ship with the software get installed:

`C:Program FilesIBMSPSSStatistics24SamplesEnglish`

A list of sample SPSS data files (those with a `.sav` extension) will be displayed. For this example, select the `bankloan.sav` file, as shown in the following screenshot, and click on **Open**:

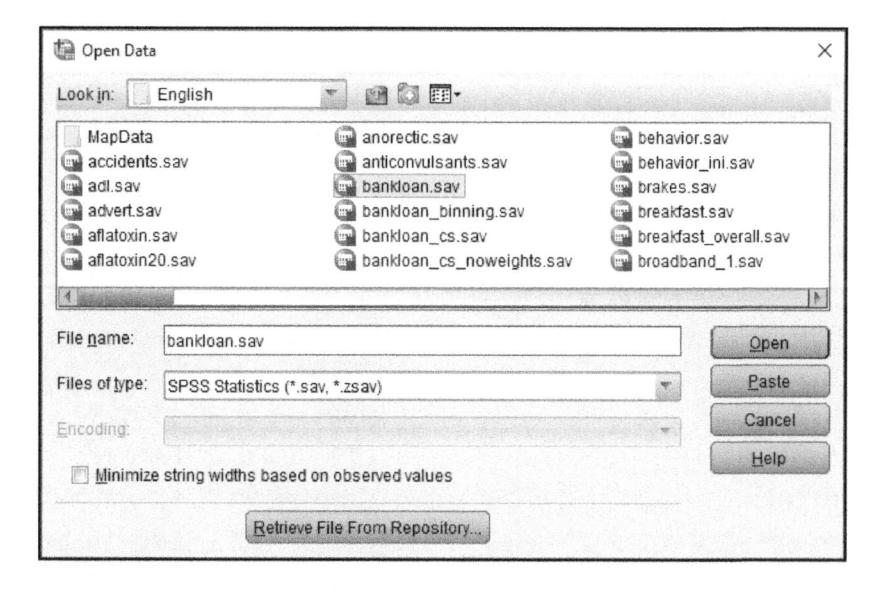

The **Data Editor** window now displays the name of the file just opened in the title bar with the fields (variables in SPSS terminology) as the column names and the actual values in the rows. Here, each row represents a bank customer and the columns contain their associated information. Only the first 12 rows are visible in the following screenshot, but after scrolling down, you will see more.

Installing and Configuring SPSS

There are 850 rows in total:

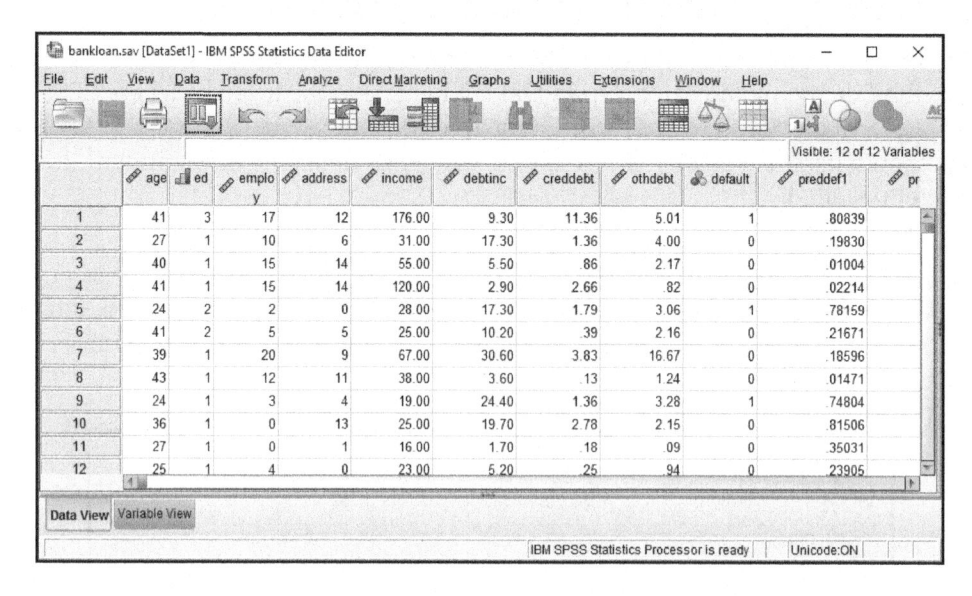

Go to the **Analyze** menu and select **Descriptive Statistics | Frequencies**, as shown in the following screenshot:

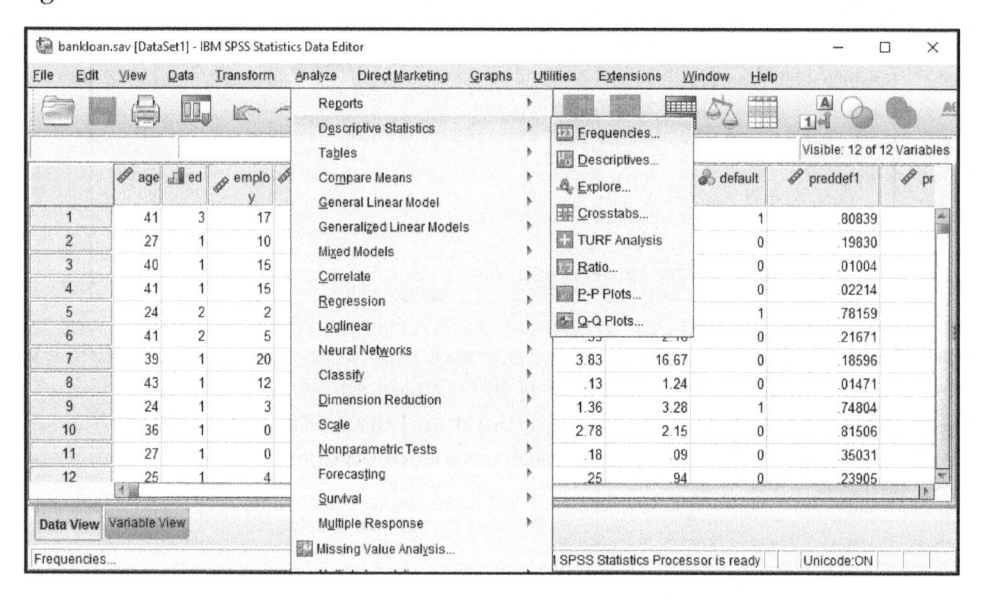

[18]

Installing and Configuring SPSS

> **TIP**
>
> The **Frequencies** dialog box shown here has a **Bootstrap** button on the lower right. This is present because the license used for this installation included the **Bootstrap** option, which results in this added feature appearing in appropriate places within SPSS.

The dialog box shown in the previous image allows you to select fields and obtain basic descriptive statistics for them.

For this initial check of the software installation, select just the education field, which is shown by its label, **Level of education**, as shown in the following screenshot. You can double-click on the label or highlight it and use the arrow in the middle of the screen to make the selection:

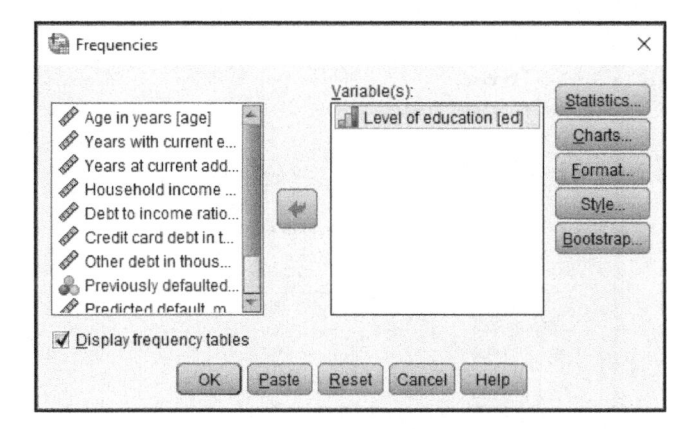

The descriptive statistics requested for the education field are presented in a new output window as shown in the following image. The left side of the output window is referred to in SPSS as the **navigation pane** and it lists the elements available for viewing in the main portion of the window. The frequency table for education shows that there are five levels of education present in the data for the bank's customers and that over half, 54.1%, of these 850 customers did not complete high school. This very simple example will confirm that the SPSS Statistics software is installed and ready to use on your machine.

Installing and Configuring SPSS

Refer to the following image for a better understanding of descriptive statistics and the navigation pane:

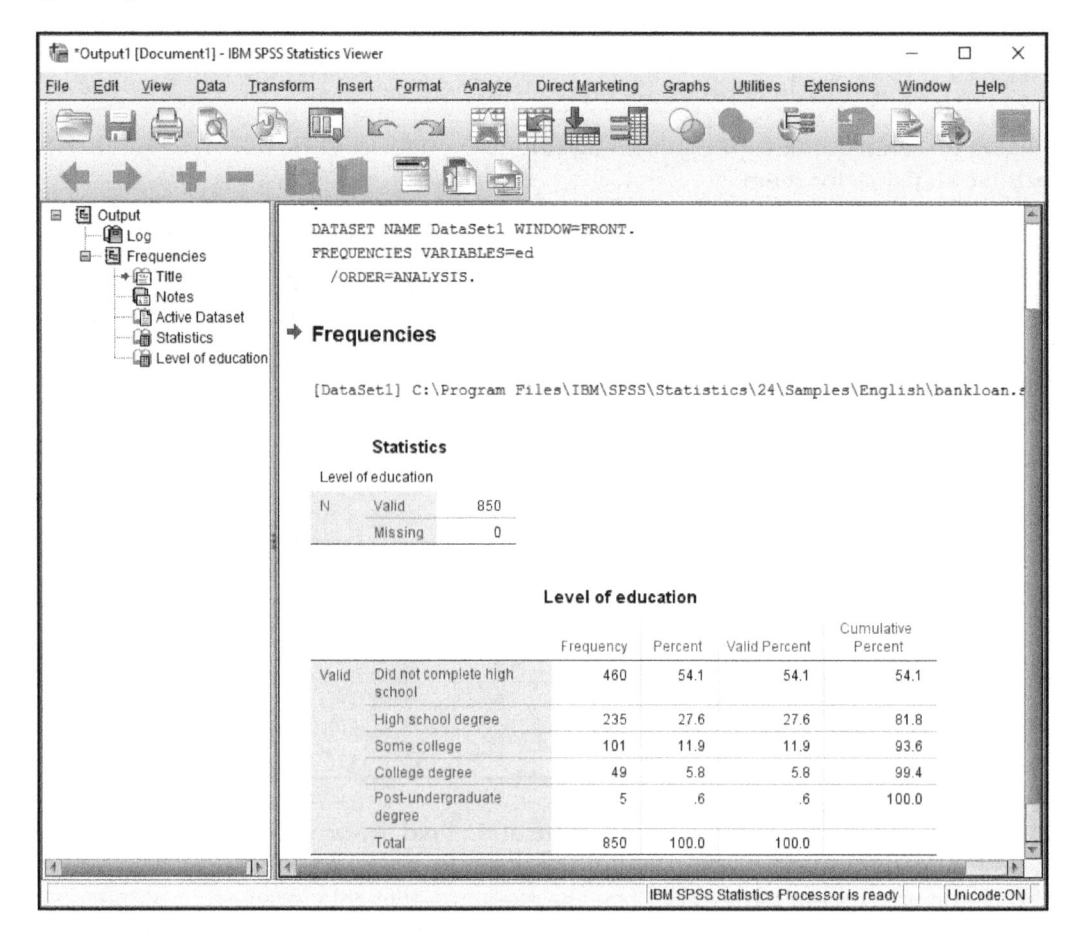

![SPSS Statistics Viewer output window showing Frequencies output for Level of education variable]

```
DATASET NAME DataSet1 WINDOW=FRONT.
FREQUENCIES VARIABLES=ed
  /ORDER=ANALYSIS.
```

Frequencies

[DataSet1] C:\Program Files\IBM\SPSS\Statistics\24\Samples\English\bankloan.s

Statistics

Level of education

N	Valid	850
	Missing	0

Level of education

		Frequency	Percent	Valid Percent	Cumulative Percent
Valid	Did not complete high school	460	54.1	54.1	54.1
	High school degree	235	27.6	27.6	81.8
	Some college	101	11.9	11.9	93.6
	College degree	49	5.8	5.8	99.4
	Post-undergraduate degree	5	.6	.6	100.0
	Total	850	100.0	100.0	

To complete this check of the installation process, go to the **File** menu and select **Exit** at the bottom. You will be prompted to save the newly-created output window, which was automatically assigned the name, ***Output1**. There is no need to save the results of the frequency table that was created, but you can do so if you like.

> The title bar of the output window shows the name ***Output1**, which was generated automatically by SPSS. The * indicates that the window contains material that has not been saved.

Summary

In this first chapter, we covered the basic installation of IBM SPSS Statistics on a local machine running Windows. The standard install includes the Python scripting component and requires licensing the software via the Internet. Although the default setting for things like files and display options were not modified, you saw how these elements can be changed later if there is a need to do so.

Once SPSS was up and running, the software was launched and a very basic example was covered. This should give you a sense of how to get started analyzing your own as well as confirm that everything is functioning as expected in terms of using the tool.

Congratulations! You are now ready to begin exploring the capabilities of SPSS Statistics on your data or using one if the sample data sets such as the one used in the sample session above. Be sure to take advantage of the tutorials within the Help system to facilitate the process of learning SPSS.

2
Accessing and Organizing Data

This chapter shows you how to read common file formats such as an Excel sheet or a delimited text file to IBM SPSS Statistics. The rationale for showing the reading of these formats is that most software programs read these file formats. In addition, many analysts use Excel for simple data activities such as data handling and producing charts. However, beyond these simple activities, Excel is limited in the data analytic capabilities it provides, so researchers have turned to IBM SPSS Statistics for its extensive statistical and analytical capabilities.

In order to use IBM SPSS Statistics, you must first read your data to the IBM SPSS Statistics Data Editor window. Once you successfully read the data, you provide variable properties to enrich the description of the data. After you have established the variable properties for the variables in your file, you have set the stage to produce informative statistical analyses and charts.

We will cover the following topics in this chapter:

- Accessing and organizing data overview
- Reading Excel files
- Reading delimited text files
- Saving IBM SPSS Statistics files
- Reading IBM SPSS Statistics files
- Looking at the data with frequencies
- Specifying variable properties

Accessing and organizing data overview

Once you read the data to IBM SPSS Statistics, you should at least do a cursory **data check** of the inputted data. Do you see numeric data? String data? Is the data in the expected scale and range? Is the data complete?

Of course, even if your data is not really very large in either the number of rows or columns, it can be difficult to assess via a simple visual inspection. For this reason, you might use SPSS Statistics to produce a tabular summary of variables showing counts and percentages. Doing so produces tables showing all the data codes in the designated variables. Once you have defined the SPSS Variable Properties such as value labels, you can control the tabular display to show data values (the data codes), value labels, or both.

A further consideration is how the data values are represented for categorical variables. Let's consider Respondent's Sex as an example.

Your categorical values in an Excel spreadsheet could be string values such as `male` or `female`. If so, then IBM SPSS Statistics can read these values.

> However, it is a common practice in the survey research community to use numeric codes to represent categories. In general, use sequential numbers starting from 1 to enumerate the categories. In this example, the data codes would be 1 and 2, although assignment to the genders of male and female is arbitrary. Say that males are represented by a 1 code and females are represented by a 2 code.

A drawback of using numeric codes is that tabular summaries such as a summary table of counts will list the number of 1s and 2s, but the reader would not know that **1** represents male and **2** represents female. The way to handle this situation is to use value labels, one of a number of Variable Properties you can define after successfully reading the data.

Another consideration is: what if Respondent's Sex is not known for a specific individual? If the variable is a string variable, you could represent an unknown value of Respondent's Sex as a string value such as 'unknown', or you might represent the absence of information with a string of blanks such as ' '.

If Respondent's Sex is a numeric field, an unknown value could be represented by a distinct number code such as **3**, assuming that males and females would be represented by **1** and **2**, respectively. In either situation, you would like your summary tables and statistics to take into account the absence of information indicated in the values 'unknown' or 3. The way to handle this situation is to use the **missing values** command. There is more on this next.

Accessing and Organizing Data

Value labels and missing values are two examples of **variable properties**, which are properties internal to IBM SPSS Statistics that are associated with each variable in the data. You can save these properties along with the data. When added, these properties inform the analysis and display of data in IBM SPSS Statistics. For example, for a variable indicating Sex of Respondent, value labels could provide gender labels 'male' and 'female' that would clarify which data code represented which gender. Or, by defining data codes as missing values, you would insure that SPSS Statistics excluded these cases from the calculation of valid percent's, for example.

> **Menus versus syntax**
> The examples in this chapter start from the menus but suggest the use of the **Paste** button to paste constructed syntax to the Syntax window. In the syntax window, you can run the just-pasted syntax. We discuss elements of the syntax, but encourage you to use the **Help** button to learn more about individual commands.

Reading Excel files

Here is a snapshot of a portion of an Excel spreadsheet:

	A	B	C	D	E
1	ID_	MARITAL	AGE	HAPPY	SEX
2	1	3	53	1	m
3	2	1	26	1	f
4	3	3	59	3	m
5	4	1	56	1	f
6	5	1	74	1	f
7	6	1	56	2	f
8	7	1	63	2	m
9	8	1	34	1	m
10	9	5	37	3	f

Note that row 1 of the Excel spreadsheet is a header row containing variable names for the columns.

> When working with Excel spreadsheets or delimited text files, use row **1** of the file to supply variable names that you intend to use in SPSS Statistics.

[25]

Accessing and Organizing Data

IBM SPSS Statistics can directly read an Excel sheet. There are different implementations in different recent releases of IBM SPSS Statistics but, in general, the capability exists on the **File** menu. In IBM SPSS Statistics 24, use the following path:

File | Import Data

Here is the **Read Excel File** dialog box:

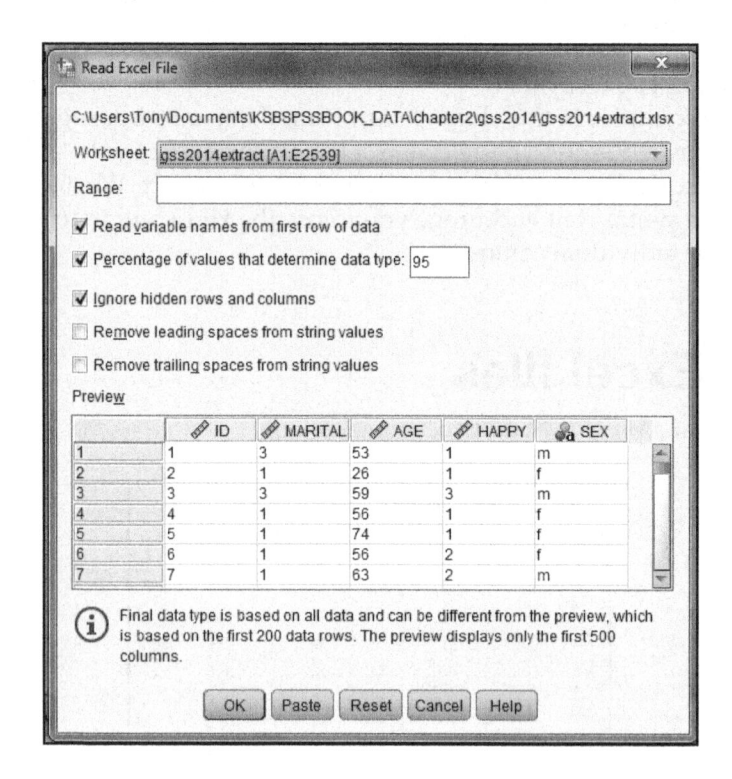

By default, IBM SPSS Statistics shows the entire range of data that it encounters in the Excel sheet. You can use the **Range** portion of the dialog box to specify a subset range. Also by default, IBM SPSS Statistics expects to find variable names in the first row of data. Additional checkboxes exist, but the default settings will work for the Excel file that we are analyzing. Finally, click on **OK** to read the file, or click on **Paste** to paste the constructed syntax to the syntax window.

Accessing and Organizing Data

Here is the pasted syntax (IBM SPSS Statistics version 24):

```
GET DATA
  /TYPE=XLSX
/FILE='C:\Users\Tony\Documents\KSBSPSSBOOK_DATA\chapter2\gss2014\gss2014ext
ract.xlsx'
  /SHEET=name 'gss2014extract'
  /CELLRANGE=FULL
  /READNAMES=ON
  /DATATYPEMIN PERCENTAGE=95.0
  /HIDDEN IGNORE=YES.
EXECUTE.
DATASET NAME DataSet1 WINDOW=FRONT.
```

The subcommands have a close correspondence with the dialog box settings in the **Read Excel File** dialog box. Note that the command is the GET DATA command, and the /TYPE subcommand specifies that the input file is an XLSX file. Note that the slash (/) is used to separate subcommands. The /SHEET subcommand points to the particular worksheet. /CELLRANGE tells IBM SPSS Statistics to read the full range of data. /READNAMES tells IBM SPSS Statistics that the first row is a header row.

The EXECUTE command in the above pasted syntax reads the active dataset and causes execution of any pending commands.

Finally, the DATASET NAME command assigns the name **Dataset1** to the active dataset and brings the SPSS Statistics Data Editor window to the front.

Running the indicated syntax populates an **IBM SPSS Statistics Data Editor** window with the data, as displayed in the following screenshot:

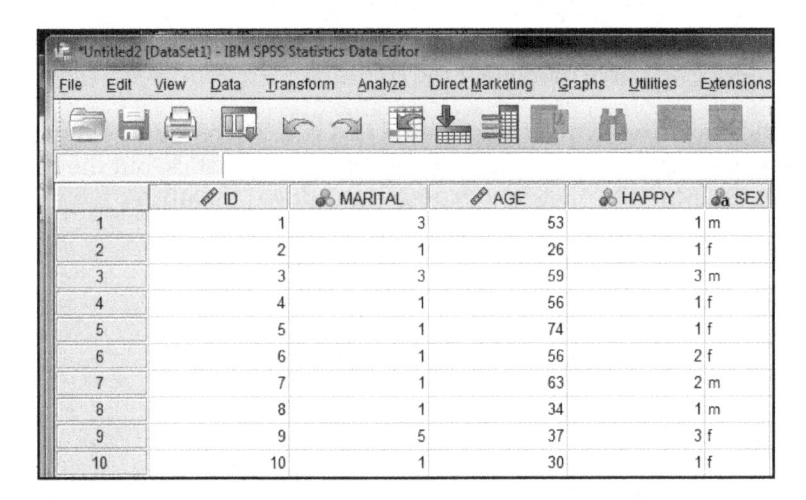

	ID	MARITAL	AGE	HAPPY	SEX
1	1	3	53	1	m
2	2	1	26	1	f
3	3	3	59	3	m
4	4	1	56	1	f
5	5	1	74	1	f
6	6	1	56	2	f
7	7	1	63	2	m
8	8	1	34	1	m
9	9	5	37	3	f
10	10	1	30	1	f

Accessing and Organizing Data

IBM SPSS Statistics uses the variable names in the header row with one minor change--the variable name **ID_** in the header row of the Excel sheet is automatically changed to **ID**. This is covered in the section with the rules to name variables.

Reading delimited text data files

Here is a snapshot of a portion of a comma-delimited text file:

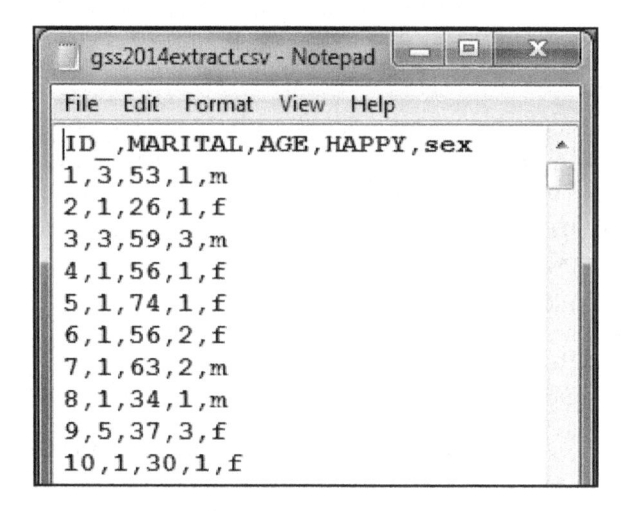

```
gss2014extract.csv - Notepad
File  Edit  Format  View  Help
ID_ ,MARITAL,AGE,HAPPY,sex
1,3,53,1,m
2,1,26,1,f
3,3,59,3,m
4,1,56,1,f
5,1,74,1,f
6,1,56,2,f
7,1,63,2,m
8,1,34,1,m
9,5,37,3,f
10,1,30,1,f
```

A **delimiter** is a character such as a comma that serves as a separator between elements across a line of data. A **text file** is a kind of computer file that is structured as a sequence of lines of electronic text, often using the ASCII character set. Such a file is easily viewed in Windows accessories such as Notepad. Note that row 1 of the comma-delimited text file is a header row containing variable names for the columns.

IBM SPSS Statistics can directly read a delimited text file. There are different implementations in different recent releases of IBM SPSS Statistics, but the capability exists on the **File** menu. In IBM SPSS Statistics 24, use the following path:

File | Import Data

Accessing and Organizing Data

Here is the **Read CSV File** dialog box:

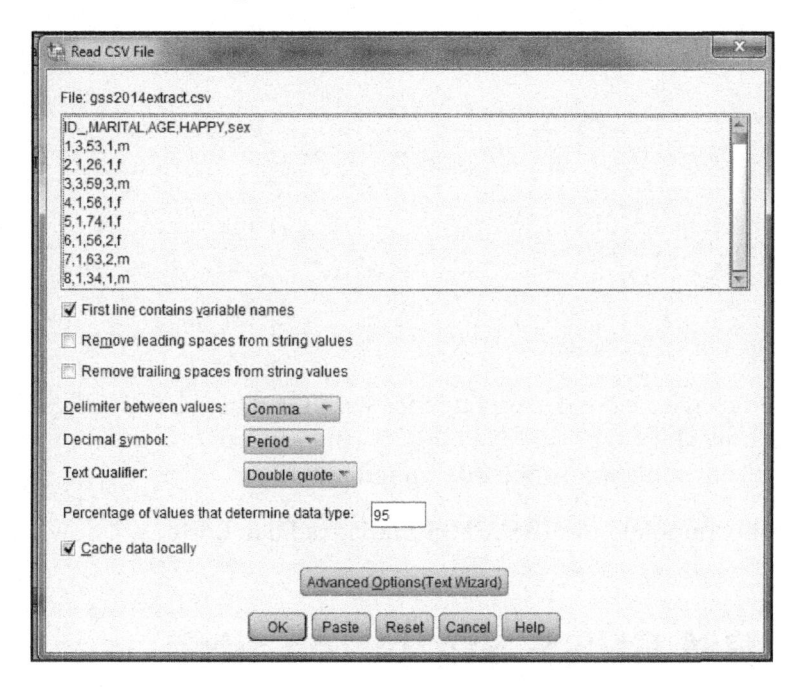

The **Read CSV File** dialog box shows the name of the file and a literal listing of what it reads from the first lines of the source file.

By default, IBM SPSS Statistics expects to find variable names in the first row of data--the checkbox for **First line contains variable names** is checked by default. Additional checkboxes exist as well as drop bars to specify the delimiter character, **Decimal Symbol**, and **Text Qualifier**. An **Advanced Options** button invokes a **Text Wizard** with additional capability to read text files formatted in a variety of ways. Here, the default settings shown in the **Read CSV File** dialog box will work for the delimited text file we are analyzing. Finally, click on **OK** to read the file, or click on **Paste** to paste the constructed syntax to the syntax window.

Here is the pasted syntax (IBM SPSS Statistics version 24):

```
PRESERVE.
SET DECIMAL DOT.
GET DATA  /TYPE=TXT
/FILE="C:\Users\Tony\Documents\KSBSPSSBOOK_DATA\chapter2\gss2014\gss2014ext
ract.csv"
  /ENCODING='UTF8'
  /DELIMITERS=","
  /QUALIFIER='"'
```

[29]

Accessing and Organizing Data

```
    /ARRANGEMENT=DELIMITED
    /FIRSTCASE=2
    /DATATYPEMIN PERCENTAGE=95.0
    /VARIABLES=
    ID AUTO
    MARITAL AUTO
    AGE AUTO
    HAPPY AUTO
    sex AUTO
    /MAP.
RESTORE.
CACHE.
EXECUTE.
DATASET NAME DataSet1 WINDOW=FRONT.
```

The subcommands have a close correspondence with the dialog box settings in the **Read CSV File** dialog box. The /TYPE, /ARRANGEMENT, and /DELIMITERS subcommands establish that the source file is a comma-delimited text file.

Running the syntax populates an **IBM SPSS Statistics Data Editor** window with the data.

Saving IBM SPSS Statistics files

Use the SAVE command to save a data file in the IBM SPSS Statistics format, which contains data plus a **dictionary**. The dictionary contains a name for each variable, plus variable metadata (variable properties) such as assigned variable labels, value labels, missing values, and formats. As an aside, the dictionary also contains text that was specified on the DOCUMENTS command, if this command is used.

To save the data file along with variable properties from the menus, specify as follows:

File | Save

This brings up the **Save Data As** dialog box:

At a minimum, specify the folder in which you wish to save the file, along with a filename. Then press either **Paste** to paste the syntax or **Save** to write the file to disk. In addition, you can use the **Variables...** button to select variables to keep or drop.

Here is an example of the pasted syntax:

```
SAVE
OUTFILE='C:\Users\Tony\Documents\KSBSPSSBOOK_DATAchapter2\gss2014\myfile.sav'
  /COMPRESSED.
```

Mark and run the pasted syntax to save the IBM SPSS Statistics data file.

> The SPSS Statistics `SAV` file is the native file format of IBM SPSS Statistics. One advantage of this format is that you can read the file directly and do not need any knowledge of its internal structure. The `SPSS Statistics` file contains the data in binary form along with variable names, formats, and other variable properties.

Reading IBM SPSS Statistics files

The IBM SPSS Statistics file is a data file created and saved in IBM SPSS Statistics. This file contains data in binary form, variable names, and other variable properties, and is directly readable by IBM SPSS Statistics.

In IBM SPSS Statistics 24, use **File** | **Open** | **Data**.

Here is the **Open Data** dialog box:

Click on **OK** to read the file, or click on **Paste** to paste the constructed syntax to the syntax window.

Here is the constructed syntax:

```
GET
FILE='C:\Users\Tony\Documents\KSBSPSSBOOK_DATA\chapter2\gss2014\gss2014extr
act170113.sav'.
DATASET NAME DataSet1 WINDOW=FRONT.
```

Running the syntax populates an **IBM SPSS Statistics Data Editor** window with the data.

Accessing and Organizing Data

Demo - first look at the data - frequencies

The GSS 2014 data extract has 2,538 rows. You can inspect the data by visually scanning and scrolling through the data window, but the sample size makes it difficult to grasp all of the data at once. For example, how many unique values are there in a given variable? Do the values in a given variable occur with about the same frequency, or do certain values predominate? Running Frequencies on the data can serve as a useful first look because it produces summary tables that show all data values on the specified variables.

To run **Frequencies** from the menus, specify as follows:

Analyze | Descriptive Statistics | Frequencies

This opens the **Frequencies** dialog box.

Move all variables except ID from the left-hand side to the right-hand side variable list. Why leave out ID? This is because the resulting frequency table is quite lengthy.

> **TIP**: Variables such as **ID** or **INCOME** measured in actual amounts can have many unique values. For this reason, you might choose to NOT display them in **Frequencies** as the resulting table can be very lengthy.

Press **Paste** to paste the syntax to a syntax window. Here is the syntax:

```
FREQUENCIES VARIABLES=MARITAL AGE HAPPY SEX
  /ORDER=ANALYSIS.
```

Mark and run the command.

To illustrate data inspection, consider the frequency table for **MARITAL**:

MARITAL

		Frequency	Percent	Valid Percent	Cumulative Percent
Valid	1	1158	45.6	45.6	45.6
	2	209	8.2	8.2	53.9
	3	411	16.2	16.2	70.1
	4	81	3.2	3.2	73.2
	5	675	26.6	26.6	99.8
	9	4	.2	.2	100.0
	Total	2538	100.0	100.0	

The frequency table shows all data codes that occur in the variable. For each code, the table shows the following points:

- **Frequency**: The number of occurrences of the code
- **Percent**: The percentage of cases having a particular value
- **Valid Percent**: The percentage of cases having a particular value when only cases with non-missing values are considered
- **Cumulative Percent**: The percentage of cases with non-missing data that have values less than or equal to a particular value

This data follows the survey research convention for categorical data--there are as many data codes as there are response categories, and there are also data codes to represent different types of non-responses. The data codes of **1** through **5** correspond to various marital statuses such as married, single, and so on, and the data code of **9** corresponds to responses in which marital status was not known.

It would be nice if the table showed the marital category names instead of or in addition to the data codes. It turns out that IBM SPSS Statistics gives us a way to do this.

In this instance, note that the **Percent** column and the **Valid Percent** column are identical because the code of **9** is treated the same as marital codes **1** through **5**. The MISSING VALUES command gives us a way to declare the **9** data code as a missing value.

Finally, the **Frequency** column shows the category counts, which, in this instance, vary widely across the categories.

Variable properties

Once you successfully read a source data file, the next steps are to establish the variable properties for each variable and then do some data checking.

Accessing and Organizing Data

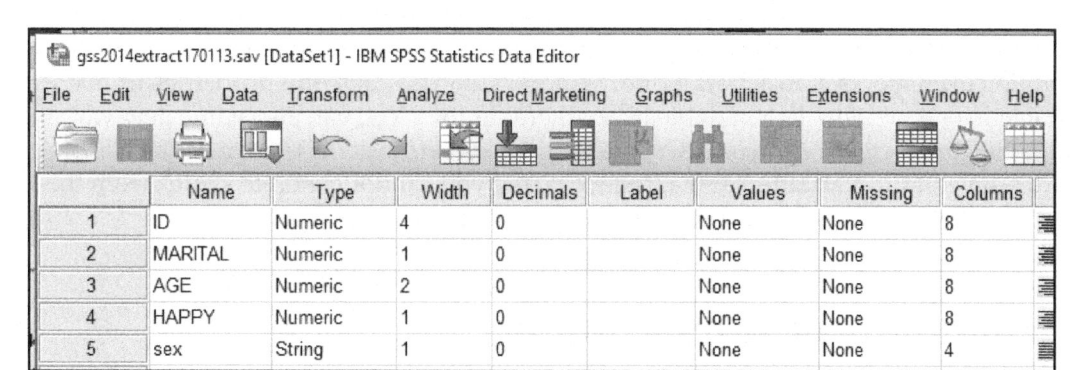

Here is an example of a portion of a **Variable View** with variable properties:

	Name	Type	Width	Decimals	Label	Values	Missing	Columns
1	ID	Numeric	4	0		None	None	8
2	MARITAL	Numeric	1	0		None	None	8
3	AGE	Numeric	2	0		None	None	8
4	HAPPY	Numeric	1	0		None	None	8
5	sex	String	1	0		None	None	4

The **IBM SPSS Statistics Data Editor** window presents two views accessible via tabs in the lower left of the window: **Data View** and **Variable View**. The **Data View** shows a flat file view of the data with observations in the rows and variables in the column. The **Variable View** shows the variables row-wise along with the variable properties. In the **Variable View**, there are as many rows as there are variables. At the time of writing this, there are 11 default variable properties, plus you can define and add custom attributes.

The variable properties are as follows:

- **Name**: Each variable must have a unique variable name
- **Type**: The type or format of the variable, for example, numeric, string, or date
- **Width**: The total number of columns of the variable values
- **Decimals**: The number of decimal positions of the variable values
- **Label**: The variable label for the variable
- **Values**: Value labels for the values of the variable
- **Missing**: User-defined values that should be flagged as missing
- **Columns**: The display width of the variable column in the **Data View**
- **Align**: The alignment of the values in the **Data View** columns
- **Measure**: The level of measurement of the variable
- **Role**: The role of the variable in analysis when used in certain IBM SPSS Statistics procedures

[35]

The **Variable View** provides an interactive interface to define and edit variable properties. You can work directly in the **Variable View** interface to add or edit properties or you can use copy and paste to copy properties from one variable to another. The copy and paste operation even works across Data Editor windows, so you can copy properties from a variable in one window to a variable in another window. You can also name new variables and define properties for the newly created variables before collecting data. One shortcoming of the **Variable View** interface is that you cannot generate syntax from this window. However, see the next section to define variable properties.

Variable properties - name

Each variable must have a unique name.

The rules for naming are as follows:

- Maximum of 64 characters
- The lead character must be a letter
- Names can be comprised of letters, numbers, a period, or most special characters
- You cannot use the following special characters: !, ?, `, *, or blanks
- The name cannot end with an underscore or a period
- You can use any combination of lower or upper-case characters

Variable properties - type

The **Variable Type** dialog box specifies the type and display format of a variable. In the **Variable View**, click in the type area of any variable. This brings up the ellipsis button. Click in this button to open the **Variable Type** dialog box:

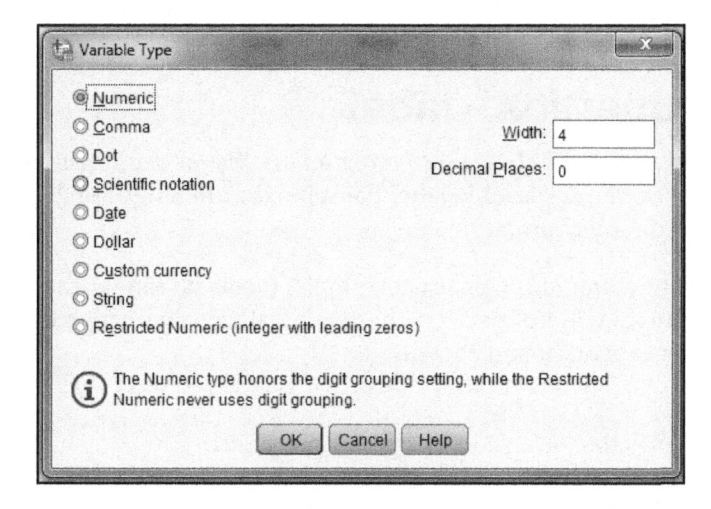

For a numeric variable, specify the width (total number of columns) and the number of decimal positions.

> Note that the width should allow for any special characters that are displayed with the requested format. For a string variable, specify the total number of characters in the string.

The equivalent syntax is the FORMATS command.

Variable properties - width

As indicated under the discussion of type, use the **Variable Type** dialog box to specify the variable width.

The equivalent syntax is the FORMATS command.

Accessing and Organizing Data

Variable properties - decimals

As indicated under the discussion of type, use the **Variable Type** dialog box to specify the number of decimal positions used to display a variable's values.

The equivalent syntax is the FORMATS command.

Variable properties - label

In the **Variable View**, use the **Label** cell to enter a variable label for each variable. Note that variable labels are optional. A variable label has a maximum length of 256 characters and can consist of spaces or any character.

> **TIP**: While the limit is 256 characters, make labels no longer than necessary as procedures will not necessarily display all 256 characters or might wrap the labels in an unsightly way.

The equivalent syntax is the VARIABLE LABELS command.

Variable properties - values

In the **Variable View**, use the **Values** cell to enter a value label for any or all values of a variable. Click in the **Values** area of any variable. This brings up the **ellipsis** button. Click in this button to open the **Value Labels** dialog box:

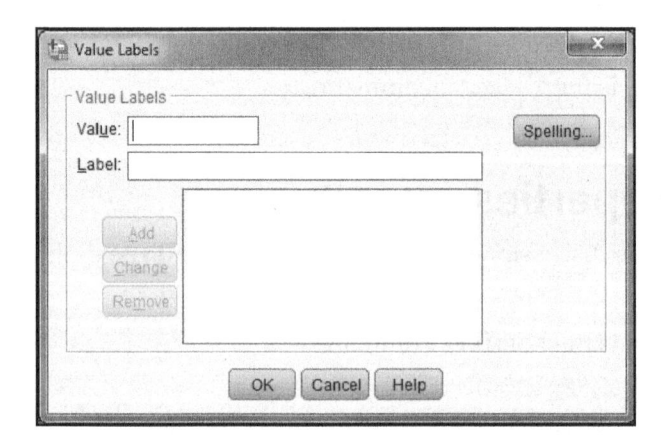

Accessing and Organizing Data

The **Value Labels** dialog box specifies one or more values and the accompanying labels. Type the data value, type the label, and click on **Add** to add a new label. You can also use **Change** to change a highlighted existing label or **Remove** to delete a highlighted label.

> Value labels are optional but are strongly recommended for categorical data or missing value data codes. Each value label can be up to 120 characters long. However, make the labels no longer than necessary. Note that SPSS's Custom tables and graph facilities produce more informative tables and charts by making use of value labels.

The equivalent syntax is the `VALUE LABELS` command.

Variable properties - missing

In the **Variable View**, use the missing cell to enter missing value codes. These are values defined as containing missing data and are designated as **user-missing** values. Click in the missing area of any variable. This brings up the **ellipsis** button. Click in the button to open the **Missing Values** dialog box:

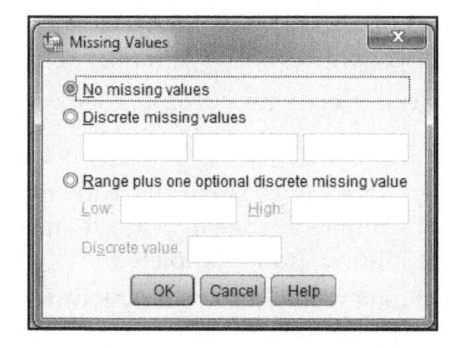

By default, there are no defined missing values. Using the dialog box, you can define up to three explicit missing values, or you can specify two data codes that are endpoints of a range along with an optional discrete missing value. The purpose of allowing multiple missing value codes is to accommodate different mechanisms for missingness.

The equivalent syntax is the `MISSING VALUES` command.

> Note that IBM SPSS Statistics has another type of missing value--the **system-missing** value. If no value is present for a numeric variable, it is assigned the system-missing value. This is represented by a period (.) in the **Data View** of the Data Editor.

[39]

Variable properties - columns

In the **Variable View**, use the columns cell to specify the display width of the column in the **Data View**. You can also change the column width directly in the **Data View** of the Data Editor by clicking and dragging the width of the column.

The equivalent syntax is the `VARIABLE WIDTH` command.

Variable properties - align

In the **Variable View**, use the Align cell to specify the alignment of the values of the variable in the **Data View** columns. The list of choices includes right, center, or left. By default, numeric variable values are right-aligned and string variable values are left-aligned.

The equivalent syntax is the `VARIABLE ALIGNMENT` command.

Variable properties - measure

In the **Variable View**, use the **Measure** cell to specify the level of measurement for the variable. Click in the **Measure** cell to activate a drop-bar list with three elements and select one:

- **Scale**: Data where the data values are intrinsically meaningful numbers reflecting order and distance. Examples are age in years, temperature in Fahrenheit units, and education as the highest grade completed.
- **Ordinal**: Categorical data where there is a rank order of categories. Ordinal data can come about through grouping of scale values into broad groups, for example, age groups obtained through binning of ages. In addition, Likert-type items with responses such as Very Satisfied, Somewhat Satisfied, Neither Satisfied Nor Dissatisfied, Somewhat Dissatisfied, and Very Dissatisfied are ordinal in measurement.
- **Nominal:** Categorical data where the categories are unordered. Examples are marital status and postal code area.

> **TIP**: Procedures such as Codebook, Tables, and Chart Builder recognize the measurement-level definitions and produce different statistics or charts for different measurement types, so make sure that you specify the correct Measure level for each variable.

Accessing and Organizing Data

The equivalent syntax is the VARIABLE LEVEL command.

Variable properties - role

In the **Variable View**, use the Role cell to specify the level of measurement for the variable. Click in the Role cell to activate a drop-bar list with six elements and select one:

- **Input**: The variable will be used as an input.
- **Target**: The variable will be used as a target variable.
- **Both**: The variable will be used as both input and target.
- **None**: The variable has no role assignment.
- **Partition**: The variable will be used to partition the data into separate samples for training, testing, and validation.
- **Split**: Included for compatibility with IBM SPSS modeler. Variables with this role are not used as split file variables in IBM SPSS Statistics.

> **TIP**
> Dialog boxes for some procedures support predefined roles that can be used to select variables for analysis. If the dialog box supports these roles, variables that meet the role requirements will automatically populate the appropriate variable list. By default, the role of all variables is set to Input, which means that all of the variables are available for analysis.

The equivalent syntax is the VARIABLE ROLE command.

Demo - adding variable properties to the Variable View

Consider that you have just read data from an Excel spreadsheet to IBM SPSS Statistics. Now, you wish to add variable properties to the **Variable View**. Here is an example using AGE.

In the IBM SPSS Statistics Data Editor, press the **Variable View** tab to go to the **Variable View**. Note that some of the properties are already filled in. Reading left to right, Name, Type, Width, and Decimals can be left as is.

In the **Label** area for AGE, type in the label, Age of respondent.

[41]

Accessing and Organizing Data

In the Values area for AGE, click on the right side to open the **Value Labels** dialog box. The AGE data codes are intrinsically meaningful and do not need labels, but we will add labels for missing values. Also, the data code of 89 represents respondent's age 89 and older, so we wish to add a label for that. In sum, use the dialog box to add the following values and value labels:

```
89     89 or older

98     Don't know

99     No answer
```

In the **Missing** area for AGE, click on the right side to open the **Missing Values** dialog box. Press the **Discrete missing values** button. Enter 98 and 99 in the first two boxes and press **OK**.

Demo - adding variable properties via syntax

Here is the syntax to specify variable labels, value labels, missing values, and levels of measurement for the GSS 2014 data extract.

Here are the `Variable Labels`:

```
VARIABLE LABELS
    ID         "Respondent id number"
    MARITAL    "Marital status"
    AGE        "Age of respondent"
    SEX        "Respondents sex"
    HAPPY      "General happiness"
.
```

You can facilitate readability by providing one variable name and label per line. Note the period in its own line. That is not required, but makes the period easy to see.

Here are the `Value Labels`:

```
VALUE LABELS
  MARITAL
       1         "Married"
       2         "Widowed"
       3         "Divorced"
       4         "Separated"
       5         "Never married"
       9         "No answer"
  / AGE
```

[42]

```
          89         "89 or older"
          98         "Don't know"
          99         "No answer"
  / SEX
         'f'          "Female"
         'm'          "Male"
  / HAPPY
          1          "Very happy"
          2          "Pretty happy"
          3          "Not too happy"
          0          "Not applicable"
          8          "Don't know"
          9          "No answer"
  .
```

For readability, enter one value and label per line. Note the use of the slash (/) as a separator. Additionally, as the codes for SEX are string values, enclose the values in matching quotes.

Here is the Missing Values specification:

```
MISSING VALUES
  MARITAL(9)
  / AGE(98,99)
  / HAPPY(0,8,9)
  .
```

For readability, specify one variable per line and use the slash as a separator.

Here is the Variable Level specification:

```
VARIABLE LEVEL
  ID,AGE(SCALE)
  / HAPPY(ORDINAL)
  / MARITAL(NOMINAL)
  .
```

As a shortcut, use lists to name variables that are the same Variable Level.

Select and run the syntax. The **Variable View** updates immediately. To see the effect of adding variable properties, here is the frequency table for **MARITAL** after executing the syntax and rerunning frequencies:

MARITAL

		Frequency	Percent	Valid Percent	Cumulative Percent
Valid	Married	1158	45.6	45.7	45.7
	Widowed	209	8.2	8.2	53.9
	Divorced	411	16.2	16.2	70.2
	Separated	81	3.2	3.2	73.4
	Never married	675	26.6	26.6	100.0
	Total	2534	99.8	100.0	
Missing	No answer	4	.2		
Total		2538	100.0		

Now, the table has nice labels for the marital status categories, and the four cases with data codes of 9 are set off in a separate part of the table where the missing data is summarized.

aeaak

Demo - defining variable properties

You have seen that you can **Define Variable Properties** either in the **Variable View** or via syntax. Yet another way is to use **Define Variable Properties** found in the **Data** menu. An advantage of using **Define Variable Properties** is that you fill in a dialog box but can use the Paste command to obtain the constructed syntax.

Here, let's consider defining variable properties for **MARITAL**.

To use **Define Variable Properties** from the menus, navigate to **Data | Define Variable Properties**.

This opens the **Define Variable Properties** dialog box. Move **MARITAL** to the right-hand side:

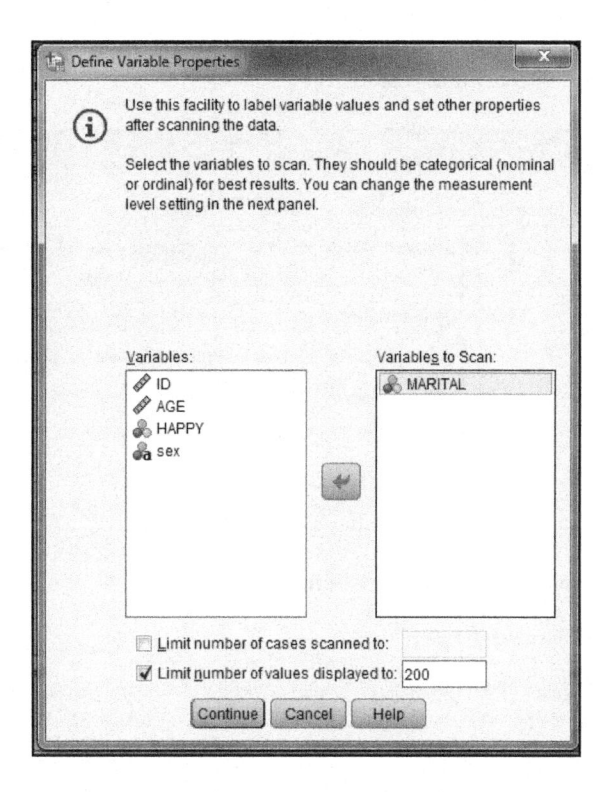

Here is a portion of the **Define Variable Properties** box after you press **Continue**:

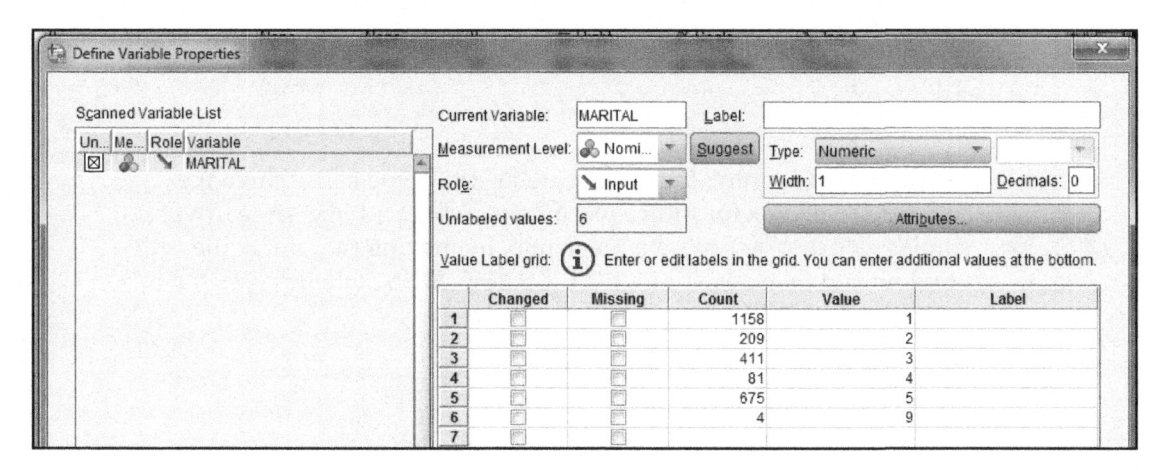

Accessing and Organizing Data

This dialog box is an all-in-one view that shows both the variable properties and the actual data summarized. You can type in this dialog box to add **Variable** properties for **MARITAL**.

Here is the dialog box with the fields filled in:

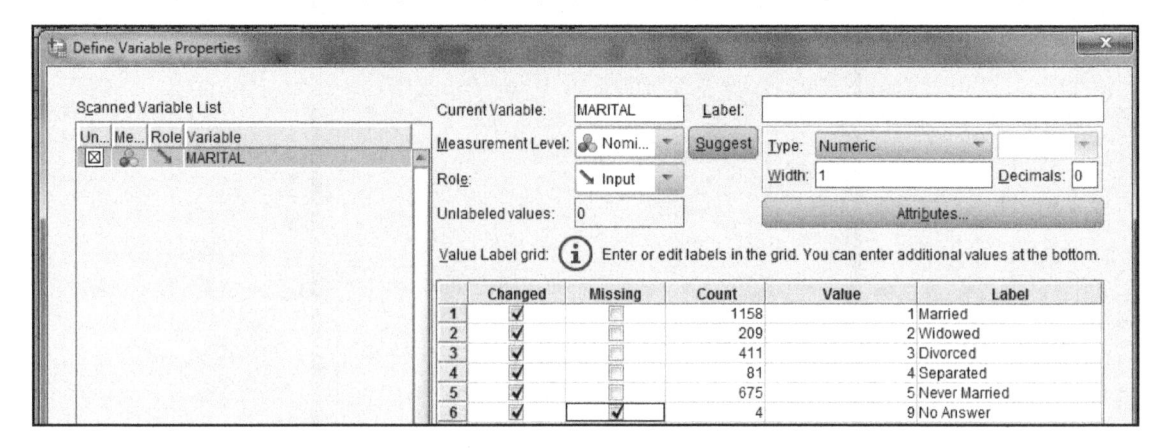

Here is the constructed syntax when you paste:

```
* Define Variable Properties.
*MARITAL.
VARIABLE LABELS  MARITAL 'Marital Status'.
MISSING VALUES MARITAL(9).
VALUE LABELS MARITAL
   1 'Married'
   2 'Widowed'
   3 'Divorced'
   4 'Separated'
   5 'Never Married'
   9 'No Answer'.
EXECUTE.
```

> In addition to running the constructed syntax, you can archive the constructed syntax for future use on a variable with the same or very similar values. You can save the syntax by making the syntax the active window and then specifying **FILE | SAVE**. SPSS Statistics uses the SPS extension for SPSS syntax files.

Summary

This chapter showed you how to read in data from two common file formats--Excel and delimited data. These are common file formats that are writeable by most software, so the ability to read these formats means that you can share data from many other applications.

This chapter also showed you how to save the data as an IBM SPSS Statistics data file. Of course, if you can save a file in that format, then you can use IBM SPSS Statistics to read that file format. The advantage of the SPSS Statistics file format is that the variable information and data are saved in a form that you can access directly. The SPSS Statistics file format is also the native file format of the IBM SPSS Modeler.

This chapter also discussed variable properties, which you can specify for the variables and then save in the IBM SPSS Statistics file format. Variable properties are important because they produce more informative and aesthetically pleasing tables and charts. In addition, the measure property is used by SPSS Statistics Custom Tables and Chart Builder.

There are several ways to specify variable properties. We demonstrated adding variable properties to the **Variable View** via syntax and via define variable properties.

Now that you know how to read your data to SPSS Statistics and establish variable properties, our next step is to learn how to summarize individual data elements using three important procedures: Frequencies, Descriptives, and Explore.

3
Statistics for Individual Data Elements

Prior to beginning analysis, it is essential to assess the data in terms of its quality and potential to yield insights. This is done initially by examining individual fields within the data and cross-checking key elements to determine the integrity of the data. This chapter will cover techniques that you can employ to establish the foundation for subsequent investigation of patterns. It will also help to introduce several of the most basic features of the SPSS Statistics software that you will make use of regularly. We will cover the following procedures in this chapter:

- Descriptives
- Frequencies
- Explore

Getting the sample data

The examples in this section will use a subset of the General Social Survey from 2016 with only 28 fields out of the original 896. After downloading and opening the General Social Survey file for 2016 in the SPSS Statistics format, you can run the following code to create a file that will produce the same results shown in this chapter. Remember to change the directory reference on the second line of the SPSS code to reflect the directory on your machine where you want to have this new file saved:

```
* create GSS2014small with 28 fields.
* change the directory reference below as needed.
SAVE OUTFILE='C:GSS DataGSS2014sm28.sav'
 /keep = happy marital hapmar age
```

```
VOTE12    PRES12 educ speduc natpark natroad NATENRGY   cappun natmass
natchld natsci
partyid degree incom16 satfin size spdeg polviews
  rincom16 res16 childs wrkstat sex region /COMPRESSED.
```

Descriptive statistics for numeric fields

The descriptives procedure in SPSS Statistics provides you with an easy way to get a comprehensive picture of all the numeric fields in a dataset. As was noted in `Chapter 2`, *Accessing and Organizing Data*, the way in which a field is coded determines how it can be used in SPSS Statistics. Data fields coded with characters will not be available for use in the **Descriptives** dialog as it produces summary statistics only. Text fields in your data will need to be examined using a different approach, which will be covered next section of this chapter.

To obtain a table with all the numeric fields from your data along with some basic information such as the count, mean, and standard deviation, select **Descriptive Statistics** under the **Analyze** menu and click on the second choice, **Descriptives**. Highlight the first field--which in this dataset is **Age**--scroll down to the last field listed on the left, **VOTE OBAMA OR ROMNEY [PRES12]**, and use *Shift-Click* to select all fields.

Click on the arrow in the middle of the dialog to move the list to the box on the left, as shown in the following image, and then click on **OK**:

Statistics for Individual Data Elements

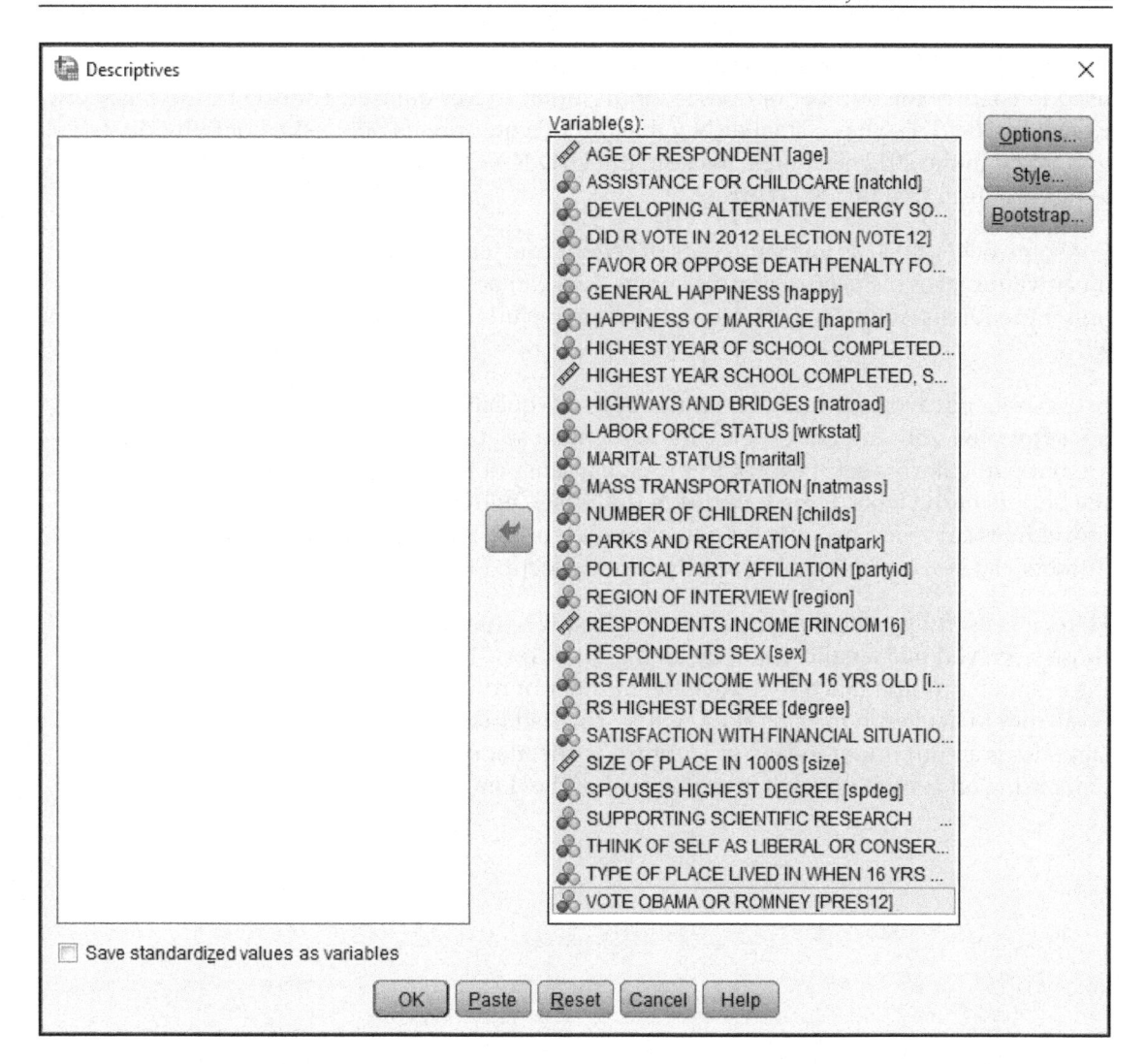

The descriptive statistics for the 28 fields in this dataset are displayed in following screenshot. One of the first pieces of information to check is the N, which indicates how many of the rows contain a valid code for each field. For the 2016 General Social Survey data, the maximum value of N is 2,867 and it is evident that most of the fields are close to this number with a few exceptions. Questions in the survey tare dependent on a person's marital status, such as **Happiness of Marriage** and the items related to spouse's education, so it makes sense that the N for these fields would be lower.

Statistics for Individual Data Elements

A check of the **Marital Status** field specifically (using the frequencies procedure) can be used to confirm the number of married individuals in this dataset. The **VOTE OBAMA OR ROMNEY** field also has a smaller N value but this question is only asked of individuals that voted in the 2012 election. Checking the **DID R VOTE IN 2012 ELECTION** field is a way to confirm that this **N** is correct.

For some fields, such as age and years of school completed, the minimum, maximum, and mean values provide useful information as they can be interpreted directly. In this survey, only individuals in the 18 to 89 age range were included and the mean age of the group was 49.

In general, however, the numeric values used for questions such as marital status or region are associated with categories relevant to the item so the minimum, maximum, and mean are not particularly useful except to provide a sense of the range of values in the data. At the bottom of the table, there is **Valid N (listwise)**, which indicates how many of the 2,867 individuals surveyed had a valid value for each of the 28 questions in the table. This number can be very helpful, especially when selecting fields to use in multivariate analysis.

Here, it is useful to note that while the smallest N value for the 28 fields is 1,195, only 422 of those surveyed had a valid value on all the questions. This illustrates how absent information can dramatically reduce the number of rows available for use in analysis. Strategies to deal with missing data will be covered in a later chapter, but descriptive statistics is an important means of identifying the magnitude of the challenge before embarking on a more detailed investigation of the data:

Descriptive Statistics

	N	Minimum	Maximum	Mean	Std. Deviation
AGE OF RESPONDENT	2857	18	89	49.16	17.693
ASSISTANCE FOR CHILDCARE	2700	1	3	1.48	.609
DEVELOPING ALTERNATIVE ENERGY SOURCES	2743	1	3	1.52	.657
DID R VOTE IN 2012 ELECTION	2810	1	3	1.43	.623
FAVOR OR OPPOSE DEATH PENALTY FOR MURDER	2695	1	2	1.40	.489
GENERAL HAPPINESS	2859	1	3	1.88	.652
HAPPINESS OF MARRIAGE	1204	1	3	1.44	.571
HIGHEST YEAR OF SCHOOL COMPLETED	2858	0	20	13.74	2.964
HIGHEST YEAR SCHOOL COMPLETED, SPOUSE	1195	0	20	13.89	2.945
HIGHWAYS AND BRIDGES	2820	1	3	1.60	.666
LABOR FORCE STATUS	2864	1	8	3.03	2.326
MARITAL STATUS	2866	1	5	2.66	1.682
MASS TRANSPORTATION	2699	1	3	1.72	.622
NUMBER OF CHILDREN	2859	0	8	1.85	1.669
PARKS AND RECREATION	2817	1	3	1.72	.568
POLITICAL PARTY AFFILIATION	2835	0	7	2.76	2.034
REGION OF INTERVIEW	2867	1	9	5.09	2.482
RESPONDENTS INCOME	1632	1	26	15.19	6.101
RESPONDENTS SEX	2867	1	2	1.55	.497
RS FAMILY INCOME WHEN 16 YRS OLD	2802	1	5	2.72	.949
RS HIGHEST DEGREE	2859	0	4	1.67	1.222
SATISFACTION WITH FINANCIAL SITUATION	2856	1	3	1.99	.749
SIZE OF PLACE IN 1000S	2867	0	8175	334.33	1149.625
SPOUSES HIGHEST DEGREE	1204	0	4	1.82	1.258
SUPPORTING SCIENTIFIC RESEARCH	2687	1	3	1.70	.663
THINK OF SELF AS LIBERAL OR CONSERVATIVE	2756	1	7	4.06	1.487
TYPE OF PLACE LIVED IN WHEN 16 YRS OLD	2861	1	6	3.63	1.498
VOTE OBAMA OR ROMNEY	1730	1	5	1.42	.625
Valid N (listwise)	422				

Controlling the descriptives display order

In addition to providing a quick overview of a dataset, descriptives can be used to focus on a set of related questions to compare them and set the stage for deeper analysis of them as a group. The General Social Survey includes a set of questions dealing with problems facing the United States and asks people to indicate whether the nation is spending too much money on the problem, too little, or the right amount. A response of **too little** is coded as **1**, a response of **about right** is coded as **2**, and a response of **too much** is coded as **3** in the dataset. To obtain a quick comparison of how some of these questions about national problems were rated in the 2016 survey, use the following menus:

Analyze | Descriptives Statistics | Descriptives

Select the six items shown in the following image from the list of fields on the left. Click on the **Options** button and, under **Display Order**, select **Ascending means**:

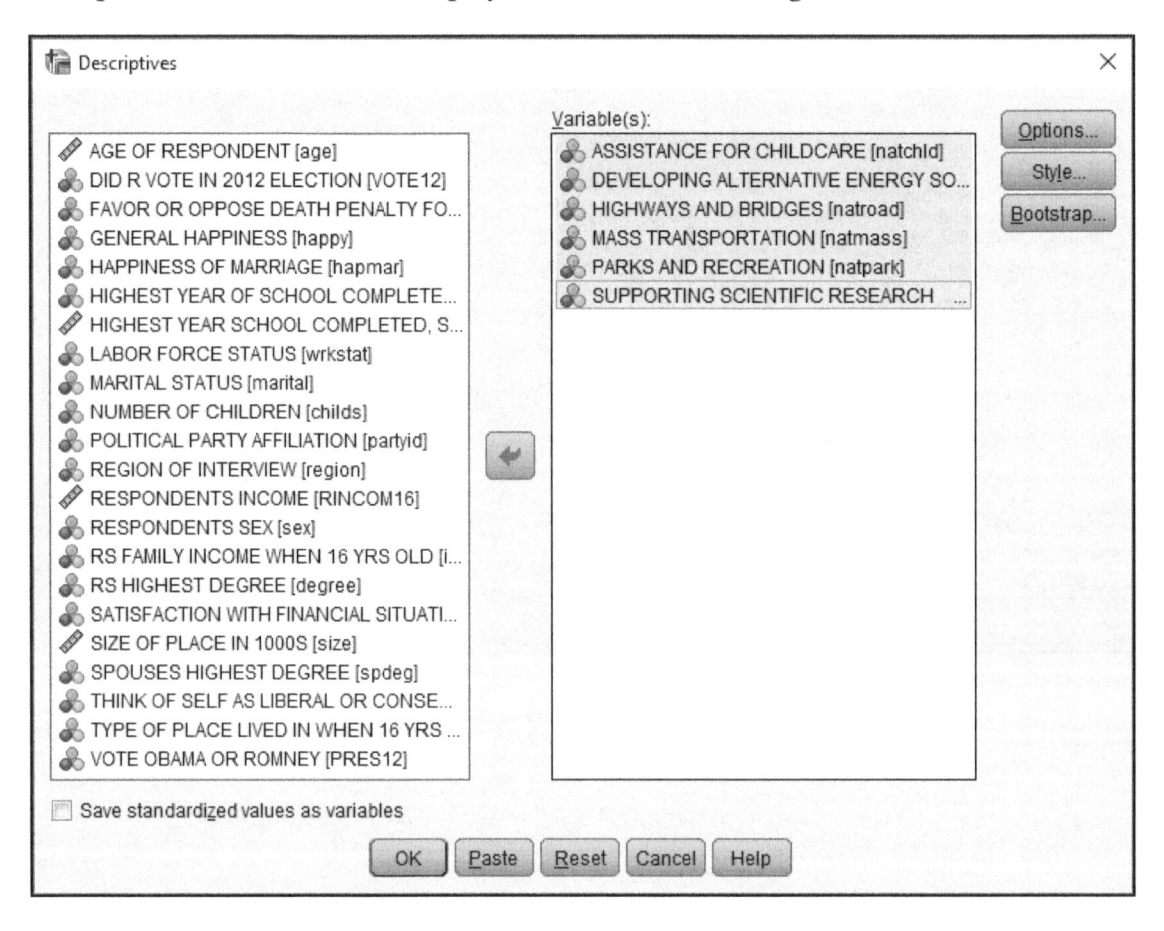

This will cause the fields to be sorted so that those with the lowest mean are at the top of the list. These are the problems that people think are receiving too little funding at present. Click on **OK** to obtain the table shown in the next image.

It is evident that childcare and alternative energy are the problems that people think should receive more funding. There are many handy features in SPSS, such as the ability demonstrated here to sort the results based on a statistic. These features are available as options so be sure to explore the secondary menus to see the choices you have:

Descriptive Statistics

	N	Minimum	Maximum	Mean	Std. Deviation
ASSISTANCE FOR CHILDCARE	2700	1	3	1.48	.609
DEVELOPING ALTERNATIVE ENERGY SOURCES	2743	1	3	1.52	.657
HIGHWAYS AND BRIDGES	2820	1	3	1.60	.666
MASS TRANSPORTATION	2699	1	3	1.72	.622
PARKS AND RECREATION	2817	1	3	1.72	.568
SUPPORTING SCIENTIFIC RESEARCH	2687	1	3	1.70	.663
Valid N (listwise)	2403				

> **TIP**
> A table of ordered means can be useful when looking at a set of questions from a customer or employee satisfaction survey. Typically, these survey questions employ a 1-5 rating from Highly Satisfied to Highly Dissatisfied so the items with the lowest mean score indicate areas of greatest satisfaction.

Frequency distributions

One of the analytic tools that you will make regular use of in SPSS Statistics is the ability to display the distribution of values for individual fields in your data.

The descriptive statistics shown in the preceding section are a convenient way to obtain an overview of the data but it is often necessary to see how many times each value is present in a set of data. This makes it possible to check the data in more detail and identify any potential issues.

To obtain a distribution of values for the **Highest Year of School Completed** field, navigate to the following path:

Analyze | Descriptive Statistics | Frequencies

Statistics for Individual Data Elements

Select this field from the list on the left, then click on **OK** to produce the table shown in the following image:

		Frequency	Percent	Valid Percent	Cumulative Percent
HIGHEST YEAR OF SCHOOL COMPLETED					
Valid	0	2	.1	.1	.1
	1	3	.1	.1	.2
	2	3	.1	.1	.3
	3	3	.1	.1	.4
	4	2	.1	.1	.5
	5	4	.1	.1	.6
	6	31	1.1	1.1	1.7
	7	18	.6	.6	2.3
	8	48	1.7	1.7	4.0
	9	59	2.1	2.1	6.1
	10	90	3.1	3.1	9.2
	11	118	4.1	4.1	13.3
	12	824	28.7	28.8	42.2
	13	242	8.4	8.5	50.6
	14	359	12.5	12.6	63.2
	15	137	4.8	4.8	68.0
	16	485	16.9	17.0	85.0
	17	108	3.8	3.8	88.7
	18	149	5.2	5.2	93.9
	19	63	2.2	2.2	96.2
	20	110	3.8	3.8	100.0
	Total	2858	99.7	100.0	
Missing	98 DK	1	.0		
	99 NA	8	.3		
	Total	9	.3		
Total		2867	100.0		

Statistics for Individual Data Elements

Given that the General Social Survey is conducted in the United States, the pattern in this table looks reasonable. The largest single group has a value of 12, which corresponds to the end of high school.

There is another sizeable group with 16 years of education, typically the time it takes to finish college. Understanding the US educational system allows us to check this data to see that it looks reasonable.

If data were collected from another country, we would expect a different distribution aligned with the structure to their educational system. In the `Descriptive Statistics` table screenshot, the mean for this field was shown as 13.74, which is useful information but not as detailed as what is provided in the **Highest Year of School Completed** table screenshot. The cumulative percentage column on the right, for example, shows the percentage that have 12 or fewer years of formal education (42.2%) as well as the percentage that have fewer than 16 years of education (68%) and both of these numbers provide some valuable information.

Discovering coding issues using frequencies

The frequency distribution for **INCOME** in the following screenshot demonstrates another reason why it is important to examine the pattern for individual data fields before diving into analytics more deeply. Navigate to **Analyze | Descriptive Statistics | Frequencies**, and select **Respondents Income** to build this table:

Statistics for Individual Data Elements

RESPONDENTS INCOME

		Frequency	Percent	Valid Percent	Cumulative Percent
Valid	1 UNDER $1 000	25	.9	1.5	1.5
	2 $1 000 TO 2 999	51	1.8	3.1	4.7
	3 $3 000 TO 3 999	32	1.1	2.0	6.6
	4 $4 000 TO 4 999	30	1.0	1.8	8.5
	5 $5 000 TO 5 999	31	1.1	1.9	10.4
	6 $6 000 TO 6 999	31	1.1	1.9	12.3
	7 $7 000 TO 7 999	24	.8	1.5	13.7
	8 $8 000 TO 9 999	34	1.2	2.1	15.8
	9 $10000 TO 12499	51	1.8	3.1	18.9
	10 $12500 TO 14999	45	1.6	2.8	21.7
	11 $15000 TO 17499	60	2.1	3.7	25.4
	12 $17500 TO 19999	52	1.8	3.2	28.6
	13 $20000 TO 22499	74	2.6	4.5	33.1
	14 $22500 TO 24999	64	2.2	3.9	37.0
	15 $25000 TO 29999	97	3.4	5.9	43.0
	16 $30000 TO 34999	118	4.1	7.2	50.2
	17 $35000 TO 39999	108	3.8	6.6	56.8
	18 $40000 TO 49999	158	5.5	9.7	66.5
	19 $50000 TO 59999	137	4.8	8.4	74.9
	20 $60000 TO 74999	141	4.9	8.6	83.5
	21 $75000 TO $89999	79	2.8	4.8	88.4
	22 $90000 TO $109999	68	2.4	4.2	92.5
	23 $110000 TO $129999	36	1.3	2.2	94.7
	24 $130000 TO $149999	21	.7	1.3	96.0
	25 $150000 TO $169999	14	.5	.9	96.9
	26 $170000 OR OVER	51	1.8	3.1	100.0
	Total	1632	56.9	100.0	
Missing	0 IAP	1136	39.6		
	27 REFUSED	85	3.0		
	98 DK	14	.5		
	Total	1235	43.1		
Total		2867	100.0		

Statistics for Individual Data Elements

> **TIP**
> The values coded in the data are displayed in Figure 3 along with the associated value labels. This was done on the **Edit | Options | Output** screen by specifying values and labels in the dropdown at the lower left under to pivot table labeling.

People are often reluctant to divulge their income so surveys typically ask them to select an income category like the groupings in this table. Notice, however, that the groups (numbered 1 through 26) represent unequal bands of income. The groups coded 3 thru 7 represent a range of only $1,000, while group 15 has a range of $5,000, and group 20 covers $15,000.

In the previous chapter, one of the properties of variables that was discussed involved the level of measurement. Income is an example of a scale variable and for these fields, it is assumed that the intervals between values are equal, which is not the case in this instance. The information in this table can be evaluated even though the categories are not uniform in terms of the dollar range they represent, but before using this field for statistical modeling, it is important to adjust the coding to reflect the actual differences in income.

In a later chapter, techniques for modifying fields will be covered but it is by examining the data along with the coding scheme used that you discover where the need for change exists.

Using frequencies to verify missing data patterns

Another advantage of scrutinizing the individual fields is the ability to see the pattern of missing data. The **Income** table in previous screenshot contains usable information for 56.9% of those surveyed. The fact that so many individuals did not have any income is undoubtedly because some are retired or currently unemployed.

This can be checked by requesting a frequency distribution for the **LABOR FORCE STATUS** field. Use frequencies to request a table as shown in the following screenshot to verify that the missing income information aligns with the employment status information:

LABOR FORCE STATUS

		Frequency	Percent	Valid Percent	Cumulative Percent
Valid	1 WORKING FULLTIME	1321	46.1	46.1	46.1
	2 WORKING PARTTIME	345	12.0	12.0	58.2
	3 TEMP NOT WORKING	57	2.0	2.0	60.2
	4 UNEMPL, LAID OFF	118	4.1	4.1	64.3
	5 RETIRED	574	20.0	20.0	84.3
	6 SCHOOL	76	2.7	2.7	87.0
	7 KEEPING HOUSE	284	9.9	9.9	96.9
	8 OTHER	89	3.1	3.1	100.0
	Total	2864	99.9	100.0	
Missing	9 NA	3	.1		
Total		2867	100.0		

Explore procedure

To thoroughly examine the distribution of scale or interval level fields, you can employ the explore procedure in SPSS Statistics. The output provided by explore is more detailed than descriptives or frequencies, and includes more information on extreme values that may influence statistical measures in an undesirable manner. Navigate to **Analyze | Descriptive Statistics | Explore** to open the dialog box in the following figure and put the **HIGHEST YEAR OF SCHOOL COMPLETED** field in the upper box labeled **Dependent List**. Select **OK** to request the default output that explore generates:

Statistics for Individual Data Elements

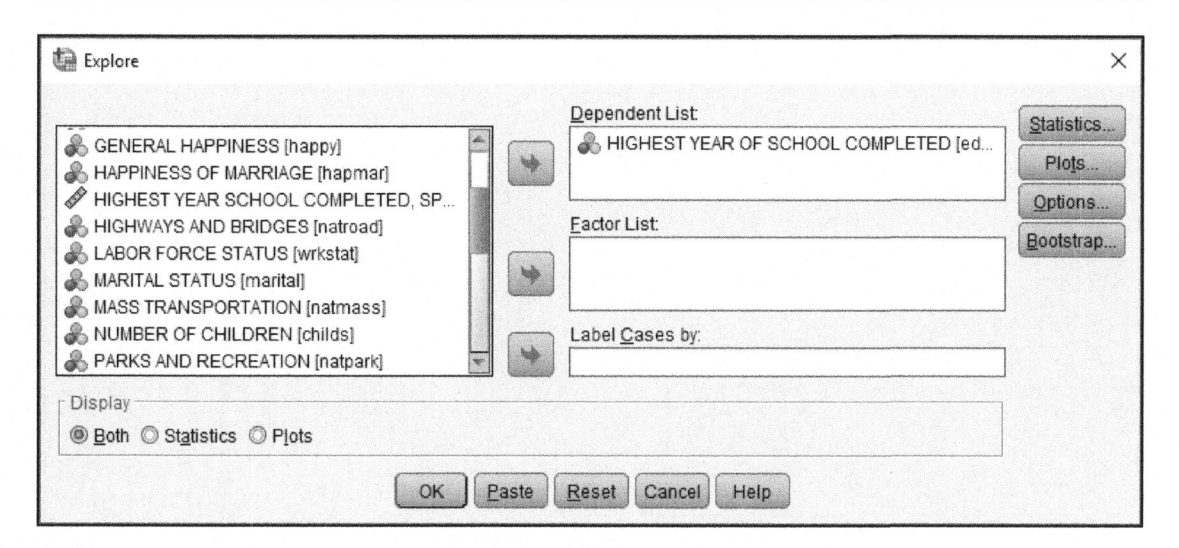

[SPSS Explore dialog box screenshot]

The first section of results produced by **Explore** contains a set of descriptive statistics related to the distribution of the values. In addition to the mean, a 5% trimmed mean is calculated to show how removing the top and bottom 2.5% of the values influences the mean.

If the mean and trimmed mean differ by an appreciable amount, outliers may need to be addressed. The results in following screenshot for years of school completed show very little difference between the mean (13.74) and the trimmed mean (13.78), suggesting that outliers are not distorting the value:

Statistics for Individual Data Elements

Descriptives

			Statistic	Std. Error
HIGHEST YEAR OF SCHOOL COMPLETED	Mean		13.74	.055
	95% Confidence Interval for Mean	Lower Bound	13.63	
		Upper Bound	13.85	
	5% Trimmed Mean		13.78	
	Median		13.00	
	Variance		8.785	
	Std. Deviation		2.964	
	Minimum		0	
	Maximum		20	
	Range		20	
	Interquartile Range		4	
	Skewness		-.186	.046
	Kurtosis		.824	.092

Stem and leaf plot

Two graphical results are included in the explore output. The first, in the following image, is a stem and leaf plot that summarizes the distribution of the field into groups using a **stem** value and showing the number of rows in the data that fall into each using a **leaf** symbol. As years of schooling has a relatively small range of values (0-20), each group in this stem and leaf plot is comprised of a single value. The legend at the bottom of the graph indicates that a **leaf** symbol represents 9 cases or, in this instance, individual people. The graph reflects the large groups at key points along the education spectrum corresponding to stopping at high school (12 years) and at completion of college (16 years). There are also 17 **extreme** values of 5 or fewer years of formal schooling:

Statistics for Individual Data Elements

```
HIGHEST YEAR OF SCHOOL COMPLETED Stem-and-Leaf Plot

 Frequency    Stem &  Leaf

     17.00 Extremes    (=<5.0)
     31.00        6 .  000
       .00        6 .
     18.00        7 .  00
       .00        7 .
     48.00        8 .  00000
       .00        8 .
     59.00        9 .  0000000
       .00        9 .
     90.00       10 .  0000000000
       .00       10 .
    118.00       11 .  000000000000
       .00       11 .
    824.00       12 .  0000000000000000000000000000000000000000000000000000000000000000000000000000000000000000000
       .00       12 .
    242.00       13 .  000000000000000000000000000
       .00       13 .
    359.00       14 .  0000000000000000000000000000000000000000
       .00       14 .
    137.00       15 .  000000000000000
       .00       15 .
    485.00       16 .  00000000000000000000000000000000000000000000000000000
       .00       16 .
    108.00       17 .  000000000000
       .00       17 .
    149.00       18 .  0000000000000000
       .00       18 .
     63.00       19 .  0000000
       .00       19 .
    110.00       20 .  000000000000

 Stem width:     1
 Each leaf:         9 case(s)
```

Boxplot

The final piece of output from explore is the box and whisker plot. I have added an image after this paragraph for your understanding. This is a visual representation of the dispersion of values around the median.

The box contains the middle 50% of the values with a heavy line at the median. In this box plot, the line is at 13, which is the median value shown in the **Descriptives** table. The bottom of the box is at 12 and the top is at 16, which is consistent with the **interquartile range** value in the **Descriptive** table. The T or whisker lines above and below the box mark the boundaries of the typical or non-extreme portion of the values. As values are bound by 0-20 and the median is at 13, the upper whisker is shorter than the lower one.

Additionally, the extreme values are all at the bottom (the 17 individuals who reported 5 or fewer years of schooling) of the range. The case numbers in the data for the extreme values are displayed on the graph if there is sufficient space to do so. Here, 16 of the 17 fit on the graph. These numbers correspond to the row in the dataset with the associated value for this field:

Statistics for Individual Data Elements

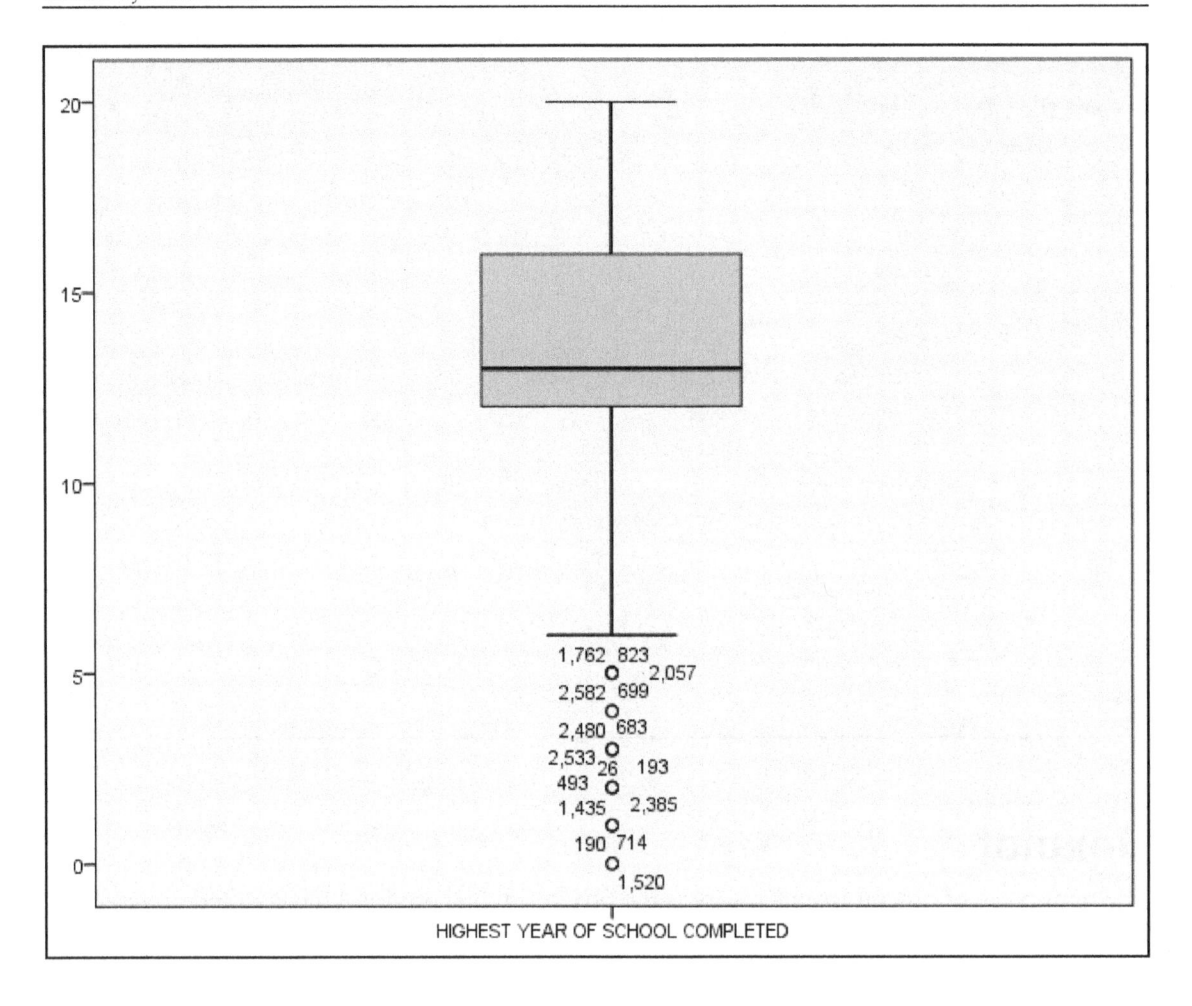

[box plot with y-axis 0–20, labeled HIGHEST YEAR OF SCHOOL COMPLETED, with outliers labeled: 1,762 823 2,057 2,582 699 2,480 683 2,533 26 193 493 1,435 2,385 190 714 1,520]

Using explore to check subgroup patterns

While explore is useful for looking at the distribution of individual fields, it is particularly helpful for the investigation of patterns across subsets of the data. We'll look at an example of this approach next. Go back to the **Explore** dialog box, the **HIGHEST YEAR OF SCHOOL COMPLETED** field should still be in the upper **Dependent List** box (if not, add it). In the lower **Factor List**, add **REGION OF INTERVIEW** and click on **OK**.

The descriptives produced by explore now contain a separate set of results for each of the nine regions used to group the states for the purposes of the survey. Values for New England (Connecticut, Maine, Massachusetts, New Hampshire, Rhode Island, and Vermont) are shown first (see Figure 12) as this region is coded with the value **1** in the data.

Statistics for Individual Data Elements

This area of the US is relatively well-educated as can be seen by the mean (14.29) and median (14) values in the table:

HIGHEST YEAR OF SCHOOL COMPLETED	1 NEW ENGLAND	Mean		14.29	.233
		95% Confidence Interval for Mean	Lower Bound	13.83	
			Upper Bound	14.75	
		5% Trimmed Mean		14.38	
		Median		14.00	
		Variance		9.530	
		Std. Deviation		3.087	
		Minimum		0	
		Maximum		20	
		Range		20	
		Interquartile Range		4	
		Skewness		-.699	.184
		Kurtosis		2.864	.365

By comparison, the West South Central region (Arkansas, Louisiana, Oklahoma, and Texas), which is coded **7** in the data, has a lower mean (12.91) and median (12) years of schooling:

7 W. SOU. CENTRAL	Mean		12.91	.177
	95% Confidence Interval for Mean	Lower Bound	12.56	
		Upper Bound	13.25	
	5% Trimmed Mean		12.94	
	Median		12.00	
	Variance		9.329	
	Std. Deviation		3.054	
	Minimum		0	
	Maximum		20	
	Range		20	
	Interquartile Range		3	
	Skewness		-.255	.141
	Kurtosis		1.290	.282

Statistics for Individual Data Elements

The stem and leaf plot for the New England region (see the figure below) indicates that there are only two extreme values and a large proportion of individuals with 14 and 16 years of education:

```
HIGHEST YEAR OF SCHOOL COMPLETED Stem-and-Leaf Plot for
region= NEW ENGLAND

 Frequency    Stem &  Leaf

     2.00 Extremes    (=<2.0)
     1.00        7 .  0
     2.00        8 .  00
     1.00        9 .  0
     4.00       10 .  0000
     3.00       11 .  000
    49.00       12 .  0000000000000000000000000000000000000000000000000
    10.00       13 .  0000000000
    24.00       14 .  000000000000000000000000
    10.00       15 .  0000000000
    36.00       16 .  000000000000000000000000000000000000
     4.00       17 .  0000
    15.00       18 .  000000000000000
     4.00       19 .  0000
    10.00       20 .  0000000000

 Stem width:     1
 Each leaf:        1 case(s)
```

The corresponding plot for the West South Central region, shown in the following figure, has 19 extreme values at the lower end, 8 or fewer years, and another 19 extreme values at the higher end, 18 or more years of schooling. It is also evident that in this area of the US, people very often finish their education after 12 years when they complete high school:

```
HIGHEST YEAR OF SCHOOL COMPLETED Stem-and-Leaf Plot for
region= W. SOU. CENTRAL

 Frequency    Stem &  Leaf

    19.00 Extremes    (=<8.0)
    12.00        9 .  000000000000
      .00        9 .
    17.00       10 .  00000000000000000
      .00       10 .
    17.00       11 .  00000000000000000
      .00       11 .
    88.00       12 .  0000000000000000000000000000000000000000000000000000000000000000000000000000000000000000
      .00       12 .
    21.00       13 .  000000000000000000000
      .00       13 .
    49.00       14 .  0000000000000000000000000000000000000000000000000
      .00       14 .
    14.00       15 .  00000000000000
      .00       15 .
    33.00       16 .  000000000000000000000000000000000
      .00       16 .
     8.00       17 .  00000000
    19.00 Extremes    (>=18)

 Stem width:     1
 Each leaf:       1 case(s)
```

The boxplot (following figure) included in the explore output provides an excellent visual depiction of the pattern across the groups and highlights potential areas to address in terms of the distribution of education. At a glance, one can see that five of the regions (New England, Middle Atlantic, South Atlantic, Mountain, and Pacific) have a similar pattern in terms of the median (14), size of the box, and small number of extreme values. By contrast, the West North Central and West South Central regions have a lower median value (12), a smaller box indicating a concentration of values just above the median, and several extreme values at both the top and bottom. These patterns are important because the variance across, groups involved in an analysis is assumed to be consistent and, when that is not the case, it can cause problems. The boxplot is a convenient means of comparing the variability of the subgroups in the data visually on a single page:

Statistics for Individual Data Elements

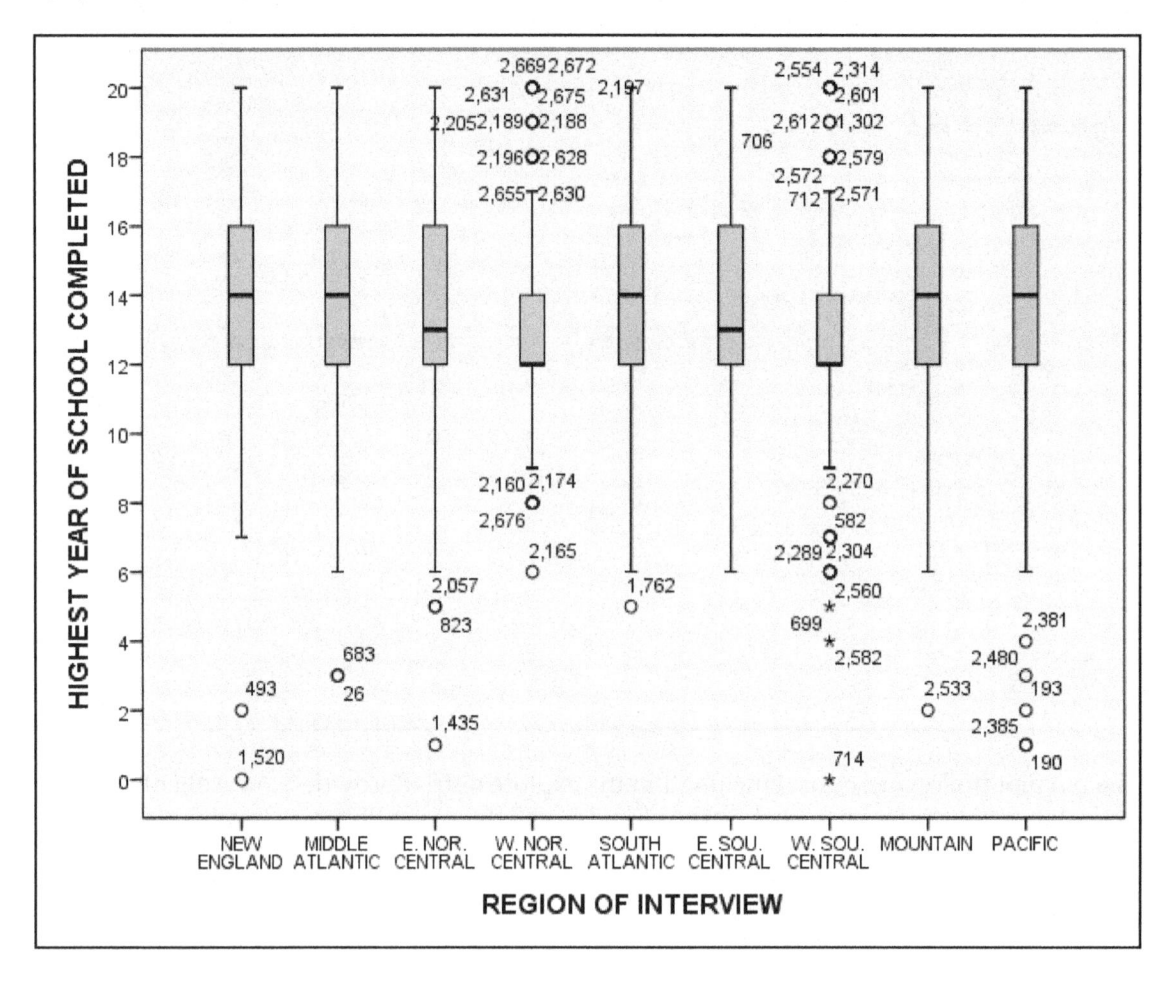

> **TIP:** The vertical axis was modified to add more values. Chapter 5, *Visually Exploring the Data*, will discuss how to modify the charts produced by SPSS.

Summary

You will find the techniques covered in this chapter valuable not only initially when working with a new set of data, but throughout the analytic journey as patterns are investigated and further exploration of the results is undertaken.

Understanding the structure of the data in detail is critical before moving on to more sophisticated analytical methods as they often characterize the relationship found into a handful of summary statistics. The diagnostics accompanying these statistics provide a means of assessing how well they capture the patterns, but appreciating in advance where issues are likely to be present helps focus the examination of the results.

The next chapter will expand on the topic of outliers touched on here and address the issue of missing values. Both of these situations occur regularly when dealing with real data and there are several approaches that can be utilized to detect their presence so that the impact on analytics can be minimized.

4
Dealing with Missing Data and Outliers

The earlier chapters showed you how to read common file formats and define Variable Properties. In any project, as you pull together the data that helps you address your business question or research question, you must spend some time gaining an understanding of your data via a data audit. Simple procedures such as Frequencies, Descriptives, or Examine can give you a summary understanding of each variable via statistical and graphical means. In addition, the data audit should focus on unusual/extreme values and the nature and extent of missing data.

The topics covered in this chapter include the following:

Outliers:

- Frequencies for a histogram and percentile values
- Descriptives for standardized scores
- The Examine procedure for extreme values and boxplot
- Detecting multivariate outliers using the Regression procedure

Missing data:

- Missing values in Frequencies
- Missing values in Descriptives
- Missing value patterns
- Replacing missing values

Outliers

An **outlier** is an observation that lies an unusual distance from other observations. There is a judgmental element in deciding what is considered unusual, and it helps to work with the subject-matter expert in deciding this. In **exploratory data analysis**, there are two activities that are linked:

- Examining the overall shape of the graphed data for important features
- Examining the data for unusual observations that are far from the mass or general trend of the data

Outliers are data points that deserve a closer look. The values could be real data values accurately recorded or the values could be misrecorded or otherwise flawed data. You need to discern what is the case in your situation and decide what action to take.

In this section, we consider statistical and graphical ways of summarizing the distribution of a variable and detecting unusual/extreme values. IBM SPSS Statistics provides many tools for this, which are found in procedures such as Frequencies, Examine, and Chart Builder. To explore these facilities, we introduce data on used Toyota Corollas and, in particular, look at the distribution of the offer prices, in Euros, of sales in the Netherlands in the year 2004.

> The Toyota Corolla data featured in this chapter is described in *Data Mining for Business Analytics: Concepts, Techniques, and Applications with XLMiner(R)*, Third Edition. Galit Shmueli, Peter C. Bruce, and Nitin R. Patel. Copyright 2016 John Wiley and Sons.

Frequencies for histogram and percentile values

You can use Frequencies to produce a histogram and percentiles along with the minimum and maximum. Here is an example of the syntax for Frequencies:

```
FREQUENCIES VARIABLES=Price
  /FORMAT=NOTABLE
  /PERCENTILES=1.0 5.0 10.0 25.0 50.0 75.0 90.0 95.0 99.0
  /STATISTICS=MINIMUM MAXIMUM
  /HISTOGRAM
  /ORDER=ANALYSIS.
```

Dealing with Missing Data and Outliers

Recall that you can use frequencies to produce a `frequency` table, a table of `statistics`, or a chart. Our purpose here is to produce statistics and a chart. The `/FORMAT` subcommand suppresses the printing of a frequency table as there are many unique values of `Price` and the resulting table would be lengthy. The `/PERCENTILES` subcommand produces a table of percentile values, which are useful for understanding numeric variables such as `Price`.

> **TIP**
> When you are analyzing a numeric variable with pronounced skewness, percentiles can be a useful summary statistic.

Here is the histogram for `Price`:

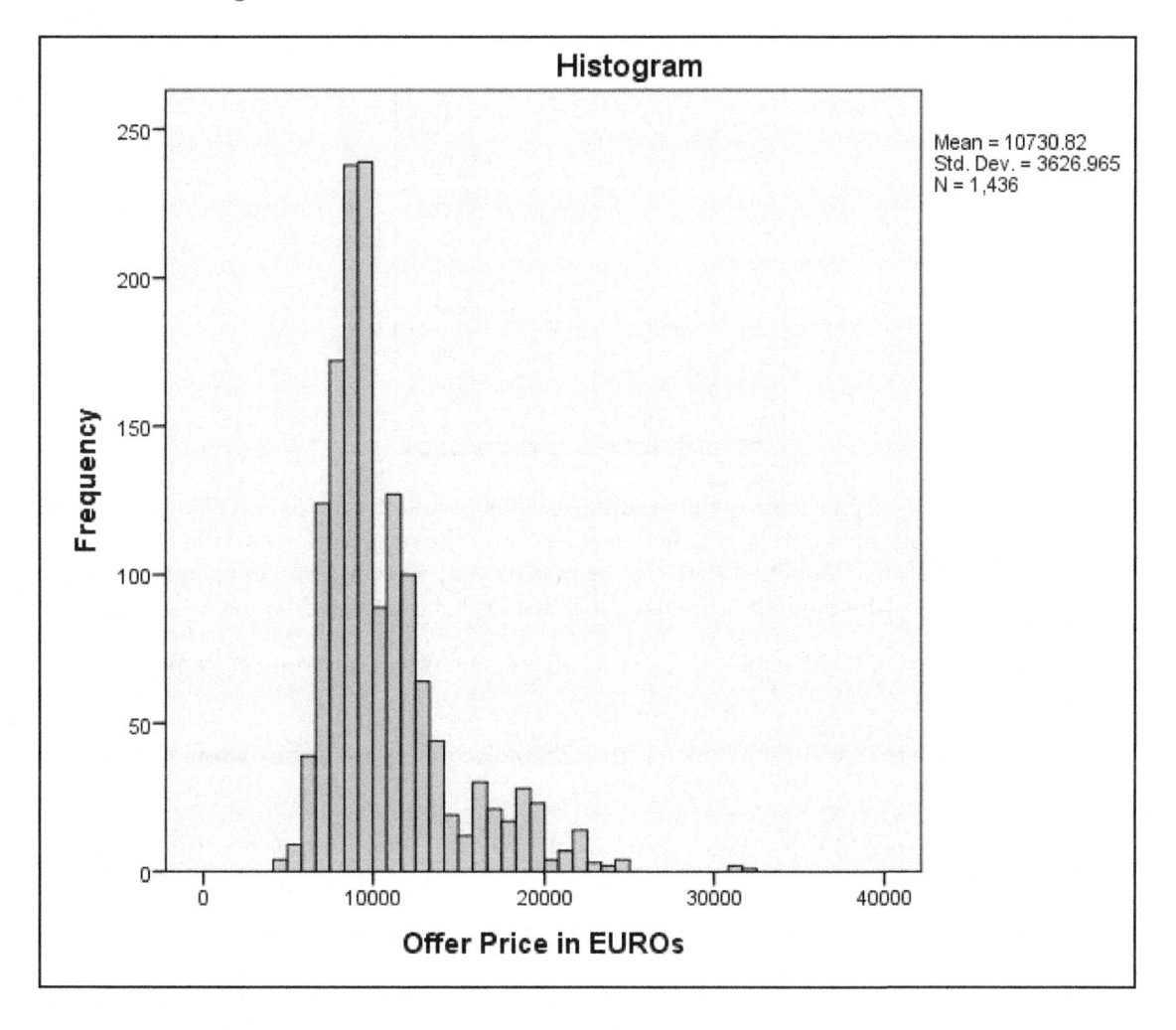

Histogram

Mean = 10730.82
Std. Dev. = 3626.965
N = 1,436

Offer Price in EUROs

[73]

Dealing with Missing Data and Outliers

The histogram has a notable peak before 10,000 and in addition, the right tail is skewed. For this reason, methods that focus on the values in the right tail can be useful. The histogram also presents summary statistics--mean, standard deviation, and number of cases. The sample size(**N**) is **1,436**, the **mean** is **10730.82**, and the standard deviation(**Std. Dev.**) is **3626.965**.

Here is the table of percentile values:

Statistics		
Price		
N	Valid	1436
	Missing	0
Minimum		4350
Maximum		32500
Percentiles	1	5865.35
	5	6900.00
	10	7450.00
	25	8450.00
	50	9900.00
	75	11950.00
	90	15950.00
	95	18950.00
	99	22407.50

The **50**th percentile--also known as the **median**--is 9,900 while the mean is 10,730.82. The **mean** is the center of mass and is obtained as the sum of the observations divided by the number of observations. Note that here the mean pulled up in value by the values in the right tail. In contrast, the median is the middle value and is unaffected by the other values.

The **90**th percentile is 15,950, which means that 10% of the prices are more extreme than this value.

The **95**th percentile is 18,950, which means that 5% of the prices are more extreme than this value.

The **99**th percentile is 22,407.50, which means that 1% of the prices are more extreme than this value. Note that the maximum price is 32,500, so there is a spread of about 10,000 in the prices in the top 1%.

Descriptives for standardized scores

Descriptives is an easy-to-use procedure that produces summary statistics for numeric fields. An added feature is that you can compute and add standardized versions of select fields to your active Data Editor window. Here, **standardization** refers to scaling a variable relative to its sample mean and standard deviation, which produces a new variable with a mean of 0 and standard deviation of 1.

The purpose of deriving standardized variables is to take advantage of known properties of the normal distribution. Note that the theoretical normal distribution is an ideal type, and the empirical distribution of the data will at best only approximate the theoretical normal distribution. In addition, the normal distribution may or may not be an appropriate reference distribution for the data.

If the empirical distribution is roughly bell-shaped, then you might derive standard scores and use cutpoints to identify outliers and extremes. For example, if you use cutpoints smaller than -2 or bigger than 2 in value, you expect to identify approximately 5% of the data that are outliers by one conventional definition. Otherwise, if you use cutpoints smaller than -3 or bigger than 3 in value, you expect to identify approximately 0.27% (about 3 points in 1,000) of the data that is extreme.

Here is the syntax to produce descriptive statistics on `Price`:

```
DESCRIPTIVES VARIABLES=Price
  /SAVE
  /STATISTICS=MEAN STDDEV MIN MAX.
```

The `/SAVE` subcommand produces a standardized `Price` variable and adds it to the active data window. By default, IBM SPSS Statistics names the new variable by concatenating an initial letter Z to the front of the existing name. Therefore, the standardized version of `Price` will be named `ZPrice`. Additionally, the newly-derived variables are added to the right of the right-most variable in the Data Editor.

Here is a snapshot of prices along with their corresponding standardized scores:

Price	ZPrice
19950	2.54184
19950	2.54184
32500	6.00204
31000	5.58847
31275	5.66429
24950	3.92041

The Price of 32,500 Euros corresponds to a standard score of about 6. You can interpret this as follows: A Toyota Corolla with an offer price of 32,500 Euros has an offer price about 6 standard deviations above the mean offer price.

As a suggested analysis, you might decide to take a closer look at any observation for which the standardized price is greater than or equal to 3.

The Examine procedure for extreme values and boxplot

Examine provides a useful collection of statistics and charts. You can use Examine either for single-variable analysis or for analysis of a numeric variable within levels of one or more categorical variables. Here, we consider Examine for univariate analysis and identification of potential outliers. In particular, we will focus on the Extreme Values table and the boxplot.

Here is the syntax for Examine:

```
EXAMINE VARIABLES=Price
  /PLOT BOXPLOT
  /COMPARE GROUPS
  /STATISTICS DESCRIPTIVES EXTREME
  /CINTERVAL 95
  /MISSING LISTWISE
  /NOTOTAL.
```

In particular, the /PLOT subcommand specifies the boxplot and the /STATISTICS subcommand specifies the Extreme Values table.

Dealing with Missing Data and Outliers

Here is the `Extreme Values` table:

Extreme Values

			Case Number	Value
Price	Highest	1	39	32500
		2	41	31275
		3	40	31000
		4	45	24990
		5	42	24950[a]
	Lowest	1	55	4350
		2	140	4400
		3	83	4450
		4	56	4750
		5	87	5150

a. Only a partial list of cases with the value 24950 are shown in the table of upper extremes.

The table shows the five highest values and five lowest values for the indicated variable along with the case number of the value. Displaying 10 observations is an arbitrary choice, but nonetheless serves to show the very extreme values at either end of the data. Note that it is possible for more than one record to have the same value. If the table cannot show all cases with a given value, the value will be flagged with a footnote. For example, case 42 has a value of 24,950 and the value is flagged with the footnote **a**, meaning that there are other values of 24,950 in the data that are not shown in the table.

Dealing with Missing Data and Outliers

Here is the boxplot for `Price`:

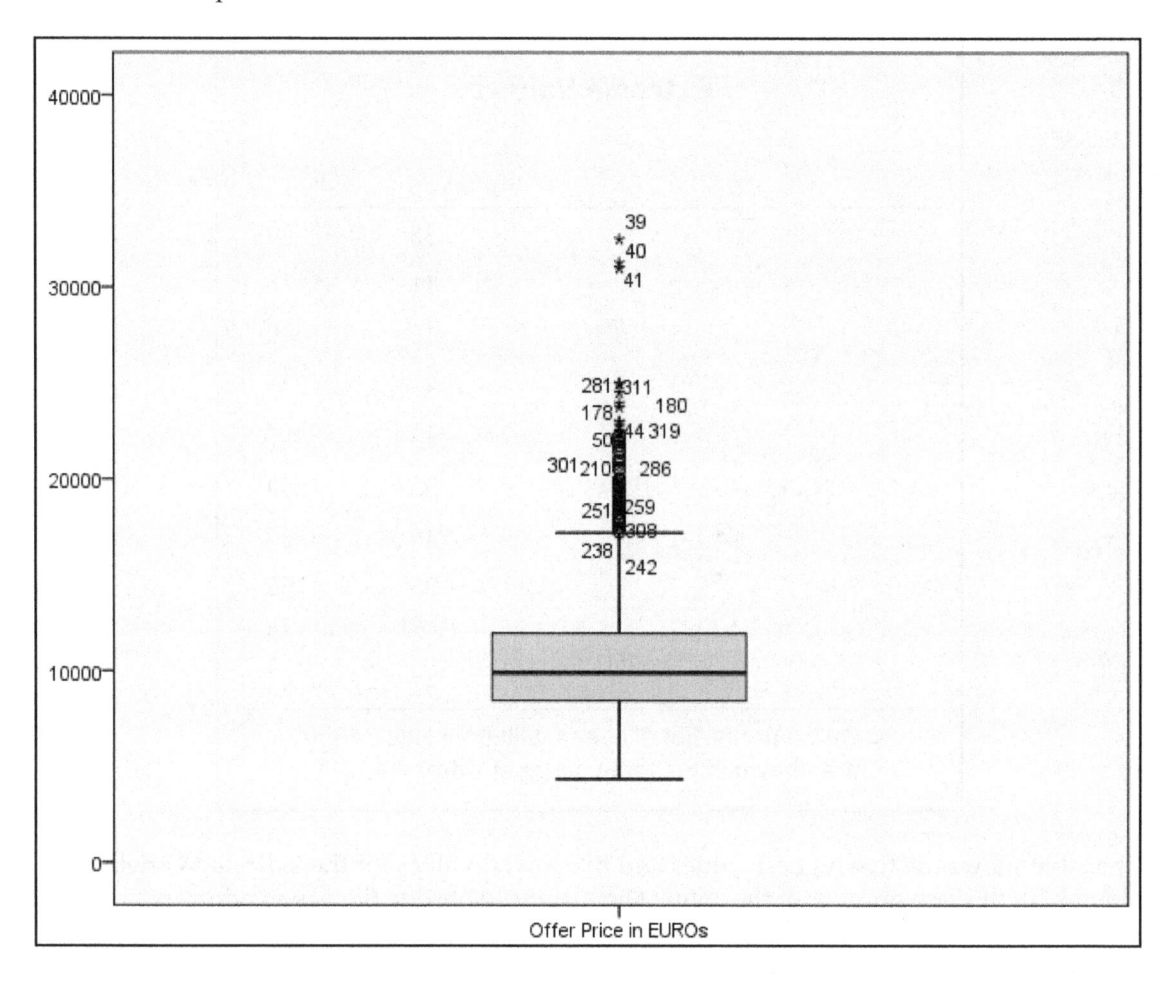

[Boxplot showing Offer Price in EUROs, with outliers labeled including 39, 40, 41 near 30000+, and numerous outliers around 18000-25000 including 281, 311, 178, 180, 50, 44, 319, 301, 210, 286, 251, 259, 308, 238, 242]

The boxplot shows five statistics: **lower whisker**, **first quartile**, **median**, **third quartile**, and **upper whisker**. The lower and upper whiskers might or might not be the true extreme values in the data, because they are determined in a way that depends on the spread in the middle of the data.

> The boxplot is useful to display the distribution of a numeric variable and pinpoint outliers. Note that the boxplot makes use of the median and interquartile range, which are robust alternatives to the mean and standard deviation.

Dealing with Missing Data and Outliers

The **median** is the middle value--half the data points are below it and half are above it. In the boxplot, the median is the thick line in the middle of the box. In the boxplot for `Price`, the median looks to be close to 10,000 in value. Inspection of the Descriptives table (not shown) shows that the median price is 9,900.

In similar fashion, the **first quartile** is the value that one-quarter of the values are below and three-quarters of the values are above. Likewise, the **third quartile** is the value such that three-quarters of the values are below and one-quarter of the values are above it. These values form the edges, or hinges, of the box in the boxplot. The middle half of the data is in the range of the box. Visual inspection of the boxplot for Price suggests that the box is in the range of about 8,500 to 12,000. The difference between these two values is called the **interquartile range (IQR)**. For Price, the IQR is about 3,500.

The whiskers in the boxplot show the minimum and maximum that might or might not be true extremes and are defined relative to the center of the data. In particular, compute the whiskers as follows:

- upper whisker = $Q3 + 1.5 * IQR$
- lower whisker = $Q1 - 1.5 * IQR$

Here, Q1 is the first quartile, Q3 is the third quartile, and IQR is the interquartile range. The value of 1.5 was specified by John Tukey, the developer of the boxplot. Outliers are points that lie outside the whiskers.

> For a variable that approximately follows a normal distribution, the points outside of the whiskers will comprise about 0.7% of the observations.

If you inspect the boxplot of `Price`, you will see that the lower whisker is a true minimum while the upper whisker is not a true maximum. Beyond the upper whisker are outliers (symbol **o**) and extremes (symbol *****). We have already seen how outliers are defined. If you extend another 1.5 times the interquartile range above the upper whisker or below the lower whisker, then you have **extremes** beyond those distances.

The numbers alongside the symbols are observation numbers. From the plot, you can see that observations **41**, **40**, and **39** have the three most extreme prices.

Detecting multivariate outliers

A histogram can reveal an unusual observation on one variable. However, sometimes a point stands out not on a single variable but instead on a combination of values on two or more variables. For this reason, approaches such as those outlined previously are not sufficient to identify unusual observations. Here, we will see how to use IBM SPSS Statistics to detect multivariate outliers.

Here is a scatterplot of simulated data following a bivariate normal distribution:

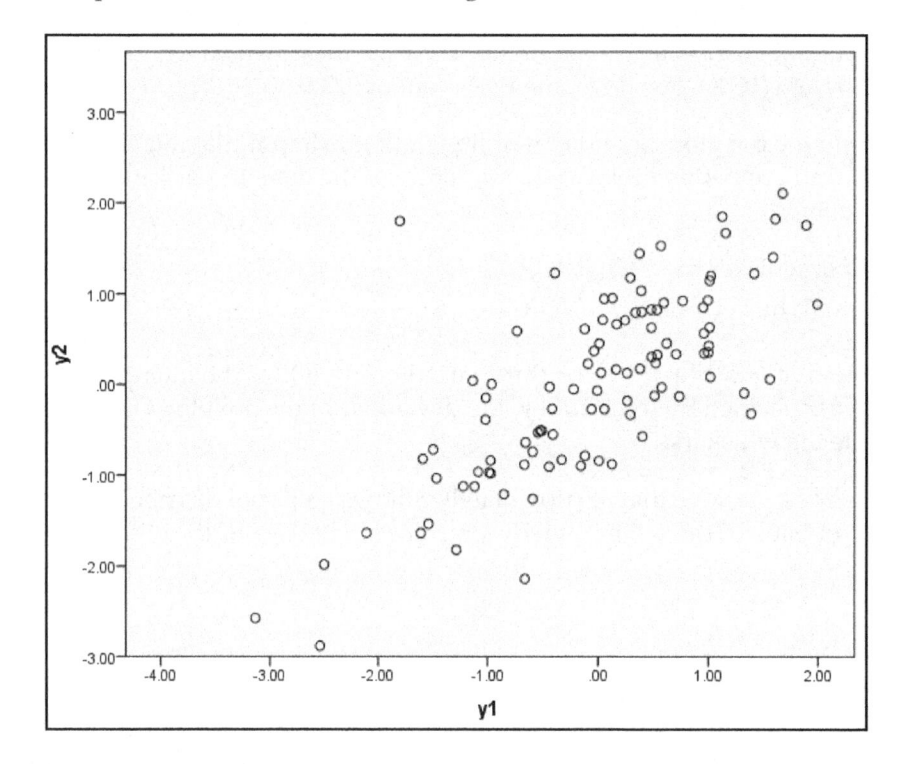

The points generally trend from the lower left to upper right, but there is one point up and to the left by itself. Note that this point would not stand out if you produced separate histograms of **Y1** or **Y2**.

One approach to detecting a multivariate outlier is to compute the **Mahalanobis** distances for each data row. The Mahalanobis distance is a multivariate extension of a Z-score.

Dealing with Missing Data and Outliers

Recall that the Z-score captures how far a point is from the center, where the center is the mean and the distance is in standard normal units. The Mahalanobis distance captures how far a point is from the centroid of the scatter of points, taking into account the variances and covariance's of the variables. Note that this makes the Mahalanobis distance different from the Euclidean distance. The Mahalanobis distance squared is referenced against a *chi-square distribution*, where the degrees of freedom parameter is based on the number of input variables in the computation.

In IBM SPSS Statistics, the Mahalanobis distance is available in Discriminant and Regression, and we will work with Regression. These two procedures are used in predictive modeling and classification, which is not our goal here, so instead we use them in a special way. The "trick" to computing the Mahalanobis distance for our purpose is to compute a random variable, use it as a dependent variable in regression, and use the variables being analyzed (Y1 and Y2 in this example) as predictors in the regression. This works because the Mahalanobis distance in regression is an individual case statistic based on the inputs only; therefore, the target variable and regression analysis are of no interest aside from computing the distances.

> Note that the MAHAL statistic as given in IBM SPSS Statistics REGRESSION is already in squared units.

Here is the syntax to set up the regression analysis for our Y1 Y2 example:

```
set seed 12345.
compute dependent=rv.normal(0,1).
REGRESSION
  /MISSING LISTWISE
  /STATISTICS COEFF OUTS R ANOVA
  /CRITERIA=PIN(.05) POUT(.10)
  /NOORIGIN
  /DEPENDENT dependent
  /METHOD=ENTER y1 y2
  /SAVE MAHAL(mahal2vars).
```

The COMPUTE command computes a variable named dependent by drawing from a random variable.

The REGRESSION code is easily produced via specification of the **Linear Regression** dialog box, available in the menus as **Analyze | Regression | Linear,** with added selection of the **Save** button. On the REGRESSION command, note that the /SAVE subcommand saves the Mahalanobis distances in a variable named mahal2vars.

Dealing with Missing Data and Outliers

Suppose that you are interested in looking at approximately 1% of the most unusual cases. The critical value for a chi-square distribution with two degrees of freedom where the right-tail area is 0.01 is equal to **9.21**. If you wish to derive this critical value in IBM SPSS Statistics, use the COMPUTE function:

```
IDF.CHISQ(.99,2)
```

By this criterion, there are two cases flagged--observation **57** has a Mahalanobis distance value of 9.69 and observation **101** has a Mahalanobis distance value of 24.23. See the scatterplot with these two points labeled:

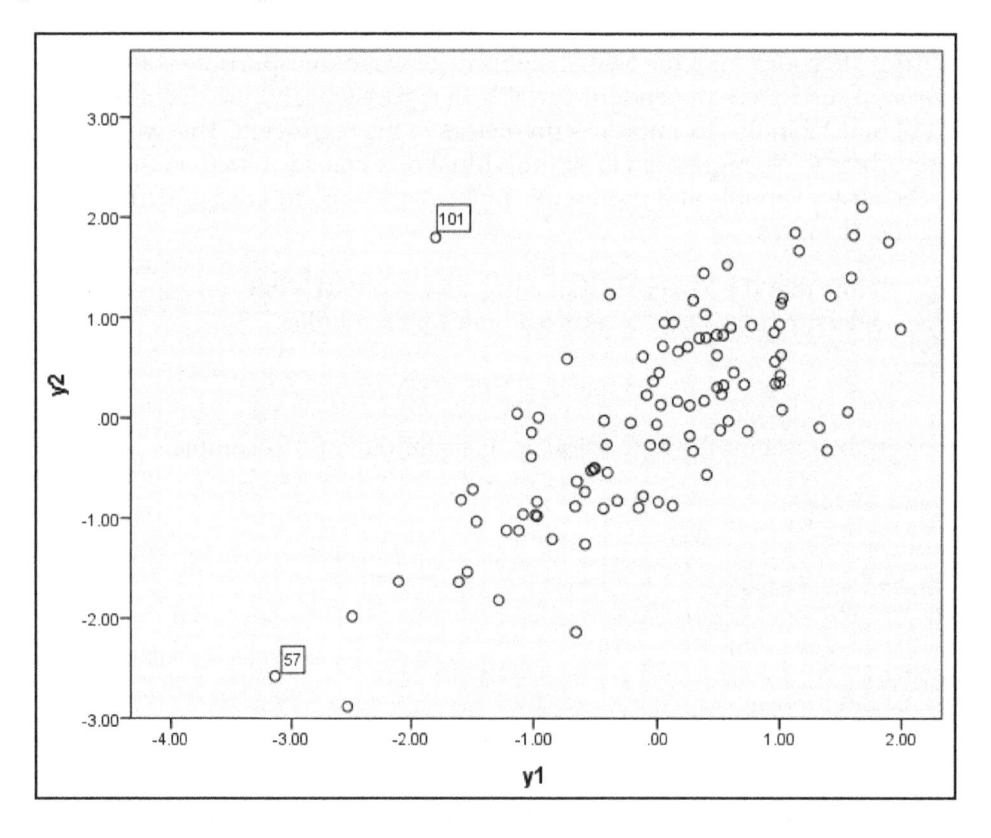

Observation **57** aligns with the main scatter of points and has the smallest value on **Y1** and the second smallest on **Y2**. Observation **101** is the point up and to the left that we saw before. In visual inspection, observation **101** might not appear that far from the mass of points, but visuals can be deceiving. The Mahalanobis distance takes into account the correlation between **Y1** and **Y2**, so distance here is not based on Euclidean distances.

Dealing with Missing Data and Outliers

Instead of visually inspecting the scatterplot or the calculated values of the Mahalanobis distances for the points, you can use a graphic approach called the **Q-Q plot**. A **Q-Q plot** is an exploratory plot used to check the validity of a distributional assumption for a dataset. Here, we wish to assess whether the Mahalanobis distances follow a chi-square distribution with a certain number of degrees of freedom. The Q-Q plot places the theoretical distribution on the horizontal axis and the sample distribution on the vertical axis. In the IBM SPSS Statistics menus, navigate to **Analyze** | **Descriptive Statistics** | **Q-Q Plots**.

In the Q-Q Plots dialog box, perform the following:

1. Place `mahal2vars` in the variables box.
2. Set the **Test distribution** drop bar to **Chi-square**.
3. Set **df** to 2.
4. Paste the syntax and run it.

Here is the plot:

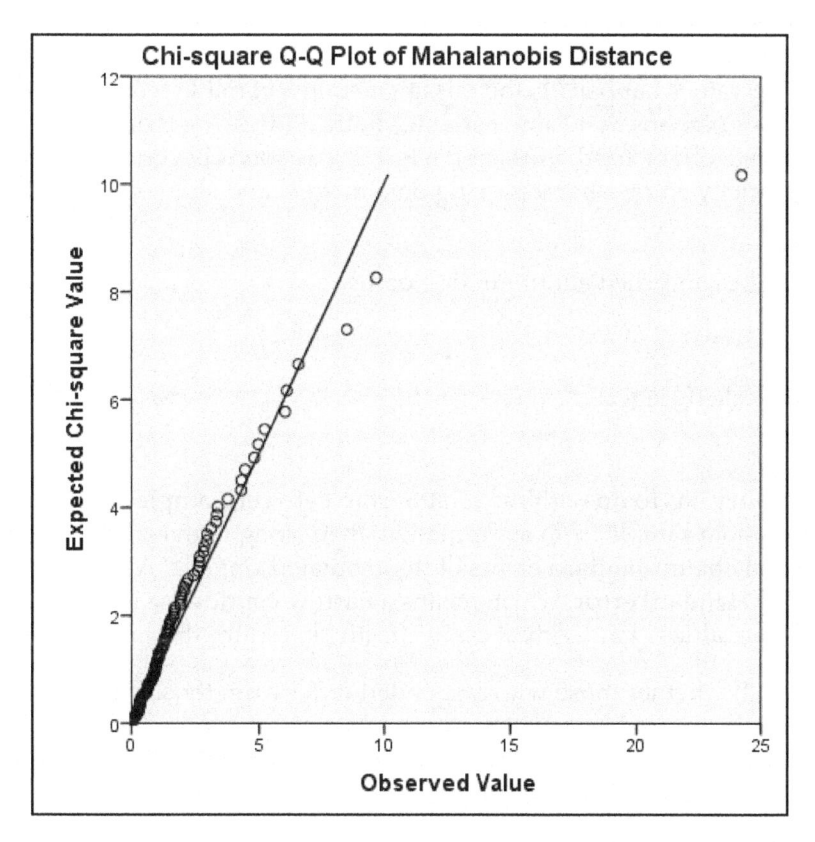

Note that case 57 and especially 101 stand out--they are the right-most two points with the largest **Observed Values**. If the data follows the assumed distribution, then the points ought to fall along the diagonal straight line that goes from the lower left to upper right. The point 101 in particular is away from this line.

Note that the Q-Q plot approach is a general approach that works with two or more input variables. It is possible that in the many-variable case, neither histograms nor bivariate scatterplots reveal unusual points, and yet there could be multivariate outliers. For this reason, the Q-Q plot is extremely useful. Additionally, this technique is best used when linearity and normality at least approximately hold. Be aware that statisticians have proposed some robust alternatives to the approach shown here.

Missing data

Just as you ought to assess outliers and extreme values in the variables being analyzed, you should also assess the missing responses in the variables being analyzed. For a given variable, what number or fraction of responses is missing? What is or are the mechanisms by which missing values happen? Is the missingness in a variable related to values on another variable or perhaps that same variable? Fully addressing these questions in the context of your data can be hard work, and a full discussion is beyond the scope of this book. Here, we briefly address why missing data matters and show some analyses that you can do.

Why should you be concerned about missing data?

There are two reasons:

- Statistical efficiency
- Bias

Statistical efficiency has to do with the relationship between sample size and precision. If your data is a random sample from a population, then along with estimates such as the sample mean, you obtain standard errors of the estimated statistic. A larger sample size leads to a smaller standard error, which means a narrow confidence interval and increased precision. Missing values in individual cases effectively reduce the sample size.

Bias has to do with whether those who responded differ from those who did not respond. In a given setting, bias might be nonexistent, small, or large. Moreover, assessing bias can be difficult. In any event, a biased estimate can give rise to misleading inferences.

Missing values in Frequencies

When you run Frequencies, by default you get a Statistics table that gives a summary breakdown of valid and missing counts for each variable.

Suppose you run Frequencies on a number of variables from GSS2014:

```
FREQUENCIES VARIABLES=AGE SEX RACE EDUC PAEDUC MAEDUC SPEDUC MARITAL
    /ORDER=ANALYSIS.
```

Here is the `Statistics` table (transposed for readability):

Statistics	N Valid	Missing
AGE	2529	9
SEX	2538	0
RACE	2538	0
EDUC	2537	1
PAEDUC	1885	653
MAEDUC	2271	267
SPEDUC	1148	1390
MARITAL	2534	4

To transpose the table, perform the following steps:

1. Find the table in the **Viewer**.
2. Right-click to show the context menu and edit in a separate window.
3. Find the **Pivot** menu in the **Pivot Table** window.
4. Select **Transpose Rows and Columns**.
5. Close the **Pivot Table** window.

Inspecting the table reveals that **AGE**, **SEX**, **RACE**, **EDUC**, and **MARITAL** are complete or nearly so. On the other hand, **PAEDUC**, **MAEDUC**, and **SPEDUC** each have sizeable missing data counts.

Dealing with Missing Data and Outliers

How did the missing data for these variables come about?

Answer: The respondent answers directly about his or her own education and through recall, provides responses for **PAEDUC**, **MAEDUC**, and **SPEDUC**. Missing values occur when the respondent does not know the answer, or does not give an answer, or the question is not applicable. You can learn the details by inspecting the Frequency table for any of the variables.

Notice that **SPEDUC** is missing on over half of the responses. Why?

Answer: This is because **SPEDUC** can only have a valid response if the respondent's marital status is married, and slightly less than half of the respondents are married.

Missing values in Descriptives

You can also obtain summary information about missing data using Descriptives. Descriptives is useful when you are analyzing scale variables. Descriptives does not produce a frequency table or chart, but simply produces summary statistics for scale variables. In addition, Descriptives produces a listwise valid number of cases.

Suppose that you run Descriptives on the scale variables previously analyzed in FREQUENCIES:

```
DESCRIPTIVES VARIABLES=AGE EDUC PAEDUC MAEDUC SPEDUC
   /STATISTICS=MEAN STDDEV MIN MAX.
```

Here is the `Descriptive Statistics` table produced by that command:

Descriptive Statistics

	N	Minimum	Maximum	Mean	Std. Deviation
AGE	2529	18	89	49.01	17.412
EDUC	2537	0	20	13.70	3.071
PAEDUC	1885	0	20	11.78	4.200
MAEDUC	2271	0	20	11.66	3.892
SPEDUC	1148	0	20	13.86	3.285
Valid N (listwise)	863				

Note that the **N** column agrees with the **Valid N** column in the Statistics table produced by Frequencies. In addition, the `Descriptive Statistics` table presents default summary statistics for each variable: **Minimum**, **Maximum**, **Mean**, and **Standard Deviation**. Finally, note the line for **Valid N (listwise)**. The **N** listed is 863. This is the number of complete rows for the variables in the list. That is, there are 863 data rows with complete information for **AGE**, **EDUC**, **PAEDUC**, **MAEDUC**, and **SPEDUC**. The other rows are missing for at least one of the variables in this list.

Suppose that you remove **AGE** from the list and rerun the Descriptives procedure. Here is the **Descriptive Statistics** table:

Descriptive Statistics

	N	Minimum	Maximum	Mean	Std. Deviation
EDUC	2537	0	20	13.70	3.071
PAEDUC	1885	0	20	11.78	4.200
MAEDUC	2271	0	20	11.66	3.892
SPEDUC	1148	0	20	13.86	3.285
Valid N (listwise)	868				

This time the **Valid N (listwise)** is 868. Evidently, **AGE** was uniquely missing for a handful of cases.

> **TIP**
> Run the DESCRIPTIVES procedure to obtain the **Valid N (listwise)**, also known as the number of complete cases for the listed variables.

Missing value patterns

It can be useful to perform a pattern analysis of valid and missing patterns across a set of variables. In this section, we will present a way to do so using IBM SPSS Statistics syntax. We will present the syntax without too much comment, as other chapters will elaborate on the commands featured here.

Dealing with Missing Data and Outliers

Here is a snapshot of the first 10 rows of GSS2014, which show the individual values for four education variables--**EDUC, PAEDUC, MAEDUC,** and **SPEDUC**:

	ID	EDUC	PAEDUC	MAEDUC	SPEDUC
1	1	16	IAP	9	IAP
2	2	16	16	14	16
3	3	13	IAP	12	IAP
4	4	16	12	12	16
5	5	17	8	17	15
6	6	17	16	14	14
7	7	12	DK	DK	NA
8	8	17	12	12	20
9	9	10	IAP	9	IAP
10	10	15	IAP	10	12

For each of these variables, valid responses range from 0 through 20, while there are various missing codes to represent "Don't know," "No Answer," and "Inapplicable." Inspection of the first 10 rows of data shows, for example, that Case ID **4** has valid responses across all four variables, while Case **ID 1** has missing values on **PAEDUC** and **SPEDUC**.

Consider that each variable can be either valid or missing and there are four variables, therefore, there are potentially 16 patterns of valid and missing across these four variables. These patterns can occur with varying frequencies, and a frequency summary of the patterns could be useful.

Here is the IBM SPSS Statistics syntax to compute a series of flag indicators that are 1 if a value is a missing code and 0 if a value is a valid code:

```
IF MISSING(EDUC)=1 EDUC_MIS=1.
IF MISSING(EDUC)=0 EDUC_MIS=0.
IF MISSING(PAEDUC)=1 PAEDUC_MIS=1.
IF MISSING(PAEDUC)=0 PAEDUC_MIS=0.
IF MISSING(MAEDUC)=1 MAEDUC_MIS=1.
IF MISSING(MAEDUC)=0 MAEDUC_MIS=0.
IF MISSING(SPEDUC)=1 SPEDUC_MIS=1.
IF MISSING(SPEDUC)=0 SPEDUC_MIS=0.
FORMATS EDUC_MIS TO SPEDUC_MIS (F1.0).
EXECUTE.
```

Dealing with Missing Data and Outliers

The `IF` commands derive new variables after testing a condition. For example, consider the first `IF` command and consider processing a single record. The `MISSING` function is a function that evaluates as true or false. A true evaluation results in a 1 while a false evaluation results in a 0. Inside the parentheses is an expression; in this case, the variable name **EDUC**. Therefore, the `MISSING` function is evaluating whether or not **EDUC** has any valid or missing value. Based on the evaluation, the flag variable `EDUC_MIS` is set to 0 or 1.

Here is a snapshot of the first 10 rows of GSS2014 showing the individual values for the four flag variables--**EDUC_MIS, PAEDUC_MIS, MAEDUC_MIS,** and **SPEDUC_MIS**:

ID	EDUC_MIS	PAEDUC_MIS	MAEDUC_MIS	SPEDUC_MIS
1	0	1	0	1
2	0	0	0	0
3	0	1	0	1
4	0	0	0	0
5	0	0	0	0
6	0	0	0	0
7	0	1	1	1
8	0	0	0	0
9	0	1	0	1
10	0	1	0	0

You can compare this figure to the previous figure to see that we have captured the patterns of valid and missing for each individual row.

The next step is to obtain summary counts of the frequency of each pattern. There are a number of approaches to doing this, but we will use aggregation, which **rolls up** similar records (as indicated by values on the **break** variables) into a summary record with a frequency count.

Here is the `AGGREGATE` command:

```
AGGREGATE
  /OUTFILE=
'C:\Users\Tony\Documents\KSBSPSSBOOK_DATA\chapter4\gssmissing\GSSExtractch4
2014\educvarsAGG.sav'
  /BREAK=EDUC_MIS PAEDUC_MIS MAEDUC_MIS SPEDUC_MIS
  /frequency=N.
```

The /OUTFILE subcommand writes the aggregated results to the specified file. Here is the aggregated file:

	EDUC_MIS	PAEDUC_MIS	MAEDUC_MIS	SPEDUC_MIS	frequency
1	0	0	0	0	868
2	0	0	0	1	905
3	0	0	1	0	51
4	0	0	1	1	61
5	0	1	0	0	186
6	0	1	0	1	312
7	0	1	1	0	42
8	0	1	1	1	112
9	1	1	1	0	1

The first row shows that the pattern **0,0,0,0** has a frequency of 868. Note that this is the number of complete cases on the four variables, and that 868 was the listwise **Valid N** that we saw in one of the DESCRIPTIVES tables. The second row shows that the pattern **0,0,0,1** has a frequency of 905. This count reflects respondents who provide their own highest grade completed, report their father's and mother's highest grade attained, but do not have a spouse.

You interpret the other rows in a similar fashion. Note that there are only nine patterns out of the sixteen possible ones. In sum, some patterns occur with relatively large frequency, some with less frequency, and some not at all.

As a final point, IBM SPSS Statistics has an add-on module called IBM SPSS Missing Values that has additional capabilities for missing value pattern detection.

Replacing missing values

IBM SPSS Statistics has a simple replace missing values facility on the **Transform** menu. Replace missing values offers the following replacement methods:

- Series mean
- Mean of nearby points
- Median of nearby points
- Linear interpolation
- Linear trend at point

It is important to note that these methods are ad hoc methods and do not necessarily have any good statistical properties. As an aside, some of these methods were originally included in IBM SPSS Statistics in the context of time series data with occasional missing data.

Filling in with the series mean is sometimes called **mean imputation**. Mean imputation has the property that the variable has the same mean before and after imputing. However, filling in with the mean will affect the variable's standard deviation and variance, and also its covariance or correlation with the other variables. For this reason, some researchers do not use it at all, while others limit its use to situations in which the variable in question has a low number or fraction of missing values.

To demonstrate the use of this facility, we look again at **AGE**. Previous inspection showed that **AGE** has nine missing responses.

Here are the descriptive statistics for **AGE**:

Descriptive Statistics

	N	Minimum	Maximum	Mean	Std. Deviation
AGE	2529	18	89	49.01	17.412
Valid N (listwise)	2529				

Here is the `Replace Missing Value` syntax:

```
RMV /AGE_imp=SMEAN(AGE).
```

Note that `RMV` creates a new variable named `AGE_imp`. This variable has the mean age filled in for the cases in which `AGE` is missing.

Here is the `RMV` output:

Result Variables

	Result Variable	N of Replaced Missing Values	Case Number of Non-Missing Values First	Case Number of Non-Missing Values Last	N of Valid Cases	Creating Function
1	AGE_imp	9	1	2538	2538	SMEAN(AGE)

Dealing with Missing Data and Outliers

The RMV output reports that 9 cases had a missing value replaced by the variable mean. Here are the **Descriptive Statistcs** for **AGE** and **AGE_IMP**:

Descriptive Statistics	N	Minimum	Maximum	Mean	Std. Deviation
AGE	2529	18	89	49.01	17.412
AGE_imp	2538	18.0	89.0	49.013	17.3810
Valid N (listwise)	2529				

AGE and **AGE_imp** have the same mean but the standard deviation for **AGE_imp** is a bit smaller than the standard deviation for AGE.

This section demonstrated mean substitution.

> **TIP**
> Note that mean substitution is easy to do but is not necessarily a good thing to do. Here, the number of missing cases on **AGE** was small.

Summary

In the early stages of working with a dataset, you gain data understanding by at least selectively performing outlier analysis and missing value analysis. IBM SPSS Statistics offers many useful facilities for outlier analysis. In this chapter, we looked at ways of generating histograms, percentiles, z-scores, and boxplots to gain an understanding of outliers. In addition, most procedures in IBM SPSS Statistics produce a simple summary table of valid and missing cases. We also saw how to look at missing value patterns and perform mean substitution. In the next chapter, we turn to visually exploring the data through charts.

5
Visually Exploring the Data

In the two preceding chapters, you saw examples of graphs used to provide visual insights regarding patterns in the data. The box and whisker plots in Chapter 3, *Statistics for Individual Data Elements* and Chapter 4, *Dealing with Missing Data and Outliers*, made it easy to see how many outliers were present in the data. The scatterplot in Chapter 4, *Dealing with Missing Data and Outliers*, singled out the multivariate outliers quite readily.

This chapter will look at graphs in more detail, both in terms of what is available in SPSS and how graphs can be modified to enhance your ability to see the key patterns in the data.

At the outset, it is worth distinguishing between graphs created to enable the analytical process of data discovery and presentation graphics designed to communicate the findings to a broader audience. The initial focus will be on using graphs for discovery as the first task is to identify the important patterns in any dataset. The techniques used to enhance graphs for discovery purposes will also be useful when it comes to creating presentation graphics.

In this chapter, we will look at the following graph types as these are the most useful for both analytical discovery and presentation:

- Bar charts
- Histograms
- Scatterplots
- Box and whisker plots

The editing methods used to improve the appearance of graphs are very similar for all the graphs so by covering a range of types, you will also learn how to make use of many of these features.

Visually Exploring the Data

Graphs available in SPSS procedures

Many of the statistical techniques under the **Analyze** menu in SPSS offer graphs as part of the optional output that you can request. In Chapter 3, *Statistics for Individual Data Elements*, a boxplot was requested as part of the Explore procedure output. Among the Descriptive Statistics procedures, Frequencies, Descriptives, Crosstabs, and Explore all have optional graphs available. As you saw in Chapter 4, *Dealing with Outliers and Missing Data*, there are also specialty graphs (P-P and Q-Q plots) available. Many of the statistical procedures, such as ANOVA and regression, also include graph options. They will be explored in the chapters that cover these topics.

Obtaining bar charts with frequencies

For this first set of graph examples, we will use a small sample of **General Social Survey** (**GSS**) data from 2016 that was the basis for the examples in Chapter 3, *Statistics for Individual Data Elements*. Open the SPSS data file you created earlier (or download and open the full GSS2016 following the steps in Chapter 3, *Statistics for Individual Data Elements*).

> In Chapter 4, *Dealing with Outliers and Missing Data*, there are many examples of using the SPSS syntax to create results. If you prefer that approach, use it here as well. The graphs shown here will use the dialog boxes to request the results but using the Paste button rather than OK, you can generate the associated SPSS syntax.

Navigate to **Analyze | Descriptive Statistics | Frequencies** and select **Region** from the list of fields on the left, then click on **Charts** and the **Bar Charts** choice, and then **Continue** and **OK**.

In the output window, double-click on the bar chart to open the chart editor window. The editor allows you to make changes to a chart. Any changes that you make will replace the original version of the graphs with your modified version when you exit the editor. Click on any of the bars and notice that all of them are highlighted with a border and the second icon in the upper left is now active. When you move the mouse over it, **Show Data Labels** is displayed. This illustrates a central feature of the chart editor--first you select an element and then the associated editing features become available.

Refer to the following diagram for a better understanding:

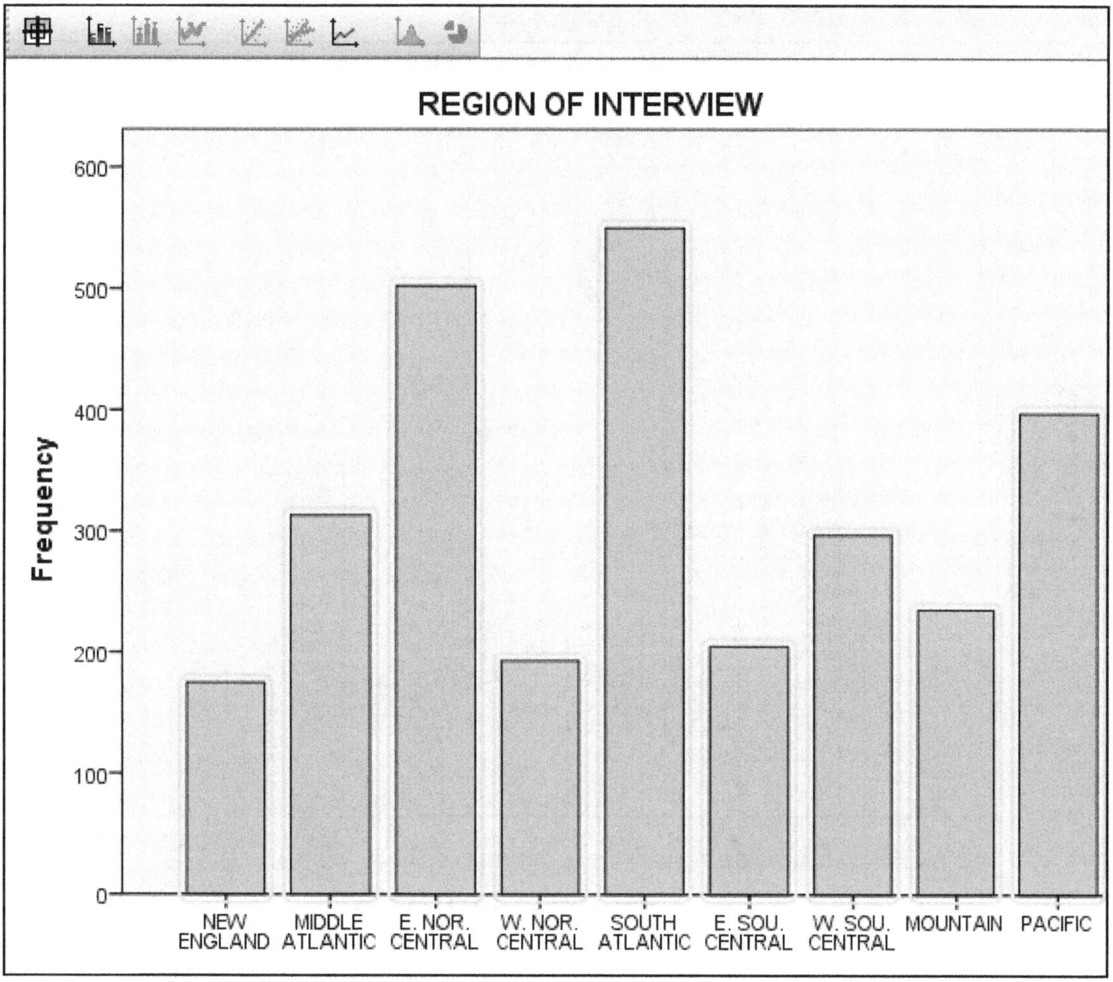
REGION OF INTERVIEW
Frequency
0
100
200
300
400
500
600
NEW ENGLAND
MIDDLE ATLANTIC
E. NOR. CENTRAL
W. NOR. CENTRAL
SOUTH ATLANTIC
E. SOU. CENTRAL
W. SOU. CENTRAL
MOUNTAIN
PACIFIC

Visually Exploring the Data

Click on the **Show Data Labels** icon and the counts will be added to each of the bars, as shown in the following image:

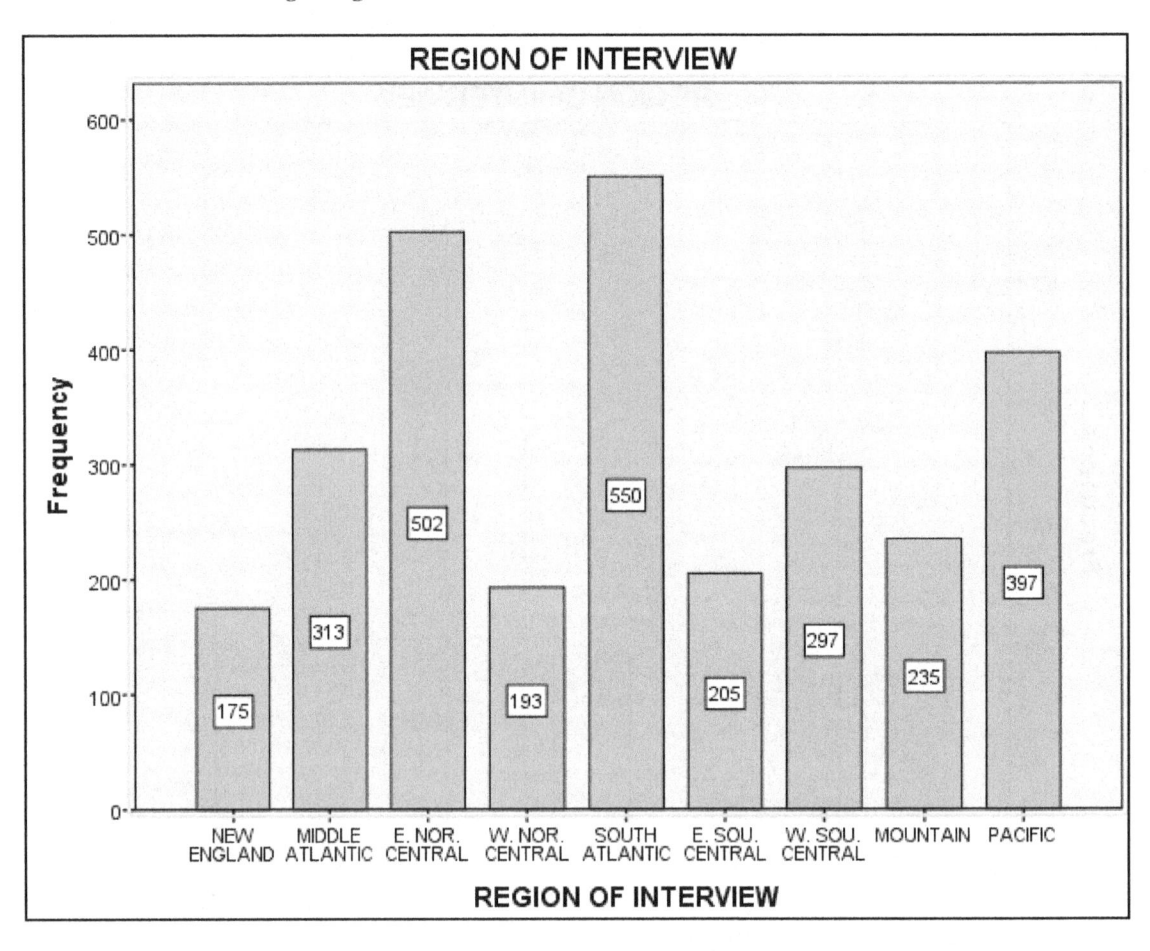

REGION OF INTERVIEW

Region	Frequency
NEW ENGLAND	175
MIDDLE ATLANTIC	313
E. NOR. CENTRAL	502
W. NOR. CENTRAL	193
SOUTH ATLANTIC	550
E. SOU. CENTRAL	205
W. SOU. CENTRAL	297
MOUNTAIN	235
PACIFIC	397

The title and horizontal axis label are redundant so double-click on **REGION OF INTERVIEW** at the bottom of the graph and backspace over the text to remove this label. The **Options** menu at the top (see the following image) provides access to many helpful editing features including adding annotation and reference lines.

The following screenshot gives a good understanding of the **Options** menu:

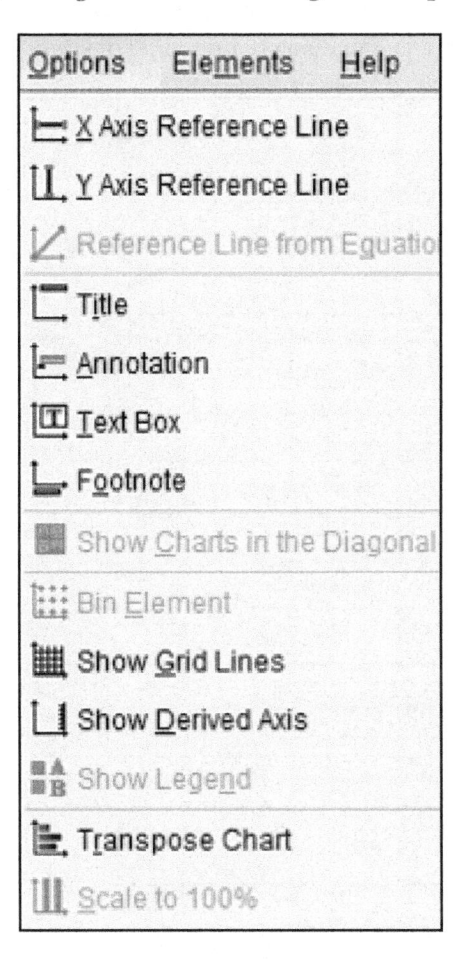

```
Options    Elements    Help
  ⊢ X Axis Reference Line
  ⊥ Y Axis Reference Line
  ∠ Reference Line from Equation
  ⌠ Title
  ⊨ Annotation
  ⊡ Text Box
  ⌞ Footnote
  ▦ Show Charts in the Diagonal
  ⋮⋮ Bin Element
  ⊞ Show Grid Lines
  ⊔ Show Derived Axis
  ▤ Show Legend
  ⊫ Transpose Chart
  ⫴ Scale to 100%
```

Select the **Transpose** option to make the bars horizontal. Note that by removing the axis label and changing the orientation, a better display of the region names is produced, which can be very useful if the graph is to be used for a presentation.

Visually Exploring the Data

You can also edit the individual bar labels if you want to spell out South and North for readability and consistency. Highlighting the labels for region, as shown in the following image, displays the font that you can also change, if so desired:

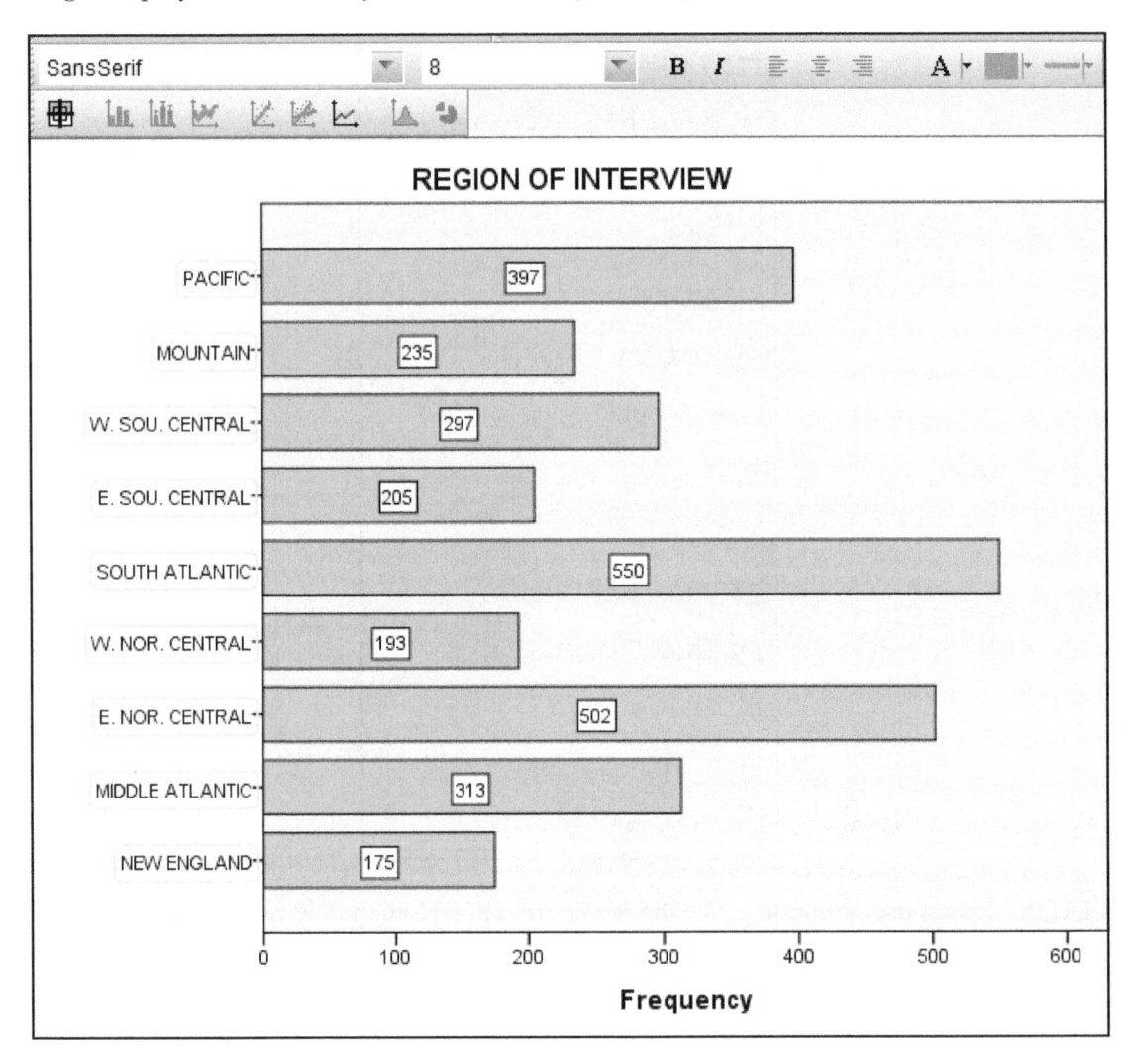

Visually Exploring the Data

Should you make a change and decide that it is not what you want, highlight the element in the graph and right-click to bring up a new menu. In the following example, the data labels added earlier are selected and the menu includes an option to hide them. It also has the **Transpose** option, which would switch the bars back to vertical in this case:

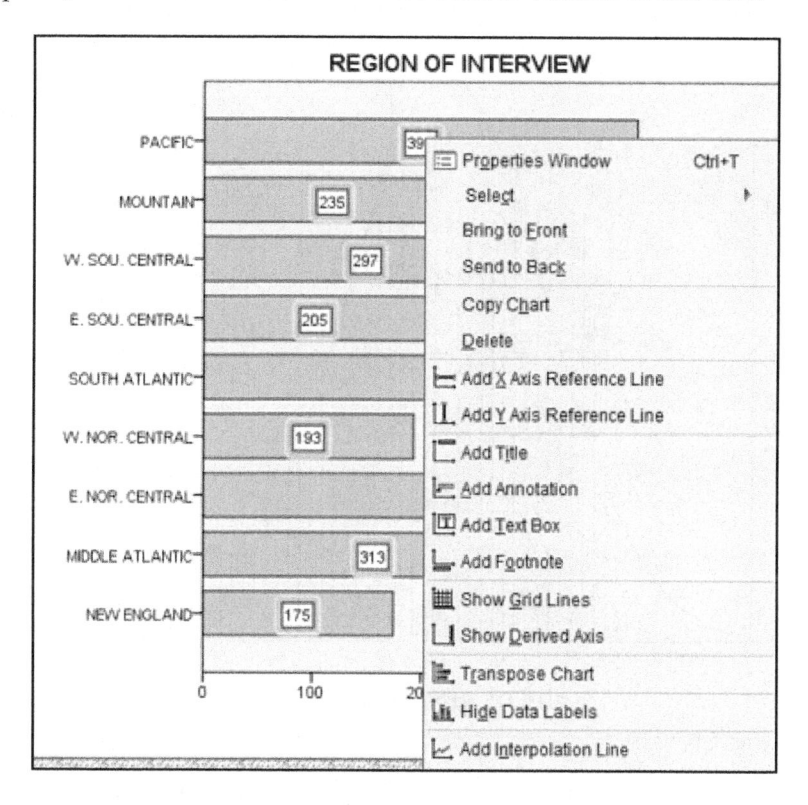

We will move on to other graph types but the techniques to edit graphs covered here for bar charts will apply in a similar manner to other chart types.

Obtaining a histogram with frequencies

In Chapter 4, *Dealing with Outliers and Missing Data*, there was an example of how to request a histogram and use it to examine the distribution of a field in the data. Here, we will expand on that by adding the normal curve for comparison purposes and making other modifications to explore the distribution in detail. To get started, navigate to **Analyze | Descriptive Statistics | Frequencies** and select **AGE** as the variable. In the **Chart** menu, specify a **Histogram** and check the box to show the normal curve.

[99]

This will produce a frequency table followed by a graph as follows:

Histogram

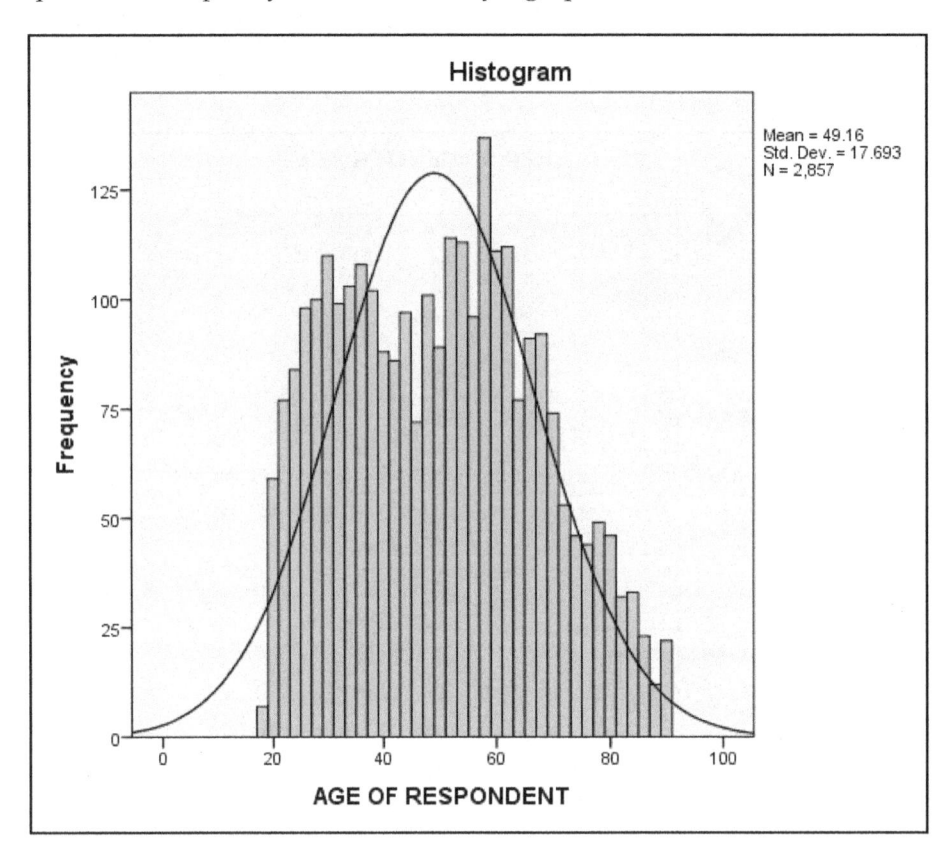

Mean = 49.16
Std. Dev. = 17.693
N = 2,857

AGE OF RESPONDENT

By superimposing the normal curve for a distribution with this mean and standard deviation it helps to emphasize that, in this instance, there are fewer people in this sample with an age near the mean than one might expect. The peaks are for ages lower and higher than the mean age of 49.

The range of the **AGE** axis goes from zero to over 100 but the frequency table makes it clear that the actual age range is from 18 to 89. To make the graph more readable, this range can be modified. Before making changes to this graph, make a copy so that you can go back to the original if you want to see the impact of the changes. Right-click on the graph icon on the left to highlight it, select **Copy**, and then **Paste After**. This is a useful way to experiment with changes to graphs while retaining the initial version so that you can start over if you desire.

Visually Exploring the Data

Activate the new copy of the histogram in the window on the right to open the **Chart Editor** window. Edit the x-axis to display the following dialog box. The data is shown as ranging from **17** to **91** because the histogram bins the values in groups (here each group contains three years):

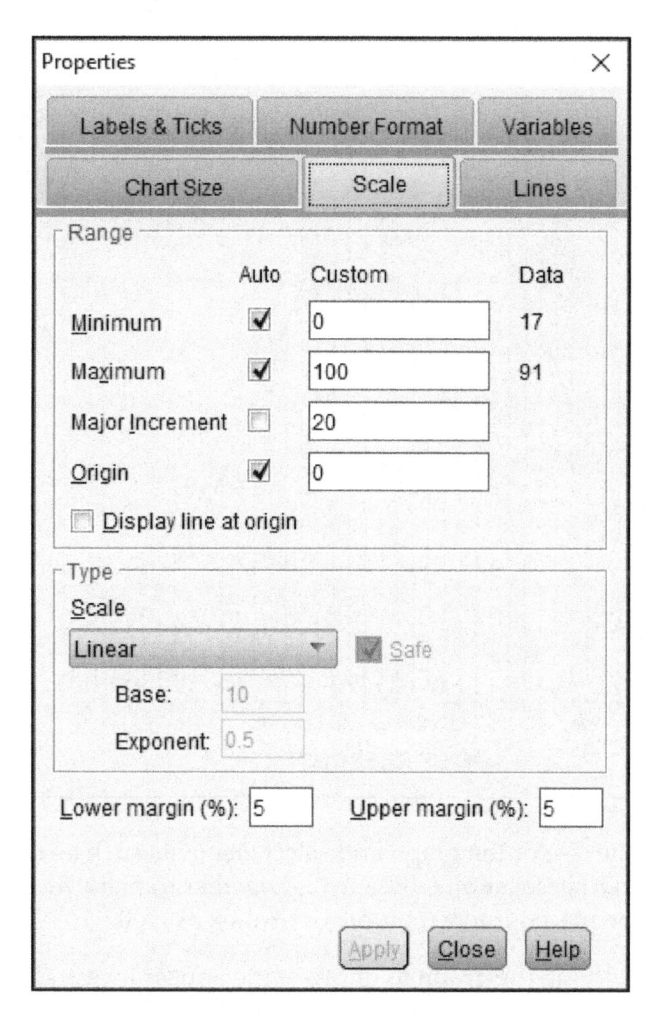

Visually Exploring the Data

Uncheck the **Auto** setting for the **Minimum** and **Maximum** and change them to 18 and 89, respectively. Change the major increment value to 5 and select **APPLY**. Your modified version of the original histogram should look like the graph in the following figure:

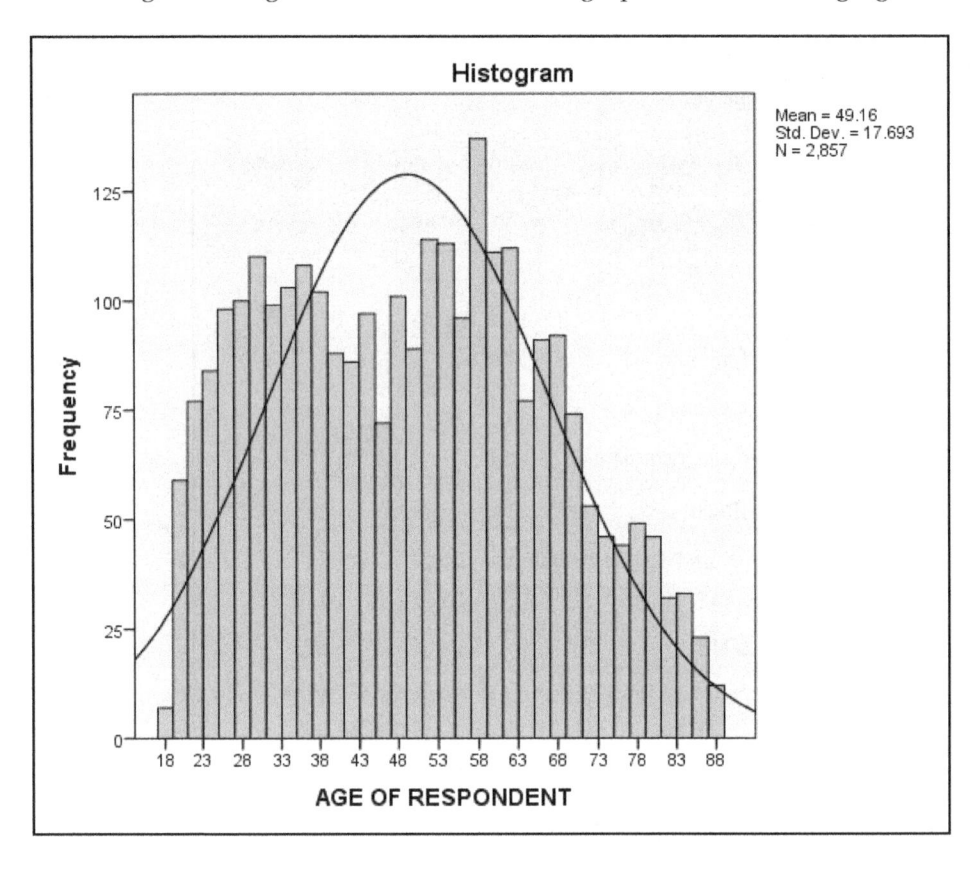

You can also change the size of the graph and select elements such as the box displaying the mean and drag it to another location or delete it altogether to make more room for the bars. Key information can be placed into a footnote or textbox as well.

> **TIP**
> Try modifying the graph to improve the appearance and to develop a sense of the chart editing process. Consider making another copy of the original graph if you want to start over from the beginning.

Creating graphs using chart builder

While it's often convenient to generate graphs using the options available with various statistical procedures in SPSS, there is an independent graphing feature that offers these same capabilities and more. In `Chapter 3`, *Statistics for Individual Data Elements*, a boxplot was shown as part of the output from Explore. This same boxplot can be requested using **Chart Builder**.

The following **Graph** menu contains several choices to produce graphs. The first option, Chart **Builder**, will be used for these examples. The second choice, **Graphboard Template Chooser**, can be useful in some situations but it makes use of a different chart editing interface with fewer capabilities. There are special graphs for specific purposes (**Weibull Plots**, **Compare Subgroups**, and **Regression Plots**) that will not be covered here. They provide graphs that are similar in many respects to those shown in this chapter but the emphasis is on the particular topic area implied by the name.

The last menu choice, **Legacy Dialogs**, is for SPSS users familiar with the earlier version of graphics and is not relevant to those getting started with SPSS currently:

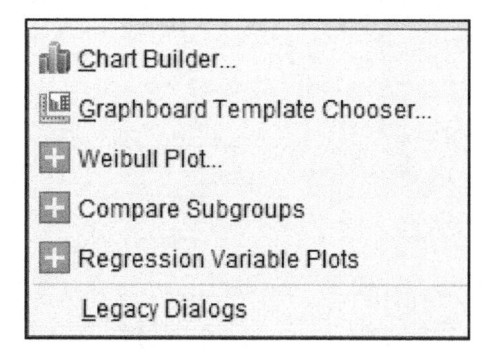

- Chart Builder...
- Graphboard Template Chooser...
- Weibull Plot...
- Compare Subgroups
- Regression Variable Plots
- Legacy Dialogs

Building a scatterplot

One of the most valuable methods for examining the relationship between two variables containing scale-level data is a scatterplot. In the previous chapter, scatterplots were used to detect points that deviated from the typical pattern--multivariate outliers. To produce a similar scatterplot using two fields from the 2016 General Social Survey data, navigate to **Graphs** | **Chart Builder**.

Visually Exploring the Data

An information box is displayed indicating that each field's measurement properties will be used to identify the types of graphs available so adjusting these properties is advisable. In this example, the properties will be modified as part of the graph specification process but you may want to alter the properties of some variables permanently so that they don't need to be changed for each use. For now, just select **OK** to move ahead.

In the main **Chart Builder** window, select **Scatter/Dot** from the menu at the lower left, double-click on the first graph to the right (**Simple Scatter**) to place it in the preview pane at the upper right, and then right-click on the first field labeled **HIGHEST YEAR OF SCHOOL**. Change this variable from **Nominal** to **Scale**, as shown in the following screenshot:

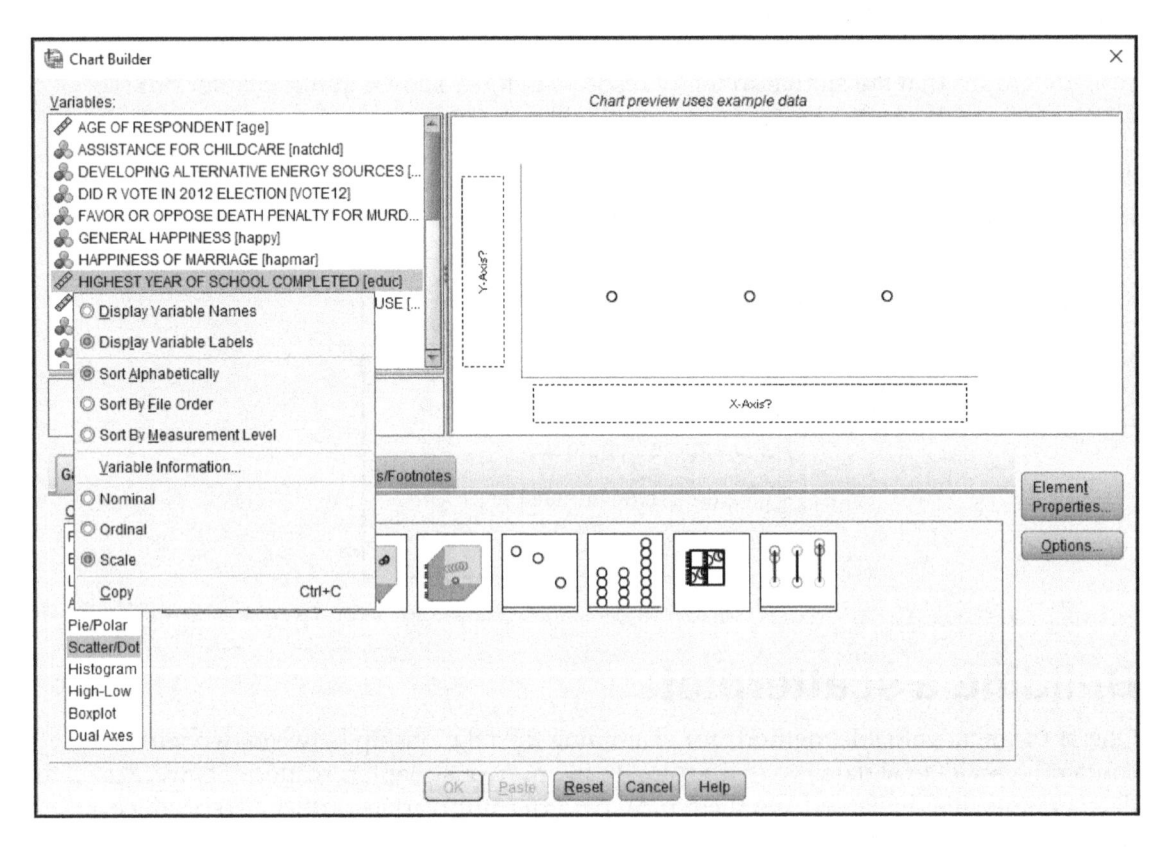

[104]

Visually Exploring the Data

> In most dialogs, only the first part of a variable's label is displayed so it may be necessary to expand the window containing the names to show enough details to select the right field. There are two variables here with similar labels, one for the respondent and one for the spouse, and showing more of the labels makes it easier to find the desired variable. Also, a variable's properties are influenced by the number of unique values and the presence of value labels. This is the reason why one of the education fields is **Nominal** and the other is **Scale**.

After changing the respondent's education to **Scale**, drag this field to the **X-Axis** location in the preview pane and drag spouse's education to the **Y-Axis** location. Once both elements are in place, the **OK** choice will become available.

Select it to produce the scatterplot in the following screenshot:

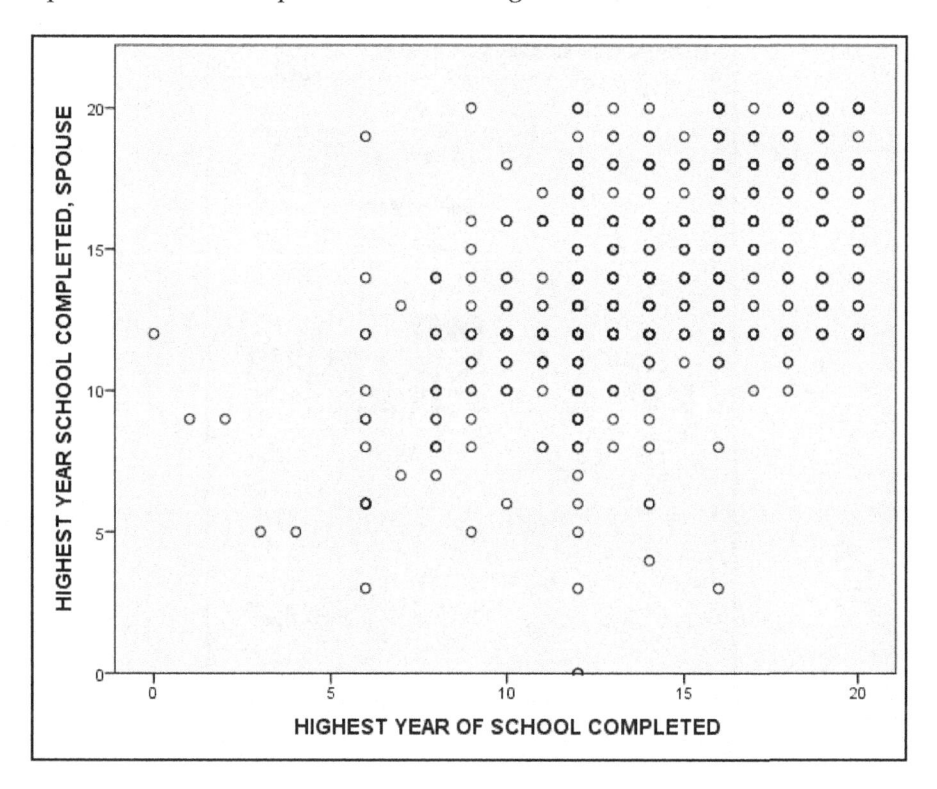

[105]

Visually Exploring the Data

The scatterplot produced by default provides some sense of the trend in that the denser circles are concentrated in a band from the lower left to the upper right. This pattern, however, is rather subtle visually. With some editing, the relationship can be made more evident.

Double-click on the graph to open the **Chart Editor** and select the X icon at the top and change the major increment to 4 so that there are numbers corresponding to completing high school and college. Do the same for the y-axis values. Select a point on the graph to highlight all the "dots" and right-click to display the following dialog. Click on the **Marker** tab and change the symbol to the star shape, increase the size to **6**, increase the border to **2**, and change the border color to a dark blue. Use **Apply** to make the changes visible on the scatterplot:

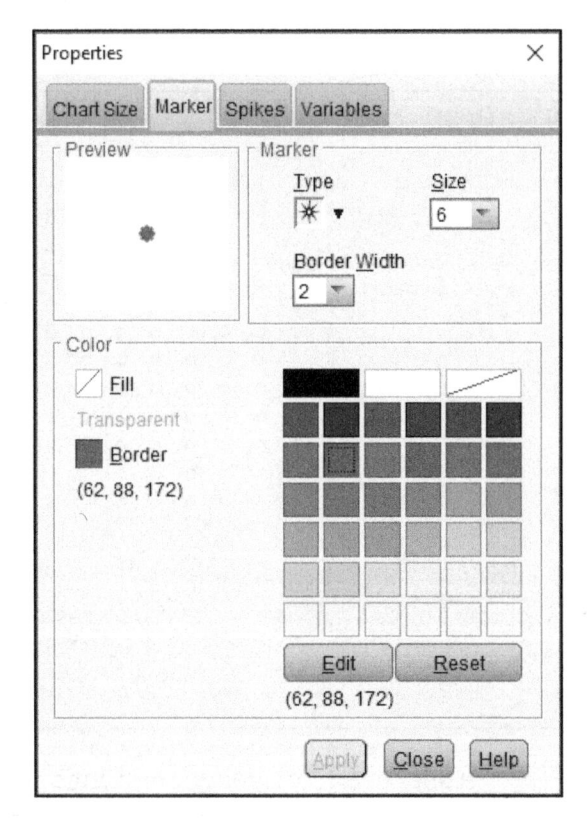

Visually Exploring the Data

Use the **Add Fit line at Total** icon above the graph to show the regression line for this data. Drag the R^2 box from the upper right to the bottom, below the graph and drag the box on the graphs with the equation displayed to the lower left away from the points:

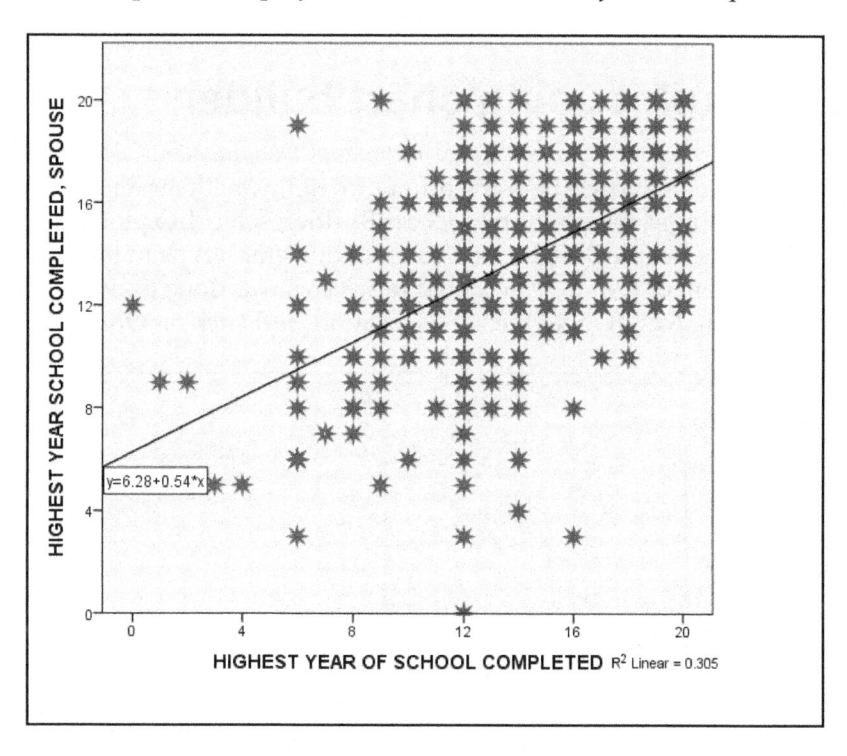

Visually Exploring the Data

The modifications to the original scatterplot make it easier to see the pattern since the "stars" near the line are darker and denser than those farther from the line indicating fewer cases are associated with those points.

Create a boxplot using chart builder

The boxplot shown in `Chapter 3`, *Statistics for Individual Data Elements*, compared educational levels by region to see both the difference in the medians and the similarity in variance. To produce this same graph from **Chart Builder**, select **Boxplot** under the **Gallery** tab, double-click on the Simple Boxplot icon to place this graph type in the preview pane, change the measurement of the education field to scale as was done previously, drag it to the y-axis location, drag **REGION** to the x-axis location, and click on **OK**:

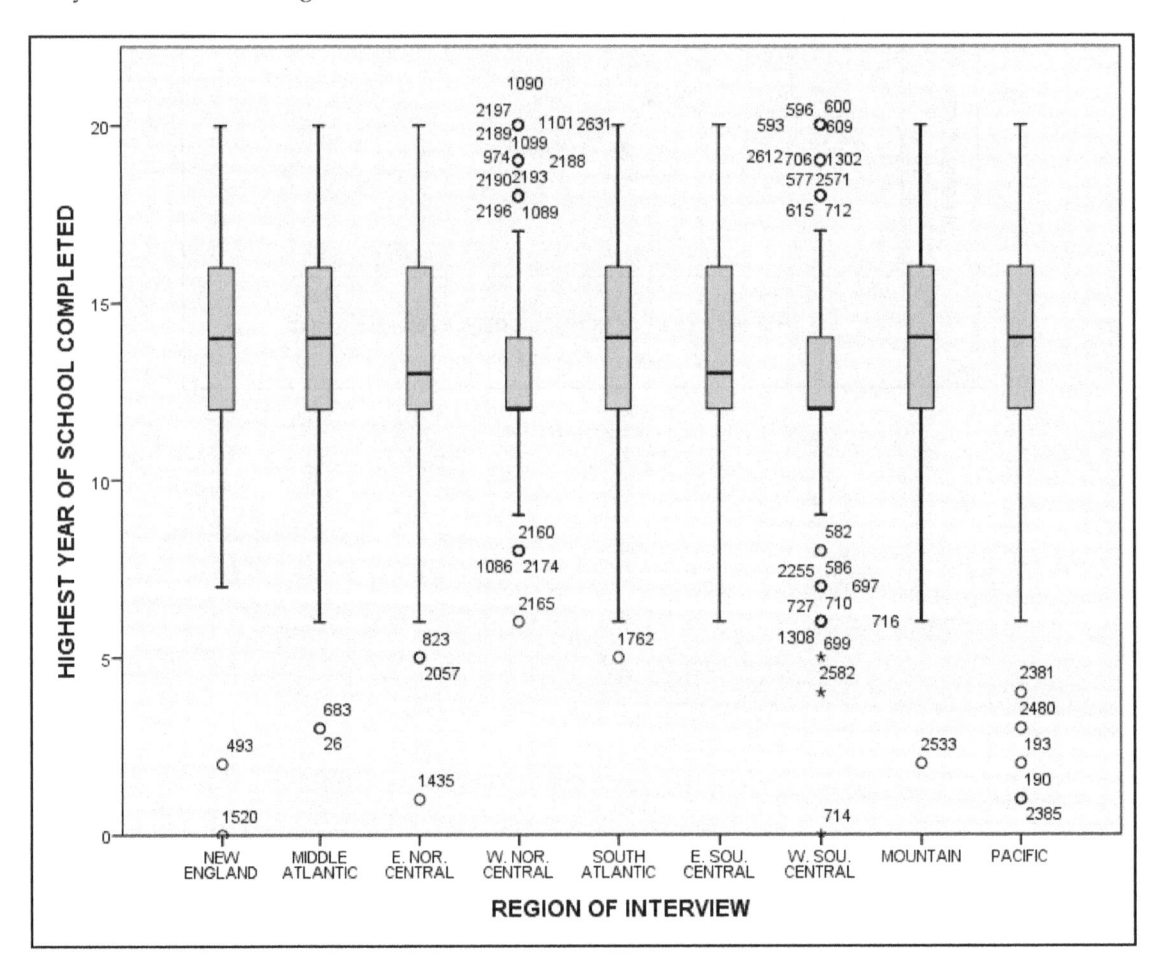

[108]

Visually Exploring the Data

In a boxplot such as the one above, there are three points of interest. First, are black bars in each box at the same point on the vertical axis. Here, all but the West North Central and West South Central regions are close to 14. Secondly, are the boxes of similar size indicating that the variance is about the same. Again, the North and South Central regions show a smaller variation. Finally, the number of outliers should be checked. The same two regions have many more outliers than the other seven. The graph makes it easy to see that these two central regions are different with respect to educational attainment compared with the rest of the U.S.

The utility of this basic boxplot can be enhanced by making some simple modifications. Use the **Options** menu to add a reference line to the y-axis at the median using the **Set to** dropdown under the **Reference Line** tab and check the box to attach a label to the line. Add a textbox, also under the **Options** menu, to indicate that 13 is the overall median and put a border on the textbox. Drag the textbox to the upper left and resize it so that it just fits the text. Change the y-axis major increment to 4. Edit the individual region labels to spell out the words completely and change the x-axis label to just **REGION**. After making these changes, the new version of the graph should look like the following boxplot:

Visually Exploring the Data

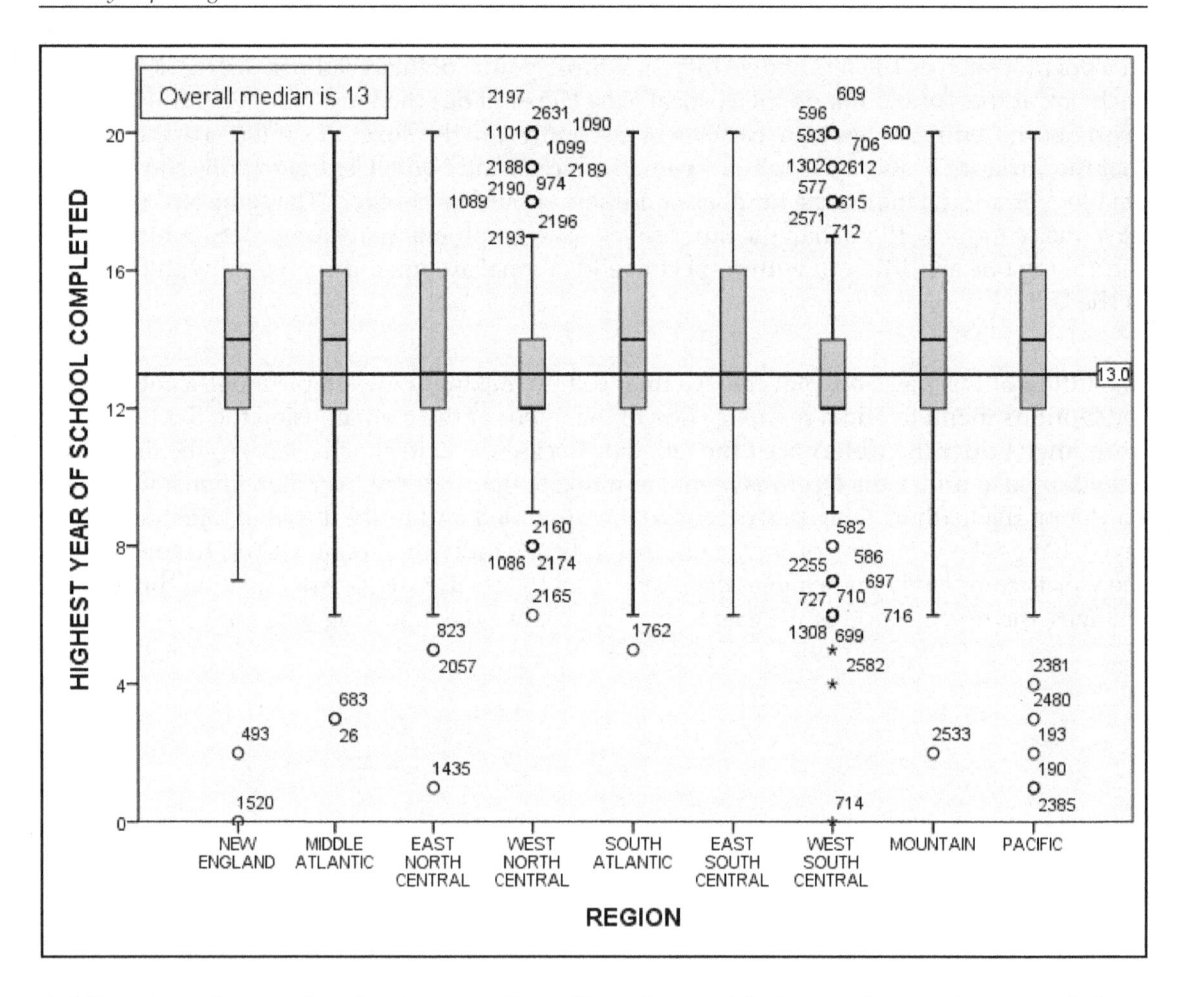

Adding the reference line for the overall median, along with the text box at the upper left, makes it visually evident which regions are higher, lower or at the national median level for education. Spelling out the labels for the individual regions will be helpful when this graph is put into a report or used for a presentation.

Summary

The SPSS capabilities with respect to graphs covered in this chapter give you a foundation to create visual representations of data for both deeper pattern discovery and to communicate results to a broader audience. There are a variety of ways to produce graphs initially in both the statistical procedures and the graph builder itself. Either approach will generate a visual that can then be tailored to your needs using the techniques introduced in the preceding examples. Several other graph types such as pie charts and multiple line charts, which were not covered in this chapter, can be built and edited using the approaches shown for the preceding charts. Explore these alternative graphs styles to see when they may be better suited to your needs.

If your objective is to prepare graphs for inclusion in a report or presentation, it is very valuable to have access to someone with an understanding of the data and analysis objective but with a limited background in analytics/statistics. Such an individual can assess whether the information communicated by a graph captures the key points clearly and effectively. Graphs that you build to share with other analysts, on the other hand, may well need to include more details and supporting information such as summary statistics in footnotes or textboxes.

In the chapter that follows, selecting subsets of the data, data sampling and weighting will be covered.

6
Sampling, Subsetting, and Weighting

You are often interested in analyzing a subset of cases and even treating that subset as a dataset in its own right. SPSS Statistics provides facilities to find subgroups of cases based on logical criteria, time or case ranges, random sampling, or values of a specific variable. This activity sometimes goes by the terms **drilling down** or **filtering**.

A related idea is **weighting**. Here, fewer records might stand in for more if you have a case weight variable that represents case replication.

In this chapter, we will consider SPSS Statistics commands that enable us to perform case selection, sampling, and weighting, in particular, the following topics:

- Various forms of case selection
- Temporary case selection with Temporary
- Random sampling of cases with Sample
- Repeating analyses in case subsets with Split File
- Weighting with Weight

Select cases dialog box

Select Cases provides several methods to select a subgroup of cases. In the main menu, navigate to **Data** | **Select Cases**.

Here is the **Select Cases** dialog box:

The **Select** radio buttons provide several methods to select a subgroup of cases. The buttons correspond to the following actions:

- **All cases**: Turns case filtering off and uses all cases.
- **If condition is satisfied**: Uses a conditional expression to select cases. If the result of the conditional expression is true, then SPSS Statistics selects the case. If the result of the conditional expression is false or missing, then SPSS Statistics does not select the case.

- **Random sample of cases**: Selects a random sample of cases.
- **Based on time or case range**: Selects cases based on a range of case numbers or a range of dates/times.
- **Use filter variable**: Uses the selected numeric variable as a filter variable. Cases with any value other than 0 or missing for the filter variable are selected.

The **Output** radio buttons control the treatment of unselected cases:

- **Filter out unselected cases**: Unselected cases are not included in the analysis but remain in the dataset and, therefore, are visible in the Data Editor Window.
- **Copy selected cases to a new dataset**: Selected cases are copied to a new dataset.
- **Delete unselected cases**: Unselected cases are deleted from the dataset. You can recover the deleted cases by exiting from the file without saving and then reopening the file.

Having shown the **Select Cases** radio buttons, let's now consider the Select alternatives in more detail.

Select cases - If condition is satisfied

If condition is satisfied invokes **Select Cases** based on a conditional expression.

From the menus, navigate to **Data | Select cases**.

Then, select the radio button **If condition is satisfied**.

Then, press the **If** button.

This brings up the **Select Cases: If** dialog box.

Sampling, Subsetting, and Weighting

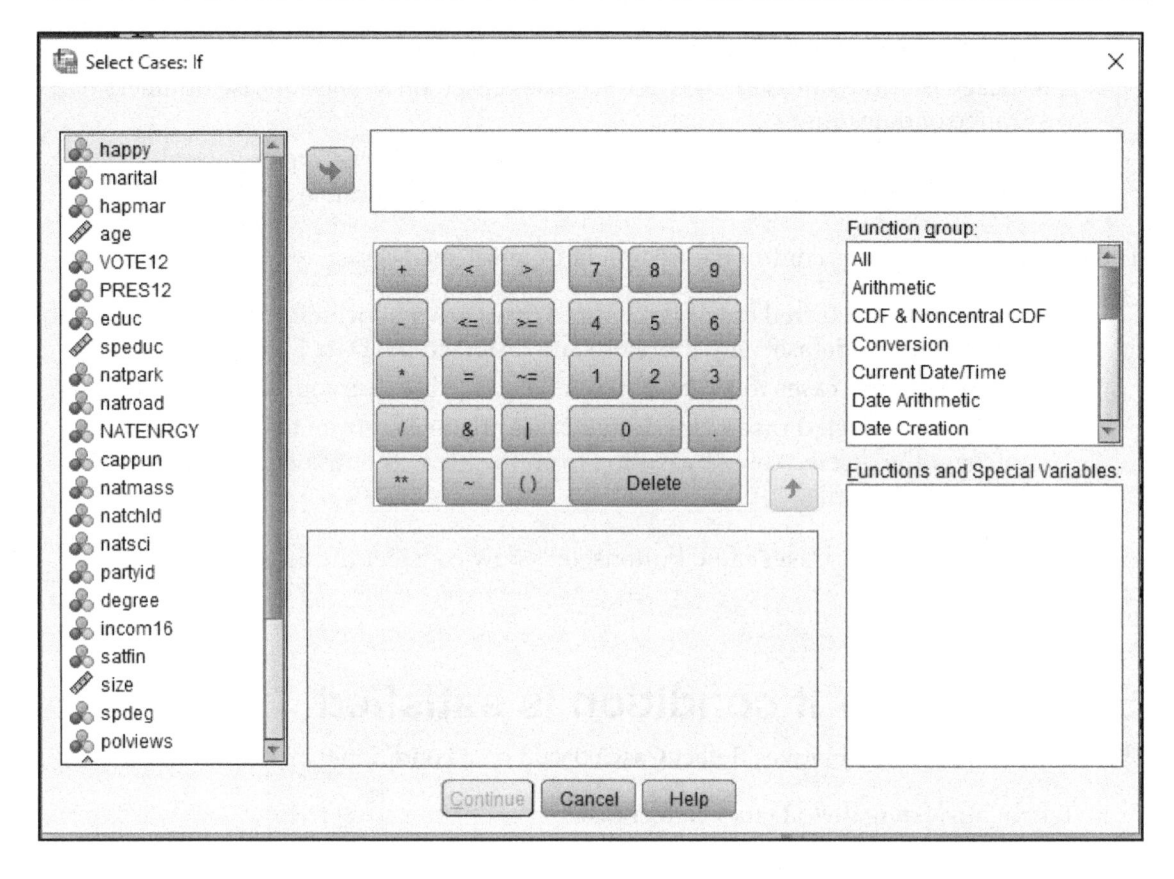

Use the box to build the expression to select cases.

> The expression can contain elements such as variable names, values, relational operators, arithmetic operators, functions, and system variables. For each case, SPSS Statistics evaluates the conditional expression and returns a value of true, false, or missing.

If the result of a conditional expression is true, the case is included in the selected subset. If the result of a conditional expression is false or missing, the case is not included in the selected subset.

> Of course, you can use the dialog boxes directly, or use them to paste syntax. As you learn SPSS Statistics, you can work directly using syntax. Next, we show the syntax forms of case selection.

Example

The data in this example is a subset of variables from the 2016 General Social Survey. We wish to create a subset of cases consisting of those respondents with **0** children in their household. A variable named `Childs` has information on the number of children. Here, we wish to demonstrate the different SPSS Statistics code as we specify the different **Output** radio buttons on **Select If**.

If condition is satisfied combined with Filter

Here is the code produced by the combination of **Select: If condition is satisfied** and **Output: Filter out unselected cases**:

```
USE ALL.
COMPUTE filter_$=(childs = 0).
VARIABLE LABELS filter_$ 'childs = 0 (FILTER)'.
VALUE LABELS filter_$ 0 'Not Selected' 1 'Selected'.
FORMATS filter_$ (f1.0).
FILTER BY filter_$.
EXECUTE.
```

Here are the comments on the SPSS Statistics code:

- `USE` designates a range of observations to be used. `USE ALL` specifies that initially all observations in the file should be used.
- The `COMPUTE` command computes a variable named `filter_$`. This is a **flag** variable that takes on a value of either a **0** or **1**, with the **1** value corresponding to true. The statement being evaluated is whether or not `Childs` is equal to **0** for a given data row. This variable name is a special SPSS Statistics variable name for the variable that is to be used in filtering.
- The next three commands (`Variable labels`, `Value labels`, and `Formats`) specify variable properties for `filter_$`.
- By default, the `Filter` command specifies `filter_$` as the filter variable. This variable is used to exclude cases from program procedures without deleting them from the active dataset. When `Filter` is in effect, cases with either a 0 or missing value for the specified variable or expression are not used in program procedures. The excluded cases are not actually deleted and are available again if you select all cases.

If you run the preceding code, by default, the commands are echoed in the log in the **Output** window. The filter is on and in effect until you undo it. To see the effect of filtering, we will run `Frequencies` on the `Childs` variable:

```
FREQUENCIES VARIABLES=childs
  /ORDER=ANALYSIS.
```

Here is the resulting frequency table:

NUMBER OF CHILDREN				
	Frequency	Percent	Valid Percent	Cumulative Percent
Valid 0	797	100.0	100.0	100.0

There are **797** filtered cases, consisting of those cases for which the number of children is equal to **0**. Note that nothing in the table explicitly tells you that filtering is on. Instead, you see that there is a count of **797** for the value **0**, and you would likely know from being familiar with the data that the overall sample size is larger than **797** and that there are values other than **0** for number of children.

Having said this, there are some ways to learn whether filtering is on.

To see if a filter is in effect, run the `SHOW` command:

```
SHOW FILTER.
```

SPSS prints the following **System Settings** table:

System Settings		
Keyword	Description	Setting
FILTER	Filter variable	childs = 0 (FILTER)

Another way to see if a filter is in effect is to look in notes.

Sampling, Subsetting, and Weighting

Here is a picture of the **Navigation Tree** in the **Output** viewer:

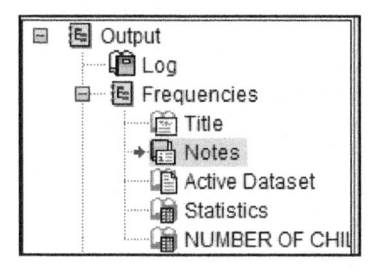

```
□ ▣ Output
    📄 Log
    □ ▣ Frequencies
        📄 Title
      → 📄 Notes
        📄 Active Dataset
        📄 Statistics
        📄 NUMBER OF CHI|
```

By default, **Notes** appears in the tree but is a **closed book** and, therefore, not visible in the Output Viewer. You can double-click on it to open it and make it viewable. Here is the **Notes** table:

		Notes
Output Created		11-APR-2017 15:39:35
Comments		
Input	Data	C:\Users\tbabinec\Documents\KSBSPSSBOOK_DATA\GSS2016\GSS2016sm28 40317.sav
	Active Dataset	DataSet1
	Filter	childs = 0 (FILTER)
	Weight	<none>
	Split File	<none>
	N of Rows in Working Data File	797
Missing Value Handling	Definition of Missing	User-defined missing values are treated as missing.
	Cases Used	Statistics are based on all cases with valid data.
Syntax		FREQUENCIES VARIABLES=childs /ORDER=ANALYSIS.
Resources	Processor Time	00:00:00.02
	Elapsed Time	00:00:00.01

You can see in the **Filter** display that a filter is in effect for the frequency table of `Childs`.

[119]

Sampling, Subsetting, and Weighting

Finally, the **SPSS Statistics Data Editor** window has a message area in the lower right border of the window. When filtering is in effect, the text **Filter On** appears in the message area.

Here is a snapshot of the Data Editor with the filter variable in effect:

	happy	childs	wrkstat	sex	region	filter_$
1	2	3	1	1	1	0
2	2	0	1	1	1	1
3	1	2	5	1	1	0
4	2	4	2	2	1	0
5	1	2	2	2	1	0
6	1	2	7	2	1	0
7	2	2	1	1	1	0
8	1	3	2	2	2	0
9	2	3	1	1	2	0
10	2	4	5	1	2	0

Looking at the first 10 rows, row number **2** has a **Childs** value of **0** and is therefore not filtered, while the other rows have non-zero values for **Childs** and are therefore filtered. It is easy to see that filtering is on because the row number in the Data Editor window has a diagonal slash in it if the row is filtered.

> Note that SPSS Statistics adds a column to the right named `filter_$` that is a 0-1 flag variable, with 1 representing selected cases and 0 representing unselected cases.

To undo the filtering, specify `FILTER OFF`:

```
FILTER OFF.
USE ALL.
EXECUTE.
```

If condition is satisfied combined with Copy

You can combine **Select: If condition is satisfied** with **Output: Copy selected cases to a new dataset**. You supply a dataset name. Then, SPSS Statistics executes the case selection and puts the selected cases in a new Data Editor window.

> Recall that, by default, you can have multiple Data Editor windows in a session, although only one is active at a time.

Here is the SPSS code for **Copy selected cases to a new dataset**:

```
DATASET COPY ChildEQ0.
DATASET ACTIVATE ChildEQ0.
FILTER OFF.
USE ALL.
SELECT IF (childs = 0).
EXECUTE.
DATASET ACTIVATE DataSet1.
```

Here are comments on the commands:

- `DATASET COPY` creates a new dataset that captures the current state of the active dataset. The new dataset gets the dataset name, `ChildEQ0`.
- `DATASET ACTIVATE` makes dataset `ChildEQ0` the active dataset.
- `FILTER OFF` turns filtering off and makes all cases available again.
- `USE ALL` defines a USE range starting with the first observation and ending with the last observation.
- `SELECT IF` permanently selects cases for analysis based on the logical condition, `childs=0`.
- `EXECUTE` forces the data to be read and executes the transformations that precede it.
- `DATASET ACTIVATE` makes (original data) `Dataset1` the active dataset.

Run the preceding commands. Here is a snapshot showing the two Data Editor windows, with `ChildEQ0` active and in front of the original file `Dataset1`:

Sampling, Subsetting, and Weighting

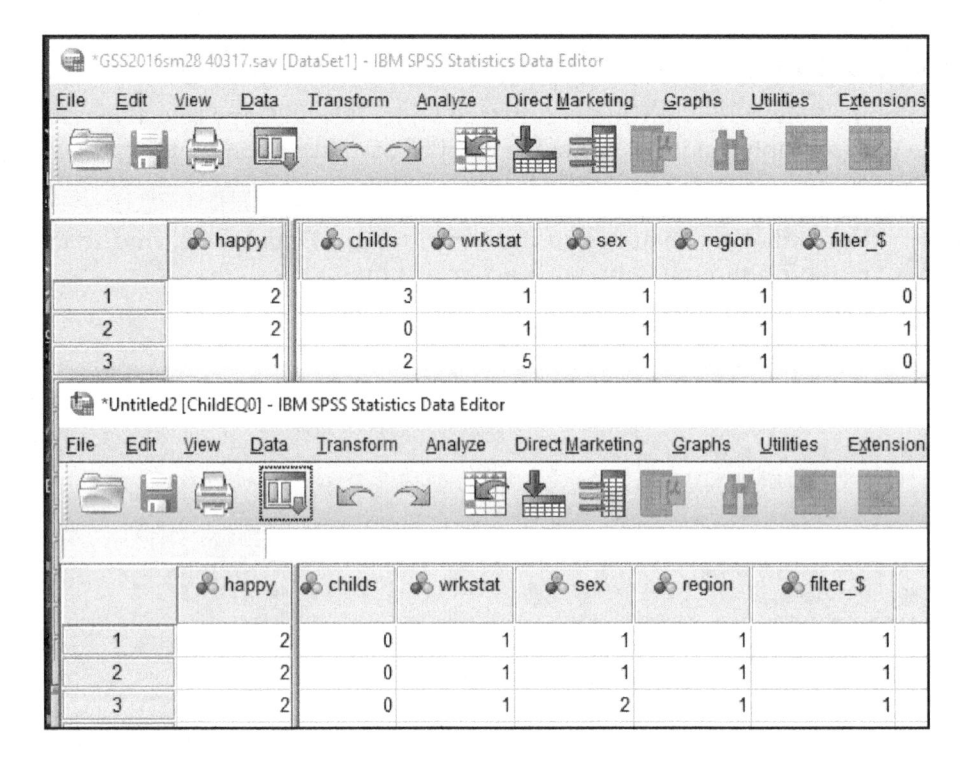

Dataset `ChildEQ0` has only the records for `childs=0`. You can make this file the focal file for analysis by SPSS by making it the active file. In the above screenshot, `ChildEQ0` is the active file, as indicated by the red plus(+) symbol. Clicking in the top margin of the Data Editor Window is one way to make it active. An advantage of the Copy approach is that you do not have to be concerned with an undo operation as you have the original file available if necessary.

If condition is satisfied combined with Delete unselected cases

In this form of case selection, SPSS Statistics deletes the unselected cases from the active file. There is no undo operation. Instead, to get back to the original file, you must exit from the file without saving and then reopen the file.

> **TIP**: Be aware that if you **Get** a file and then perform a **File Save** after this form of case selection, you will replace your original file with the subset file. There is no undo operation for this. You should use **File Save As** instead. Having said this, while there are precautions that you can take, this

> **TIP:** process is error-prone and you might be better off using one of the other case selection approaches to avoid an unintended outcome such as overwriting your original file.

Here is the SPSS code to perform case selection **if a condition is satisfied** coupled with **deletion of the unselected cases**:

```
FILTER OFF.
USE ALL.
SELECT IF (childs = 0).
EXECUTE.
```

The Temporary command

A command that might prove useful in the context of case selection is the `Temporary` command. Note that `Temporary` is only available in syntax--there is no menu equivalent. `Temporary` has no arguments. Instead, place it at the beginning of a block of transformations that are in effect for only the next procedure. You can use `Temporary` in conjunction with `Select If` to make case selections that you intend to be in effect for only the next procedure. After that next procedure, the case selection goes away.

For example, consider the following code:

```
TEMPORARY.
SELECT IF (childs = 0).
FREQUENCIES VAR=childs.
FREQUENCIES VAR=childs.
```

`SELECT IF` is a transformation, while `FREQUENCIES` is a procedure. For the first `FREQUENCIES` command, SPSS selects cases for which `childs=0`. After the first `FREQUENCIES` command, SPSS reverts to all cases. Therefore, the second `FREQUENCIES` command produces the full frequency table for `childs`.

Next, consider the following code:

```
TEMPORARY.
SELECT IF (childs = 0).
FREQUENCIES VAR=childs.
TEMPORARY.
SELECT IF (childs = 1).
FREQUENCIES VAR=childs.
```

Sampling, Subsetting, and Weighting

The first `FREQUENCIES` command produces a frequency table for `CHILDS` equals 0. The second `FREQUENCIES` command produces a frequency table for `CHILDS` equals 1. After the second `FREQUENCIES`, SPSS reverts to all cases. Therefore, this is a preferred way of writing code when you want to run the same procedure code in different subgroups.

Finally, consider the following code:

```
SELECT IF (childs = 0).
FREQUENCIES VAR=childs.
SELECT IF (childs = 1).
FREQUENCIES VAR=childs.
```

The first `FREQUENCIES` command produces a frequency table for `CHILDS` equals 0. This is based on a permanent case selection. The second `FREQUENCIES` table produces an empty frequency table. This is probably not what you intend.

> **TIP**
> If you are not careful, using `TEMPORARY` can produce unintended consequences if you make syntax mistakes or even if you don't. Sometimes, when writing and testing SPSS code, users will comment out the `TEMPORARY` command and forget to undo the commenting, or an omitted period at the end of a command could lead to a wrong selection.

Select cases based on time or case range

Another form of selection is to select cases based on either a time range or case range. We illustrate this form of selection by selecting the first 10 cases in a way that filters out the unselected cases.

Here is the code:

```
FILTER OFF.
USE 1 thru 10.
EXECUTE.
```

The `USE` command designates the first 10 rows of data as data to be used with procedures. Cases outside this range are filtered but not deleted from the active dataset.

Sampling, Subsetting, and Weighting

Here is a snapshot of a portion of the Data Editor window with this Use selection in place:

	happy	marital	hapmar
1	2	1	1
2	2	5	0
3	1	1	1
4	2	1	1
5	1	1	1
6	1	1	1
7	2	1	1
8	1	1	1
9	2	1	2
10	2	3	0
~~11~~	8	5	0
~~12~~	3	2	0
~~13~~	1	1	1

To get all cases back, specify USE ALL:

```
FILTER OFF.
USE ALL.
EXECUTE.
```

> **TIP**
> USE has a special purpose in time series analysis. Typically, the data rows are ordered by time or date. USE can be used to select a training sample that stops short of data rows at the bottom, which is presumably the most recent data. Then, you develop a model on the USE cases and make predictions into the holdout data. If the data is not time series data, you could order the data using a computed random variable and then specify a USE period, in a similar way to what is shown in creating a training sample, to model.

[125]

Using the filter variable

You can use any numeric variable from the data file as the filter variable. Cases with any value other than 0 or missing for the filter variable are selected.

For example, here we use the previously-created variable `filter_$`.

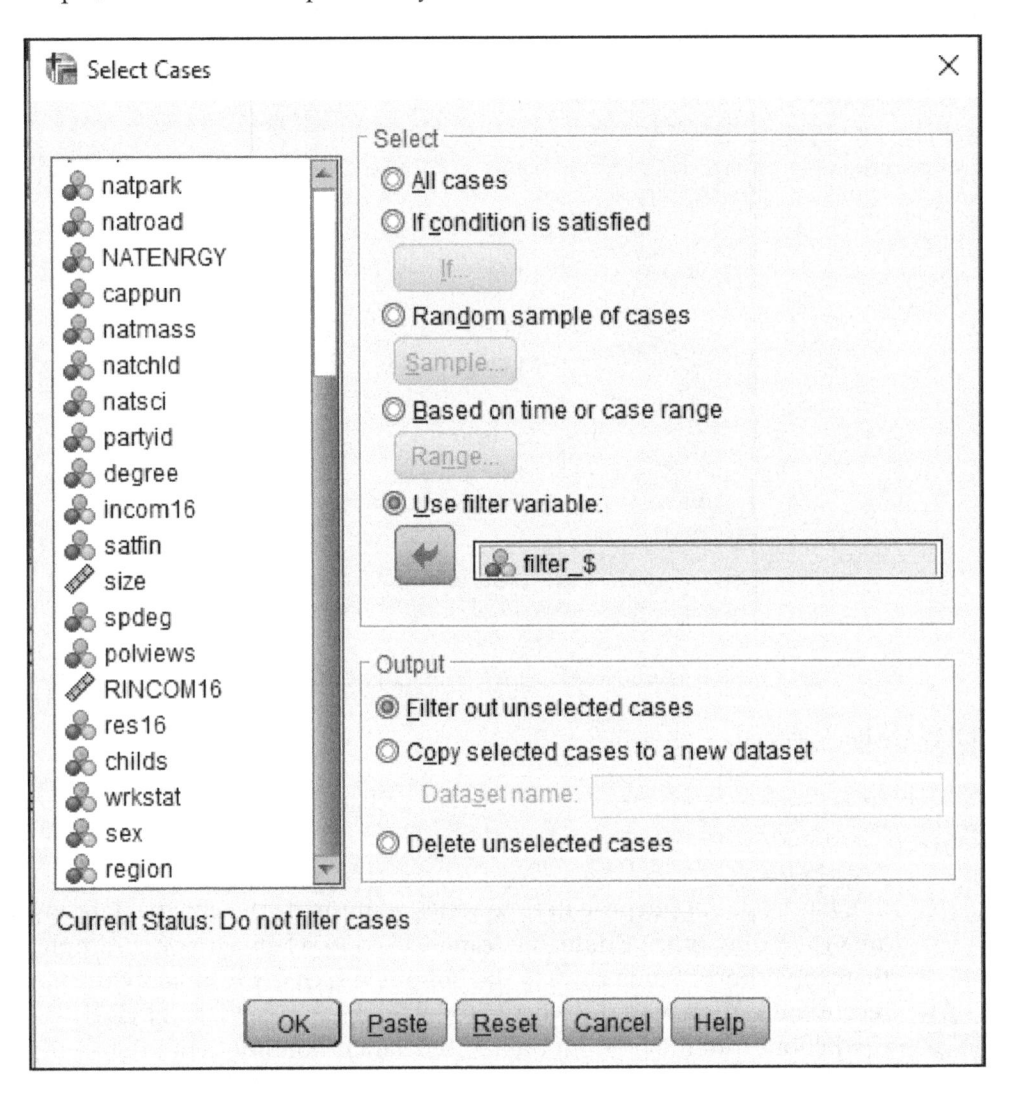

Selecting a random sample of cases

Sample permanently draws a random sample of cases to process in all the subsequent procedures. Use Sample to draw a random sample of cases.

Sample allows two different specifications. One way to run it is to specify a decimal value between 0 and 1 reflecting the approximate fraction of cases that you would like to see in the sample. The second is to select an exact-size random sample, specify a positive number that is less than the file size, and follow it with the keyword FROM and the active dataset size.

To illustrate sampling, suppose you want to draw an approximately 30 percent sample from the GSS2016 active file. We will demonstrate the effect of sampling by obtaining statistics on age before and after sampling.

Here is the SPSS code:

```
DESCRIPTIVES VARIABLES=age
 /STATISTICS=MEAN STDDEV MIN MAX.
FILTER OFF.
USE ALL.
SAMPLE .30.
DESCRIPTIVES VARIABLES=age
 /STATISTICS=MEAN STDDEV MIN MAX.
```

The command sequence FILTER through the final DESCRIPTIVES command shows the syntax way of deleting unsampled cases. That is, combine **Select Random sample of cases** with **Output Delete unselected cases** in the **Select Cases** dialog box.

Sampling, Subsetting, and Weighting

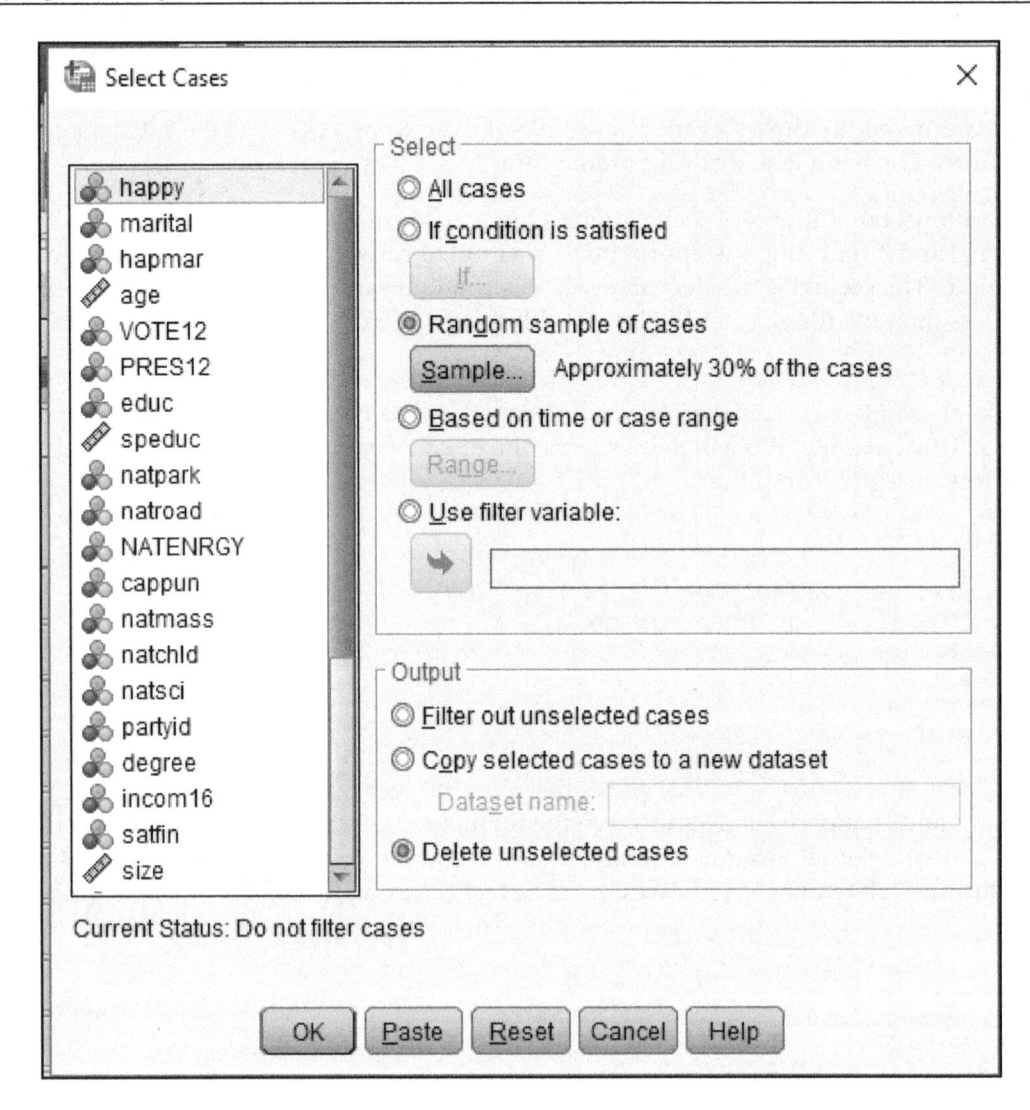

Here is the `Descriptive Statistics` table from the first `DESCRIPTIVES` command:

Descriptive Statistics

	N	Minimum	Maximum	Mean	Std. Deviation
AGE OF RESPONDENT	2857	18	89	49.16	17.693
Valid N (listwise)	2857				

The sample size (**N**) is the full sample of 2,857.

Here is the `Descriptive Statistics` table from the second `DESCRIPTIVES` command:

Descriptive Statistics

	N	Minimum	Maximum	Mean	Std. Deviation
AGE OF RESPONDENT	840	19	89	48.96	17.253
Valid N (listwise)	840				

Note that the sample size of 840 is about 29.4 percent of 2,857, which is not exactly 30% but close. There is a random element to the sampling such that the sampled number of cases is not exactly 30 percent. This sample size is in effect from this point forward in the SPSS session.

While we do not illustrate them here, you have alternative specifications for the sampling that are similar to those that we showed for case selection earlier--filtering, copying the sample to a new Data Editor window, or combining sampling with `Temporary`.

Sampling in SPSS is based on a pseudo-random-number generator that depends on a starting value called a `SEED`. By default, in recent versions of SPSS, the seed is set to 2,000,000. This ensures that there is repeatability in multiple runs of SPSS. To see the seed value in effect, use the following command:

```
SHOW SEED.
```

> **TIP**: To set the seed to another value, use the `SET` command. See the IBM SPSS Statistics Command Syntax Reference or SPSS Statistics Help for more details.

Split File

Split File splits the active dataset into subgroups that can be analyzed separately. Note that the file stays intact. The subgroups are sets of adjacent cases in the file that have the same values for the split variable or variables.

> In order for Split File to work correctly, cases must be sorted by the values of the split variable or variables. Split File can be an efficient alternative to the repeated invocation of `Select If` when you are interested in repeating the same analysis in each level of a split variable.

As an example, we will contrast the running of `Descriptives` on several numeric variables without and with Split File in effect. As the splitting variable, we will use `VOTE12`, which indicates whether or not the respondent voted in the 2012 US Presidential Election.

First, here are `Descriptive Statistics` for several numeric variables from the small `GSS2016` file:

Descriptive Statistics

	N	Minimum	Maximum	Mean	Std. Deviation
AGE OF RESPONDENT	2857	18	89	49.16	17.693
HIGHEST YEAR OF SCHOOL COMPLETED	2858	0	20	13.74	2.964
SIZE OF PLACE IN 1000S	2867	0	8175	334.33	1149.625
Valid N (listwise)	2848				

Here is the `Split Files` syntax for the **compare groups** output option, followed by the `Descriptives` specification:

```
SORT CASES BY VOTE12.
SPLIT FILE LAYERED BY VOTE12.
DESCRIPTIVES VARIABLES=age educ size
  /STATISTICS=MEAN STDDEV MIN MAX.
```

Here is a snapshot of a portion of the resulting `Descriptive Statistics` table (omitting the missing categories of `VOTE12`):

Descriptive Statistics

DID R VOTE IN 2012 ELECTION		N	Minimum	Maximum	Mean	Std. Deviation
1 Voted	AGE OF RESPONDENT	1805	21	89	53.82	16.644
	HIGHEST YEAR OF SCHOOL COMPLETED	1807	1	20	14.38	2.793
	SIZE OF PLACE IN 1000S	1809	0	8175	317.57	1154.317
	Valid N (listwise)	1803				
2 Did not vote	AGE OF RESPONDENT	796	22	89	43.47	15.680
	HIGHEST YEAR OF SCHOOL COMPLETED	798	0	20	12.56	2.922
	SIZE OF PLACE IN 1000S	800	0	8175	339.18	1145.143
	Valid N (listwise)	794				
3 Ineligible	AGE OF RESPONDENT	200	18	82	29.15	13.165
	HIGHEST YEAR OF SCHOOL COMPLETED	200	1	20	12.82	2.931
	SIZE OF PLACE IN 1000S	201	1	8175	421.70	1073.756
	Valid N (listwise)	199				

Looking at the descriptive statistics, you would conclude, for example, that those who did not vote appear to be younger and less educated on average than those who did vote. To produce the subgroup statistics without using Split File, you would have to repeatedly invoke `Select If`. This would generate descriptive statistics on each VOTE12 subgroup, although the descriptive tables would be separate tables and not part of the same display.

You can also run Split File in a way that it produces separate tables, with the Split File **organize output by groups** output option.

Here is a portion of the output produced, showing the first two **Descriptive Statistics** tables:

```
SORT CASES BY VOTE12.
SPLIT FILE SEPARATE BY VOTE12.
DESCRIPTIVES VARIABLES=age educ size
  /STATISTICS=MEAN STDDEV MIN MAX.
```

DID R VOTE IN 2012 ELECTION = Voted

Descriptive Statistics[a]

	N	Minimum	Maximum	Mean	Std. Deviation
AGE OF RESPONDENT	1805	21	89	53.82	16.644
HIGHEST YEAR OF SCHOOL COMPLETED	1807	1	20	14.38	2.793
SIZE OF PLACE IN 1000S	1809	0	8175	317.57	1154.317
Valid N (listwise)	1803				

a. DID R VOTE IN 2012 ELECTION = 1 Voted

DID R VOTE IN 2012 ELECTION = Did not vote

Descriptive Statistics[a]

	N	Minimum	Maximum	Mean	Std. Deviation
AGE OF RESPONDENT	796	22	89	43.47	15.680
HIGHEST YEAR OF SCHOOL COMPLETED	798	0	20	12.56	2.922
SIZE OF PLACE IN 1000S	800	0	8175	339.18	1145.143
Valid N (listwise)	794				

a. DID R VOTE IN 2012 ELECTION = 2 Did not vote

In this form of output, each VOTE12 subgroup gets its own **Title** and **Descriptive Statistics** table with a footnote.

Weighting

Use the Weight command to give cases different weights for statistical analysis. Typically, the Weight variable brings about simulated case replication. For example, if a case has a weight of 5, it would be as if the case occurred five times in the data even though the case is physically a single record. You can use Weight to weight a sample up to a population, or you might use Weight to enter cell counts for an example table in a publication. If there is no explicit Weight variable, then the weight for each case is 1.

When SPSS Statistics reports the number of cases, it reports the weighted number of cases. With no explicit weight variable, the case weights are all 1 and the sum of the 1s equals the number of active rows. With an explicit Weight variable, the sum of the weights is the effective sample size, and in general is not equal to the number of rows.

Here is an example:

```
data list / freq 1 row 3 column 5.
begin data.
6 1 1
4 1 2
4 2 1
6 2 2
end data.
weight by freq.
CROSSTABS
 /TABLES=row BY column
 /FORMAT=AVALUE TABLES
 /STATISTICS=CHISQ
 /CELLS=COUNT
 /COUNT ROUND CELL.
compute freq2=10*freq.
weight by freq2.
CROSSTABS
 /TABLES=row BY column
 /FORMAT=AVALUE TABLES
 /STATISTICS=CHISQ
 /CELLS=COUNT
 /COUNT ROUND CELL.
```

Sampling, Subsetting, and Weighting

Here are the comments on the syntax:

- `DATA LIST` reads four lines of data. The first column, named `FREQ`, represents case-replicating weights.
- Following `END DATA`, the `WEIGHT` command weights by `FREQ`.
- `CROSSTABS` specifies a two-way table.
- `COMPUTE` creates a variable named `FREQ2` by multiplying `FREQ` by 10.
- `CROSSTABS` specifies the same two-way table as before.

Here is the table produced by the first `CROSSTABS` command:

row * column Crosstabulation

Count

		column 1	column 2	Total
row	1	6	4	10
	2	4	6	10
Total		10	10	20

In the syntax, you see four rows of data. Yet, the table reports the table total count as 20, which is the sum of the four cell counts. The four cell counts come from the `FREQ` column and the fact that we weighted by `FREQ`.

Here is the table produced by the second `Crosstabs` command:

row * column Crosstabulation

Count

		column 1	column 2	Total
row	1	60	40	100
	2	40	60	100
Total		100	100	200

[133]

The second `Crosstabs` specification is identical to the first, but the table is based on the use of `FREQ2` as a `Weight` variable, and `FREQ2` has values of **60**, **40**, **40**, and **60**, respectively.

You can use the preceding approach to enter published tables into SPSS Statistics.

As illustrated, use the `Weight` command to invoke case-replicating weighting. In research, weighting can arise in other contexts. If your data arises from a complex multistage probability sample, then SPSS Statistics has a Complex Samples module that could prove useful. If you are interested in post-stratifying by known population numbers, then SPSS Statistics has an extension command for a technique known as **raking**. These topics are beyond the scope of this text.

Summary

This chapter has shown you how to use SPSS Statistics for case selection, sampling, and weighting.

For case selection and sampling, you have a number of ways of handling the unselected and selected cases. As selected cases are viewed in a Data Editor window, you can use all the functionality of SPSS on a subset of cases just as you would for an entire file.

Having covered case selection, sampling, and weighting, we next turn to creating new data elements via `Compute`.

7
Creating New Data Elements

New fields can be created in SPSS using a variety of different methods. In Chapter 4, *Dealing with Outliers and Missing Data,* the SAVE subcommand on both the DESCRIPTIVES and REGRESSION commands resulted in the addition of fields to the original dataset. This same chapter contained an example of using a set of IF commands to create new fields that were designed to address specific missing value issues in the data. In this chapter, the commands available in SPSS for creating new fields will be demonstrated in detail.

Deriving new fields is central to the analytic process since this is how subject matter knowledge is incorporated into the predictive modeling. Ratios and differences of specific data elements, for example, can be very useful as predictors but do not typically exist in the source data.

The four most heavily used commands available on the **Transform** menu will be covered in the chapter and shown using detailed examples:

- RECODE
- COMPUTE
- IF
- DO IF/ELSE IF

Several of the other commands that are designed for special situations will be discussed as well.

Creating New Data Elements

Transforming fields in SPSS

The Transform menu in SPSS Statistics (explained in the following screenshot) provides access to the core set of commands that all users use to modify existing fields or create new fields by applying a range of approaches.

In addition to the capabilities that will be covered in detail in this chapter, there are facilities to handle things such as assigning ranks and working with time series data. The SPSS syntax language gives you access to an even broader set of features, and one of those--DO IF/ELSE IF--will demonstrated towards the end of the chapter.

Following is the screenshot of the **Transform** menu:

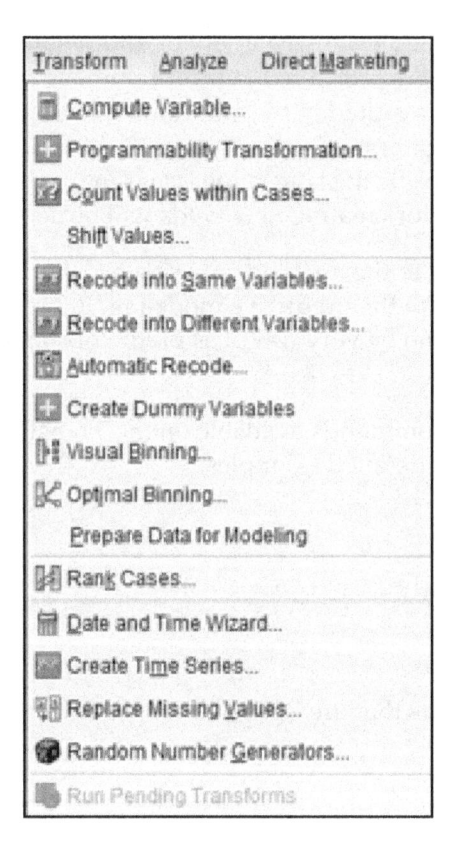

The RECODE command

A common task that analysts need to tackle involves modifying the original codes assigned to a field. There are a variety of reasons to revise values of a variable, and SPSS Statistics provides a handy command designed to meet this need. For this example, consider the `SATISF.SAV` file that ships with the software and can be found in the `SAMPLES` folder.

This dataset contains a set of fields related to customer satisfaction with their shopping experience. The following screenshot shows the details for the **Overall Satisfaction** question:

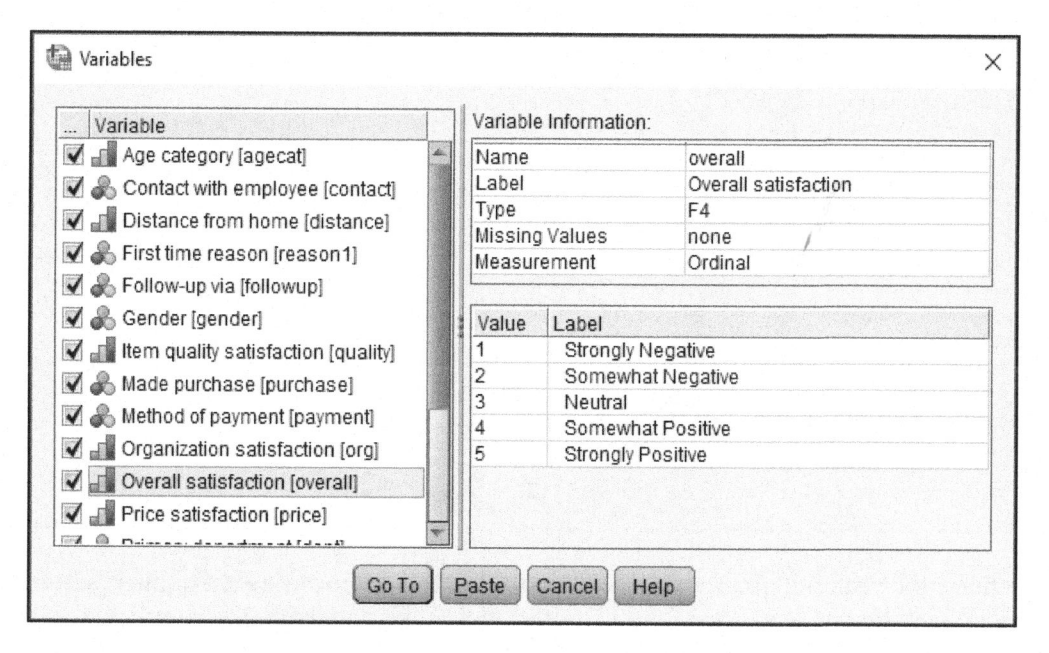

As we can see from the preceding screenshot, this has five response categories ranging from **Strongly Positive** (5) to **Strongly Negative** (1).

Creating a dummy variable using RECODE

To create a field that indicates whether a shopper gave a positive response or not, the `RECODE` transformation can be used.

Creating New Data Elements

While there are occasions when it is reasonable to reassign the code of an existing variable, it is generally a better strategy to map the new values into a new field and retain the original field in its unaltered form. Use the following step to use `RECODE`:

Transform | Recode into Different Variables

This will display the dialog as shown in the following screenshot:

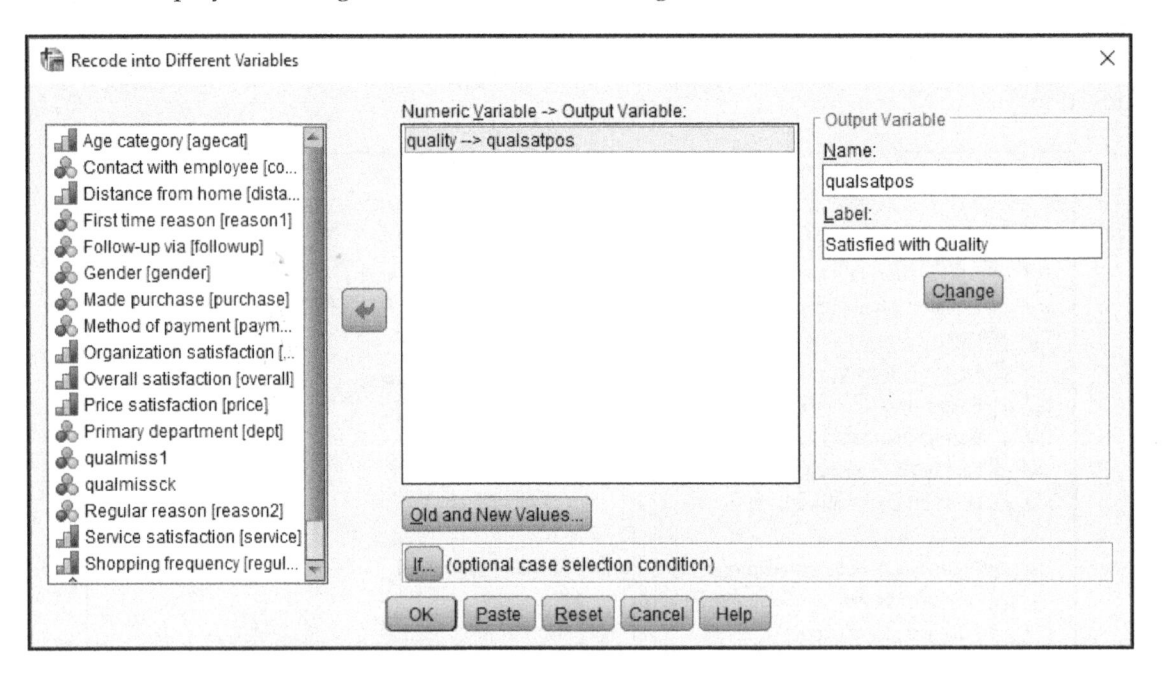

The satisfaction with the quality field will be used in this example. Select quality, assign the new field the name `qualsatpos`, and give it a label. Click on **Change** to complete this first step and then on **Old and New Values**.

Creating New Data Elements

The original values are specified on the right side of the dialog box, as shown in the following screenshot, and the new values on the left side:

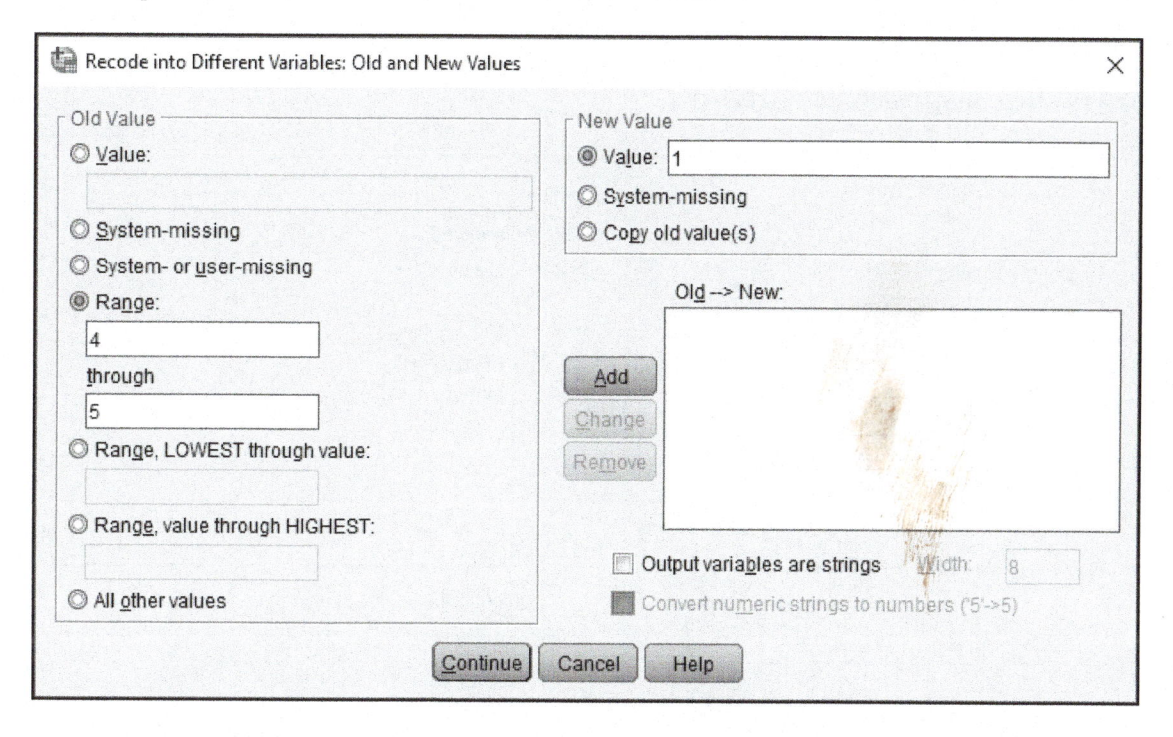

[Screenshot: Recode into Different Variables: Old and New Values dialog box. Old Value section has Range selected with 4 through 5. New Value section has Value set to 1.]

Here, the two top values of the field are assigned the value 1, and the **Add** button is used to complete the first step.

Values 1 through 3 are assigned the value zero to effectively create a dummy variable that indicates a positive response to the question regarding satisfaction with the quality of products available at the store.

There are choices for assigning missing values to a new value, which could be the system missing value if so desired. Be aware that the **All other values** choice on the left could be used to handle all the values, other than the two positive values (4 and 5), but this would mean that any customer with a missing value in the question would also end up in the zero group.

Creating New Data Elements

By explicitly specifying, only values 1 through 3 are assigned a zero on the new field; any value, including any missing values, not covered by the RECODE specifications will be missing in the new field:

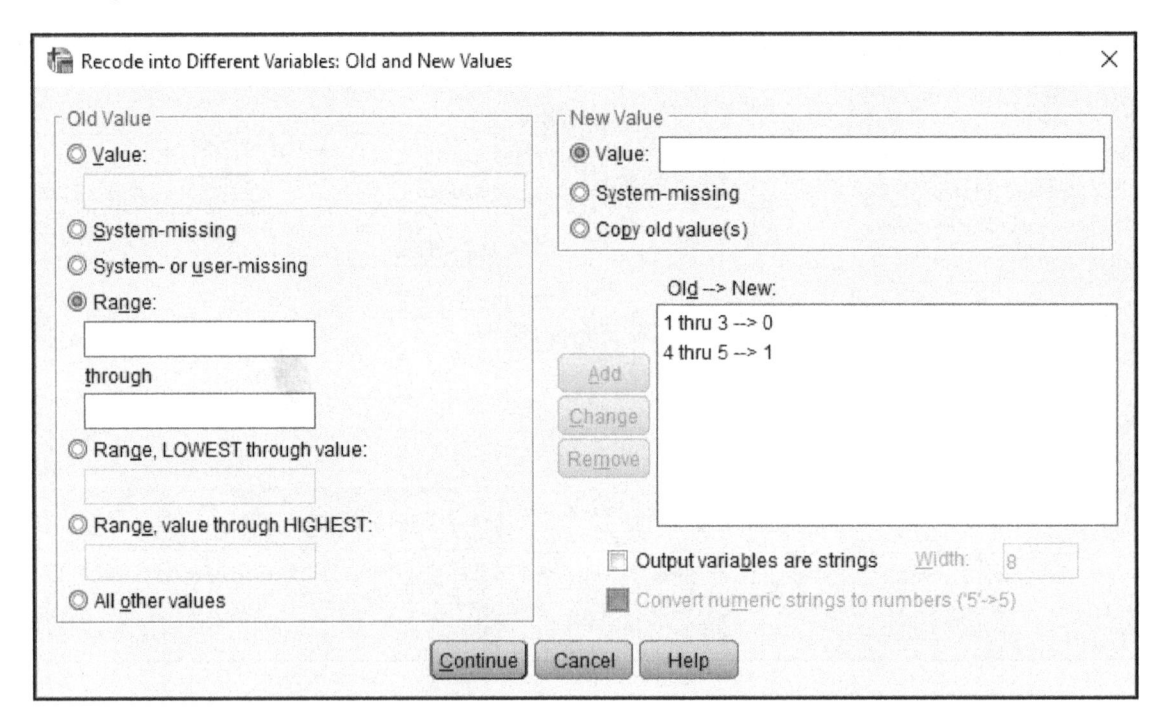

[Dialog box: Recode into Different Variables: Old and New Values, showing Old Value options (Value, System-missing, System- or user-missing, Range selected with "through", Range LOWEST through value, Range value through HIGHEST, All other values) and New Value options (Value selected, System-missing, Copy old value(s)). Old --> New list shows: "1 thru 3 --> 0" and "4 thru 5 --> 1". Buttons: Add, Change, Remove. Checkboxes: Output variables are strings, Width 8, Convert numeric strings to numbers ('5'->5). Buttons at bottom: Continue, Cancel, Help.]

Select **Continue** and then paste to place the SPSS syntax created via these dialogs into a command window. It is best to use SPSS syntax to apply transformations to a dataset, even when the commands themselves are produced using the dialog boxes. This provides an audit trail of the changes made and stores the commands so they can be applied in a consistent manner to future data of the same type.

Customer satisfaction data, such as those used in this example, are generally collected on a regular basis so any transformations will need to be applied to each new wave of responses:

```
RECODE quality (1 thru 3=0) (4 thru 5=1) INTO qualsatpos.
VARIABLE LABELS qualsatpos 'Satisfied with Quality'.
```

There are six satisfaction questions in the sample survey file, and it would be useful to create a new field that captures whether the response fell into the positive section of the range for each question. This could be accomplished with separate RECODE commands, but it is simpler to name all the original fields, provide the recoding scheme, the keyword INTO, and then the six corresponding new fields as shown in the following syntax.

[140]

Creating New Data Elements

A `VARIABLE LABELS` command could be added after the `RECODE` command to provide extended labels to each of the new variables.

```
RECODE quality price numitems org service overall (1 thru 3=0) (4 thru 5=1)
INTO qualsatpos pricesatpos numitemsatpos orgsatpos servicesatpos
overallsatpos.
```

Dummy (or binary) fields such as these may be more useful predictors in modeling than the original variables, and make it easier to assess the impact of a positive satisfaction level.

If you are recoding non-integer values, be aware that since decimals are stored to many digits of precision, it is possible for a value to fall between two specified values. This can be addressed by overlapping values in `RECODE`. For example, 1.55 through 2.55=2 and 2.55 through 3.55=3 results in values that are exactly 2.55 being assigned a 2 and values even slightly greater than 2.55, such as 2.5500001, being assigned a 3. The values of a variables are compared with the recoding scheme in the order it was specified and the first time a match is found for a value, the is recoding is performed.

Using RECODE to rescale a field

`Chapter` 3, *Statistics for Individual Data Elements*, showed the distribution of an income field in which survey respondents were asked to place themselves into one of 26 income categories. The ranges associated with the assigned codes of 1 to 26 covered varying dollar amounts so that the income levels did not rise evenly as the values increased. To more accurately reflect the differences in income, the original values can be replaced with the midpoint of the corresponding range. The following `RECODE` command accomplishes this and maps the values into a new field:

```
RECODE RINCOM16
(1=750) (2=2000) (3=3500) (4=4500) (5=5500) (6=6500) (7=7500) (8=9000) (9=11250) (10
=
13750) (11=16250) (12=18750) (13=21250) (14=23750) (15=27500) (16=32500) (17=37500
) (18
=45000) (19=55000) (20=67500) (21=82500) (22=95500) (23=120000) (24=140000) (25=16
0000) (26=200000)  INTO RINCOME_MIDPT.
VARIABLE LABELS RINCOME_MIDPT
```

Creating New Data Elements

Respondent's income using the midpoint of a selected category

These rescaled values displayed in the following screenshot make it possible to more precisely detect correlations between income and other attributes in the data:

		Frequency	Percent	Valid Percent	Cumulative Percent
Valid	750.00	25	.9	1.5	1.5
	2000.00	51	1.8	3.1	4.7
	3500.00	32	1.1	2.0	6.6
	4500.00	30	1.0	1.8	8.5
	5500.00	31	1.1	1.9	10.4
	6500.00	31	1.1	1.9	12.3
	7500.00	24	.8	1.5	13.7
	9000.00	34	1.2	2.1	15.8
	11250.00	51	1.8	3.1	18.9
	13750.00	45	1.6	2.8	21.7
	16250.00	60	2.1	3.7	25.4
	18750.00	52	1.8	3.2	28.6
	21250.00	74	2.6	4.5	33.1
	23750.00	64	2.2	3.9	37.0
	27500.00	97	3.4	5.9	43.0
	32500.00	118	4.1	7.2	50.2
	37500.00	108	3.8	6.6	56.8
	45000.00	158	5.5	9.7	66.5
	55000.00	137	4.8	8.4	74.9
	67500.00	141	4.9	8.6	83.5
	82500.00	79	2.8	4.8	88.4
	95500.00	68	2.4	4.2	92.5
	120000.00	36	1.3	2.2	94.7
	140000.00	21	.7	1.3	96.0
	160000.00	14	.5	.9	96.9
	200000.00	51	1.8	3.1	100.0
	Total	1632	56.9	100.0	
Missing	System	1235	43.1		
Total		2867	100.0		

Creating New Data Elements

The values chosen to represent the midpoint of the first and last values can be adjusted depending on what one regards as reasonable for the under $1000 and $170000 plus groups.

Values for new fields are assigned a display format by default that shows two decimal places even if the values are integers. The FORMATS command can be used to modify the display, and it can also be done via the Variables tab on the data window.

The COMPUTE command

The COMPUTE command is the workhorse of the transformation capability within SPSS. It provides access to a very broad set of functions that allow one to create logical expressions of virtually any type.

The following figure shows the basic dialog for this command, including a partial list of the many functions you can use and the calculator section with logical operators available:

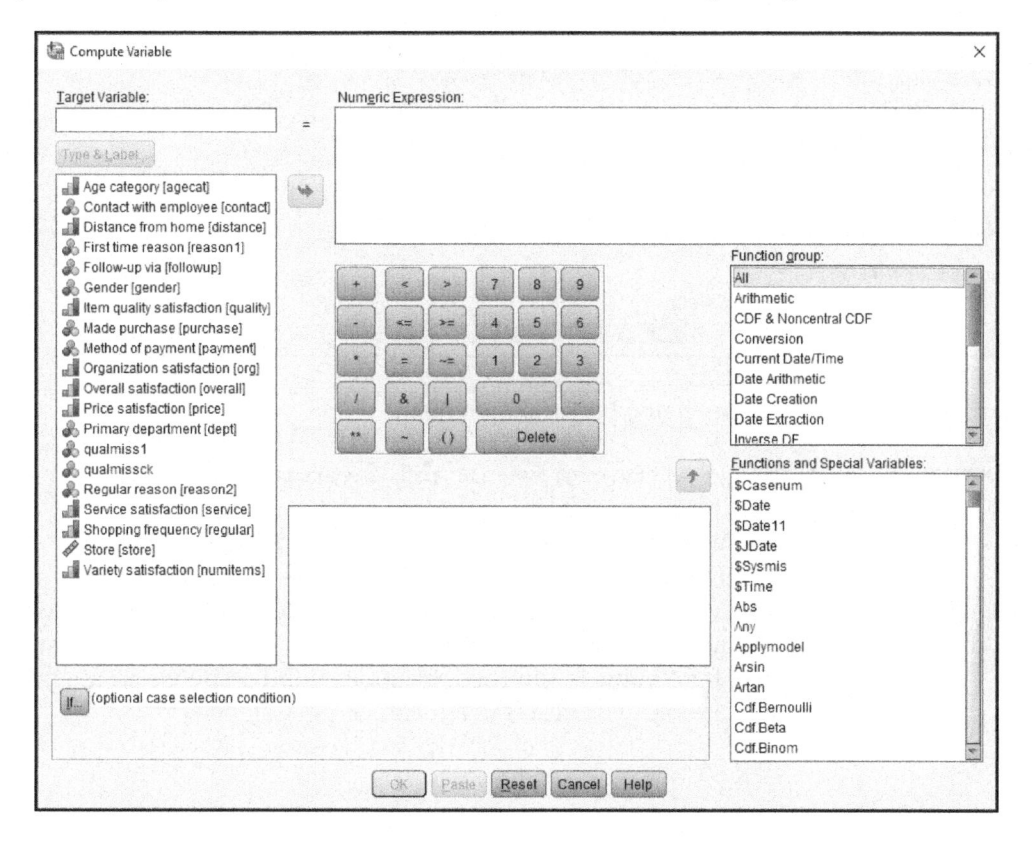

[143]

Creating New Data Elements

The MEAN function can be used to create a new field containing each customer's average across the six satisfaction questions included in the survey (refer to following screenshot). Any of the six questions that has a missing value for a row in the data is excluded from the calculation, and the denominator is automatically adjusted to reflect the number of variables used as the basis for the mean:

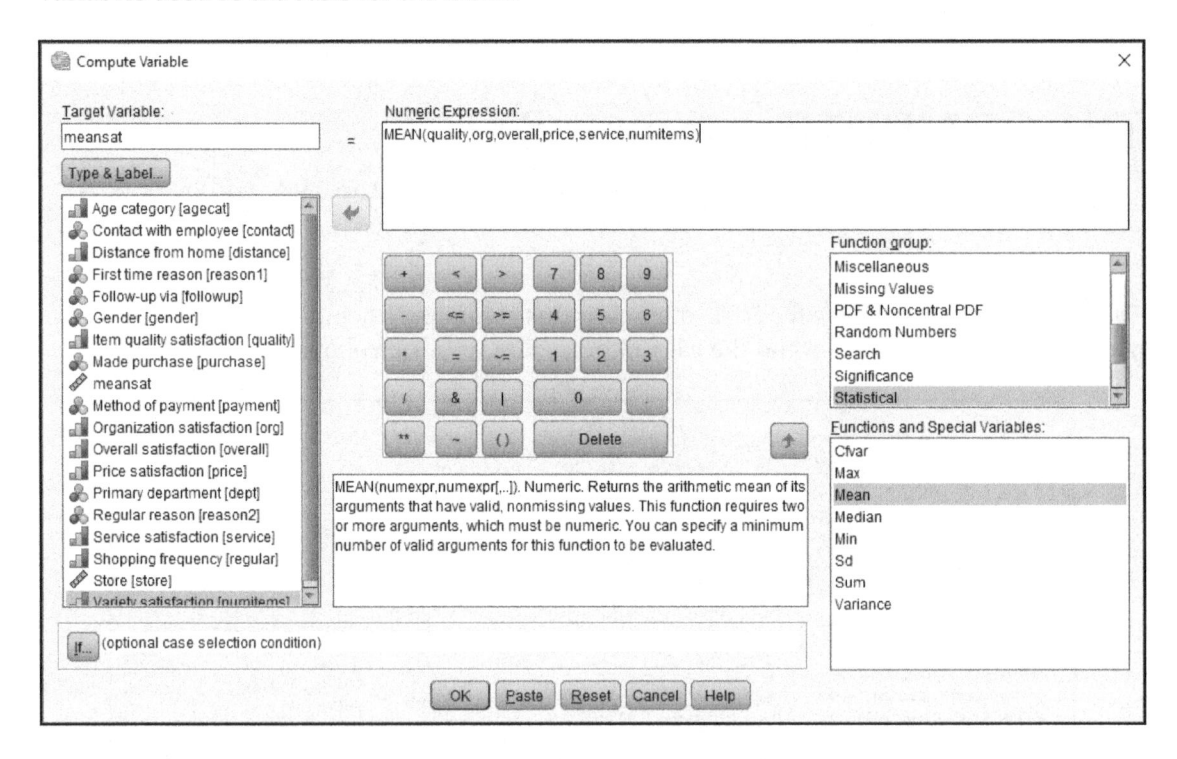

[Compute Variable dialog box screenshot showing Target Variable "meansat" and Numeric Expression "MEAN(quality,org,overall,price,service,numitems)"]

The syntax produced from the dialog box is shown next:

```
COMPUTE   meansat=MEAN(quality,org,overall,price,service,numitems).
```

> **TIP**
> The MEAN function can include a value indicating how many of the variables specified need to have valid codes for the calculation to be performed. MEAN.4, for example, requires that at least 4 of the variables named have a non-missing code, or the new field is assigned the system missing value. If no value is specified, even one valid response across the set of named variables will result in a mean being assigned.

Creating New Data Elements

New fields created by transformations can be used in subsequent commands. The following COMPUTE statement makes use of the six new fields defined by the RECODE command shown earlier:

```
COMPUTE satisf_cnt=SUM(qualsatpos, pricesatpos, numitemsatpos, orgsatpos,
servicesatpos, overallsatpos).
```

Here is the result of the same:

satisf_cnt

		Frequency	Percent	Valid Percent	Cumulative Percent
Valid	.00	115	19.8	19.8	19.8
	1.00	108	18.6	18.6	38.3
	2.00	86	14.8	14.8	53.1
	3.00	72	12.4	12.4	65.5
	4.00	78	13.4	13.4	78.9
	5.00	70	12.0	12.0	90.9
	6.00	53	9.1	9.1	100.0
	Total	582	100.0	100.0	

One of the special purpose transformation commands is COUNT, and it provides an alternative method for performing the same calculation as was just demonstrated using the COMPUTE command with the fields created by RECODE.

The following COUNT example uses the six original satisfaction fields and specifies that if the value is a four or five, the new field, satisfy_count, should be incremented by one. It is important to be aware that a field defined on a COUNT command is set to zero for each row in the dataset and the value is increased by one when the values listed for the variables match. This means that any row without any "hits" will have a value of zero on the new field.

```
COUNT satisf_count=quality price numitems org service overall(4,5).
```

There is a subtle but important difference in the way missing values are handled by the COMPUTE and COUNT commands. If all the fields listed after the SUM function on the COMPUTE command are missing for a given row, the system's missing value will be assigned for the new field being created. The COUNT command initializes the new field to zero, and that remains the value if all the input variables are missing.

Creating New Data Elements

The IF command

At the bottom of the COMPUTE dialog is an optional IF choice you can use to bring up the dialog, as shown in the following screenshot. This feature allows you to make the calculation defined in the COMPUTE portion conditional:

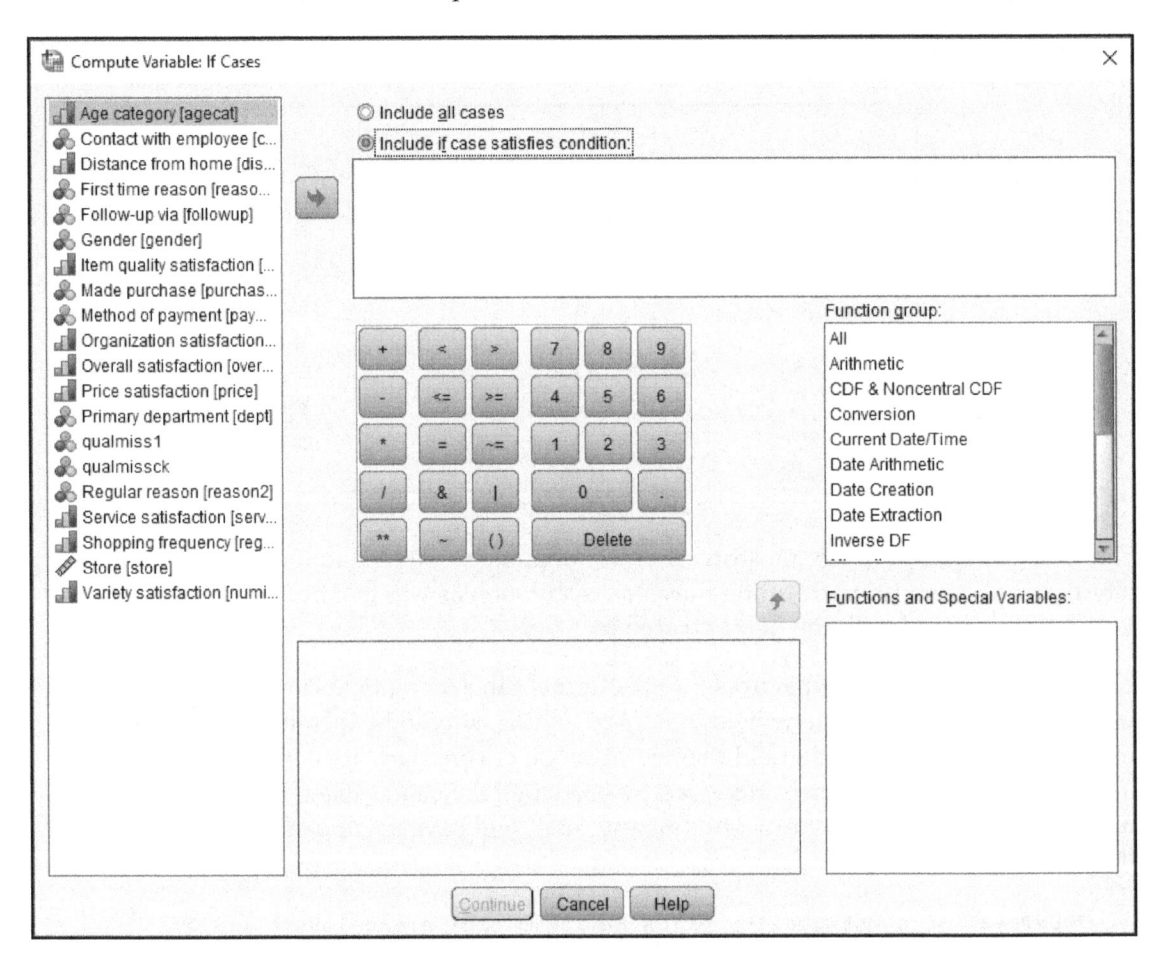

Creating New Data Elements

The cross-tabulation shown in following screenshot displays the relationship between shopping frequency and the distance to a customer's home store. This information can be used to form customer categories that can be used to target specific groups.

Shopping frequency * Distance from home Crosstabulation

Count

		Distance from home					Total
		1 < 1 mile	2 1-5 miles	3 5-10 miles	4 10-30 miles	5 > 30 miles	
Shopping frequency	0 First time	5	20	11	9	7	52
	1 < 1/month	18	43	38	40	14	153
	2 1/month	30	78	43	42	8	201
	3 1/week	18	65	34	23	2	142
	4 > 1/week	1	18	7	7	1	34
Total		72	224	133	121	32	582

The following six `IF` statements map customers into categories based on the two fields shown in the preceding screenshot. For operations such as "less than or equal to", the mnemonic LE or the symbol <= can be used. The parentheses in the third and fourth `IF` commands indicate that both the regular and distance fields are to be evaluated to assign a new value. Each portion of a statement enclosed in parentheses is evaluated as either true or false. All the conditions specified in an `IF` statement return a `true` result for the assignment portion that follows the equal sign to be executed.

```
IF regular=0 and distance le 2 custcategory=1.
 IF regular=0 and distance gt 2 custcategory=2.
 IF (regular=1 or regular=2) and distance le 2 custcategory=3.
 IF (regular=1 or regular=2) and distance gt 2 custcategory=4.
 IF regular >=3 and distance <=2 custcategory=5.
 IF regular >=3 and distance >2 custcategory=6.
 value labels custcategory 1 'New_near' 2 'New_far' 3'Monthly_near'
4'Monthly_far' 5'Weekly_near' 6'Weekly_far'.
```

The following screenshot shows the distribution of the new field defined by these `IF` statements:

custcategory

		Frequency	Percent	Valid Percent	Cumulative Percent
Valid	1.00 New_near	25	4.3	4.3	4.3
	2.00 New_far	27	4.6	4.6	8.9
	3.00 Monthly_near	169	29.0	29.0	38.0
	4.00 Monthly_far	185	31.8	31.8	69.8
	5.00 Weekly_near	102	17.5	17.5	87.3
	6.00 Weekly_far	74	12.7	12.7	100.0
	Total	582	100.0	100.0	

In the preceding example, the assignment portion of the `IF` command is very simple; expressions such as the `MEAN` and `SUM` shown earlier can be used as well. You can think of the `IF` command as a conditional `COMPUTE` statement where the expression after the equal sign is executed when the condition is evaluated as true.

If any of the fields referenced in the conditional statement are missing, a `false` evaluation is returned. The `IF` commands are processed in sequential order, so if a case meets multiple conditions for assigning a value for a new field, the last `TRUE` condition will determine the value assigned for that case. When none of the conditions used to assign a value to a new field are met by a case, the system missing value is assigned.

The DO IF/ELSE IF command

The `DO IF` command is part of the SPSS syntax language, and it is a structure in that it must be accompanied by an `END IF` command further down in the syntax file. The help system provides an overview of this command along with examples as shown in the following screenshot. This feature provides a level of program control that can be very useful when dealing with situations that require more complex transformation logic:

Creating New Data Elements

[Screenshot of IBM SPSS Help window showing DO IF command syntax reference with search results in the left pane and documentation in the right pane reading:]

> Reference > Command Syntax Reference
>
> **DO IF**
>
> The DO IF-END IF structure conditionally executes one or more transformations on subsets of cases based on one or more logical expressions. The ELSE command can be used within the structure to execute one or more transformations when the logical expression on DO IF is not true. The ELSE IF command within the structure provides further control.
>
> ```
> DO IF [(]logical expression[)]
>
> transformation commands
>
> [ELSE IF [(]logical expression[)]]
>
> transformation commands
>
> [ELSE IF [(]logical expression[)]]
> ```

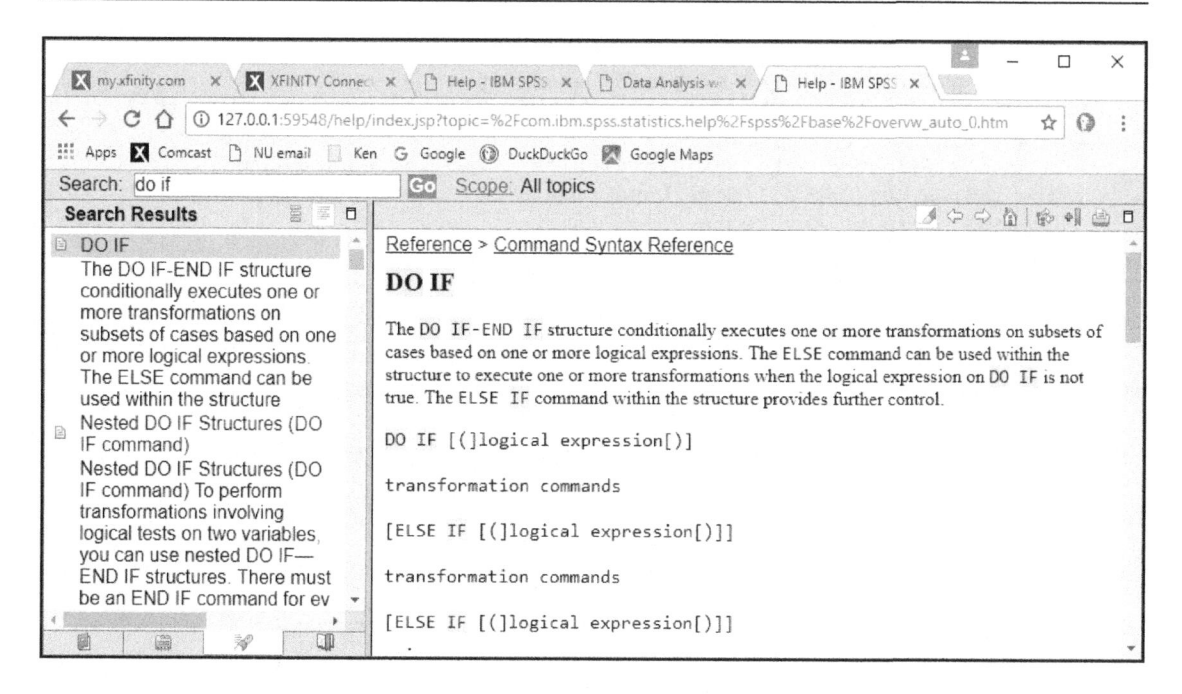

In the customer satisfaction data, for example, each store may have its own unique characteristics in terms of customer demographics and competitive environment. Store managers may want to calculate satisfaction levels and product categories in a manner that reflects these factors.

The following DO IF example uses STORE to determine how departments should be grouped into core and convenience groups. Mean satisfaction is also calculated using a different approach for each store. Note that for store three, the manager wants to emphasize the importance of price due to the competitive environment she deals with, so this variable is named twice in the COMPUTE statement.

This effectively weights the satisfaction level for PRICE twice when the mean is calculated. The following is the code:

```
DO IF STORE=1.
 RECODE dept(1,4,6,=1)(2,3,5,7=2) INTO Key_Depts.
 COMPUTE meanstoresat=MEAN(quality,price,service,numitems).
ELSE IF STORE=2.
 RECODE dept(1,4,6,=1)(2,3,5,7=2) INTO Key_Depts.
 COMPUTE meanstoresat=MEAN(quality,overall,price,numitems).
ELSE IF STORE=3.
 RECODE dept(4,5=1)(1,2,3,6,7=2) INTO Key_Depts.
 COMPUTE meanstoresat=MEAN(quality,org,price,price,service,numitems).
```

Creating New Data Elements

```
ELSE IF STORE=4.
RECODE dept(2,3,5,7,=1)(1,4,6=2) INTO Key_Depts.
COMPUTE meanstoresat=MEAN(quality,org,overall,price,service,numitems).
END IF.
var labels meanstoresat 'Satisfaction tailored for each store'.
value lables Key_Depts 1'Core Departments' 2'Convenience Departments'.
CROSSTABS store by Key_Depts.
descriptives meanstoresat.
```

The CROSSTAB and DESCRIPTIVES commands create results that can be used to check the results. Each store has both **Core Departments** and **Convenience Departments** in the table, as shown in the following figure, which is what would be expected:

Store * Key_Depts Crosstabulation

Count

		Key_Depts		Total
		Core Departments	Convenience Departments	
Store	Store 1	67	79	146
	Store 2	43	93	136
	Store 3	64	74	138
	Store 4	88	74	162
Total		262	320	582

The descriptive results in following screenshot serve as a basic check to make sure that all the cases have a value on the new variable created by the COMPUTE commands:

Descriptive Statistics

	N	Minimum	Maximum	Mean	Std. Deviation
Satisfaction tailored for each store	582	1.00	5.00	3.1256	1.00554
Valid N (listwise)	582				

The preceding example is a relatively simple DO IF command, with only two transformation commands and a single condition to be checked, but the same logic can be employed to include additional commands as well as to meet more involved conditions. The DO IF statements can also be nested to handle more complex situations.

The DO IF/ELSE IF statements are processed in order, and once a case meets the specified conditions, the commands associated with that condition are processed and the remainder of the DO IF structure is skipped. Observations that do not meet any of the conditions specified on the DO IF/ELSE IF commands will have a missing value on new fields defined.

When one (or more) of the variables named on the initial DO IF command is missing for a case, the commands within the DO IF/END IF structure are skipped, and processing up with the first command after the END IF command.

The example shown here does not make use of an ELSE command, but if you do use this feature, it must be the last condition before the END IF command, and any case that has failed all the previous condition tests will have the commands following the ELSE statement executed. The ELSE command can be very useful, but it is essential to check the results to make sure that only the appropriate rows in the data reach this point in the DO IF structure.

General points regarding SPSS transformation commands

We are going to discuss a few pointers of the tranform commands from the discussion so far:

- Any of the basic transformation commands (RECODE, COMPUTE, COUNT, and IF) can be included within a DO IF structure. Statistical procedures and special purpose procedures such as AUTORECODE and OPTIMAL BINNING cannot be put inside a DO IF structure.
- Transformation commands, unlike statistical procedures, are not executed immediately. If you create a command such as RECODE or COMPUTE using a dialog box, an EXECUTE command is included automatically, so the command gets processed. If you create a COMPUTE command in syntax and run the command, a **Tranformations pending** message appears at the bottom of each SPSS window you have open.

Creating New Data Elements

- New variables created by transformation commands are added to the active data file and can be saved to the file when you end a session. If you do not save a new version of the original file, the fields created will not be available in the future unless they are created again. Saving a syntax file with all the transformations is important since it not only allows them to be recreated if necessary, but also provides an audit trail of how the new fields were built.

Summary

The original data available to a data scientist/analyst is only the starting point of the discovery process. Building additional fields, both to address issues in the data and to incorporate subject matter expertise by creating derived variables, is central to predictive analytics. SPSS provides a range of tools to facilitate the development of new data fields, using a very comprehensive set of mathematical and statistical functions. Essential tasks, such as revising or grouping codes can be handled using specially designed transformation commands that simplify the process. Transformations that require more complex rules can be performed using conditional logic and the nesting of the appropriate commands.

In this chapter, the most commonly used transformation commands--RECODE, COMPUTE and IF--were explored in detail. The more complex DO IF/END IF structure was introduced as a means of tackling more demanding modifications to the data. With these tools in hand, you will be positioned to address most of the data transformation needs you are likely to encounter. The SPSS Help system includes many examples of building transformations, so make use of it as you start working with these commands.

The SPSS code created to transform the original data can be stored in a separate file, so it is available for use with new data in the future, and to document the steps taken to transition from the initial fields to the modified versions, which often prove to be the most useful for statistical analysis purposes.

In the chapter that follows, the file management of SPSS Statistics that allow you to match and add files together will be addressed.

8
Adding and Matching Files

You often need to combine data from multiple sources. For example, you might have customer information such as personal characteristics and purchase history in a customer database. Then, you learn that the marketing department has conducted an attitudinal survey on a subset of your customers, giving rise to new measures on some of your customers. Combining these two data sources enables you to analyze all of the variables together, which can lead to new insights and better predictions of customer behavior.

The preceding scenario describing customer data and survey data is an example of **relational data**, which means that there are relationship between pairs of datasets. In these datasets, there exist one or more variables called **keys** that are used to connect each pair of datasets. A **key** is a variable (or variables) that uniquely identifies an observation. An example of a key variable is an ID variable that uniquely identifies each customer. Across files, the ID variable should have the same name, and its values should be consistent and meaningful across files. That is, a code of, say, 10002 in an ID field in two or more files would refer to the same individual.

If the data in a pair of files is at the same level, say, customers, then a **one-to-one** merge is possible, provided that the keys' values are identical for the records being considered for the merge. If the data in a pair of files is at different levels, say, customers and orders (where multiple orders per customer are possible), then a **one-to-many** merge, each customer record to each order record for that customer, is possible, provided that the keys are equal in the records being matched.

In the preceding situations, you are combining variables. The SPSS commands for this are as follows:

- `MATCH FILES`
- `STAR JOIN`

Adding and Matching Files

Another situation is possible: You have multiple data sources for which the observed variables are at least partly overlapping, but the rows are distinct. In this situation, you wish to combine cases. The SPSS Statistics command for this is `ADD FILES`.

In this chapter, we will present several examples of joining files. Here is the topic outline:

- SPSS Statistics commands to merge files
- Example of one-to-many merge-`Northwind` database
- Example of one-to-one merge-two data subsets from GSS2016
- Example of combining cases

SPSS Statistics commands to merge files

For a one-to-one merge, use `MATCH FILES`. The basic general form is as follows:

```
MATCH FILES FILE=file1/FILE=file2/BY key_variable
```

While this example is for two files, `MATCH FILES` can merge up to 50 files at a time. `MATCH FILES` can perform a **parallel** match in which records from each file align sequentially. `MATCH FILES` can also perform a **nonparallel** match in which records are matched when key variables are equal.

Note that there are additional subcommands and features documented in IBM SPSS Statistics Help. You can keep variables, drop variables, rename variables, and produce a variable map, among other things.

In order for `MATCH FILES` to work correctly, all source files must be sorted in ascending order on the key variables. As `MATCH FILES` is not a procedure, you must follow it with either a procedure or the `EXECUTE` command.

For a one-to-many merge, you could also use `MATCH FILES`. The basic general form is as follows:

```
MATCH FILES FILE=file1/TABLE=file2/BY key_variable
```

The `/TABLE` subcommand specifies a **table lookup** file. A lookup file contributes variables, but not cases, to the new active dataset. Variables from the table file are added to all cases from the case file when key variables match in value. All specified files must be sorted in ascending order of the key variables. A table file cannot contain duplicate cases (as indicated by the key variables).

For a one-to-many merge, you could also use `STAR JOIN`, which was added to IBM SPSS Statistics in version 21. The basic general form is as follows:

```
STAR JOIN /FROM file1/JOIN file2 ON key_variable
```

The `/FROM` file is the case file while the `/JOIN` file is the table lookup file. Additional capabilities exist and are documented in SPSS Statistics Help.

`STAR JOIN` has several features not found in `MATCH FILES`:

- The files do not have to be presorted in ascending order of the key values
- Different keys can be specified for different table lookup files
- The defined width of string keys does not have to be the same in both the case file and table lookup file
- `STAR JOIN` reads the active dataset and causes the execution of any pending transformations

Finally, to combine cases, use `ADD FILES`. The basic general form is as follows:

```
ADD FILES FILE=file1/FILE=file2
```

Additional capabilities exist and are documented in SPSS Statistics Help. `ADD FILES` can combine up to 50 files at a time. Files do not have to have exactly the same variables, but it makes sense to combine files if there are at least some variables in common. As `ADD FILES` is not a procedure, you must follow it with either a procedure or the `EXECUTE` command.

> **TIP**: `ADD FILES` aligns variables of the same name. An additional requirement is that matching string variables must have the same string format.

Example of one-to-many merge - Northwind database

The **Northwind sample database** is a publicly-available fictitious simple transaction processing database that is used here to illustrate the recording, storing, retrieving, and editing of data related to procurement and fulfillment activities of the company, Northwind Traders. If you have access to recent versions of Microsoft Access, you can install the database from a built-in Database Template.

Adding and Matching Files

The `Northwind` database contains a set of data tables. For our purposes, we will work with two tables from the `Northwind` database: `Customers` and `Orders`. Note that the original creators of the database and its tables have taken shortcuts in creating some of the fields and field values in the sense that values don't vary in some places in which they ought to in reality. For our purposes, we have converted the original source tables to SPSS Statistics save files.

> **TIP**
> For a thorough discussion of the `Northwind` database, see *Teaching Case: Adapting the Access Northwind Database to Support a Database Course* by John N. Dyer and Camille Rogers, Department of Information Systems, Georgia Southern University, Statesboro, Georgia 30460.

Customer table

Here is a screenshot of a portion of the `Customer` table:

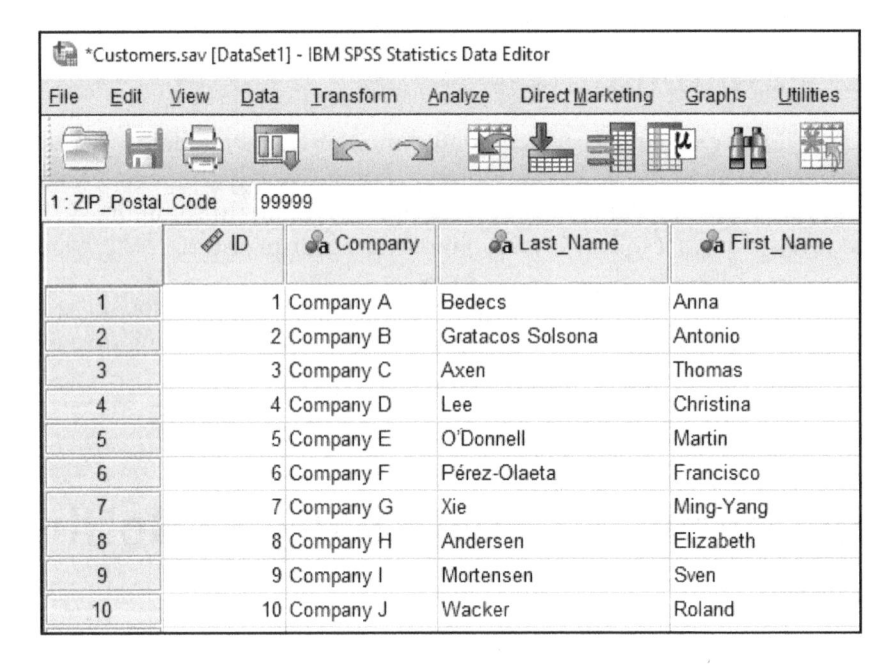

	ID	Company	Last_Name	First_Name
1	1	Company A	Bedecs	Anna
2	2	Company B	Gratacos Solsona	Antonio
3	3	Company C	Axen	Thomas
4	4	Company D	Lee	Christina
5	5	Company E	O'Donnell	Martin
6	6	Company F	Pérez-Olaeta	Francisco
7	7	Company G	Xie	Ming-Yang
8	8	Company H	Andersen	Elizabeth
9	9	Company I	Mortensen	Sven
10	10	Company J	Wacker	Roland

The `Customer` table consists of 29 observations and 18 fields. Most of the fields are strings. Here is a list of the variables:

- ID
- Company
- Last_Name
- First_Name
- E_mail_Address
- Job_Title
- Business_Phone
- Home_Phone
- Mobile_Phone
- Fax_Number
- Address
- City
- State_Province
- ZIP_Postal_Code
- Country_Region
- Web_Page
- Notes
- Attachment

The **ID** field is a numeric field that serves as a unique customer identifier. That is, the name is **ID** and it is a customer ID.

Adding and Matching Files

Orders table

Here is a screenshot of a portion of the Orders table:

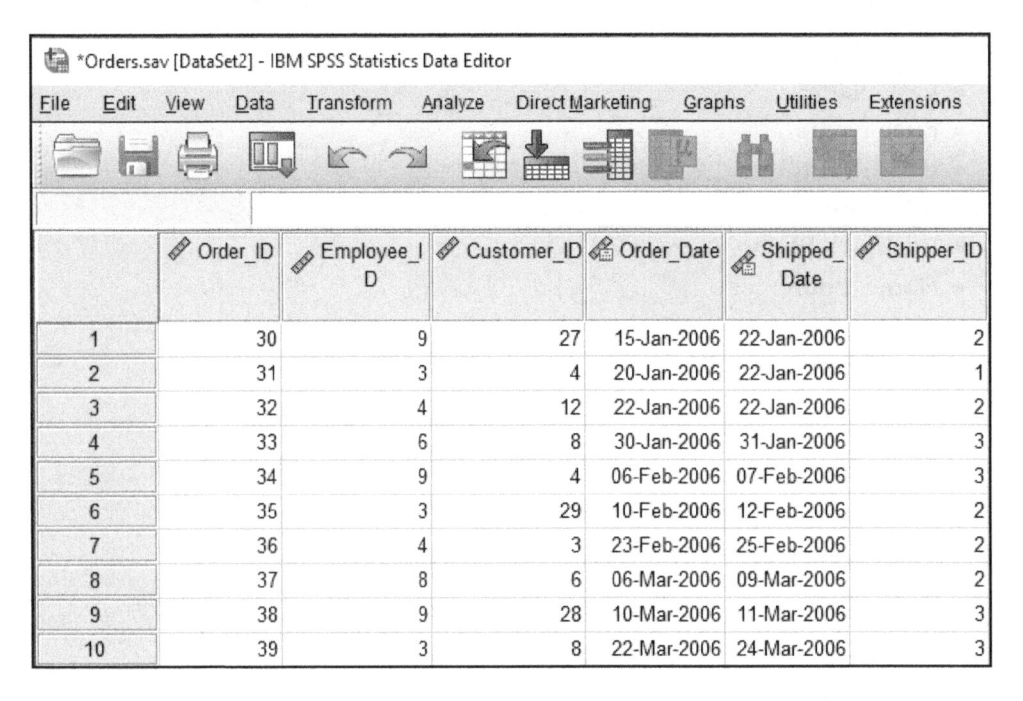

	Order_ID	Employee_ID	Customer_ID	Order_Date	Shipped_Date	Shipper_ID
1	30	9	27	15-Jan-2006	22-Jan-2006	2
2	31	3	4	20-Jan-2006	22-Jan-2006	1
3	32	4	12	22-Jan-2006	22-Jan-2006	2
4	33	6	8	30-Jan-2006	31-Jan-2006	3
5	34	9	4	06-Feb-2006	07-Feb-2006	3
6	35	3	29	10-Feb-2006	12-Feb-2006	2
7	36	4	3	23-Feb-2006	25-Feb-2006	2
8	37	8	6	06-Mar-2006	09-Mar-2006	2
9	38	9	28	10-Mar-2006	11-Mar-2006	3
10	39	3	8	22-Mar-2006	24-Mar-2006	3

The **Orders** table consists of 48 observations and 20 fields. Here is a list of the variables:

- Order_ID
- Employee_ID
- Customer_ID
- Order_Date
- Shipped_Date
- Shipper_ID
- Ship_Name
- Ship_Address
- Ship_City
- Ship_State_Province
- Ship_ZIP_Postal_Code
- Ship_Country_Region
- Shipping_Fee

- Taxes
- Payment_Type
- Paid_Date
- Notes
- Tax_Rate
- Tax_Status
- Status_ID

There are a number of ID fields that could serve as possible primary match keys for a match. Note especially the existence of **Customer_ID** and **Shipper_ID**. Inspection of the preceding screenshot shows that multiple records can have the same **Customer_ID** value, for example, see rows **2** and **5** in the `Orders` data.

The Customer-Orders relationship

From our inspection of the individual tables, we have seen that **ID** in the `Customer` table is logically the same variable as **Customer_ID** in the `Orders` table. These fields can serve as a primary key for matching; however in order for the match to work, they must have the same name.

In addition, we must understand whether the relationship between the records in the two files is one-to-one or one-to-many.

The `Customer` table has one record per customer with ID ranging from 1 to 29 consecutively.

The `Orders` table has all orders placed in the first six months of 2006. Not all customers have placed orders in this time period. Of those customers who placed orders, the number of orders ranges from 2 to 6. Therefore, the relationship between the tables is one customer to possibly many orders.

Several merges are possible. Examples include the following:

- Perform a one-to-many merge of Customer records to Order records.
- Aggregate the order records by customer, and then merge these with customer records. In this setting, different merges are possible.
- Keep the most recent order record and merge with customer information.

Here, we will show you how to do a one-to-many merge of customer records to order records.

Adding and Matching Files

SPSS code for a one-to-many merge

Suppose you wish to merge selected Customer information to Orders information. Specifically, from the `Customers` file, you wish to retain the following fields:

- First_Name
- Last_Name
- Company
- Address
- City
- State_Province
- ZIP_Postal_Code

From the `Orders` file, you wish to retain the following fields:

- Order_ID
- Shipper_ID
- Order_Date
- Shipped_Date

You can proceed as follows:

1. Recall that each file in the merge must have a match key with the same name and meaning. Additionally, depending on your approach, you might need to ensure that each file is sorted in ascending order on the key variable. Recall that MATCH FILES requires sorting while STAR JOIN does not. As we intend to demonstrate the use of both commands, we will ensure that the cases are sorted in each file.
2. Inspect the `Customers` table. Ensure that the file is ordered by `ID`, which is the primary match key. You can rename `ID` at this point or you can rename it while merging. We will demonstrate the latter:

```
*Make sure that the two files are open(Orders, then Customers) and that the
cases are sorted by ID.
*Make Customers file active. File is already sorted.
DATASET ACTIVATE DataSet2.
DATASET NAME Customers.
```

3. Select the **Orders** table. Make sure that orders is sorted in ascending order on `Customer_ID` and, nested within that, on `Order_Date`. `Customer_ID` is the primary match key, while sorting by `Order_Date` will list records in time order within each customer:

```
*Make Orders file active.
DATASET ACTIVATE DataSet1.
SORT CASES BY Customer_ID(A) Order_Date(A).
DATASET NAME Orders.
```

4. Here is the STAR JOIN command to merge the two files:

```
STAR JOIN
 /SELECT t0.Order_ID, t0.Shipper_ID, t0.Order_Date,  t0.Shipped_Date,
t1.First_Name, t1.Last_Name,
 t1.Company, t1.Address, t1.City, t1.State_Province,  t1.ZIP_Postal_Code
 /FROM * AS t0
 /JOIN 'Customers' AS t1
 ON t0.Customer_ID=t1.ID
 /OUTFILE FILE=*.
```

The STAR JOIN command performs the equivalent of a SQL left outer join:

- /SELECT specifies the fields to be included from all data sources that are specified in the /FROM and /JOIN subcommands, except for the key fields. The /SELECT subcommand is required and must be the first subcommand. Note the use of t0 and t1 as stand-in names for the data sources. Note the use of commas as separators for the fields.
- /FROM specifies the case data file in the join. The asterisk (*) is the symbol for the active file, which is the Orders file, and t0 is the alias or stand-in name for the Orders file. Note the use of the keyword, AS.
- /JOIN specifies the table lookup file. This is the source file for the one-to-many match. The dataset name Customers specifies the file. AS is followed by the alias t1. ON is followed by the key field. Here, the expression renames ID to Customer_ID. This ensures that each file in the match has the same primary key field.
- /OUTFILE makes the combined file the active file.

Adding and Matching Files

Since the active file has changed in content, you should consider saving it under a new name and you might also change its dataset name. Here is a SAVE command followed by DATASET NAME:

```
SAVE  OUTFILE='C:\Users\tbabinec\Documents\KSBSPSSBOOK_DATA\chap
ter8\NorthwindTables\Orders_and_Customers.sav'
 /COMPRESSED.
DATASET NAME OrdersandCustomers.
```

Here is a screenshot of a portion of the combined file:

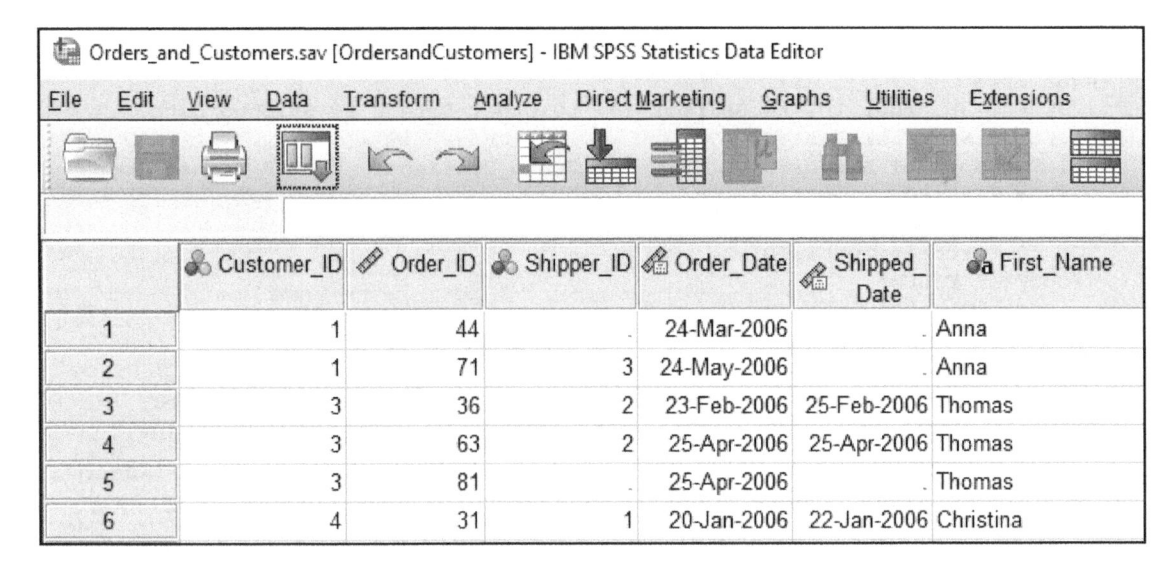

	Customer_ID	Order_ID	Shipper_ID	Order_Date	Shipped_Date	First_Name
1	1	44	.	24-Mar-2006	.	Anna
2	1	71	3	24-May-2006	.	Anna
3	3	36	2	23-Feb-2006	25-Feb-2006	Thomas
4	3	63	2	25-Apr-2006	25-Apr-2006	Thomas
5	3	81	.	25-Apr-2006	.	Thomas
6	4	31	1	20-Jan-2006	22-Jan-2006	Christina

Note the positional order of the variables: Customer_ID is first, followed by the retained variables from the Orders file, followed by the retained variables from the Customers file.

Alternate SPSS code

A one-to-many match can also be specified via the MATCH FILES command. Here is the sample code:

```
*alternate syntax for Merge.
*Make sure that the two files are open(Orders, then Customers) and that the
cases are sorted by ID.
*Make Customers file active. File is already sorted.
DATASET ACTIVATE DataSet2.
DATASET NAME Customers.
RENAME VARIABLES (ID=Customer_ID).
```

```
*Make Orders file active.
DATASET ACTIVATE DataSet1.
SORT CASES BY Customer_ID(A) Order_Date(A).
DATASET NAME Orders.
*Do the match.
MATCH FILES FILE=*/TABLE='Customers'/BY Customer_ID.
EXECUTE.
```

Here are a couple of comments on the SPSS Statistics code:

- We use `RENAME VARIABLES` to rename `ID` to `Customer_ID`
- On `MATCH FILES`, the `/TABLE` subcommand specifies `Customers` as the source file for the one-to-many match

One-to-one merge - two data subsets from GSS2016

This example draws on the General Social Survey 2016 data. For this example, we created two data files from the `GSS2016` data, and we will act as if they are two original files that we would like to merge.

Here is file 1:

	id	sex	age	marital	wrkstat	educ
1	1	1	47	1	1	16
2	2	1	61	5	1	12
3	3	1	72	1	5	16
4	4	2	43	1	2	12
5	5	2	55	1	2	18

Adding and Matching Files

File 1 has five rows and six variables. Note that **id** consists of sequential numbers 1 through 5, while the variables measure personal characteristics of the respondents.

Here is file 2:

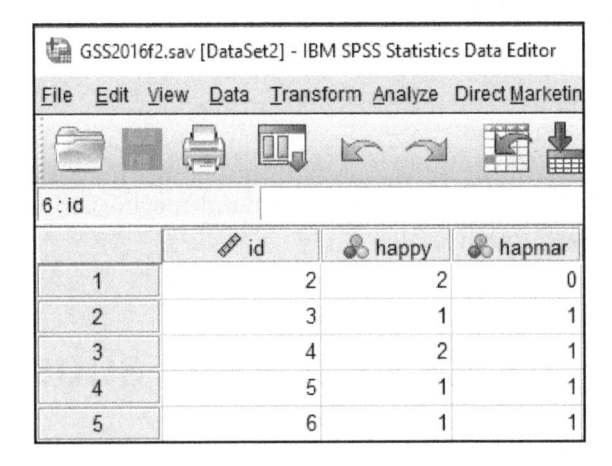

	id	happy	hapmar
1	2	2	0
2	3	1	1
3	4	2	1
4	5	1	1
5	6	1	1

File 2 has five rows and three variables. Note that **id** consists of sequential numbers 2 through 6, while the variables measure two forms of happiness.

The primary match key, **id**, has the same name in each file and the data codes have the same meaning. For example, an **id** value of 2 in each file refers to the same individual.

Several joins are possible. You could merge the files in such a way that the combined file has the following attributes:

- Records 1 through 6: An outer join. The combined file has a record if any contributing file has one.
- Records 2 through 5: An inner join. The combined file has a record only if each contributing file has it.
- Records 1 through 5: A partial join. File 1 is the focal file, and records from file 2 are matched to file 1.
- Records 2 through 6: A partial join. File 2 is the focal file, and records from file 1 are matched to file 2.

Adding and Matching Files

We will show the first approach. We proceed as follows:

1. First, ensure that both files are sorted in ascending order by `id`.
2. Make `GSS2016f1` the active file.
3. Run the `MATCH FILES` command:

```
MATCH FILES /FILE=*
 /FILE='DataSet2'
 /BY id.
EXECUTE.
```

4. Save the combined file and give it a `DATASET` name:

```
SAVE
OUTFILE='C:\Users\tbabinec\Documents\KSBSPSSBOOK_DATA\chapter8\GSS2016f1and
f2Outer.sav'
 /COMPRESSED.
 DATASET NAME f1andf2Outer.
```

Here is the combined file:

	id	sex	age	marital	wrkstat	educ	happy	hapmar
1	1	1	47	1	1	16	.	.
2	2	1	61	5	1	12	2	0
3	3	1	72	1	5	16	1	1
4	4	2	43	1	2	12	2	1
5	5	2	55	1	2	18	1	1
6	6	.	.	.	.	.	1	1

The combined file has a record if any contributing file has a record, which demonstrates that SPSS Statistics `MATCH FILES` performs an outer join when you invoke a one-to-one merge.

What if you desire an inner join? The answer is that you can make use of SPSS Statistics data and transformation statements to select or deselect records based on whether certain fields are observed or missing. We leave that as an exercise.

Example of combining cases using ADD FILES

In this example, we have GSS2014 and GSS2016 files that have some variables in common. Using ADD FILES, we create a combined file.

Following is a screenshot of the first five rows of data from a GSS2014 extract:

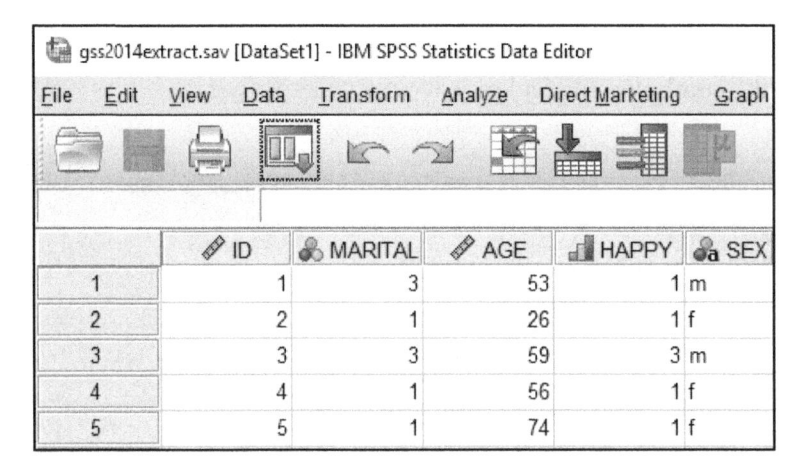

	ID	MARITAL	AGE	HAPPY	SEX
1	1	3	53	1	m
2	2	1	26	1	f
3	3	3	59	3	m
4	4	1	56	1	f
5	5	1	74	1	f

The file has 2,538 rows and five variables.

Here is a screenshot of the first five rows of data from a GSS2016 extract:

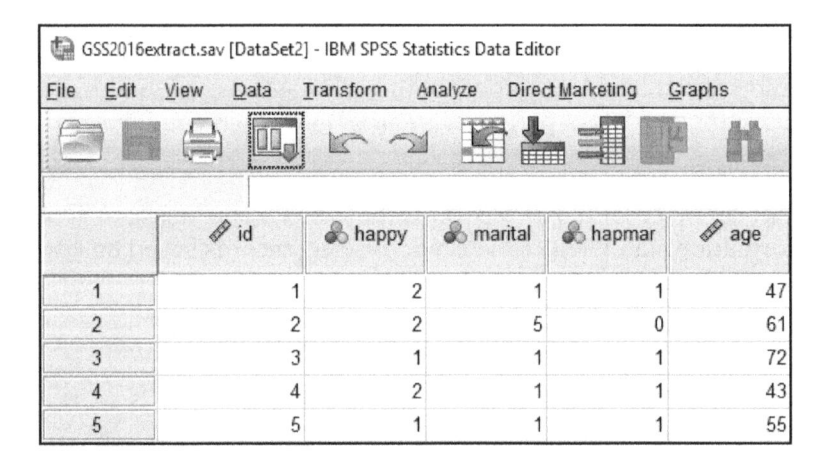

	id	happy	marital	hapmar	age
1	1	2	1	1	47
2	2	2	5	0	61
3	3	1	1	1	72
4	4	2	1	1	43
5	5	1	1	1	55

The file has 2,867 row and 29 variables.

Suppose that you wish to combine the files. While the 2016 image does not show all the fields, it turns out that the 2016 file has the same five variables as the 2014 file (along with many others). Considering the five variables in more detail, there are a couple things to take care of in the merge.

First, the **ID** fields have duplicate values across the two files because the **ID** numbers are internal to each file. In this situation, you should take some action to make the **ID** values unique across files. An easy thing to do is add a number to the IDs in one or both files. We illustrate this in the example.

Second, sex is a string variable in the 2014 file, while it is a numeric variable in the 2016 file. If you want to include sex in the combined file, you must recode one of these to make the variables conform.

Third, variable names, variable labels, and value labels use uppercase and lowercase in the 2014 file, while the corresponding items use uppercase in the 2016 file. An easy way to resolve this is to make the file with the desired dictionary items the active file in the ADD FILES merge.

Here is how we go about it:

1. Start with the 2016 file.
2. Make the ID field unique (relative to the 2014 ID variable) by adding a constant:

   ```
   DATASET ACTIVATE DataSet2.
   COMPUTE ID=ID+160000.
   FORMATS ID(F8).
   EXECUTE.
   ```

   Here are comments on the SPSS commands:

   - DATASET ACTIVATE makes the 2016 **SPSS Statistics Data Editor** window the active window
   - COMPUTE adds a large number to the IDs, which has the effect of inserting a 16 in front of the ID numbers
   - FORMATS formats the **ID** field as whole numbers
   - EXECUTE forces SPSS Statistics to read the data and process the transformations

3. Next, make the 2014 file the active file.

Adding and Matching Files

4. Transform the ID field in analogous fashion to the transformation of the ID field in the 2016 file. Then, recode the `sex` variable and tidy things up. Here are the commands:

```
DATASET ACTIVATE DataSet1.
COMPUTE ID=ID+140000.
FORMATS ID(F8).
EXECUTE.
RECODE SEX ('m'=1) ('f'=2) INTO SEXN.
FORMATS SEXN(f8).
EXECUTE.
DELETE VARIABLES SEX.
RENAME VARIABLES (SEXN=SEX).
VALUE LABELS SEX 1 'Male' 2 'Female'.
```

Here are comments on the SPSS commands:

- `DATASET ACTIVATE` makes the 2014 data file the active file.
- `COMPUTE` adds a constant to the `ID` field to make the digits **14** the lead digits of the numeric `ID` field. `FORMATS` makes `ID` a whole number. `EXECUTE` causes SPSS to read the data and perform the transformation.
- `RECODE INTO` recodes the string variable `SEX` into the numeric variable `SEXN`.
- `DELETE VARIABLES` and `RENAME VARIABLES` ensure that the numeric-coded sex codes reside in a variable named `SEX`. This ensures conformance of name and type with `SEX` in the 2016 data.
- `VALUE LABELS` establishes value labels in uppercase and lowercase for `SEX`.

Now, specify the `ADD FILES` command, along with some analysis of the combined data:

```
ADD FILES /FILE=*
 /FILE='DataSet2'
 /IN=source
 /DROP=cappun childs degree educ hapmar incom16 natchld  NATENRGY natmass
natpark natroad natsci
 partyid polviews PRES12 region res16 RINCOM16 satfin size spdeg   speduc
VOTE12 wrkstat.
VARIABLE LABELS source
 ' '.
VALUE LABELS source 0 '2014' 1 '2016'.
FORMATS source(f8).
EXECUTE.
DATASET NAME Combined2014and2016.
CROSSTABS
 /TABLES=HAPPY BY source
 /FORMAT=AVALUE TABLES
```

```
/CELLS=COUNT COLUMN
/COUNT ROUND CELL.
```

Here are some comments on the SPSS commands:

- `ADD FILES` has a `/FILE` subcommand for each file. The active file, indicated by the asterisk, is the first file. `/IN` specifies a source variable named **source**. Source is a 0,1 indicator assigned to each row, indicating whether the record is from the first- or second-named file. `/DROP` specifies which variables to exclude from the combined file.
- `VARIABLE LABELS` specifies an empty label for source.
- `VALUE LABELS` assigns the years to the source codes.
- The `CROSSTABS` command runs on the combined data.

Here is the result of running `CROSSTABS`:

			source 2014	2016	Total
General happiness	Very happy	Count	786	806	1592
		% within source	31.1%	28.2%	29.5%
	Pretty happy	Count	1403	1601	3004
		% within source	55.5%	56.0%	55.7%
	Not too happy	Count	341	452	793
		% within source	13.5%	15.8%	14.7%
Total		Count	2530	2859	5389
		% within source	100.0%	100.0%	100.0%

Inspection of the table indicates an apparent slight downward shift of the responses toward the **Not too happy** end of the happiness responses in 2016 relative to 2014.

Summary

SPSS Statistics provides you with several commands to merge files. You can perform a one-to-many merge using either `STAR JOIN` or `MATCH FILES`. `STAR JOIN` is a more recent addition to SPSS Statistics and is more flexible.

You can perform a one-to-one merge using `MATCH FILES`, which enables you to perform both parallel and non-parallel matches. Any of the aforementioned merges rely on key fields for the matching.

Finally, you can use `ADD FILES` to combine cases from multiple file sources.

In the next chapter, we turn to two important topics: aggregating and restructuring data.

9
Aggregating and Restructuring Data

There are many instances in which the data provided initially needs to be changed before analysis can begin. `Chapter 7`, *Creating New Data Elements*, described a variety of SPSS capabilities to create new variables using the transformations commands and `Chapter 8`, *Adding and Matching files*, dealt with the capabilities available to match and add files. This chapter builds on what was covered in these two chapters by introducing the use of aggregation to create summary variables by calculating statistics such as the mean, sum, minimum and maximum across a set of cases in the data. This information can be used to add fields for analytical purposes, and the aggregated file itself can be used to conduct investigations using a different unit of analysis.

The key topics that will be addressed in this chapter are as follows:

- Adding aggregated fields back to the original file
- Aggregating up one level
- Aggregating to a second level
- Matching the aggregated file back to find specific records
- Restructuring a file and switching rows to columns

Aggregating and Restructuring Data

Using aggregation to add fields to a file

A dataset contains information that is readily evident in the fields themselves, but it also has useful content that is inherent in data. Often, it is important to place specific values in a broader context to make them more meaningful. Personal income, for example, can be an important predictor in many situations but comparing someone's income with the average income in their area provides a more nuanced view of their relative economic situation. Similarly, a student score on a reading test can be compared to the national average but it is also useful to compare their score with other students in their district or school. A student's score may be just slightly preceding to the national norm but they may have one of the top scores in their school and they could benefit by being included in an advanced reading program.

For the first aggregation example, the General Social Survey data introduced in Chapter 3, *Statistics for Individual Data Elements*, will be used.

The examples in this chapter will use the 33-variable subset of General Social Survey data from 2016 that was the basis for the examples in Chapter 3, *Statistics for Individual Data Elements*, and Chapter 4, *Dealing with Missing Data and Outliers*. Open the SPSS data file that you created earlier (or download and open the full GSS2016 following the steps in Chapter 3, *Statistics for Individual Data Elements*). Before proceeding to the aggregation of the data, create the income field with the midpoint of the range as the value. This was one of the RECODE examples in Chapter 7, *Creating New Data Elements*, but the code is shown here as well:

```
RECODE RINCOM16
(1=750) (2=2000) (3=3500) (4=4500) (5=5500) (6=6500) (7=7500) (8=9000)
(9=11250) (10=13750) (11=16250) (12=18750) (13=21250) (14=23750) (15=27500) (16=32
500)
(17=37500) (18=45000) (19=55000) (20=67500) (21=82500) (22=95500) (23=120000)
(24=140000) (25=160000) (26=200000)  INTO RINCOME_MIDPT.
VARIABLE LABELS RINCOME_MIDPT Respondents income using midpoint of selected
category.
```

> ⓘ If you saved a version of the GSS data with this field included after performing RECODE, it will already be there. You can confirm this by checking the variables tab on the data window after opening your file.

Aggregating and Restructuring Data

Verify that the new income field is ready to be used by asking for a Frequency table and see that the distribution shows the midpoint values. Next, go to the **Data** menu and select **Aggregate Data** (it is near the bottom of the list).

The objective in this example is to obtain the mean of education and income for the region in which the respondent lives. This information can be used to compare their value to the average for their region. Specify **REGION** as the **Break Variable(s)** to be used to divide the cases into the relevant subsets and select education along with the new income field as the **Aggregated Variables**, as shown in the following dialog box:

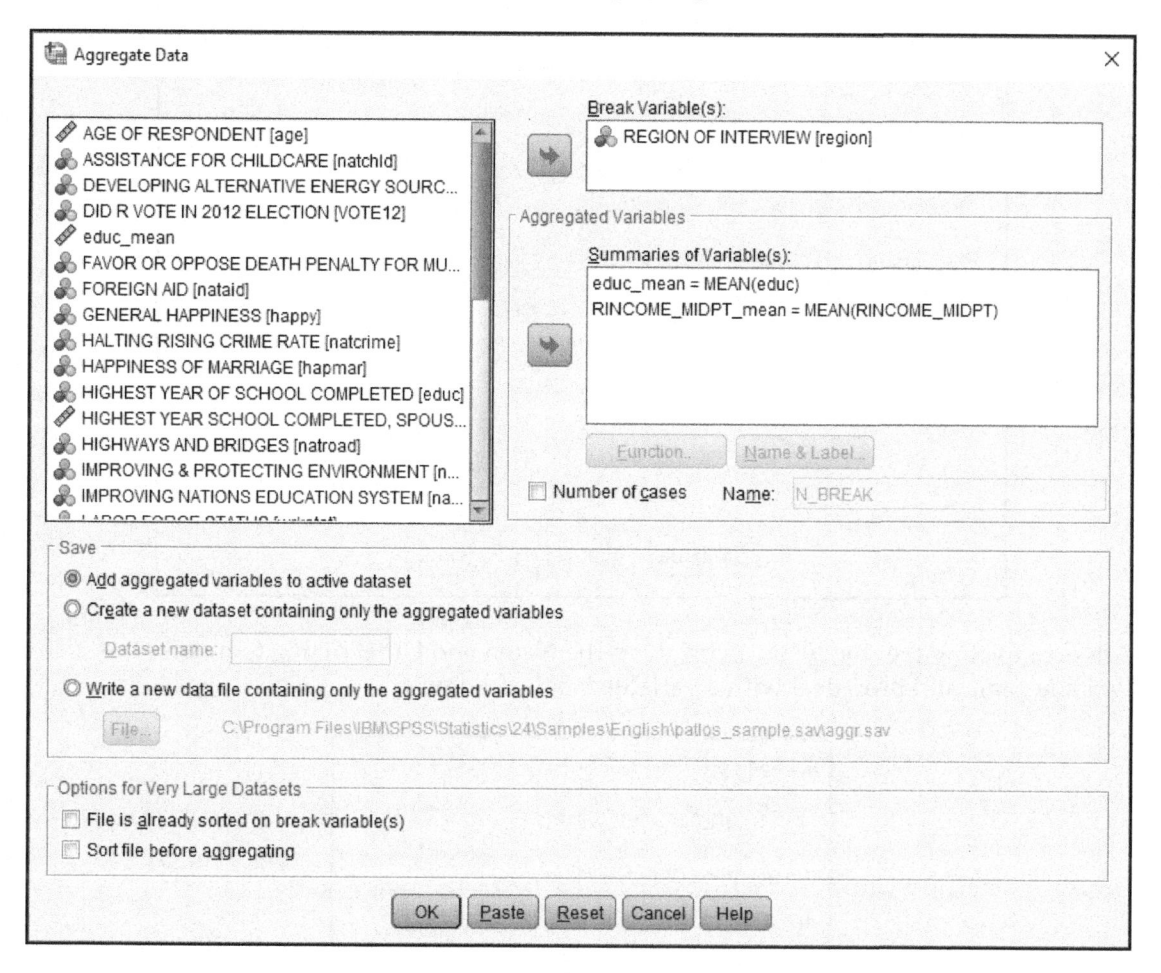

Aggregating and Restructuring Data

The `mean` is the default summary function so it is automatically selected and a new field name is provided with `mean` as a suffix to the original variable name. To create standardized scores tailored for each region, we need both the mean and standard deviation for a field. This can be obtained by adding the new income field, `RINCOME_MIDPT`, again and then using the **Function** button to change the summary statistic to standard deviation in the associated dialog, as displayed in the following screenshot:

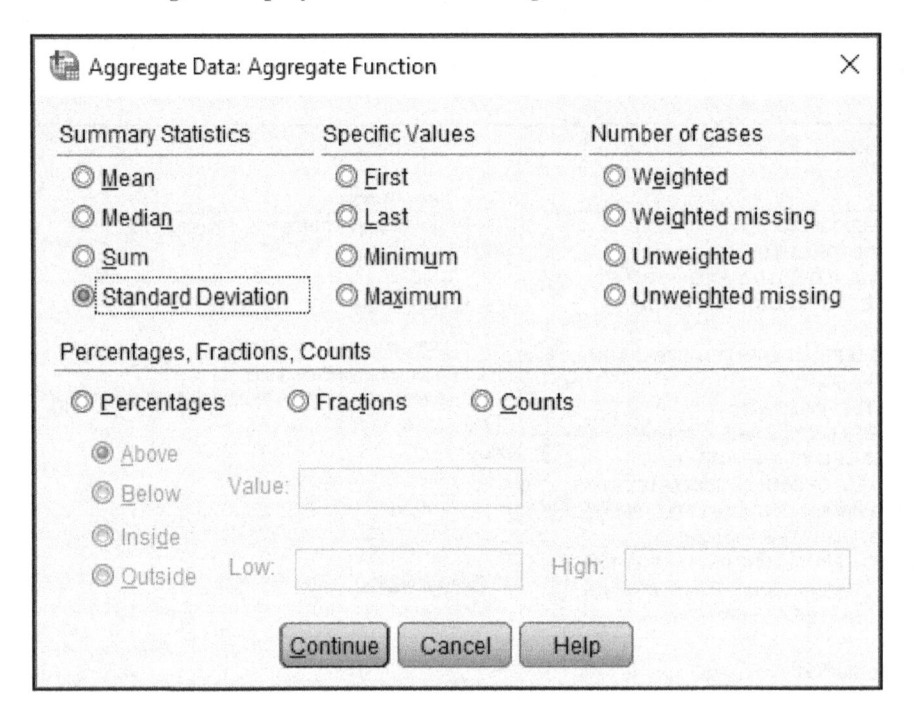

After completing the step, you can bring up the **Name and Label** dialog to modify the variable name and provide it with a variable label, as follows:

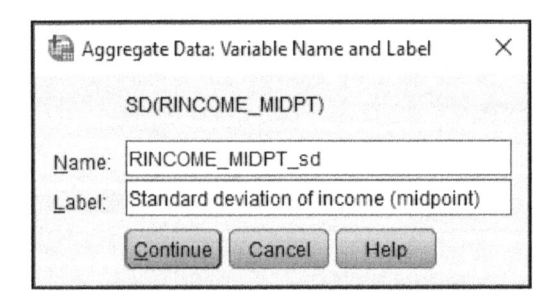

Aggregating and Restructuring Data

The **Aggregate Data** dialog shown in the following image reflects these modifications. It also indicates in the **Save** section on the lower left that the variables created by the aggregation will be added back to the active dataset--in this instance, the GSS file for 2016 used as the basis for the example:

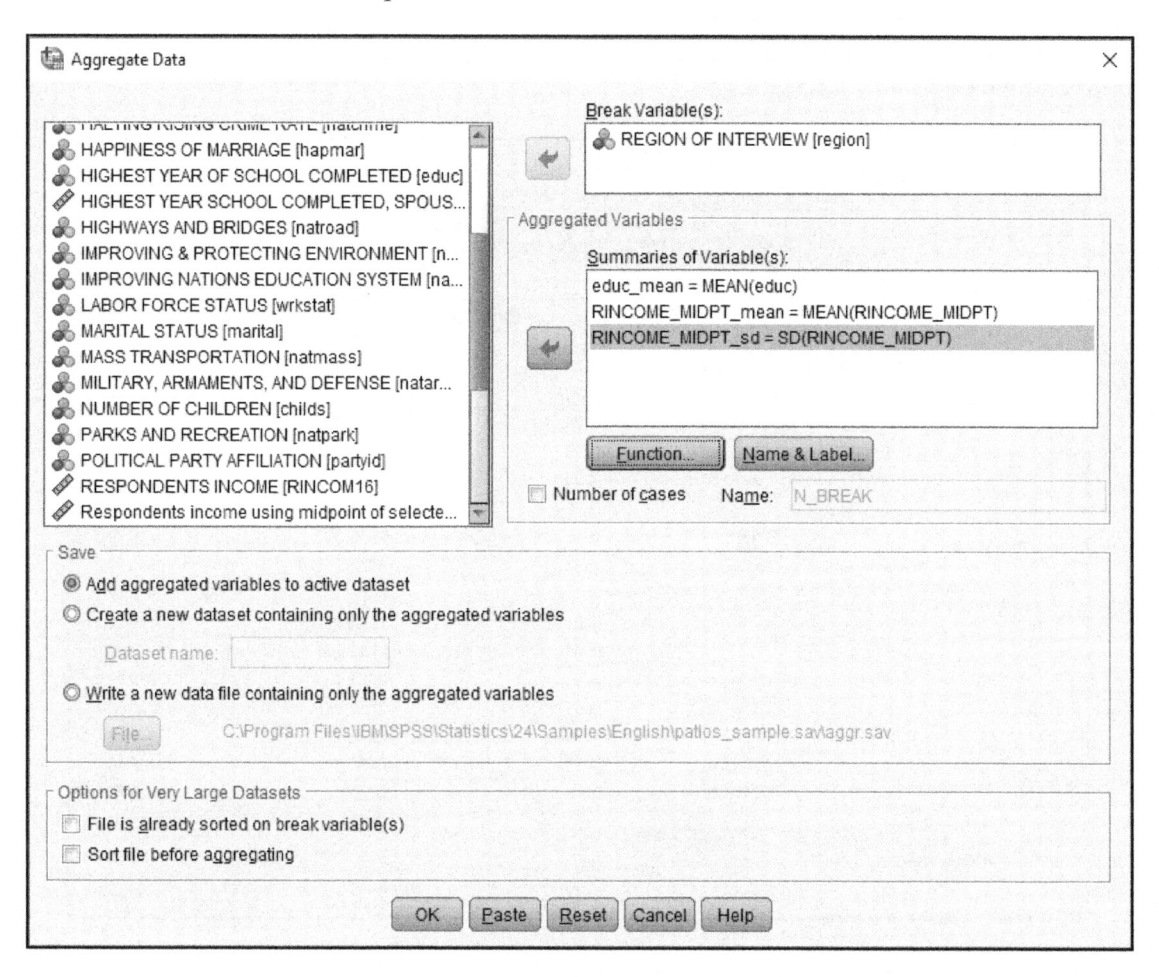

Using aggregated variables to create new fields

The following screenshot of the active dataset shows that all the rows with a region value of 1 have the same values for the three new fields added, and this is the case for region 2 as well. This new information was implicit in the original data and, by adding the appropriate values to each case, we now have contextual data that can be used to create more refined derived fields:

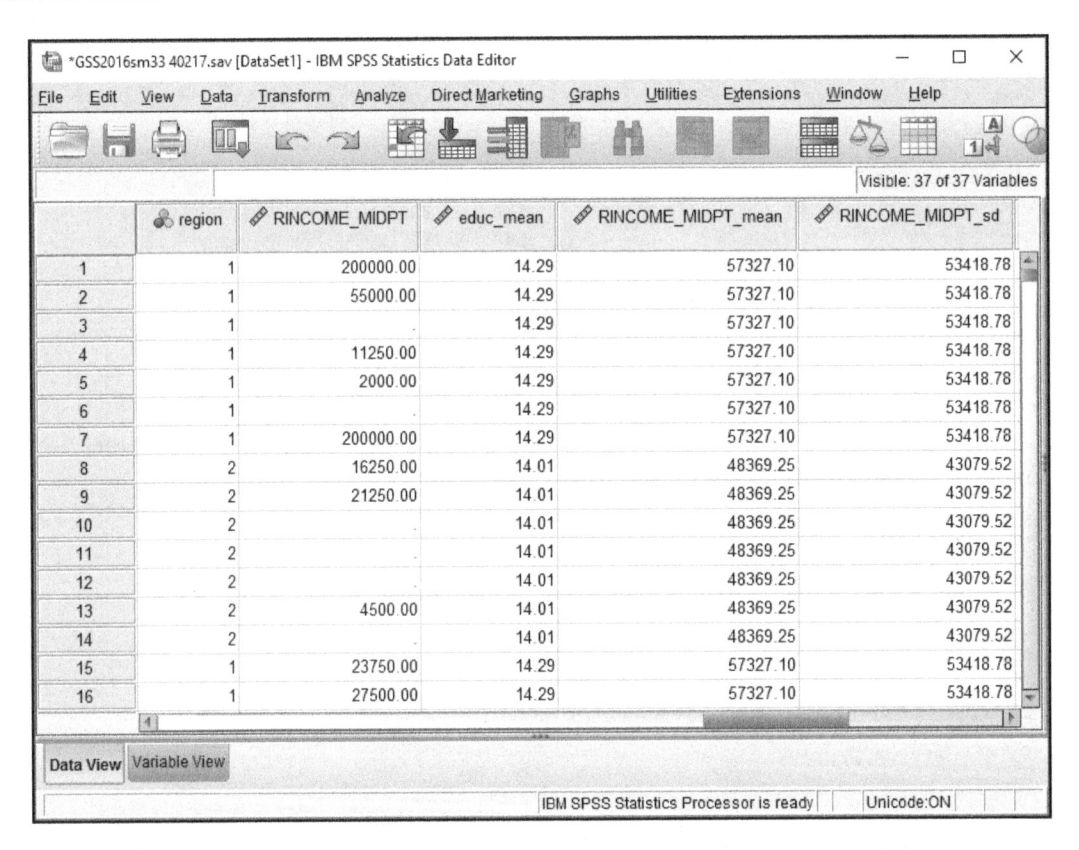

	region	RINCOME_MIDPT	educ_mean	RINCOME_MIDPT_mean	RINCOME_MIDPT_sd
1	1	200000.00	14.29	57327.10	53418.78
2	1	55000.00	14.29	57327.10	53418.78
3	1	.	14.29	57327.10	53418.78
4	1	11250.00	14.29	57327.10	53418.78
5	1	2000.00	14.29	57327.10	53418.78
6	1	.	14.29	57327.10	53418.78
7	1	200000.00	14.29	57327.10	53418.78
8	2	16250.00	14.01	48369.25	43079.52
9	2	21250.00	14.01	48369.25	43079.52
10	2	.	14.01	48369.25	43079.52
11	2	.	14.01	48369.25	43079.52
12	2	.	14.01	48369.25	43079.52
13	2	4500.00	14.01	48369.25	43079.52
14	2	.	14.01	48369.25	43079.52
15	1	23750.00	14.29	57327.10	53418.78
16	1	27500.00	14.29	57327.10	53418.78

It is possible now, for example, to create a standardized income measure using the mean and standard deviation for the region rather than just using the overall mean and standard deviation. The following `compute` command uses the fields from the aggregation to build a standardized income variable adjusted for regional differences:

```
compute zincome_region= (RINCOME_MIDPT - RINCOME_MIDPT_mean) /
RINCOME_MIDPT_sd.
descriptives zincome_region.
```

A standardized measure has a mean of zero and standard deviation of 1, which is reflected in the descriptive statistics for the created variable in the following figure:

Descriptive Statistics

	N	Minimum	Maximum	Mean	Std. Deviation
zincome_region	1632	-1.17	5.23	.0000	.99754
Valid N (listwise)	1632				

Income values less than the mean result in negative standardized scores, which is what we see for cases 2, 4, and 5 in the following screenshot of the **Data Editor** window:

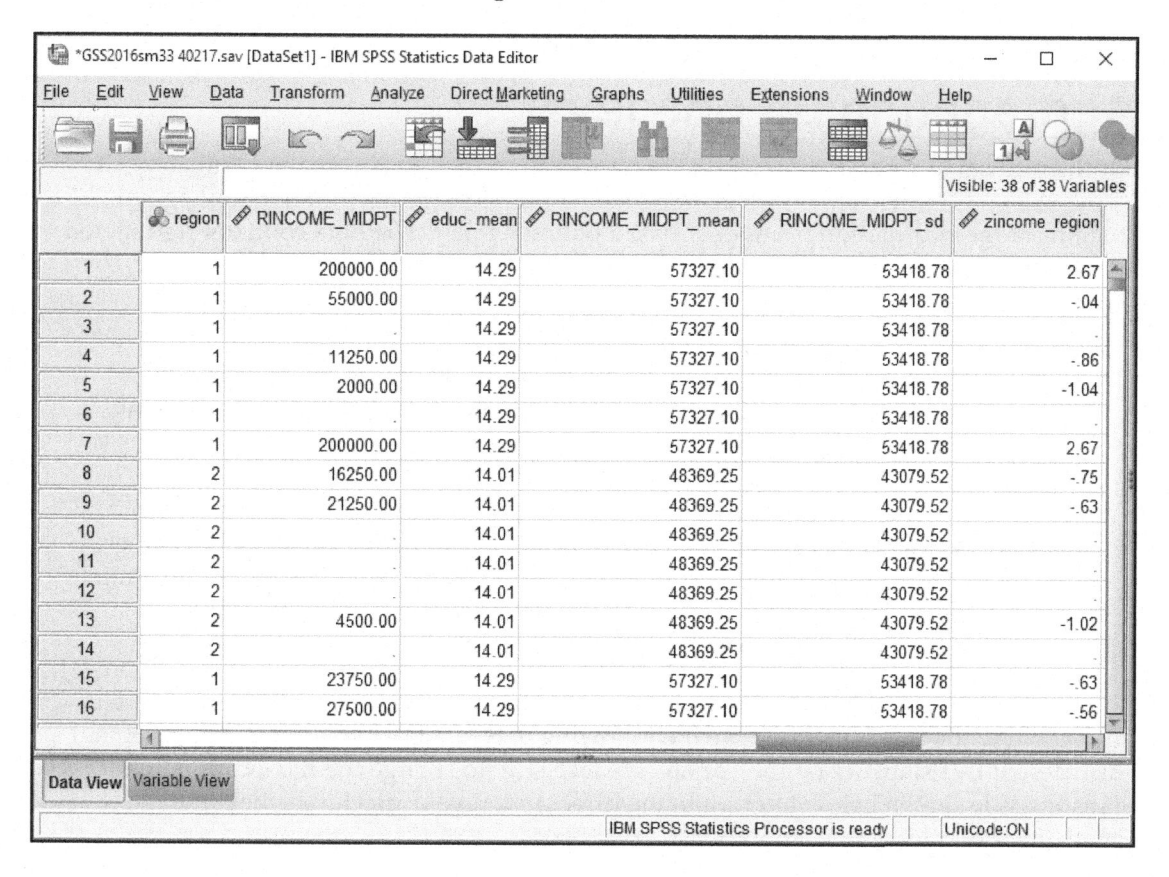

	region	RINCOME_MIDPT	educ_mean	RINCOME_MIDPT_mean	RINCOME_MIDPT_sd	zincome_region
1	1	200000.00	14.29	57327.10	53418.78	2.67
2	1	55000.00	14.29	57327.10	53418.78	-.04
3	1		14.29	57327.10	53418.78	
4	1	11250.00	14.29	57327.10	53418.78	-.86
5	1	2000.00	14.29	57327.10	53418.78	-1.04
6	1		14.29	57327.10	53418.78	
7	1	200000.00	14.29	57327.10	53418.78	2.67
8	2	16250.00	14.01	48369.25	43079.52	-.75
9	2	21250.00	14.01	48369.25	43079.52	-.63
10	2		14.01	48369.25	43079.52	
11	2		14.01	48369.25	43079.52	
12	2		14.01	48369.25	43079.52	
13	2	4500.00	14.01	48369.25	43079.52	-1.02
14	2		14.01	48369.25	43079.52	
15	1	23750.00	14.29	57327.10	53418.78	-.63
16	1	27500.00	14.29	57327.10	53418.78	-.56

Aggregating and Restructuring Data

In this example, the standard deviation was requested only for the income variable, but the same could have been done for education if so desired. This example represents one of the most common uses of Aggregate and it is the simplest type of aggregation, as the new data elements become part of the data file from which they were built. Creating an income measure relative to the regional mean and standard deviation position each individual economically in a manner that makes it possible to conduct comparisons across regions that differ in the cost of living. Someone whose income is below the national mean my be a standard deviation above the mean for their region.

> The key is recognizing that the data has the potential to support the creation of this type of information and deciding how to make use of it as part of the overall analysis strategy.

Aggregating up one level

For the next set of Aggregate examples, a dataset from the repository maintained by UC Irvine will be used. This data can be downloaded in Excel format at the following link. It contains order information from a UK based online retailer. The data contains eight fields and 541,909 rows:

https://archive.ics.uci.edu/ml/datasets/Online+Retail

> **Source**: Dr. Daqing Chen, Director: Public Analytics group. chend '@' lsbu.ac.uk, School of Engineering, London South Bank University, London SE1 0AA, UK.
>
> **Dataset Information**: This is a transnational dataset with data from 37 countries that contains all the transactions occurring between December 1, 2010 and December 9, 2011 for a UK-based and registered non-store online retail. The company mainly sells unique all-occasions gifts. Many customers of the company are wholesalers.

To read the data into SPSS, you can use the menus to open the Microsoft Excel file after downloading the file or you can use the following SPSS syntax to read the file and obtain basic descriptive statistics on the variables. Make sure to change the file location in the SPSS Statistics code shown below to point to the directory on your machine where the file was saved after downloading it from the UC Irvine site.

```
GET DATA
  /TYPE=XLSX
  /FILE='C:\Data\Online Retail.xlsx'
```

[178]

Aggregating and Restructuring Data

```
/SHEET=name 'Online Retail'
/CELLRANGE=FULL
/READNAMES=ON
/DATATYPEMIN PERCENTAGE=95.0
/HIDDEN IGNORE=YES.
Descriptives all.
```

> **TIP**: If you open the file in Excel to check it out, be sure to close it before opening it in SPSS as Excel will lock the file and it will not be accessible in SPSS.

The `Descriptives` command will automatically exclude the fields that are not numeric. The **Warnings** in the following figure indicates the fields that were excluded:

Warnings

No statistics are computed for the following variables because they are strings: StockCode, Description, Country.

The **Descriptive Statistics** in the following figure provide an overview of the fields and confirm the time period of the orders (December 1, 2010 through December 9, 2011):

Descriptive Statistics

	N	Minimum	Maximum	Mean	Std. Deviation
InvoiceNo	532618	536365	581587	559965.75	13428.417
Quantity	541909	-80995	80995	9.55	218.081
InvoiceDate	541909	01-DEC-10	09-DEC-11	04-JUL-11	115 21:05:0...
UnitPrice	541909	-11062.0600	38970.00000	4.611113626	96.75985306
CustomerID	406829	12346	18287	15287.69	1713.600
Valid N (listwise)	397924				

It is also evident that some rows are missing the **InvoiceNo** and **CustomerID**. The fact that the **Quantity** field has some negative values suggests that there may be returns included along with initial orders. Note also the extra decimal places for the **UnitPrice** field. This is based on the format inherited from Microsoft Excel.

Aggregating and Restructuring Data

On the **Variable** tab in the **Data Editor** window, we can see the properties of each field including the 15 decimal places for **UnitPrice**:

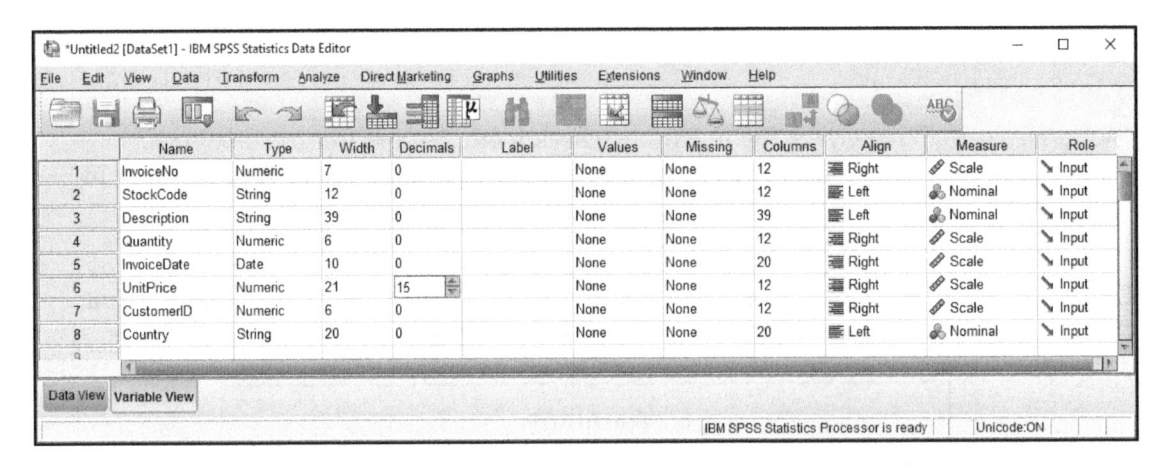

	Name	Type	Width	Decimals	Label	Values	Missing	Columns	Align	Measure	Role
1	InvoiceNo	Numeric	7	0		None	None	12	Right	Scale	Input
2	StockCode	String	12	0		None	None	12	Left	Nominal	Input
3	Description	String	39	0		None	None	39	Left	Nominal	Input
4	Quantity	Numeric	6	0		None	None	12	Right	Scale	Input
5	InvoiceDate	Date	10	0		None	None	20	Right	Scale	Input
6	UnitPrice	Numeric	21	15		None	None	12	Right	Scale	Input
7	CustomerID	Numeric	6	0		None	None	12	Right	Scale	Input
8	Country	String	20	0		None	None	20	Left	Nominal	Input

Change **UnitPrice** to two decimal places so that the subsequent output looks reasonable:

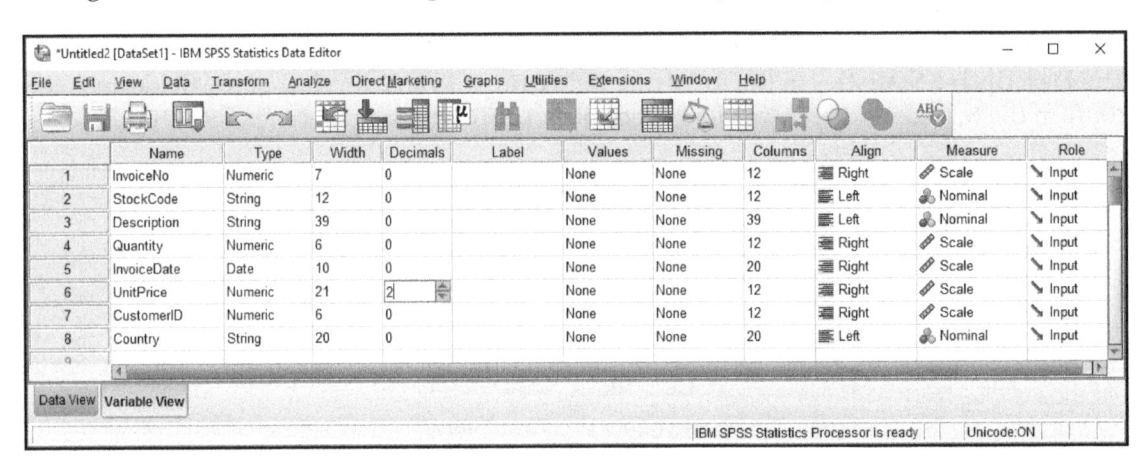

	Name	Type	Width	Decimals	Label	Values	Missing	Columns	Align	Measure	Role
1	InvoiceNo	Numeric	7	0		None	None	12	Right	Scale	Input
2	StockCode	String	12	0		None	None	12	Left	Nominal	Input
3	Description	String	39	0		None	None	39	Left	Nominal	Input
4	Quantity	Numeric	6	0		None	None	12	Right	Scale	Input
5	InvoiceDate	Date	10	0		None	None	20	Right	Scale	Input
6	UnitPrice	Numeric	21	2		None	None	12	Right	Scale	Input
7	CustomerID	Numeric	6	0		None	None	12	Right	Scale	Input
8	Country	String	20	0		None	None	20	Left	Nominal	Input

Aggregating and Restructuring Data

Switch to the Data View to examine the actual data structure and values, as shown in the following screenshot:

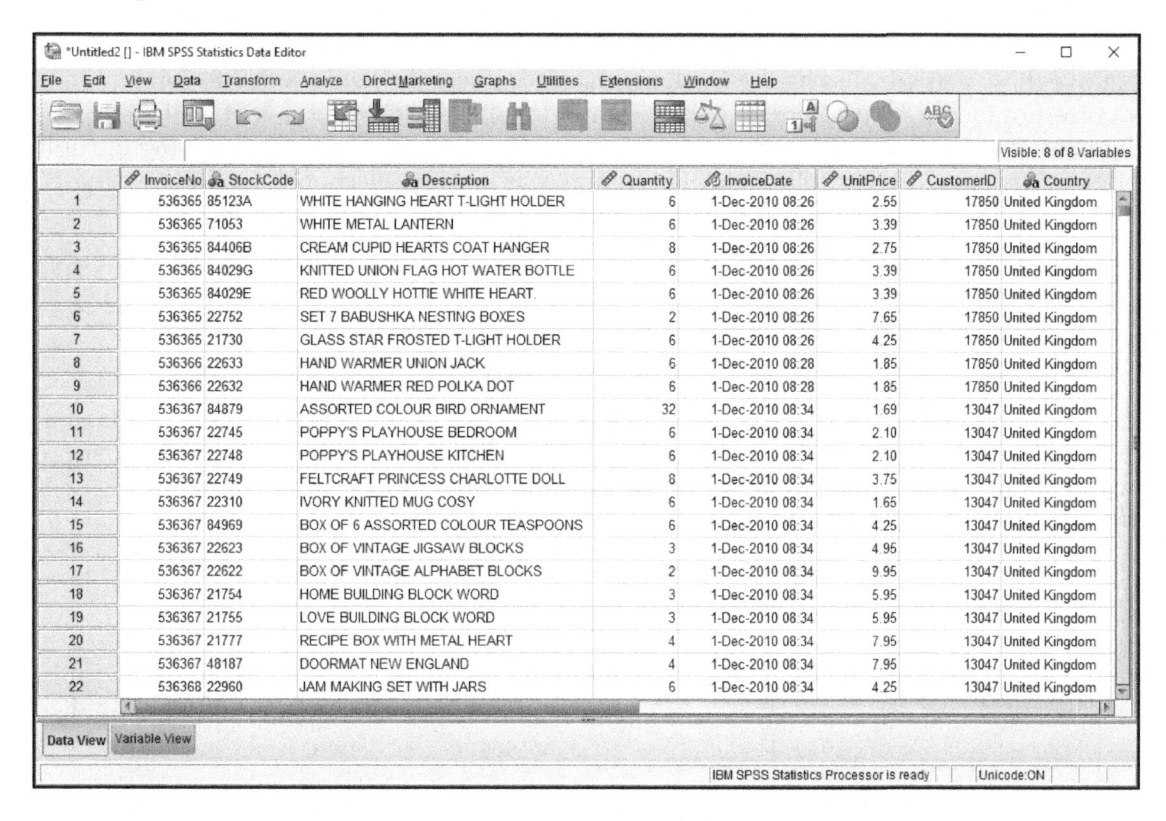

	InvoiceNo	StockCode	Description	Quantity	InvoiceDate	UnitPrice	CustomerID	Country
1	536365	85123A	WHITE HANGING HEART T-LIGHT HOLDER	6	1-Dec-2010 08:26	2.55	17850	United Kingdom
2	536365	71053	WHITE METAL LANTERN	6	1-Dec-2010 08:26	3.39	17850	United Kingdom
3	536365	84406B	CREAM CUPID HEARTS COAT HANGER	8	1-Dec-2010 08:26	2.75	17850	United Kingdom
4	536365	84029G	KNITTED UNION FLAG HOT WATER BOTTLE	6	1-Dec-2010 08:26	3.39	17850	United Kingdom
5	536365	84029E	RED WOOLLY HOTTIE WHITE HEART.	6	1-Dec-2010 08:26	3.39	17850	United Kingdom
6	536365	22752	SET 7 BABUSHKA NESTING BOXES	2	1-Dec-2010 08:26	7.65	17850	United Kingdom
7	536365	21730	GLASS STAR FROSTED T-LIGHT HOLDER	6	1-Dec-2010 08:26	4.25	17850	United Kingdom
8	536366	22633	HAND WARMER UNION JACK	6	1-Dec-2010 08:28	1.85	17850	United Kingdom
9	536366	22632	HAND WARMER RED POLKA DOT	6	1-Dec-2010 08:28	1.85	17850	United Kingdom
10	536367	84879	ASSORTED COLOUR BIRD ORNAMENT	32	1-Dec-2010 08:34	1.69	13047	United Kingdom
11	536367	22745	POPPY'S PLAYHOUSE BEDROOM	6	1-Dec-2010 08:34	2.10	13047	United Kingdom
12	536367	22748	POPPY'S PLAYHOUSE KITCHEN	6	1-Dec-2010 08:34	2.10	13047	United Kingdom
13	536367	22749	FELTCRAFT PRINCESS CHARLOTTE DOLL	8	1-Dec-2010 08:34	3.75	13047	United Kingdom
14	536367	22310	IVORY KNITTED MUG COSY	6	1-Dec-2010 08:34	1.65	13047	United Kingdom
15	536367	84969	BOX OF 6 ASSORTED COLOUR TEASPOONS	6	1-Dec-2010 08:34	4.25	13047	United Kingdom
16	536367	22623	BOX OF VINTAGE JIGSAW BLOCKS	3	1-Dec-2010 08:34	4.95	13047	United Kingdom
17	536367	22622	BOX OF VINTAGE ALPHABET BLOCKS	2	1-Dec-2010 08:34	9.95	13047	United Kingdom
18	536367	21754	HOME BUILDING BLOCK WORD	3	1-Dec-2010 08:34	5.95	13047	United Kingdom
19	536367	21755	LOVE BUILDING BLOCK WORD	3	1-Dec-2010 08:34	5.95	13047	United Kingdom
20	536367	21777	RECIPE BOX WITH METAL HEART	4	1-Dec-2010 08:34	7.95	13047	United Kingdom
21	536367	48187	DOORMAT NEW ENGLAND	4	1-Dec-2010 08:34	7.95	13047	United Kingdom
22	536368	22960	JAM MAKING SET WITH JARS	6	1-Dec-2010 08:34	4.25	13047	United Kingdom

Examining the pattern of the first 22 rows, we can see that 1 through 7 are part of a single purchase made at 8:26 on December 1, 2010 by customer 17850. This same customer made another purchase, rows 8 and 9, at 8:28 the same day. Rows 10 through 21 represent a purchase by customer 13047 and this same customer has another purchase with the same date value but a different invoice number starting in row 22.

In this form, the data can be used to perform some types of analysis. One could, for example, identify which items sold the most in a specific month in each country. A more useful type of analysis, however, could be performed if the data is aggregated up to the purchase or customer level.

Aggregating and Restructuring Data

Preparing the data for aggregation

Before summarizing the data at the purchase level, there is some preparatory work to be done. Rows missing the invoice number need to be excluded and it makes sense to also remove those that are missing the **CustomerID** since this is the field needed to combine invoices for the same customer and invoices missing this information cannot be linked together. It will also be useful to calculate the total cost for each row by multiplying the unit price by the quantity. The following SPSS syntax was used to select only the non-missing rows for the `CustomerID` and `InvoiceNo` fields. It also creates the total cost field (`itemcost`) and requests an updated set of descriptive statistics:

```
SELECT IF (not(missing(CustomerID)) and not(missing(InvoiceNo))).
COMPUTE itemcost=Quantity * UnitPrice.
descriptives all.
```

The uniform number of cases, 397924, for all the fields is a result of SELECT that eliminated those rows with missing information on the key fields that will be used in the subsequent aggregation. As we can see from the following screenshot, in some instances, as the **UnitPrice** is zero, there are some **itemcost** amounts of zero as well:

Descriptive Statistics

	N	Minimum	Maximum	Mean	Std. Deviation
InvoiceNo	397924	536365	581587	560617.13	13106.168
Quantity	397924	1	80995	13.02	180.420
InvoiceDate	397924	01-DEC-10	09-DEC-11	10-JUL-11	112 19:45:3...
UnitPrice	397924	.00	8142.75	3.1162	22.09679
CustomerID	397924	12346	18287	15294.32	1713.170
itemcost	397924	.00	168469.60	22.3947	309.05559
Valid N (listwise)	397924				

With this preparation done, the file is ready to be aggregated to the purchase-level using the invoice number.

The **Aggregate Data** dialog shown in the following screenshot uses `InvoiceNo` as the **Break variable(s)** and picks up the **CustomerID** along with the date from the first row in each **InvoiceNo** group:

Aggregating and Restructuring Data

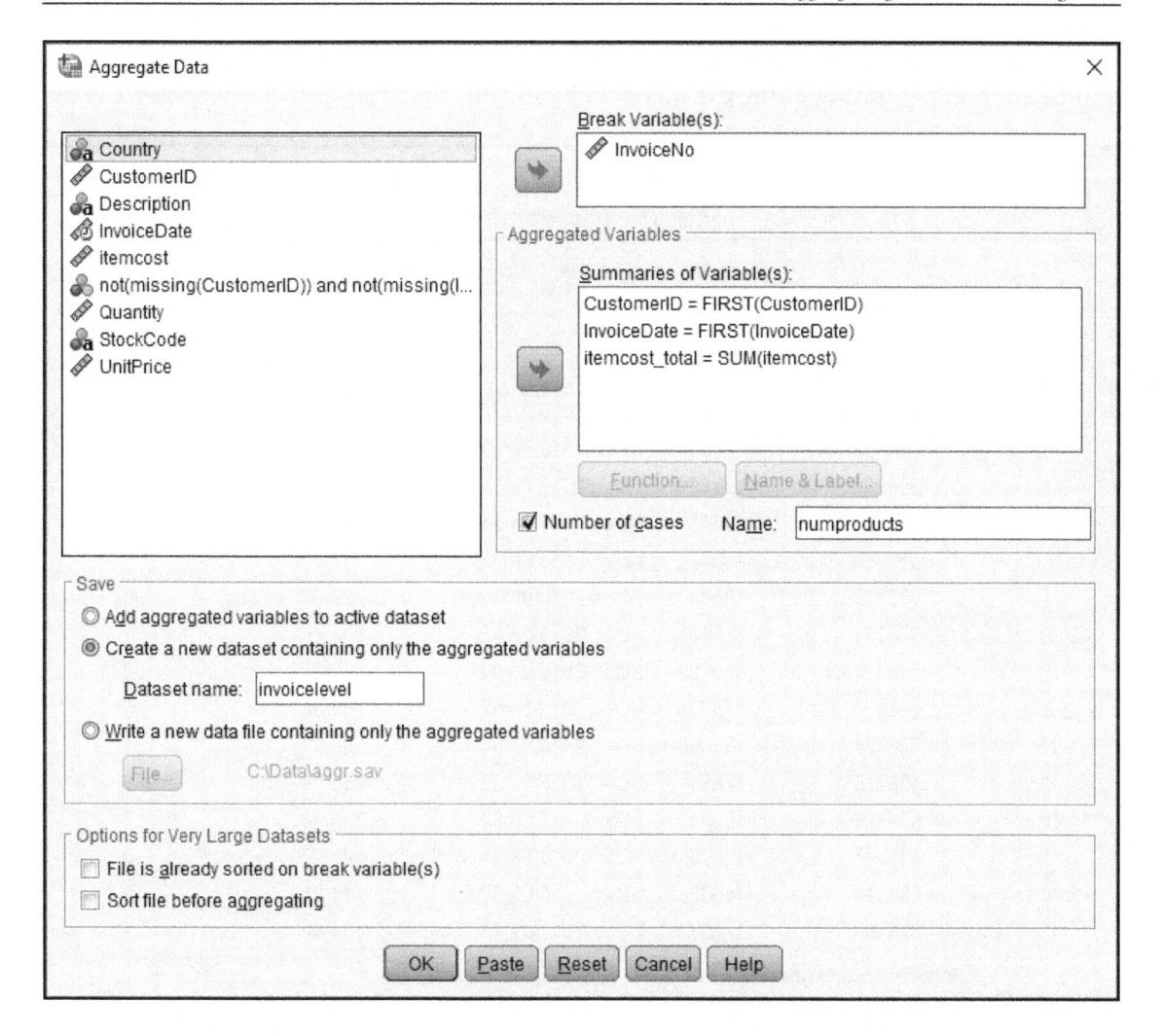

The First function is a convenient way to obtain this type of information although the Last function would have worked, as well, as all the rows have the same values for these fields. By summing the **itemcost** field for all the rows associated with an invoice, the total amount of the purchase becomes available. Checking the number of cases box and assigning a variable name captures the number of different products for the purchase.

Here, the objective is to create a new dataset with invoice level data, so in the Save section, the second radio button is chosen and a dataset name is provided.

Aggregating and Restructuring Data

In the following screenshot, the two purchases made by customer 17850, invoices 536365 and 536366, are at the top of the file followed by the three purchases from customer 13047:

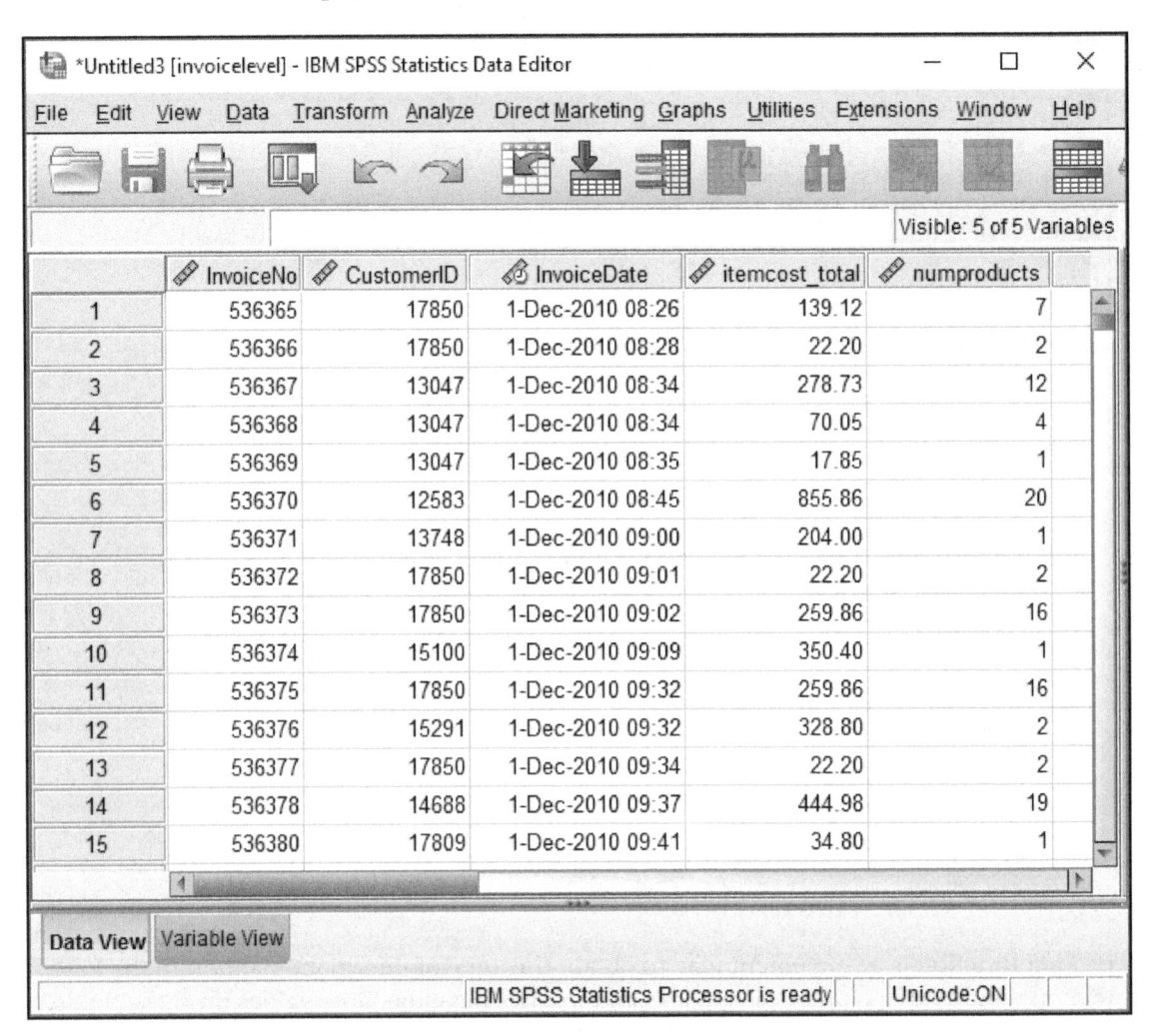

	InvoiceNo	CustomerID	InvoiceDate	itemcost_total	numproducts
1	536365	17850	1-Dec-2010 08:26	139.12	7
2	536366	17850	1-Dec-2010 08:28	22.20	2
3	536367	13047	1-Dec-2010 08:34	278.73	12
4	536368	13047	1-Dec-2010 08:34	70.05	4
5	536369	13047	1-Dec-2010 08:35	17.85	1
6	536370	12583	1-Dec-2010 08:45	855.86	20
7	536371	13748	1-Dec-2010 09:00	204.00	1
8	536372	17850	1-Dec-2010 09:01	22.20	2
9	536373	17850	1-Dec-2010 09:02	259.86	16
10	536374	15100	1-Dec-2010 09:09	350.40	1
11	536375	17850	1-Dec-2010 09:32	259.86	16
12	536376	15291	1-Dec-2010 09:32	328.80	2
13	536377	17850	1-Dec-2010 09:34	22.20	2
14	536378	14688	1-Dec-2010 09:37	444.98	19
15	536380	17809	1-Dec-2010 09:41	34.80	1

This file structure supports analytics at the purchase event level, which could provide some useful insights related to when large purchases are made and how many separate products typically make up a purchase above a certain dollar value.

Descriptive statistics for this new file in the following figure indicate that there are 18536 purchase events in the data with an average value of $480:

Descriptive Statistics

	N	Minimum	Maximum	Mean	Std. Deviation
InvoiceNo	18536	536365	581587	559528.00	13040.284
CustomerID	18536	12346	18287	15266.22	1734.179
InvoiceDate	18536	01-DEC-10	09-DEC-11	01-JUL-11	112 17:31:3...
itemcost_total	18536	.00	168469.60	480.7622	1678.02935
numproducts	18536	1	542	21.47	24.919
Valid N (listwise)	18536				

The average number of products included in a single invoice is around 21 but the range is quite large.

Second level aggregation

While this invoice level file might be of some use in terms of analytics, it is more likely to be valuable as a means of gaining better insight regarding customer behavior. To obtain such insights, more preparation needs to be done before aggregating up to the customer level. Sorting the invoice file by **CustomerID** and date will make it possible to calculate the number of days between purchases, which could be used for a wide range of marketing/promotional decisions. It could also help identify customers that appear to have been lost due to lack of activity relative to their typical purchase pattern.

Preparing aggregated data for further use

To calculate the number of days between purchases, the **Shift Values** option on the **Transform** menu can be used. Obtaining the **CustomerID** and date from the prior record in the sorted data creates the foundation to calculate the days between each purchase and the preceding one by the same customer. The **CustomerID** needs to be compared to determine whether the preceding invoice was for the same customer. Also, the first row in the data will be missing the value of the preceding **CustomerID**, so this needs to be addressed. The second condition on the following `Do if` command handles this special situation.

This syntax also makes use of the *Do IF...End IF* structure discussed in `Chapter 7`, *Creating New Data Elements*:

```
sort cases by customerid invoicedate.
```

Aggregating and Restructuring Data

```
SHIFT VALUES VARIABLE=InvoiceDate RESULT=priorinvoicedate LAG=1
 /VARIABLE=CustomerID RESULT=priorcustID LAG=1.
Do if customerid ne priorcustid or missing(priorcustid).
compute daysincepurchase=0.
else if customerid=priorcustid.
compute daysincepurchase=datediff(invoicedate,priorinvoicedate,"days").
end if.
descriptives all.
```

The following descriptive statistics summarize the invoice-level file after the preceding transformations have been performed:

Descriptive Statistics

	N	Minimum	Maximum	Mean	Std. Deviation
InvoiceNo	18536	536365	581587	559528.00	13040.284
CustomerID	18536	12346	18287	15266.22	1734.179
InvoiceDate	18536	01-DEC-10	09-DEC-11	01-JUL-11	112 17:31:3...
itemcost_total	18536	.00	168469.60	480.7622	1678.02935
numproducts	18536	1	542	21.47	24.919
Lag(InvoiceDate,1)	18535	01-DEC-10	09-DEC-11	01-JUL-11	112 17:31:0...
Lag(CustomerID,1)	18535	12346	18287	15266.06	1734.083
daysincepurchase	18536	.00	365.00	30.2625	48.35697
Valid N (listwise)	18535				

The rows labeled Lag(**InvoiceDate, 1**) and Lag(**CustomerID, 1**) correspond to the **priorinvoicedate** and **priorcustid** created by the SHIFT VALUES command in the code block just explained. Variable labels are generated automatically for these fields.

The next step is to roll the data up to the customer level using the Aggregate facility. **CustomerID** is used as the break variable and the invoice date for the first invoice for each customer provides the value for **First_purchase_date**. This works because the data was already sorted by date within CustomerID. The following screenshot also shows the use of the MAX function to get the last purchase date (the Last function would have worked as well) and the greatest number of days between purchases:

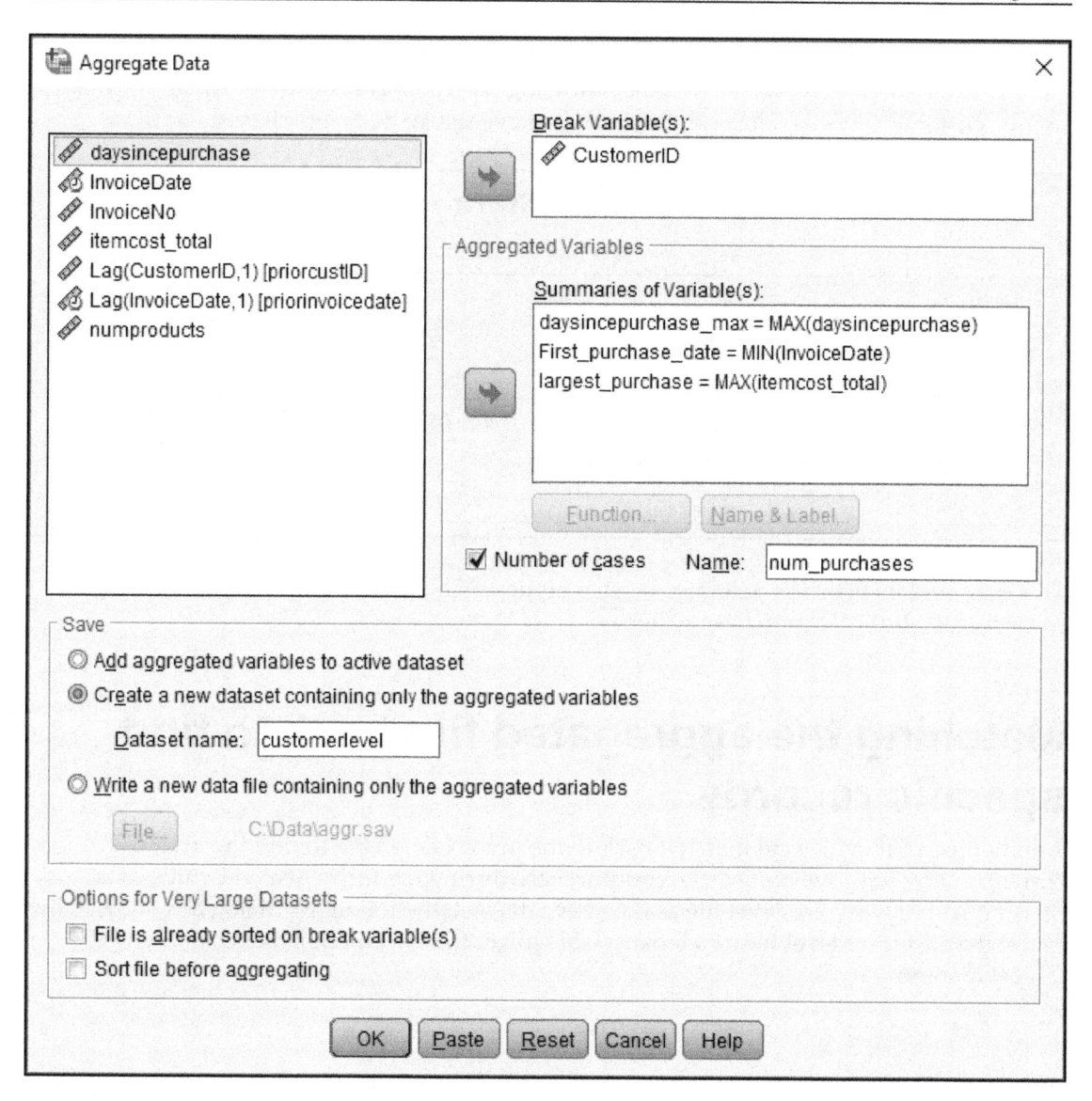

The number of purchases, invoice in this data, is also stored in a new variable.

The results of the preceding Aggregate are put into a new dataset named `customerlevel`. Descriptive statistics on this file (see the following screenshot) show that there are 4,339 unique customers in this data and they made an average of 4.27 purchases:

Descriptive Statistics

	N	Minimum	Maximum	Mean	Std. Deviation
CustomerID	4339	12346	18287	15299.94	1721.890
daysincepurchase_max	4339	.00	365.00	70.1634	78.15513
First_purchase_date	4339	01-DEC-10	09-DEC-11	30-APR-11	117 21:18:2...
largest_purchase	4339	.00	168469.60	655.8172	3088.94802
num_purchases	4339	1	210	4.27	7.705
Valid N (listwise)	4339				

This file could be used for customer-level analytics such as the example mentioned earlier regarding the typical repurchase pattern.

Matching the aggregated file back to find specific records

Another use of this file is to match it back to the invoice-level file to find the invoice corresponding to the customer's largest purchase during the time covered by this data. Starting with the invoice-level file as the active dataset, the following dialog box shows how to use the customer-level file as a lookup table to get the information associated with the largest invoice:

Aggregating and Restructuring Data

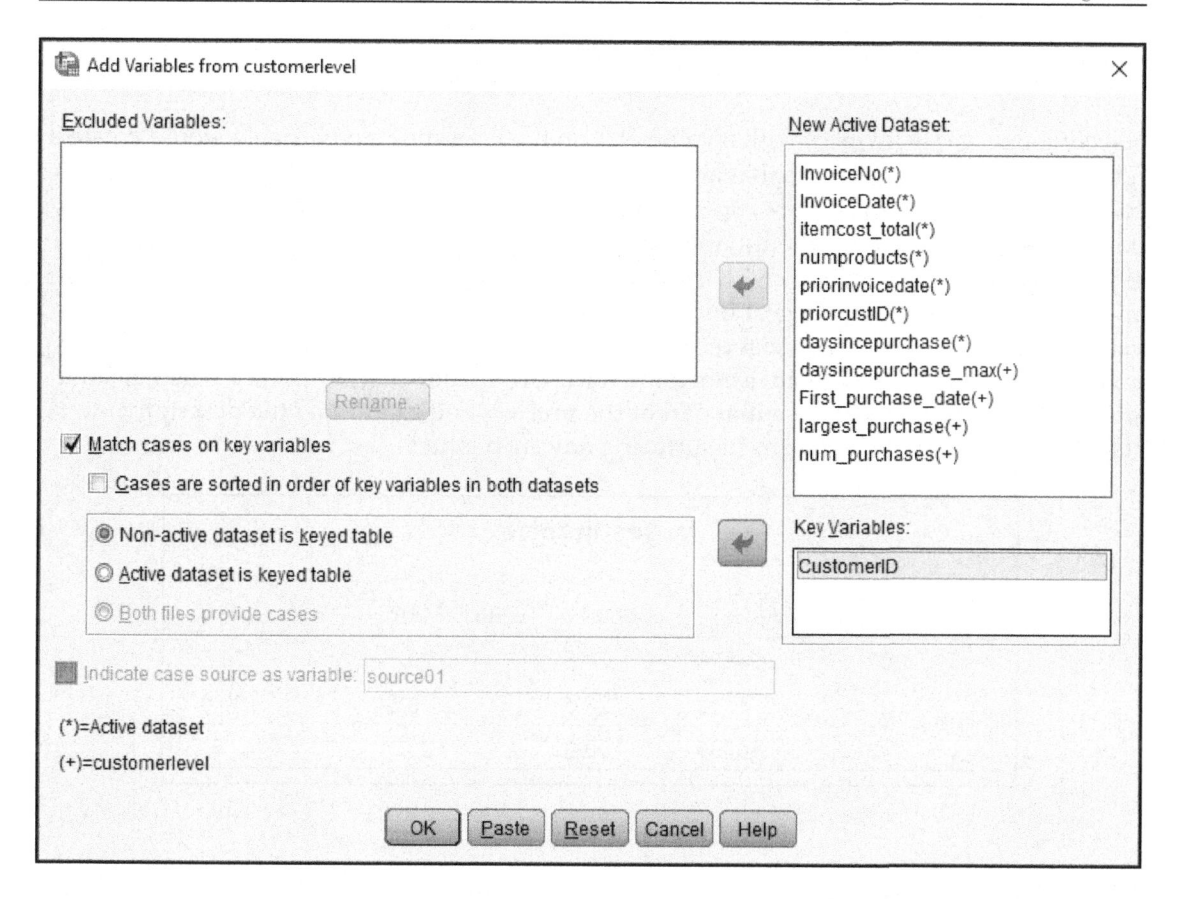

CustomerID serves as the match key in this one-to-many match. The * and + symbols indicate which file was the source for each of the variables in the resulting file.

The SPSS syntax to perform this match is shown here along with the transformation commands used to identify the largest invoice for each customer:

```
STAR JOIN
  /SELECT t0.InvoiceNo, t0.InvoiceDate, t0.itemcost_total, t0.numproducts,
t0.priorinvoicedate,
  t0.priorcustID, t0.daysincepurchase, t1.daysincepurchase_max,
t1.First_purchase_date,
  t1.largest_purchase, t1.num_purchases
  /FROM * AS t0
  /JOIN 'customerlevel' AS t1
  ON t0.CustomerID=t1.CustomerID
  /OUTFILE FILE=*.
* find the invoice for each customer that is their largest purchase.
compute largestinvoice=0.
```

```
if itemcost_total=largest_purchase largestinvoice=1.
FREQUENCIES largestinvoice.
```

Selecting only those invoices with a value of 1 on the largestinvoice variable would create a file with just those invoices, so that an analysis of these important purchase events could be conducted. Note that there are 4,358 invoices (see the following figure) that have been flagged as the largest, even though there are only 4,339 unique customers. This is because 19 customers had two invoices with an identical maximum purchase amount. This could be addressed by selecting the largest invoices, sorting by date, and then selecting the LAST value of each field to use the most recent invoice with the largest dollar value. As this only involves 19 customers, the issue is not all that important, but checking to see whether such situations are present is an essential part of the process, and examining the descriptive statistics provides an easy means of surfacing any such issues.

largestinvoice

		Frequency	Percent	Valid Percent	Cumulative Percent
Valid	.00	14178	76.5	76.5	76.5
	1.00	4358	23.5	23.5	100.0
	Total	18536	100.0	100.0	

Restructuring rows to columns

There are situations in which the way the data is structured needs to be altered before analytics can be conducted. This is related to the unit of analysis required for certain types of statistical comparisons. In most cases, the fact that the organization of the original data will not work is obvious but the way to address the problem is not immediately evident. SPSS Statistics includes a feature to restructure data to address the most common types of challenges.

Aggregating and Restructuring Data

There are three basic types of data restructuring that can be performed in SPSS using the restructure data wizard accessible via the **Restructure** choice on the **Data** menu. These choices can be seen along with a brief description in the following screenshot. By comparing the structure of the data you have with the structure necessary for the analysis you want to perform, the best approach to try can be identified.

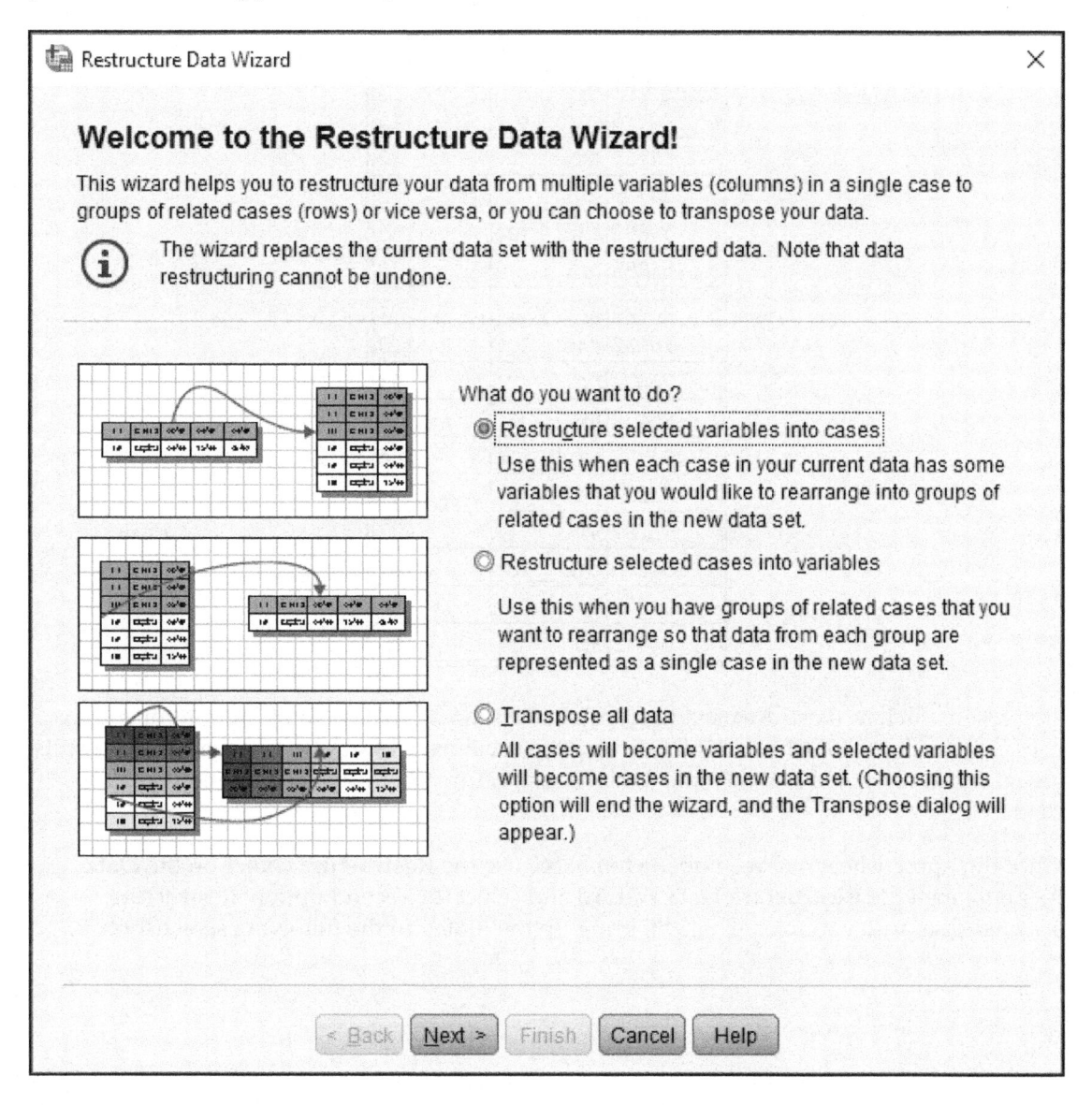

[191]

Patient test data example

The most direct way to gain familiarity with the data restructuring techniques in SPSS is to work through an example. In the sample data shown in the following screenshot, cholesterol test results for five patients are provided with separate rows for total cholesterol, HDL, and LDL:

PatientID	test	result
24785	chol_tot	129
24785	hdl	42
24785	ldl	72
51893	chol_tot	136
51893	hdl	39
51893	ldl	67
76432	chol_tot	119
76432	hdl	33
76432	ldl	59
41287	chol_tot	166
41287	hdl	47
41287	ldl	72
64973	chol_tot	207
64973	hdl	61
64973	ldl	105

Test results such as these are used to calculate the ratio of HDL to total cholesterol and to calculate the non-HDL cholesterol. Deriving these values requires that all the patient results are on the same record and the data must be restructured before the calculations can be made.

Once this spreadsheet has been opened in SPSS, use the **Restructure** choice on the **Data** menu to open the **Restructure Data Wizard** and select the second option, Restructure selected cases into variables. This will bring up the dialog in the following screenshot:

Aggregating and Restructuring Data

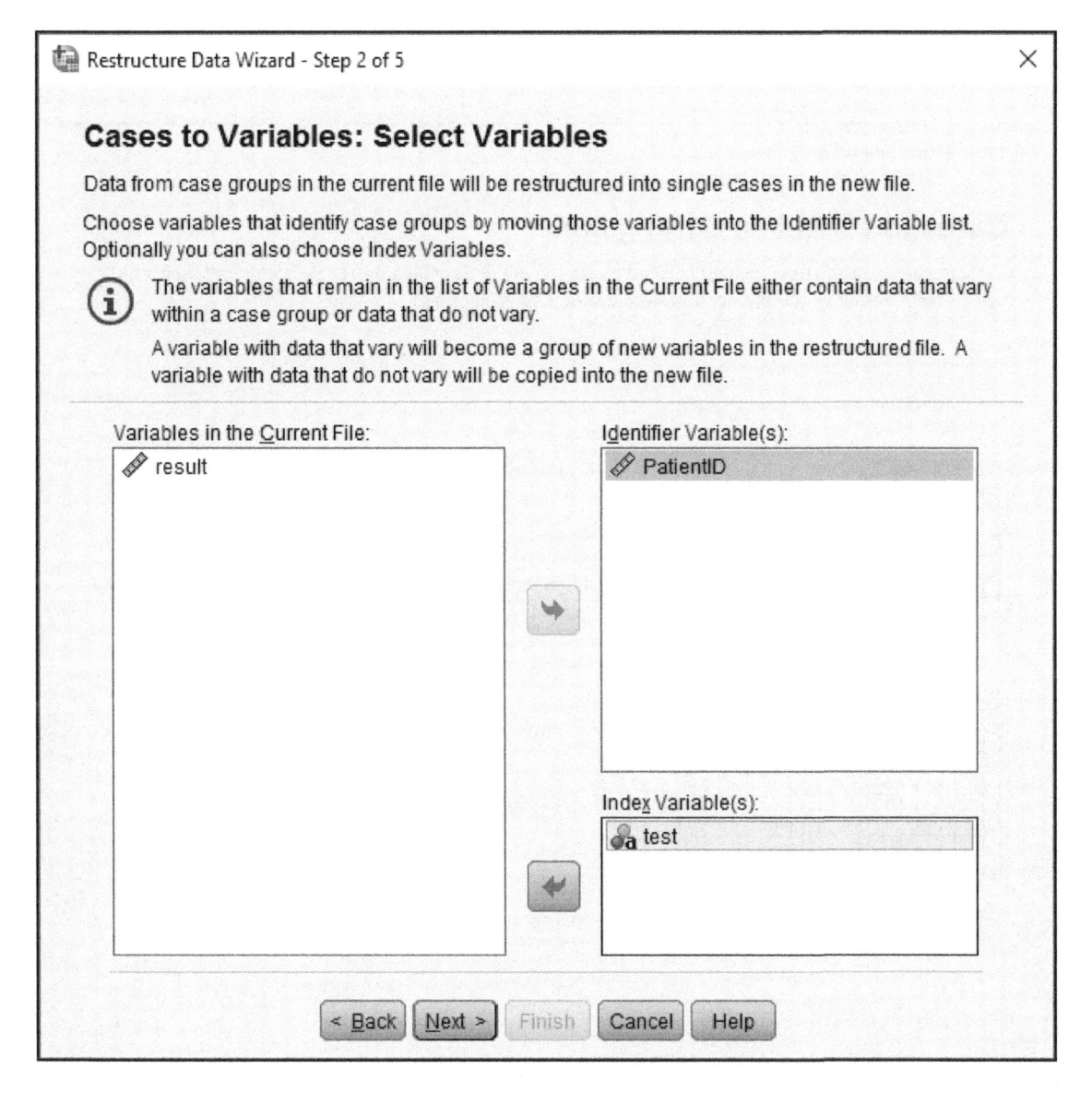

PatientID serves as the identifier linking the rows for the same patient, and *test* is the index variable, as we need a separate set of variables for each type of test.

Aggregating and Restructuring Data

After specifying the identifier and index fields, choose the default option to have the file sorted when you get to the dialog box shown in the following figure:

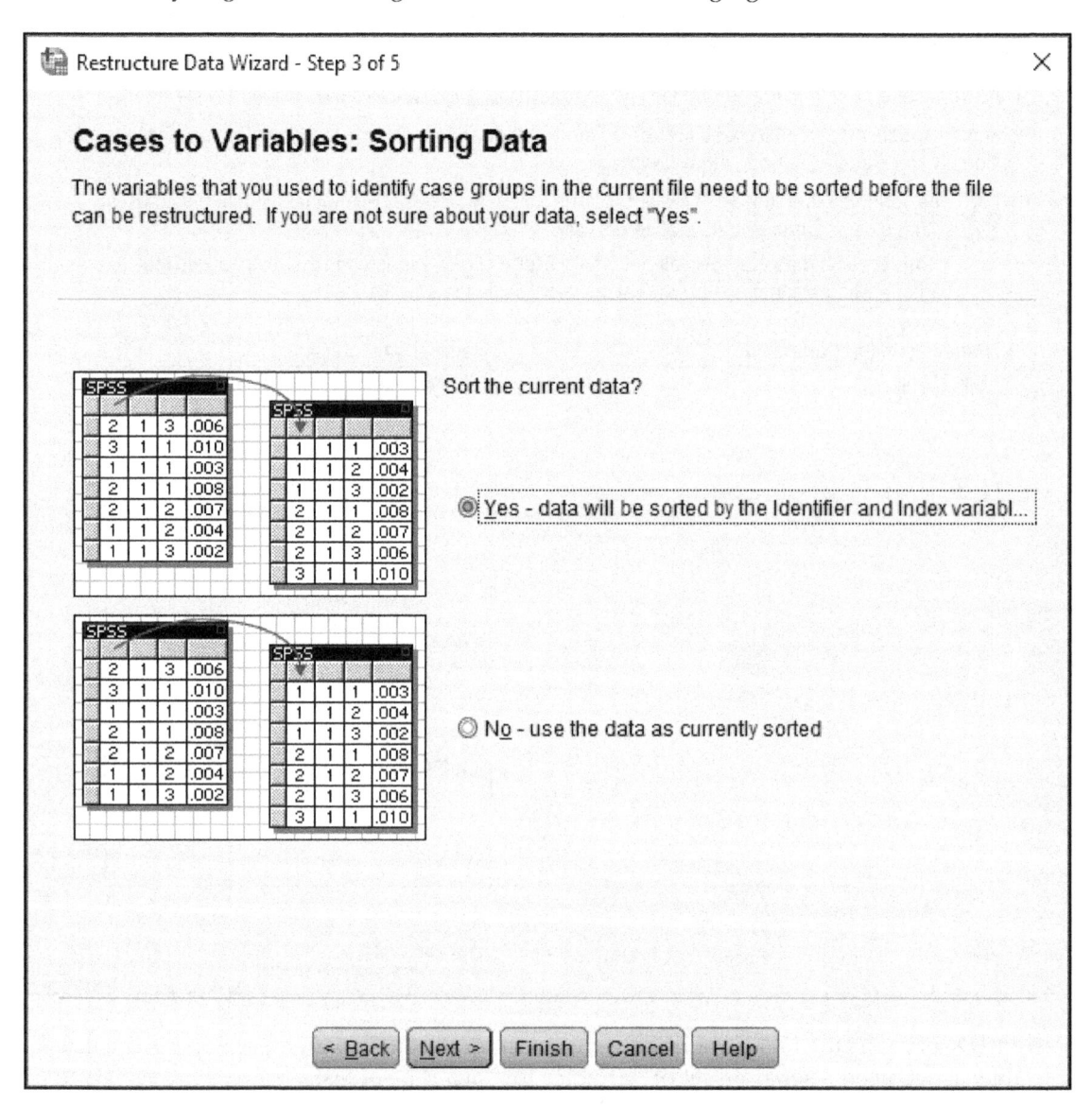

Cases to Variables: Sorting Data

The variables that you used to identify case groups in the current file need to be sorted before the file can be restructured. If you are not sure about your data, select "Yes".

Sort the current data?

◉ Yes - data will be sorted by the Identifier and Index variabl...

○ No - use the data as currently sorted

Aggregating and Restructuring Data

The fourth step in the process allows you to select how the newly-created fields are organized in the resulting file, and to request a count variable to keep track of the original rows summarized to build each case in the new file. You can also request that indicator variables be created for each unique value of the index, as shown in the following screenshot:

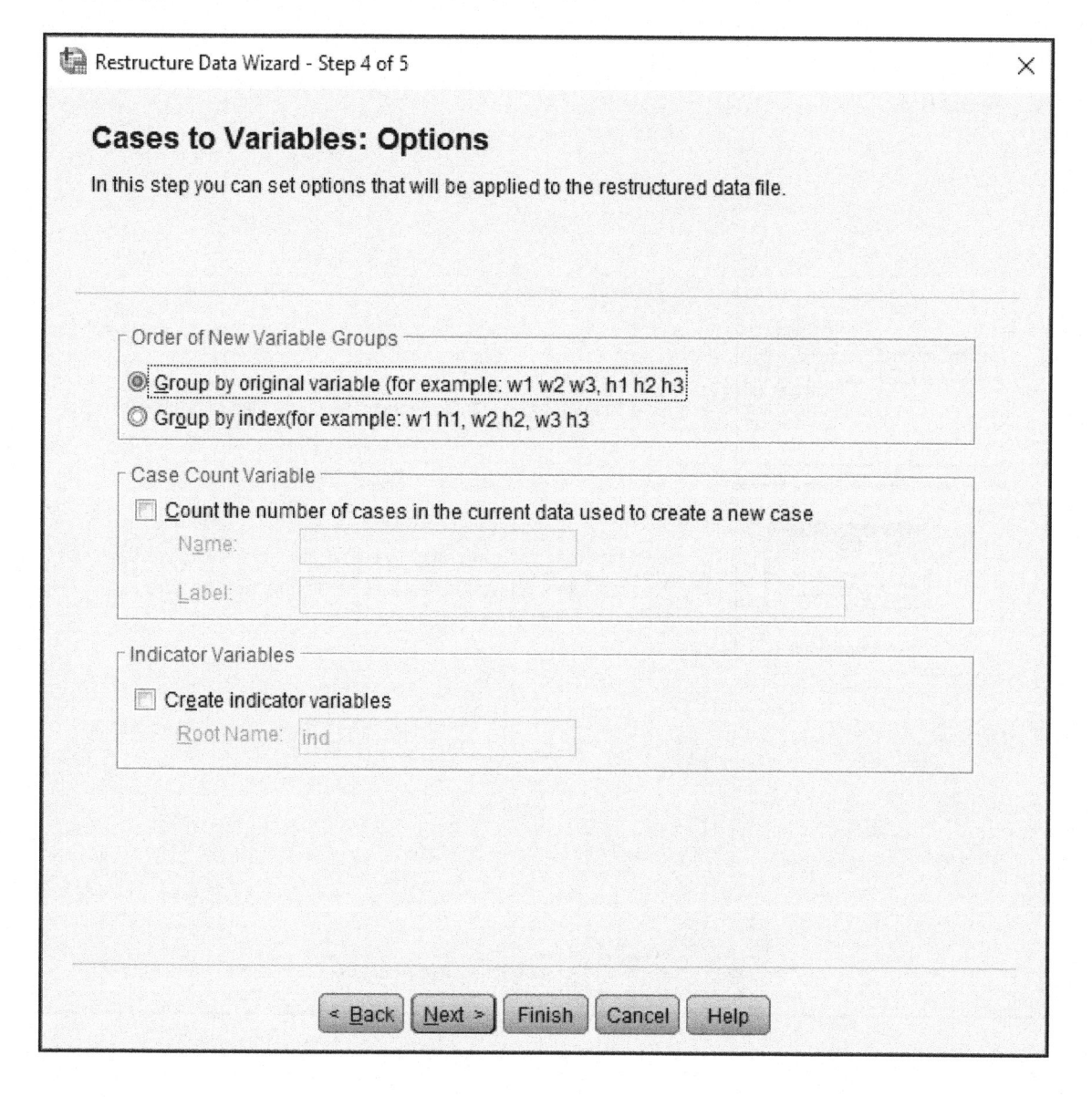

Restructure Data Wizard - Step 4 of 5

Cases to Variables: Options

In this step you can set options that will be applied to the restructured data file.

Order of New Variable Groups
- ◉ Group by original variable (for example: w1 w2 w3, h1 h2 h3)
- ○ Group by index (for example: w1 h1, w2 h2, w3 h3)

Case Count Variable
- ☐ Count the number of cases in the current data used to create a new case
  - Name:
  - Label:

Indicator Variables
- ☐ Create indicator variables
  - Root Name: ind

< Back | Next > | Finish | Cancel | Help

Aggregating and Restructuring Data

The default options work well for this example, so they have been left in place.

In this example, the choice was made to paste the syntax to restructure so that it could be saved for future use. The following screenshot reflects this selection:

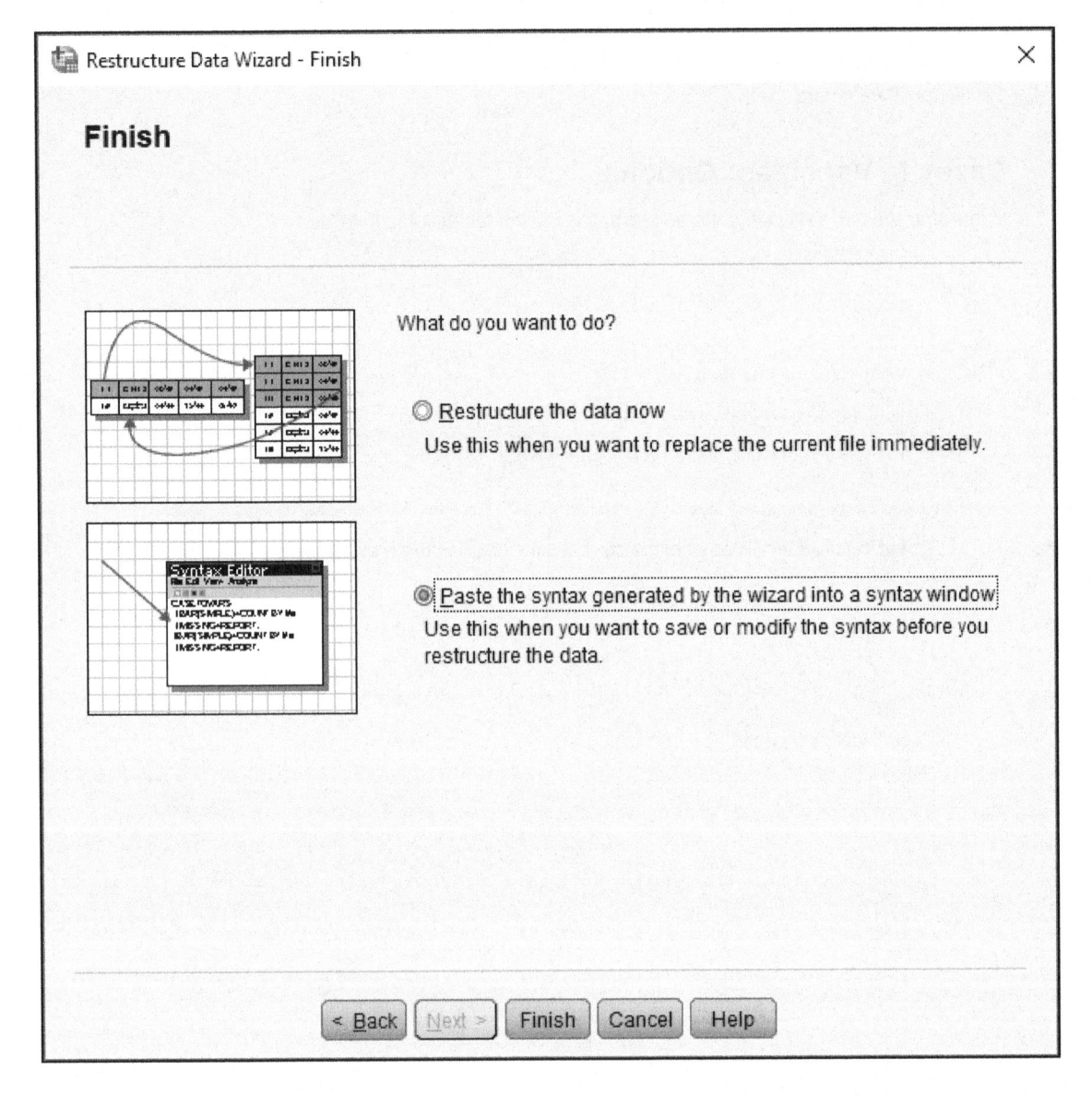

Aggregating and Restructuring Data

Here is the syntax to perform both the sorting and restructuring of the data:

```
SORT CASES BY PatientID test.
CASESTOVARS
 /ID=PatientID
 /INDEX=test
 /GROUPBY=VARIABLE.
```

The following screenshot is of the new data file created by the cases to variables restructuring:

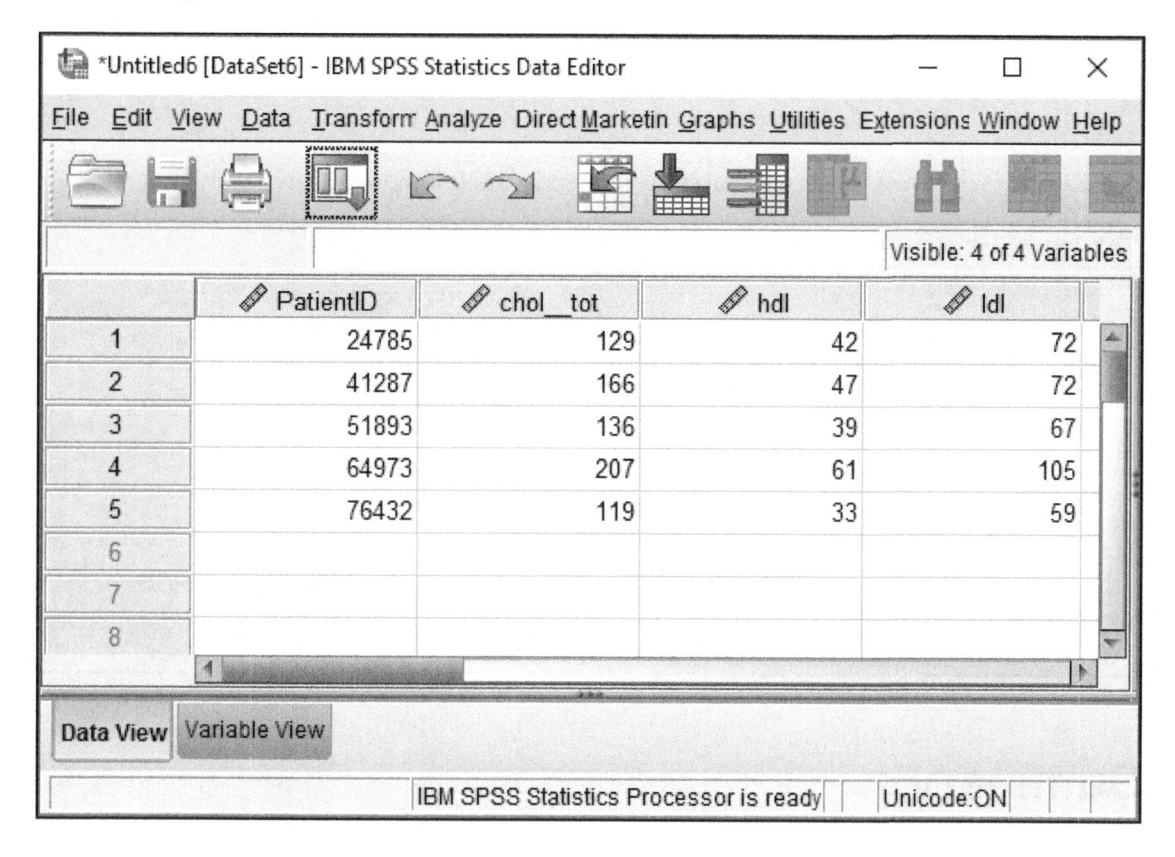

	PatientID	chol_tot	hdl	ldl
1	24785	129	42	72
2	41287	166	47	72
3	51893	136	39	67
4	64973	207	61	105
5	76432	119	33	59

Aggregating and Restructuring Data

There are five rows corresponding to the five patients with separate variables for each value of the *test* variable in the spreadsheet.

Performing calculations following data restructuring

The desired calculations can now be made to create the derived fields using the following syntax:

```
compute CHOL_HDL_RATIO= chol_tot/hdl.
compute NON_HDL_CHOL= chol_tot - hdl.
EXECUTE.
```

The data file with the two new variables is shown in the following figure:

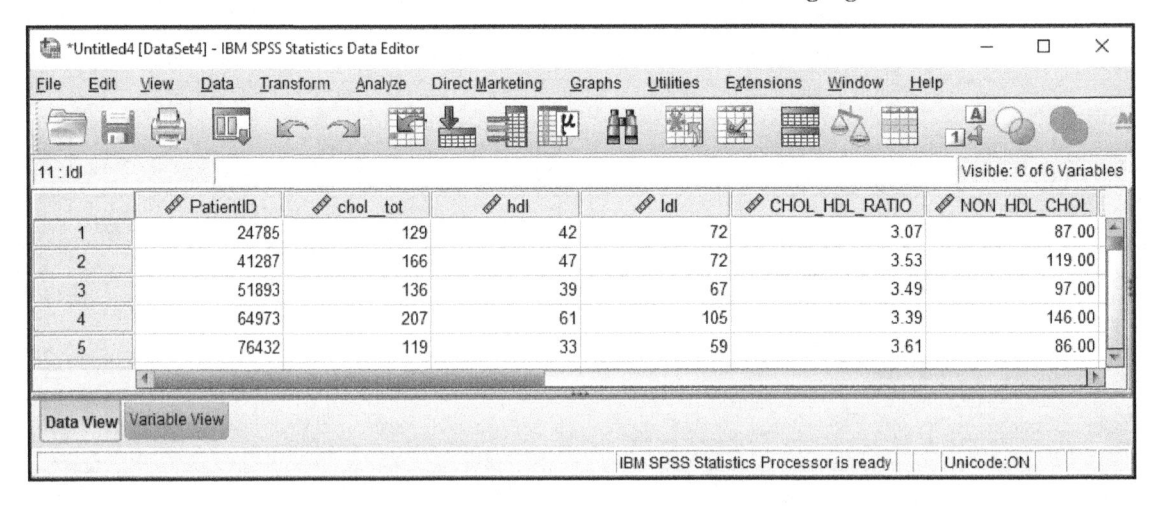

	PatientID	chol_tot	hdl	ldl	CHOL_HDL_RATIO	NON_HDL_CHOL
1	24785	129	42	72	3.07	87.00
2	41287	166	47	72	3.53	119.00
3	51893	136	39	67	3.49	97.00
4	64973	207	61	105	3.39	146.00
5	76432	119	33	59	3.61	86.00

Summary

This chapter focused on the various ways aggregation can be utilized to extract implicit information from the data and make it available for use in constructing derived fields that have the potential to yield deeper analytical insights. Adding aggregated variables back to the original dataset is a simple but powerful technique that supports the creation of fields better tailored for predictive modeling. Examples of one- and two-level aggregation were used to show how new datasets can be created to allow modeling at a different unit of analysis. Leveraging the high-level aggregations to identify key records in the original data was also demonstrated.

Finally, the data structuring capabilities in SPSS Statistics was introduced using a basic cases-to-rows consolidation example that illustrated how this allows calculations that would not otherwise be possible. With these data handling techniques covered, we can move on to exploring patterns in categorical data using crosstabulation.

10
Crosstabulation Patterns for Categorical Data

Discovering relationships among data fields that are categorical in nature is an important first step along the analytical journey. It is often necessary to factor into the predictive process controls for interactions, among various characteristics, to determine what is driving the outcomes. The crosstabs procedure in SPSS Statistics is designed to examine patterns between categorical variables.

In this chapter, we will explore the capabilities of this procedure and discuss the interpretation of the results:

- Percentages in crosstabs
- Testing differences in column proportions
- Using a Chi-square test
- Ordinal measures of association
- Nominal measures of association

Percentages in crosstabs

The examples in this chapter will use the small version of the General Social Survey data from 2016 that was the basis for the examples in Chapters 3, *Statistics for Individual Data Elements* and Chapter 4, *Dealing with Outliers and Missing Data*. Open the SPSS data file you created earlier (or download and open the full GSS2016 following the steps in Chapters 3, *Statistics for Individual Data Elements*).

Crosstabulation Patterns for Categorical Data

Go to **Analyze** | **Descriptives Statistics** | **Crosstabs** to bring up the dialog box in the following figure:

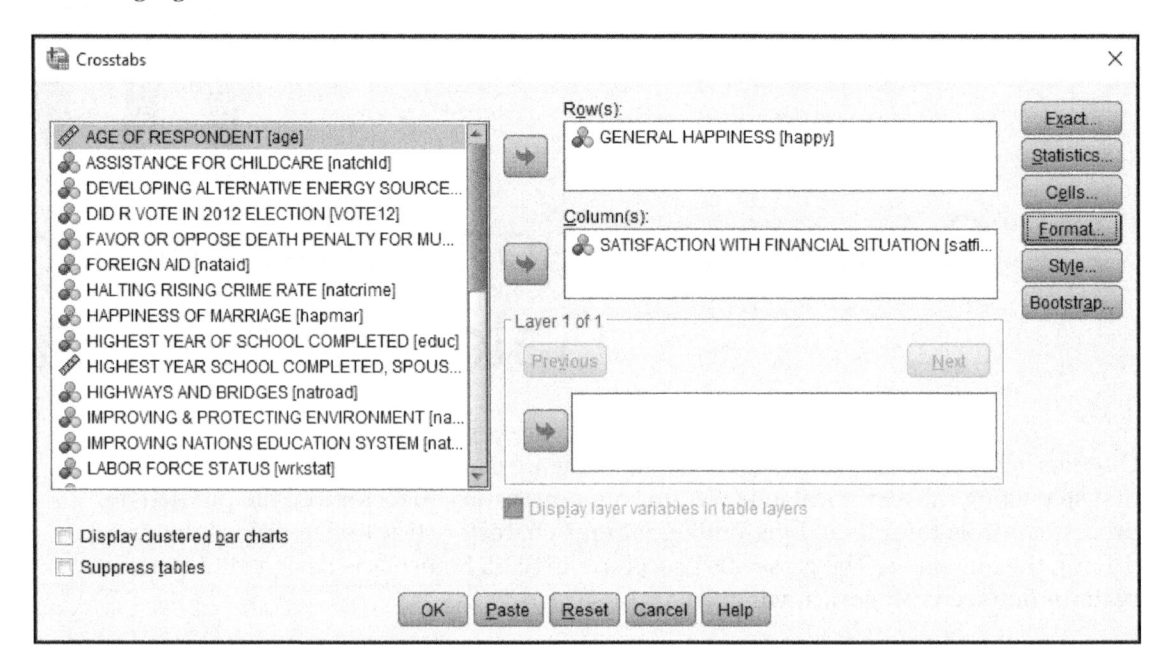

Add the GENERAL HAPPINESS variable to the row box and the SATISFACTION WITH FINANCIAL SITUATION variable to the column box. Typically, the independent variable is placed in the column position, and the dependent variable in the row position for a crosstabulation. Here, one might posit that a person's financial situation may have an impact on their level of overall happiness.

Use the **Cells...** button to bring up the dialog box in following screenshot, and check the **Column** box under **Percentages**:

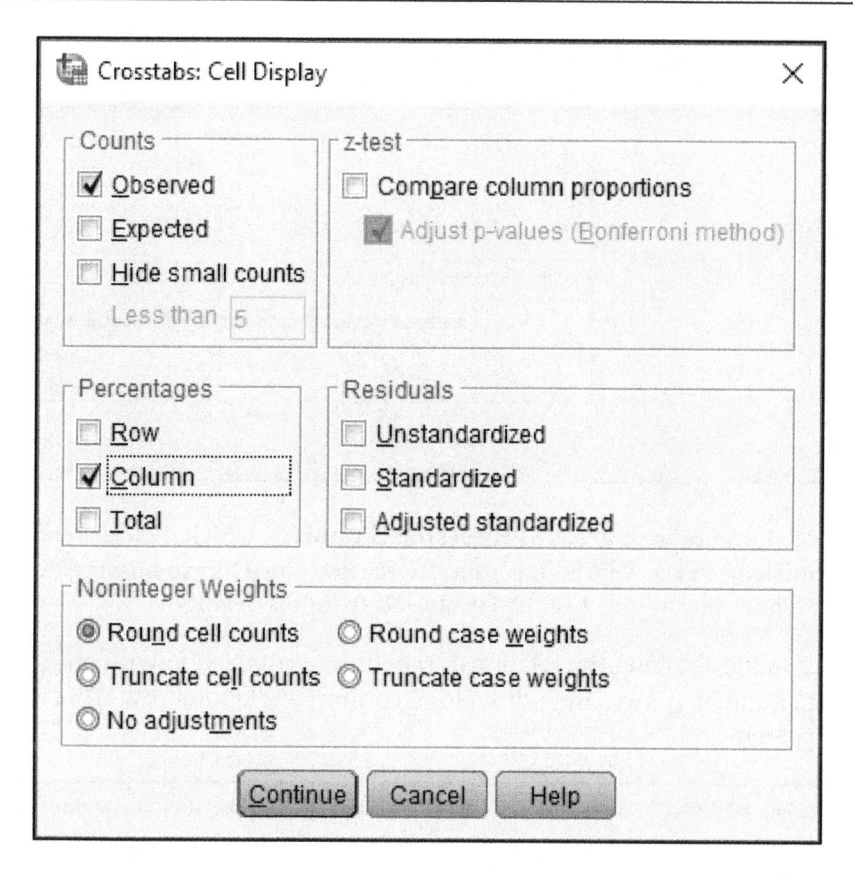

This dialog provides access to many useful features that will be examined later in this chapter, but for now, just make this one change, and select **Continue** to return the main dialog box.

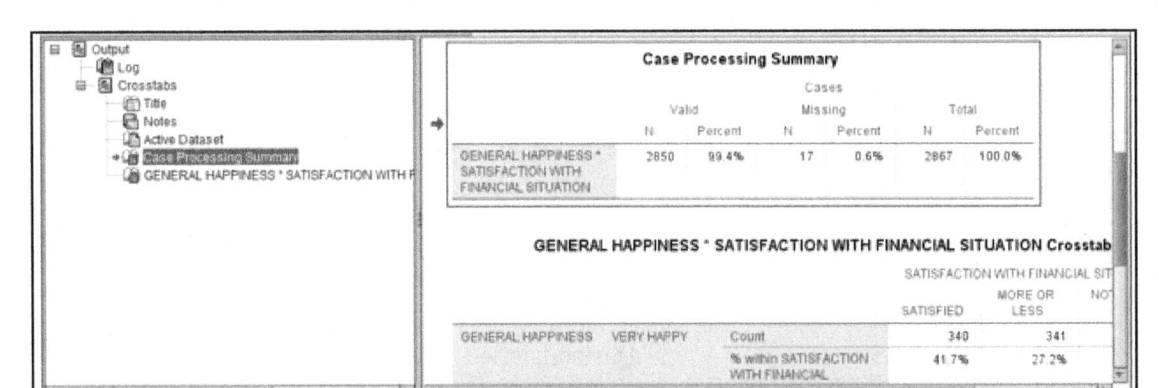

Crosstabulation Patterns for Categorical Data

Click on **OK** to generate the output shown in the following screenshot:

Above the `Crosstabs` table is a **Case Processing Summary** which includes information on the valid and missing cases. This is important to review since a case missing on any of the variables in a `Crosstabs` request will be excluded from the results.

The `Crosstabs` table showing the relationship between satisfaction with one's financial situation and general happiness includes a total column and a total row. This is shown in the following screenshot:

			SATISFACTION WITH FINANCIAL SITUATION			
			SATISFIED	MORE OR LESS	NOT AT ALL SAT	Total
GENERAL HAPPINESS	VERY HAPPY	Count	340	341	120	801
		% within SATISFACTION WITH FINANCIAL SITUATION	41.7%	27.2%	15.3%	28.1%
	PRETTY HAPPY	Count	417	761	419	1597
		% within SATISFACTION WITH FINANCIAL SITUATION	51.2%	60.7%	53.6%	56.0%
	NOT TOO HAPPY	Count	58	151	243	452
		% within SATISFACTION WITH FINANCIAL SITUATION	7.1%	12.1%	31.1%	15.9%
Total		Count	815	1253	782	2850
		% within SATISFACTION WITH FINANCIAL SITUATION	100.0%	100.0%	100.0%	100.0%

GENERAL HAPPINESS * SATISFACTION WITH FINANCIAL SITUATION Crosstabulation

Crosstabulation Patterns for Categorical Data

The counts and percentages in the totals are like a frequency distribution for the column and row variables, except that they do not include any cases missing on either survey question. These totals are referred to as **marginals** and are used as the basis for comparison purposes and for the calculation of statistics.

It is important to keep in mind the overall breakdown of the variables being investigated. The majority of people in this survey (56%) selected **PRETTY HAPPY** as their response, and more were **VERY HAPPY** (801) than **NOT TOO HAPPY** (243).

As we build more complex tables, the data will get spread over more cells, and the numbers in each category limit how many splits of the data are feasible.

By comparing the column percentages for each category of financial satisfaction with the percentages to the right in the **Total** column, you can see whether there is evidence of a relationship between happiness and financial wellbeing. In the **SATISFIED** column, the percentage for **VERY HAPPY** is 41.7% compared with an overall percentage of 28.1% for this row. The **NOT TOO HAPPY** row under Satisfied shows a much smaller percentage (7.1%) than the total column (15.9%), which also supports the presence of a relationship between these two variables.

The percentages in each row under the **MORE OR LESS** column are reasonably similar to the percentages in the total column, and this is the largest group of cases (1253 out of 2850). The **NOT AT ALL SAT** column, like the first column, shows a clear deviation from the overall percentages, but in the opposite direction. For now, it is sufficient to note the pattern in the table. Later, we will look at statistics that test the strength of the relationship.

Testing differences in column proportions

There are many factors that might have an impact on someone's level of happiness beyond their financial situation. These other factors may interact with each other and with one's financial situation. Another additional factor to consider is marital status. Request a crosstab with **MARITAL STATUS** as the column variable and **GENERAL HAPPINESS** as the row variable.

In the cells dialog, check the column under percentages, and in the upper right, check **Compare column proportions** and **Adjust p-values (Bonferroni method)**, as shown in the following screenshot:

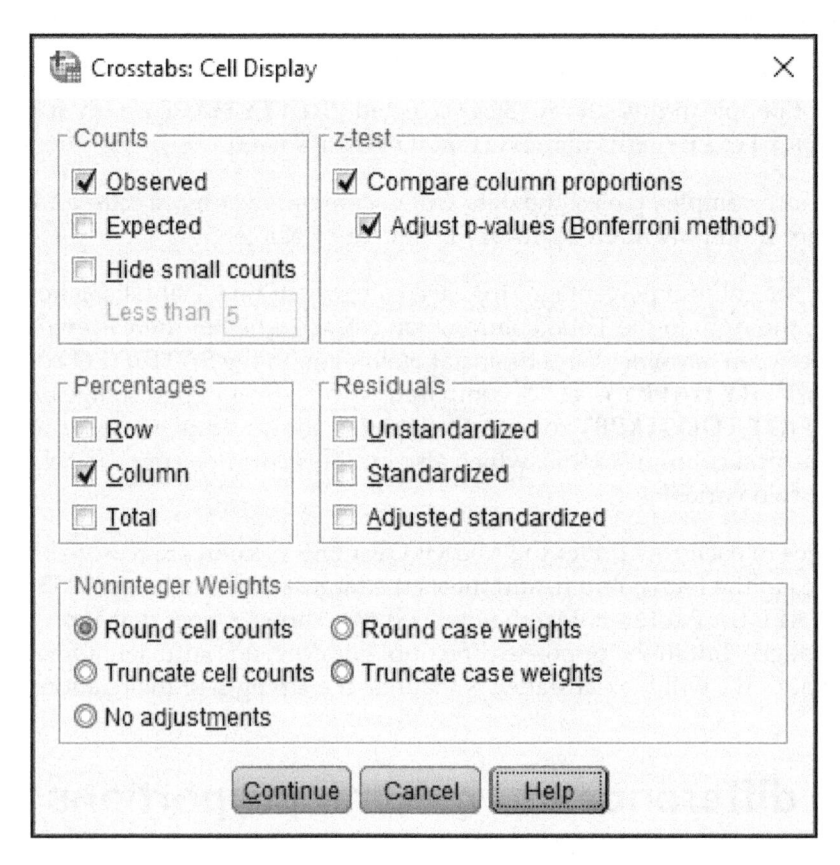

The crosstab produced includes subscripts in the individual cells, indicating where significant differences are present. The pattern of the subscripts indicates that the **WIDOWED, DIVORCED**, and **SEPARATED** groups are not significantly different from one another in any of the rows. This information is useful, since these are the three smallest groups, and it would be useful to combine them for subsequent comparisons. The evidence here supports doing so.

The **Help** choice within the Cells dialog box gives you access to the following information on the **Compare column proportions** option. You can use this information to decide which statistics to use, and you can include it as appendix material in reports if you want:

- **Compare column proportions**: This option computes pairwise comparisons of column proportions and indicates which pairs of columns (for a given row) are significantly different. Significant differences are indicated in the crosstabulation table with APA-style formatting using subscript letters, and are calculated at the 0.05 significance level.
- **Adjust p-values (Bonferroni method)**: Pairwise comparisons of column proportions make use of the Bonferroni correction, which adjusts the observed significance level for the fact that multiple comparisons are made.

GENERAL HAPPINESS * MARITAL STATUS Crosstabulation

			MARRIED	WIDOWED	DIVORCED	SEPARATED	NEVER MARRIED	Total
GENERAL HAPPINESS	VERY HAPPY	Count	465a	59b	100b	26a, b	156b	806
		% within MARITAL STATUS	38.5%	23.5%	20.2%	25.7%	19.4%	28.2%
	PRETTY HAPPY	Count	657a	126a	281a, b	46a	490b	1600
		% within MARITAL STATUS	54.4%	50.2%	56.8%	45.5%	61.0%	56.0%
	NOT TOO HAPPY	Count	86a	66b	114b	29b	157b	452
		% within MARITAL STATUS	7.1%	26.3%	23.0%	28.7%	19.6%	15.8%
Total		Count	1208	251	495	101	803	2858
		% within MARITAL STATUS	100.0%	100.0%	100.0%	100.0%	100.0%	100.0%

Each subscript letter denotes a subset of MARITAL STATUS categories whose column proportions do not differ significantly from each other at the .05 level.

Another potential factor influencing responses to the happiness question could be the gender of the respondent. Marital status may also be something to take into consideration when exploring the relationship between financial well-being and happiness. We will explore how crosstabulation can be used to examine both situations.

Crosstabulation Patterns for Categorical Data

Create a crosstab using **RESPONDENTS SEX** as the column variable and **GENERAL HAPPINESS** as the row variable. Just request column percentages for this table. We get the result as shown in the following screenshot:

GENERAL HAPPINESS * RESPONDENTS SEX Crosstabulation

			RESPONDENTS SEX MALE	RESPONDENTS SEX FEMALE	Total
GENERAL HAPPINESS	VERY HAPPY	Count	364	442	806
		% within RESPONDENTS SEX	28.6%	27.9%	28.2%
	PRETTY HAPPY	Count	718	883	1601
		% within RESPONDENTS SEX	56.4%	55.7%	56.0%
	NOT TOO HAPPY	Count	191	261	452
		% within RESPONDENTS SEX	15.0%	16.5%	15.8%
Total		Count	1273	1586	2859
		% within RESPONDENTS SEX	100.0%	100.0%	100.0%

On the main crosstab dialog, select **Display clustered bar charts** in the lower left.

The percentages in the following figure show very little difference in **GENERAL HAPPINESS** between males and females:

Bar Chart

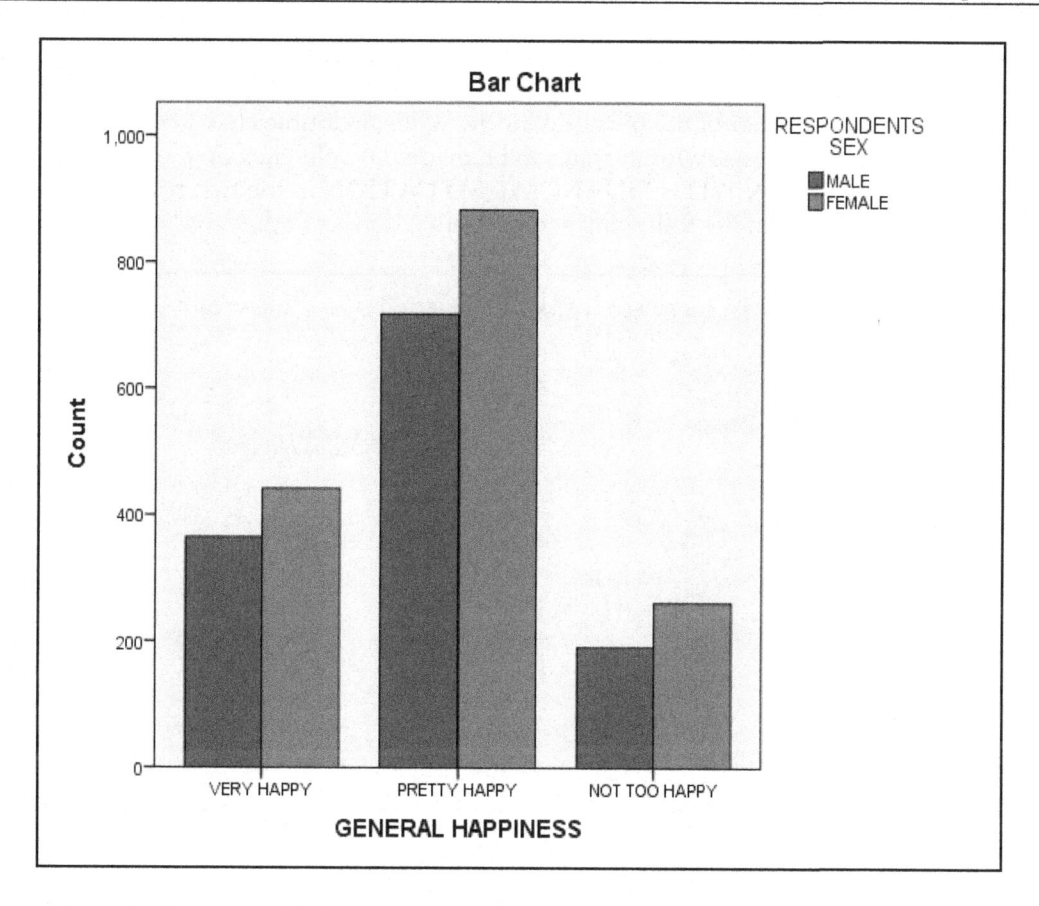

(Bar chart showing counts of General Happiness by Respondents Sex: Male and Female. Very Happy: ~370 male, ~440 female. Pretty Happy: ~720 male, ~880 female. Not Too Happy: ~190 male, ~260 female.)

The totals at the bottom of the table indicate that there are 313 more women than men in this group of survey respondents. This 55% versus 44% split is not critical, but it is something to keep in mind when making visual comparisons of table results.

Crosstab pivot table editing

The output from a crosstab request is presented in the form of a pivot table and, optionally, a graph. To make crosstab results more compact, it is useful to edit the initial table. This is especially important for larger tables that are a challenge to examine and to include in presentations without first making them more compact.

Crosstabulation Patterns for Categorical Data

Recreate the first crosstab table produced (**SATISFACTION WITH FINANCIAL SITUATION** and **GENERAL HAPPINESS**), and double-click on the table to open it up for editing. The lower left corner of the output window will say double click to edit pivot table, indicating that the table is ready for changes to be made. Double-click on the variable label **% within SATISFACTION WITH FINANCIAL SITUATION** in the first row. The text will be highlighted, as shown in the following screenshot:

Type **% within FinSat**, and hit enter to register the change.

The variable labels in each of the rows change to the new text. Go to the General Happiness label in the upper left corner of the table, double-click to highlight the text, and hit enter to erase it. Grab the column border to the left of the label **PRETTY HAPPY** and pull it to the left. The revised table should look like the crosstab in the following screenshot:

GENERAL HAPPINESS * SATISFACTION WITH FINANCIAL SITUATION Crosstabulation

		SATISFIED	MORE OR LESS	NOT AT ALL SAT	Total
VERY HAPPY	Count	340	341	120	801
	% within FinSat	41.7%	27.2%	15.3%	28.1%
PRETTY HAPPY	Count	417	761	419	1597
	% within FinSat	51.2%	60.7%	53.6%	56.0%
NOT TOO HAPPY	Count	58	151	243	452
	% within FinSat	7.1%	12.1%	31.1%	15.9%
Total	Count	815	1253	782	2850
	% within FinSat	100.0%	100.0%	100.0%	100.0%

(SATISFACTION WITH FINANCIAL SITUATION)

This table is considerably more compact than the original version but still has sufficient labeling to make the information clear. The variable labels for these two fields could have been changed in the data editor, which would eliminate the need to make these edits each time a table is produced. The advantage of modifying the table after it is produced is that the full labels are used in the title that provides a more complete description of the field. The original variable label is also available for use with any other procedures one might use.

It will frequently be necessary to copy a crosstab result, or some other SPSS pivot table, and paste it into a document or into a slide. Larger tables will often not fit well if copied using the simple **Copy** option. Right-clicking on the table will give you the options shown in the following screenshot:

Crosstabulation Patterns for Categorical Data

Select the **Copy Special** choice for the options available. The image format generally produces the best copy in terms of fitting into a report, as shown in the following screenshot:

If you right-click on a pivot table while it is open for editing, the menu in the following screenshot is presented:

Selecting **Toolbar** at the bottom will add an editing toolbar above the pivot table.

The formatting toolbar shown in the following screenshot can be used to change the font style and color of specific cells in a table to highlight them:

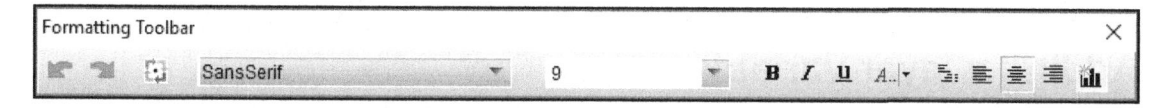

Tables generally contain many numbers, and this is an effective way to call attention to the ones you want to receive the most attention to. This is something you will want to do before copying a table as an image and pasting into a report or slideshow.

There is also a **Pivoting Trays** option on the preceding menu, but that functionality can be accessed from the **Formatting Toolbar**, using the icon next to the font type drop-down. The **Pivoting Trays** shown in the following screenshot allows you to reorder rows and columns as well as layers:

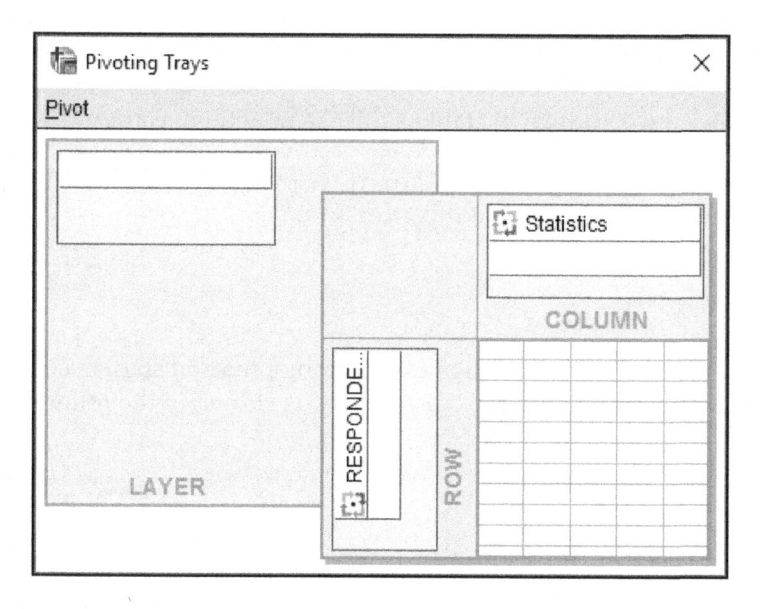

The tables shown in this chapter have not used layers, but an example will be provided in the following section.

[213]

Crosstabulation Patterns for Categorical Data

> **TIP**: It is a good idea to copy a `crosstab` table and use the Paste After option to create a duplicate in the output tree in the left window. This will allow you to experiment with various editing strategies, and you always have the option of starting over again with another copy of the original table.

Adding a layer variable

To explore the relationship between happiness and financial wellbeing in more detail, it is useful to look at the pattern with in categories of marital status. Based on the results from the earlier crosstab of happiness with marital status, it is reasonable to combine the widowed, divorced, and separated groups into a single category.

This will make for a more compact and readable table, but it will also keep the count from getting low in individual cells. By adding a third variable with three categories, the number of cells in the table will grow from nine to twenty-seven, and this spreads the smaller categories out considerably. The following RECODE was used to create a new field, marstat3, based on the values of the original marital status variable (Chapter 7, *Creating New Data Elements*, contains examples of recoding into a new variable if you want to do this using the dialog box rather than the SPSS code). In the following example, the RECODE is the CROSSTAB syntax used to produce the table, with the new field as the `layer` variable:

```
RECODE marital (1=1) (2 thru 4=2) (5=3) INTO marstat3.
value labels marstat3 1'Married' 2'Wid/Div/Sep' 3'Never Married'.
CROSSTABS
  /TABLES=happy BY satfin BY marstat3
  /CELLS=COUNT COLUMN.
```

Alternatively, after you have created the new version of marital status using either the syntax or a dialog box, you can use the crosstab dialog shown in the following screenshot to produce the table:

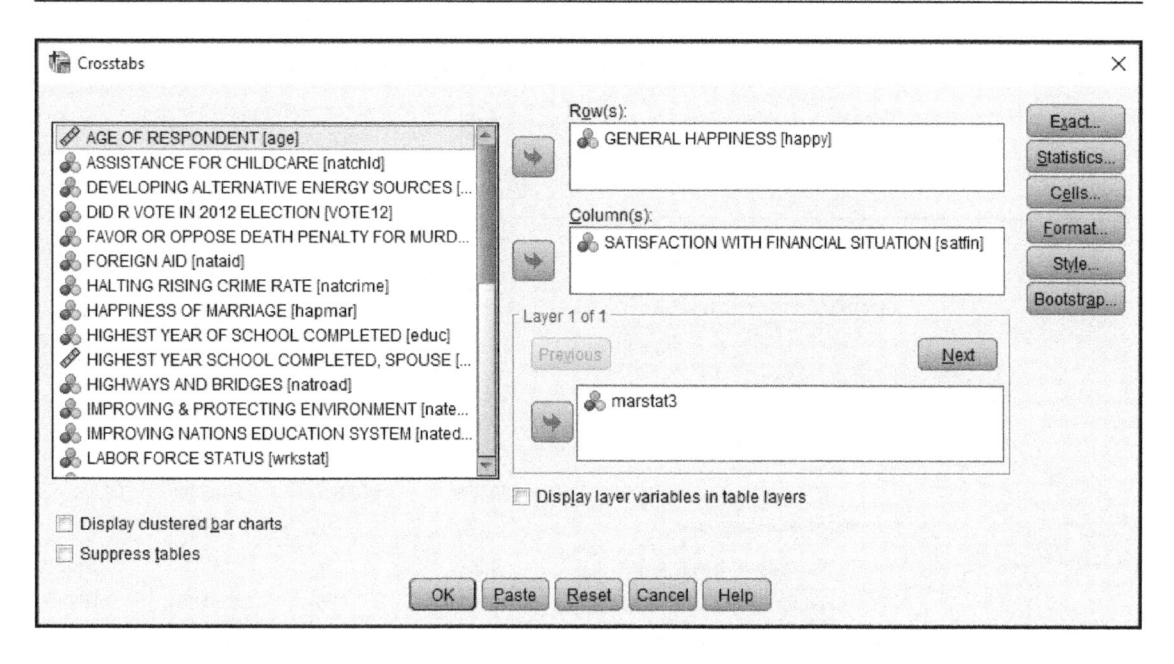

Crosstabulation Patterns for Categorical Data

The table in the following figure is similar to the first table shown at the beginning of the chapter but with separate subtables for each of the three marital status groups (the table produced originally was edited to make it more compact). Controlling marital status reveals larger differences, especially among those least satisfied with their financial situation.

While 16.5% of the married individuals in this subset reported being **NOT TOO HAPPY**, 39.1% of the widowed/divorced/separated group and 35.5% of the never married group gave the same response. This suggests that marital status interacts with financial satisfaction to influence happiness levels:

GENERAL HAPPINESS * SATISFACTION WITH FINANCIAL SITUATION * marstat3

marstat3				SATISFIED	MORE OR LESS	NOT AT ALL SAT	Total
Married	VERY HAPPY	Count		214	186	62	462
		% within SatFin		50.6%	34.1%	26.3%	38.4%
	PRETTY HAPPY	Count		196	325	135	656
		% within SatFin		46.3%	59.6%	57.2%	54.5%
	NOT TOO HAPPY	Count		13	34	39	86
		% within SatFin		3.1%	6.2%	16.5%	7.1%
	Total	Count		423	545	236	1204
		% within SatFin		100.0%	100.0%	100.0%	100.0%
Wid/Div/Sep	VERY HAPPY	Count		76	78	31	185
		% within SatFin		34.9%	22.5%	11.0%	21.9%
	PRETTY HAPPY	Count		117	195	140	452
		% within SatFin		53.7%	56.2%	49.8%	53.4%
	NOT TOO HAPPY	Count		25	74	110	209
		% within SatFin		11.5%	21.3%	39.1%	24.7%
	Total	Count		218	347	281	846
		% within SatFin		100.0%	100.0%	100.0%	100.0%
Never Married	VERY HAPPY	Count		50	77	27	154
		% within SatFin		28.9%	21.3%	10.2%	19.3%
	PRETTY HAPPY	Count		103	241	144	488
		% within SatFin		59.5%	66.8%	54.3%	61.1%
	NOT TOO HAPPY	Count		20	43	94	157
		% within SatFin		11.6%	11.9%	35.5%	19.6%
	Total	Count		173	361	265	799
		% within SatFin		100.0%	100.0%	100.0%	100.0%
Total	VERY HAPPY	Count		340	341	120	801
		% within SatFin		41.8%	27.2%	15.3%	28.1%
	PRETTY HAPPY	Count		416	761	419	1596
		% within SatFin		51.1%	60.7%	53.6%	56.0%
	NOT TOO HAPPY	Count		58	151	243	452
		% within SatFin		7.1%	12.1%	31.1%	15.9%
	Total	Count		814	1253	782	2849
		% within SatFin		100.0%	100.0%	100.0%	100.0%

Crosstabulation Patterns for Categorical Data

Adding a second layer

To dig more deeply into the relationship between satisfaction with one's financial situation and happiness, a second control can be introduced to check the influence of gender. Use the **Crosstabs** dialog, as shown in the following screenshot, to add the variable RESPONDENT SEX to the previous table as a second layer field:

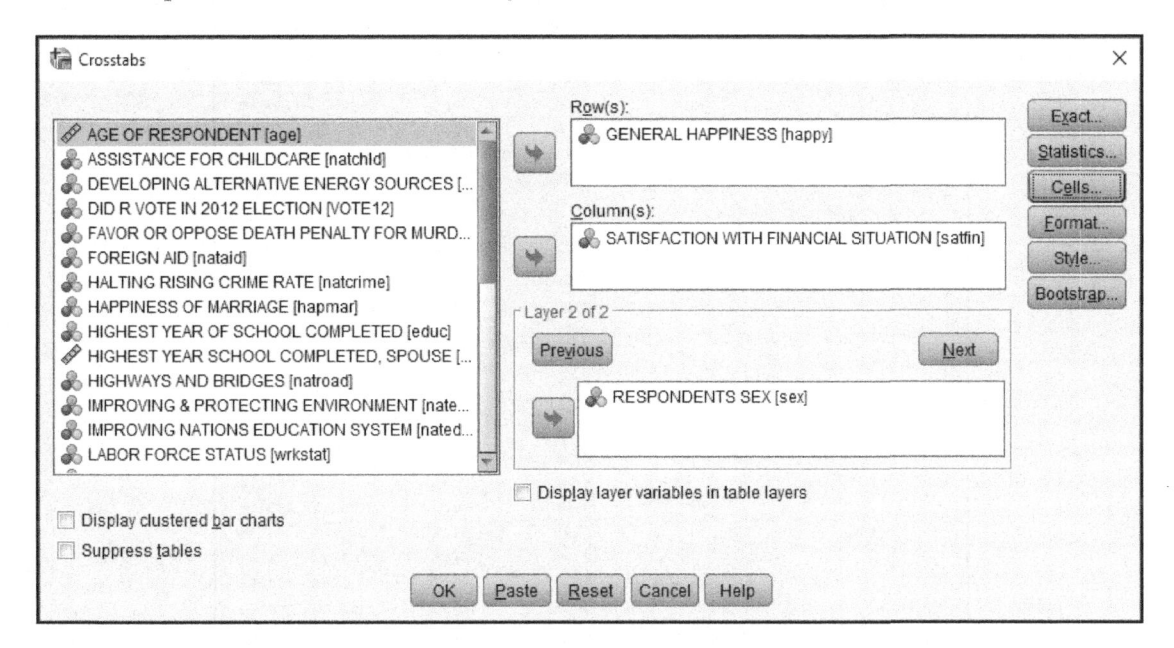

In the cells dialog, check off the **Observed** box so that only column percentages are shown. This will make for a smaller table, and the counts for each of the main groups are already known from the last table produced.

If you prefer, use the following syntax to produce the crosstab with two layer variables and no count values. The RECODE that created marstat3 should still be in effect, but if not, you will need to include that syntax again here:

```
CROSSTABS
  /TABLES=happy BY satfin BY marstat3 BY sex
  /CELLS=COLUMN.
```

GENERAL HAPPINESS * SATISFACTION WITH FINANCIAL SITUATION * marstat3 * Gender

% within SATISFACTION WITH FINANCIAL SITUATION

sex	marstat3			SATISFIED	MORE OR LESS	NOT AT ALL SAT	Total
MALE	Married		VERY HAPPY	47.3%	34.7%	26.9%	37.9%
			PRETTY HAPPY	50.2%	58.6%	51.0%	54.1%
			NOT TOO HAPPY	2.4%	6.8%	22.1%	8.0%
		Total		100.0%	100.0%	100.0%	100.0%
	Wid/Div/Sep		VERY HAPPY	34.1%	23.4%	9.5%	22.0%
			PRETTY HAPPY	56.5%	51.6%	49.5%	52.3%
			NOT TOO HAPPY	9.4%	25.0%	41.1%	25.7%
		Total		100.0%	100.0%	100.0%	100.0%
	Never Married		VERY HAPPY	25.7%	22.8%	10.5%	20.1%
			PRETTY HAPPY	64.4%	67.4%	54.4%	62.9%
			NOT TOO HAPPY	9.9%	9.8%	35.1%	17.0%
		Total		100.0%	100.0%	100.0%	100.0%
	Total		VERY HAPPY	38.9%	28.3%	15.7%	28.4%
			PRETTY HAPPY	55.2%	59.9%	51.8%	56.5%
			NOT TOO HAPPY	5.9%	11.8%	32.6%	15.1%
		Total		100.0%	100.0%	100.0%	100.0%
FEMALE	Married		VERY HAPPY	53.7%	33.7%	25.8%	38.8%
			PRETTY HAPPY	42.7%	60.5%	62.1%	54.8%
			NOT TOO HAPPY	3.7%	5.8%	12.1%	6.4%
		Total		100.0%	100.0%	100.0%	100.0%
	Wid/Div/Sep		VERY HAPPY	35.3%	22.0%	11.8%	21.8%
			PRETTY HAPPY	51.9%	58.7%	50.0%	54.1%
			NOT TOO HAPPY	12.8%	19.3%	38.2%	24.2%
		Total		100.0%	100.0%	100.0%	100.0%
	Never Married		VERY HAPPY	33.3%	19.8%	9.9%	18.5%
			PRETTY HAPPY	52.8%	66.1%	54.3%	59.3%
			NOT TOO HAPPY	13.9%	14.1%	35.8%	22.3%
		Total		100.0%	100.0%	100.0%	100.0%
	Total		VERY HAPPY	44.4%	26.4%	15.1%	27.9%
			PRETTY HAPPY	47.3%	61.4%	54.8%	55.7%
			NOT TOO HAPPY	8.3%	12.2%	30.1%	16.5%
		Total		100.0%	100.0%	100.0%	100.0%
Total	Married		VERY HAPPY	50.6%	34.1%	26.3%	38.4%
			PRETTY HAPPY	46.3%	59.6%	57.2%	54.5%
			NOT TOO HAPPY	3.1%	6.2%	16.5%	7.1%
		Total		100.0%	100.0%	100.0%	100.0%
	Wid/Div/Sep		VERY HAPPY	34.9%	22.5%	11.0%	21.9%
			PRETTY HAPPY	53.7%	56.2%	49.8%	53.4%
			NOT TOO HAPPY	11.5%	21.3%	39.1%	24.7%
		Total		100.0%	100.0%	100.0%	100.0%
	Never Married		VERY HAPPY	28.9%	21.3%	10.2%	19.3%
			PRETTY HAPPY	59.5%	66.8%	54.3%	61.1%
			NOT TOO HAPPY	11.6%	11.9%	35.5%	19.6%
		Total		100.0%	100.0%	100.0%	100.0%
	Total		VERY HAPPY	41.8%	27.2%	15.3%	28.1%
			PRETTY HAPPY	51.1%	60.7%	53.6%	56.0%
			NOT TOO HAPPY	7.1%	12.1%	31.1%	15.9%
		Total		100.0%	100.0%	100.0%	100.0%

Crosstabulation Patterns for Categorical Data

The percentages in the following screenshot provide some evidence of gender influence on happiness under certain conditions. Among those satisfied financially, more **Married** women (53.7%) than **Married** men (47.3%) were **VERY HAPPY**. Similarly, among the financially satisfied, **Never Married** women were more likely (33.3%) than **Never Married** men (25.7%) to be **VERY HAPPY**. Teasing patterns such as these out of data requires the kind of detailed investigation that can only be done by closely examining patterns in tables with multiple control variables.

Another useful feature when working with pivot tables in SPSS is the ability to modify the cell properties. Activate the table in the output window, right click to bring up the menu shown in the preceding screenshot and select **Cell Properties**. The dialog box in the following screenshot shows the three main options available for tailoring selected cells in a table:

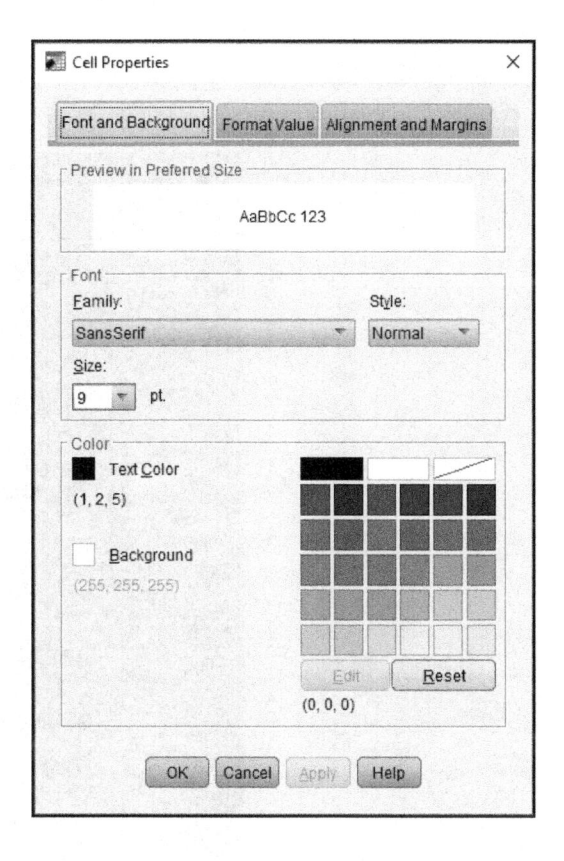

Crosstabulation Patterns for Categorical Data

This is where you can highlight specific cells by changing the font and background color to make them stand out.

> **TIP**: Check out the **Table Properties** and **Tablelooks** options on the menu from which you selected **Cell Properties** to see additional capabilities that can be used with pivot tables.

Select all the cells with percentages, right-click and select **Cell Properties**, go to the **Format Value** tab, and change the number of decimal places to zero. Click on **Apply** to make the changes, as shown in the following screenshot:

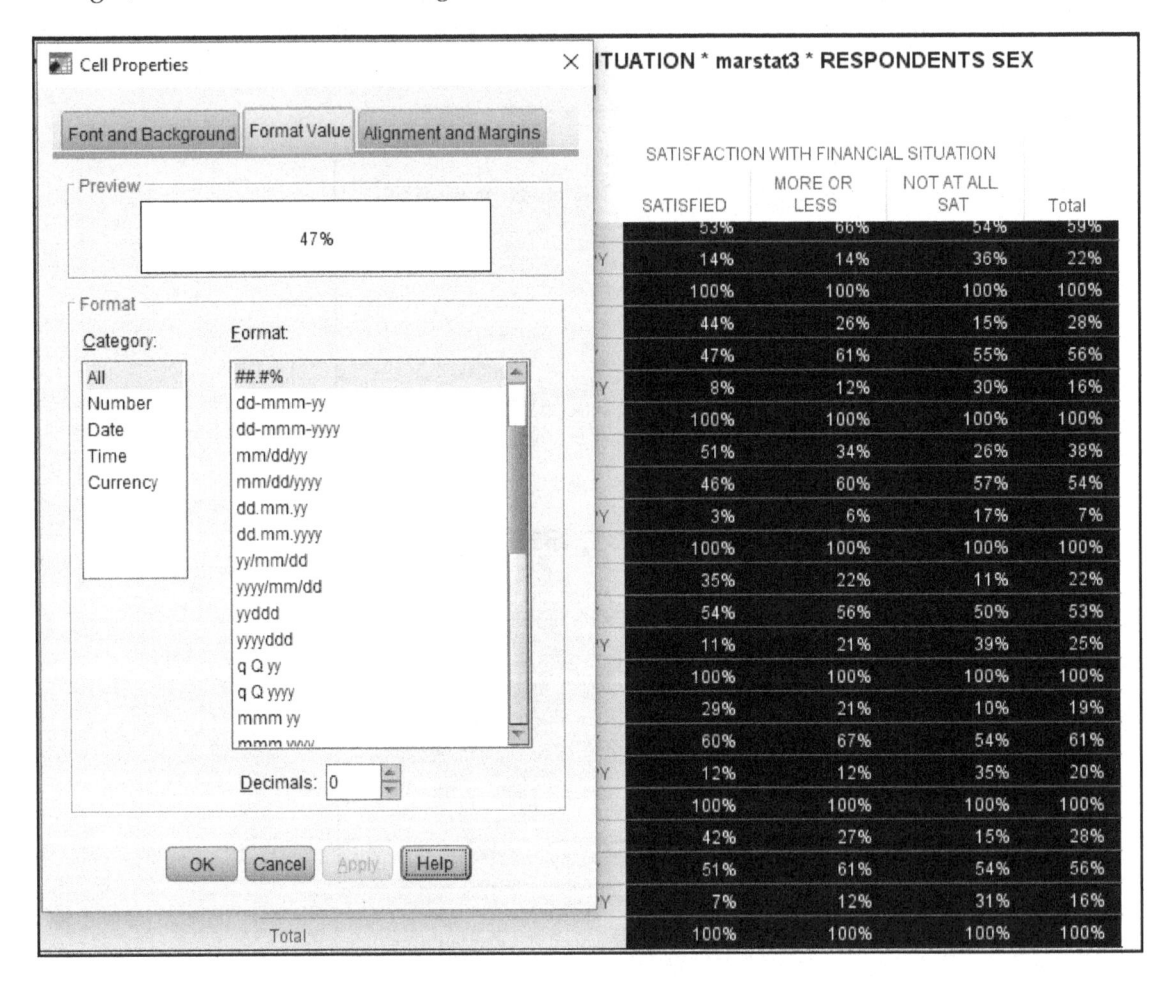

Crosstabulation Patterns for Categorical Data

The percentages are now displayed as whole numbers rounded to the nearest value. This more compact table is easier to read and will fit the page better when included in a document.

Something you may find of use when exploring `Crosstabs` interactively using SPSS is the **Display layer variables in table layers** option towards the bottom of the dialog box.

This creates a table that you can drill into to see specific combinations of the variables specifieds as layer fields.

The following screenshot illustrates how you can select individual values of the layer fields to show a specific subtable:

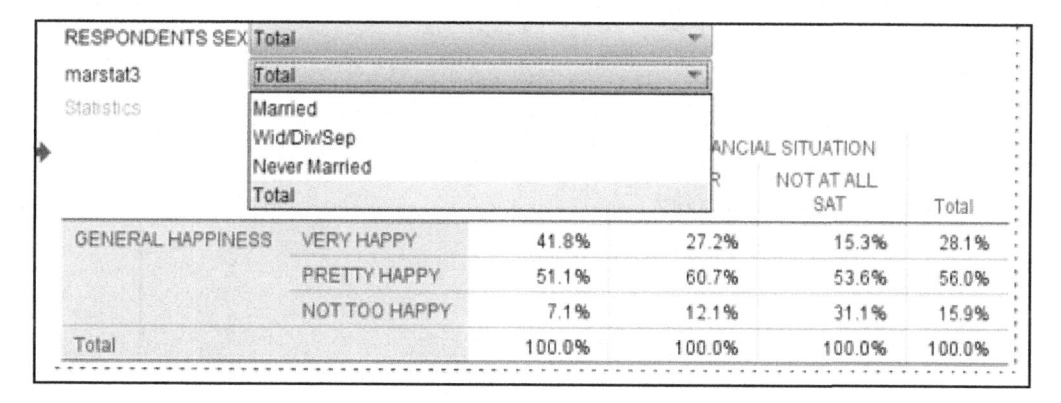

RESPONDENTS SEX	Total					
marstat3	Total					
Statistics	Married					
	Wid/Div/Sep			ANCIAL SITUATION		
	Never Married				NOT AT ALL	
	Total			R	SAT	Total
GENERAL HAPPINESS	VERY HAPPY	41.8%	27.2%		15.3%	28.1%
	PRETTY HAPPY	51.1%	60.7%		53.6%	56.0%
	NOT TOO HAPPY	7.1%	12.1%		31.1%	15.9%
Total		100.0%	100.0%		100.0%	100.0%

The SPSS syntax to request the crosstab for a table you can drill into is shown next:

```
CROSSTABS
  /TABLES=happy BY satfin BY marstat3 BY sex
  /SHOWDIM=2
  /CELLS=COLUMN.
```

> If you have access to the **Custom Tables** option for SPSS Statistics, there are additional capabilities for producing presentation quality tables. Multiple column and row fields can be defined and nested to create very detailed tables.

Crosstabulation Patterns for Categorical Data

Using a Chi-square test with crosstabs

So far, we have been looking at percentages to determine whether there is a relationship between the two principal variables being used in the crosstab tables: financial satisfaction and happiness. To answer this question statistically, the chi-square associated with the table can be obtained. Start by defining the initial crosstab shown at the beginning of the chapter, with happiness in the rows and financial satisfaction as the `column` variable.

In the cell dialog, check **Expected** count and **Column** percentages, as shown in the following screenshot:

Check the Chi-square box in the statistics dialog, and then use the **Help** button to bring up the information in the following screenshot:

Crosstabulation Patterns for Categorical Data

> **Crosstabs statistics**
>
> **Chi-square.** For tables with two rows and two columns, select **Chi-square** to calculate the Pearson chi-square, the likelihood-ratio chi-square, Fisher's exact test, and Yates' corrected chi-square (continuity correction). For 2 × 2 tables, Fisher's exact test is computed when a table that does not result from missing rows or columns in a larger table has a cell with an expected frequency of less than 5. Yates' corrected chi-square is computed for all other 2 × 2 tables. For tables with any number of rows and columns, select **Chi-square** to calculate the Pearson chi-square and the likelihood-ratio chi-square. When both table variables are quantitative, **Chi-square** yields the linear-by-linear association test.

This provides valuable information on when to use this statistic and how the values may be interpreted.

Expected counts

The expected counts that are added to the table shown in the following screenshot are calculated by multiplying count by the **Column** percentage for the row:

GENERAL HAPPINESS * SATISFACTION WITH FINANCIAL SITUATION Crosstabulation

			SATISFACTION WITH FINANCIAL SITUATION			
			SATISFIED	MORE OR LESS	NOT AT ALL SAT	Total
VERY HAPPY		Count	340	341	120	801
		Expected Count	229.1	352.2	219.8	801.0
		% within SatFin	41.7%	27.2%	15.3%	28.105263
		Residual	110.9	-11.2	-99.8	
PRETTY HAPPY		Count	417	761	419	1597
		Expected Count	456.7	702.1	438.2	1597.0
		% within SatFin	51.2%	60.7%	53.6%	56.0%
		Residual	-39.7	58.9	-19.2	
NOT TOO HAPPY		Count	58	151	243	452
		Expected Count	129.3	198.7	124.0	452.0
		% within SatFin	7.1%	12.1%	31.1%	15.9%
		Residual	-71.3	-47.7	119.0	
Total		Count	815	1253	782	2850
		Expected Count	815.0	1253.0	782.0	2850.0
		% within SatFin	100.0%	100.0%	100.0%	100.0%

Crosstabulation Patterns for Categorical Data

For the first cell, this calculation is as follows:

Expected count Row 1, *Column 1 = 815 * .281 = 229.1*

Note that when you double-click on a percentage, such as 28.1%, in the Total column, you will see the actual value displayed with more decimal places. This more precise value is used in the Chi-square calculations. Double-clicking on the 229.1 value for the **Expected** count in the first cell will reveal the actual value of 229.057895.

The Chi-square formula is relatively straightforward. The expected value in each cell (*m*) is subtracted from the actual value in a cell (*x*), the result is squared (so negative and positive differences do not cancel each other out), and the result is divided by the expected value:

$$X^2 = \sum_{i=1}^{k} \frac{(x_i - m_i)^2}{m_i}$$

By summing these deviations across the table, a value reflects the extent to which the numbers in the cells, as a whole differ from what would be present if the counts were distributed proportionately based on the marginals.

> **TIP**
> When you double-click on a percentage such as 28.1% in the Total column, you will see the actual value displayed with more decimal places. This more precise value is used in the Chi-square calculations. Double-clicking on the 229.1 value for the expected count in the first cell will reveal the actual value of 229.057895.

The second component of the Chi-square is the degrees of freedom. In this example, the table has three columns and three rows. The row and column counts are determined by the joint distribution of the two variables, so once two values in any row or column are set, the remaining value can only be the difference between the sum of the two values and the total count.

The degrees of freedom values are *Row count-1 * Column count-1*. In the case of a 3x3 table, the DF value will always be four. This value, along with the Chi-square values, is compared with a standard table of Chi-square values, and associated DF values, to obtain the significance level.

A significance of .001 means that one time in 1,000, you will find a value of this size for a table with this DF value when there is no association between the variables. A significance of .000 means that the likelihood that there is no relationship is less than one in a thousand.

Context sensitive help

SPSS produces many statistics, and it is likely for some of them to be unfamiliar to many users. The information contained in the **Help** system can be valuable in deciding which statistics to choose, but it is also useful to be able to obtain information while examining the results. Activating a pivot table containing statistical output, as shown in the following screenshot, gives you the option of bringing up the menu with the **What's This?** choice at the top:

Crosstabulation Patterns for Categorical Data

The text you highlight, pearson Chi-square in this instance, is linked to the **Help** system to produce the textbox, as shown in the following screenshot:

There are several versions of the Chi-square statistic provided, but typically, it is the Pearson Chi-square that is reported. In most instances, all of them will lead to the same conclusion when it comes to assessing whether a significant relationship is present. To obtain more detail on the likelihood ratio and linear by linear (also referred to as the Mantel-Haenszel chi-square), highlight each of them, and use the **What's This?** option.

Ordinal measures of association

The happiness and financial satisfaction variables are both ordinal measures, so the strength of the relationship can be quantified using one of the ordinal association statistics. The preceding screenshot shows the patterns of responses for these two attributes, and the Chi-square indicates that there is a significant relationship. Request this same table and select the **Gamma** statistic, as shown in the following screenshot:

[226]

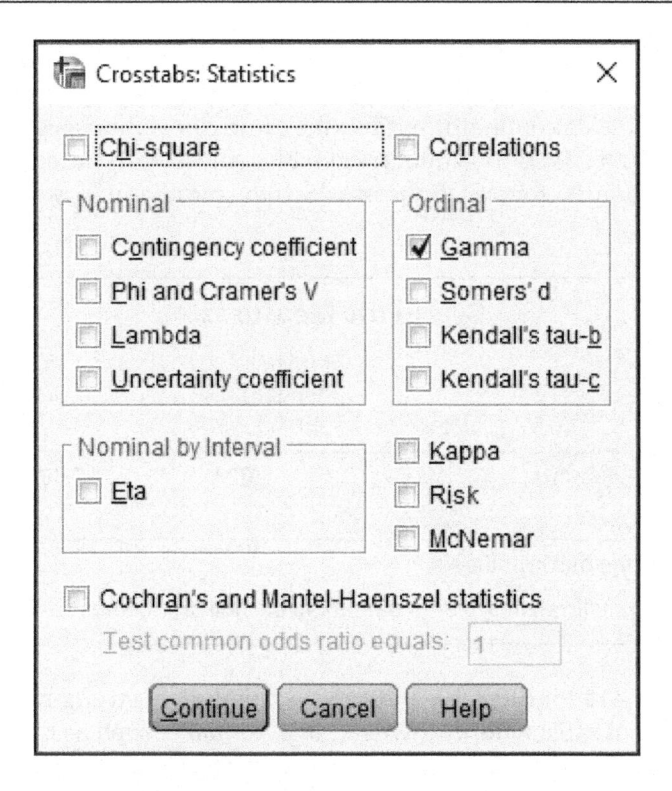

Crosstabulation Patterns for Categorical Data

The **Gamma** statistic is like the **Kendall's tau-b** and **Kendall's tau-c**, except that it ignores any ties. These measures compare the number of concordant pairs (the case with the higher value on the independent variable also has a higher value on the dependent variable) and the number of discordant pairs (the case with the higher value on the independent variable has a value that is equal or lower than the dependent variable). If for all possible pairs, it is always the case that a higher value on one variable is associated with a higher value on the other variable, these measures will all have a value of one.

Gamma subtracts the number of discordant pairs from the number of concordant pairs and divides the result by the sum of the concordant and discordant pairs. The tau measures add the number of ties to the denominator but use the same calculation as gamma for the numerator. Tau-b is best suited to symmetrical tables (those with the same number of rows and columns). Tau-c adjusts for situations in which the number of rows and columns are not equal:

Symmetric Measures

		Value	Asymptotic Standard Error[a]	Approximate T[b]	Approximate Significance
Ordinal by Ordinal	Gamma	.414	.024	15.694	.000
N of Valid Cases		2850			

a. Not assuming the null hypothesis.
b. Using the asymptotic standard error assuming the null hypothesis.

The **Gamma** value of .414 for this table indicates a moderately strong relationship between happiness and financial satisfaction. However, in a 3x3 table, such as this one for happiness with financial satisfaction, there are likely to be many ties; the gamma value overestimates the magnitude of the relationship.

Interval with nominal association measure

To gauge the strength of the relationship between an interval-level variable and a nominal field, you can use the Eta statistic in `Crosstabs`. Interval-level fields, such as age or income, generally have many unique values, which produce a very large table. In this example, the variable age (72 different values in this dataset) and 2012 vote status (three values) will be used.

Crosstabulation Patterns for Categorical Data

This would produce a table with 216 cells, so the table will be suppressed. Check the **Eta** box in the statistics dialog so the statistic gets produced. Note that by checking the **Suppress tables** box, the **Cells** and **Format** buttons become unavailable. You can see this happening in the following screenshot:

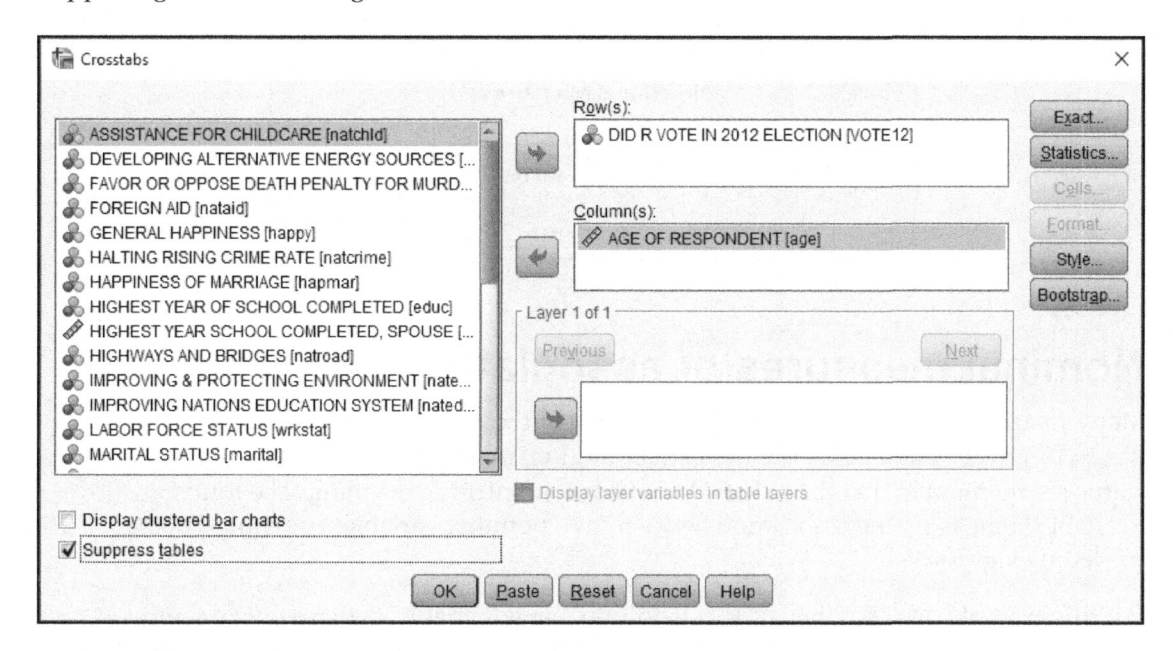

The syntax to produce the results is as follows:

```
CROSSTABS
  /TABLES=VOTE12 BY age
  /FORMAT=NOTABLES
  /STATISTICS=ETA.
```

Crosstabulation Patterns for Categorical Data

The **Eta** statistic is directional in the sense that either variable could be the dependent measure. In this situation, the hypothesis is that age may have an impact on whether someone voted in the 2012 presidential election, so the first row in the table shown in the following screenshot is the one of interest. **Eta** ranges from 0 to 1, so the value of .568 is relatively large.

Directional Measures

			Value
Nominal by Interval	Eta	DID R VOTE IN 2012 ELECTION Dependent	.568
		AGE OF RESPONDENT Dependent	.407

Nominal measures of association

Many categorical variables are nominal in terms of their measurement level. In the `General Social Survey` data, fields such as gender, region, marital status, vote status, and work status are nominal in that the values do not have an intrinsic meaning. The four statistics available to measure the association between two nominal variables are shown in the preceding Figure 29.

For this example, `RECODE` the `VOTE12` field into a new variable so that `1=Voted` and `2=Did not vote`. Those that responded `ineligible` should be left as missing on this new field. Request a crosstab of the new `voted` field with the gender variable. Request both row and column percentages and check all four nominal statistics. The code used to generate the results is as follows:

```
RECODE VOTE12 (1=1) (2=2) into Voted2012.
variable label voted2012 'Voted in 2012 Presidential Election'.
value labels voted2012 1'Voted' 2'Did not vote'.
CROSSTABS
 /TABLES=Voted2012 BY sex
 /STATISTICS=CC PHI LAMBDA UC CMH (1)
 /CELLS=COUNT ROW COLUMN.
```

By including both the row and column percentages, it is evident that 57% of the voters in 2012 were women and 71% of women voted. This appears as a strong pattern until compared with the row totals, which show that 56% of all the respondents were women, so the fact that they made up 57% of the voters is not a surprise. The following screenshot illustrates our point:

Voted in 2012 Presidential Election * RESPONDENTS SEX Crosstabulation

			RESPONDENTS SEX MALE	RESPONDENTS SEX FEMALE	Total
Voted		Count	776	1033	1809
		% within Voted in 2012	43%	57%	100%
		% within Gender	67%	71%	69%
Did not vote		Count	381	419	800
		% within Voted in 2012	48%	52%	100%
		% within Gender	33%	29%	31%
Total		Count	1157	1452	2609
		% within Voted in 2012	44%	56%	100%
		% within Gender	100%	100%	100%

The **Lambda** statistic makes use of the modal value (the largest category) as the basis of its calculations, so it is not surprising that here, the significance cannot be determined. The **Voted in 2012 Election** is the dependent pattern of interest. While the significance level of both the **Goodman and Kruskal tau** statistic and the **Uncertainty Coefficient** are below the standard .05 level, the relationship is weak at best. This is consistent with what the percentages in the table show.

Crosstabulation Patterns for Categorical Data

The contingency coefficient, Phi and Cramer's V statistics in Figure 35, exhibit a pattern like the statistics in the following table:

Directional Measures

			Value	Asymptotic Standard Error[a]	Approximate T[d]	Approximate Significance
Nominal by Nominal	Lambda	Symmetric	.000	.000	[b]	[b]
		Voted in 2012 Election Dependent	.000	.000	[b]	[b]
		RESPONDENTS SEX Dependent	.000	.000	[b]	[b]
	Goodman and Kruskal tau	Voted in 2012 Election Dependent	.002	.002		.025[c]
		RESPONDENTS SEX Dependent	.002	.002		.025[c]
	Uncertainty Coefficient	Symmetric	.001	.001	1.119	.025[e]
		Voted in 2012 Election Dependent	.002	.001	1.119	.025[e]
		RESPONDENTS SEX Dependent	.001	.001	1.119	.025[e]

a. Not assuming the null hypothesis.
b. Cannot be computed because the asymptotic standard error equals zero.
c. Based on chi-square approximation
d. Using the asymptotic standard error assuming the null hypothesis.
e. Likelihood ratio chi-square probability.

The values are marginally significant, but the coefficients are quite small:

Symmetric Measures

		Value	Approximate Significance
Nominal by Nominal	Phi	-.044	.025
	Cramer's V	.044	.025
	Contingency Coefficient	.044	.025
N of Valid Cases		2609	

Summary

This chapter focused on the capabilities of the crosstabs procedure in SPSS Statistics. Exploring relationships among categorical fields is central to many data analysis projects. Crosstabs provides both tabular results, which can be visually evaluated, and summary statistics, which assess the presence and the strength of the relationship between the measures under consideration. Categorical fields can be nominal, ordinal, or interval in terms of their measurement level, and the statistics appropriate for each of these were reviewed.

Crosstabs results are presented in the form of pivot tables and the SPSS capabilities for editing these tables was covered in this chapter. Understanding what to include in a table and how to interpret the patterns in a table, as well as the associated statistics for the table, are important topics addressed in the preceding sections. As you gain familiarity with your data and the type of data analysis reporting required for various projects, the flexibility of crosstabs to create compact tables, with the key cells highlighted, will become an increasingly valuable tool. The optional graphs can also be used to supplement the tables with a visual summary of the main differences you wish to emphasize.

In the next chapter, we will look at the procedures in SPSS Statistics that you can use to compare means and perform analysis of variance (ANOVA).

11
Comparing Means and ANOVA

One of the fundamental techniques used to check for patterns among data fields involves comparing means across a set of groups. In Chapter 3, *Statistics for Individual Data Elements*, Means were one of the statistics used as part of the investigation of individual data elements, and they were also included in the group comparison done using the Explore procedure. Here, we will examine mean comparison more formally using significance tests to assess the importance of differences that are present.

Metrics captured for individual units in a dataset, such as length of stay for hospital patients, or sales for a chain of retail stores, can be examined to identity deviations from the overall mean, as well as differences between a pair of subset Means. SPSS Statistics provides a set of procedures designed for various types of mean comparisons. This chapter will cover each of these procedures and discuss the underlying techniques. The topics covered include the following:

- Comparing Means across subsets
- One-sample t-test
- Independent-samples t-test
- Paired-comparison t-test
- One-way ANOVA for comparison of Means
- Planned comparison of Means
- Post-hoc comparison of Means
- Testing the homogeneity of variance assumption
- The ANOVA procedure

SPSS procedures for comparing Means

The individual procedures available for conducting mean comparisons can be found under the **Compare Means** group within the **Analyze** menu, as shown in the following screenshot:

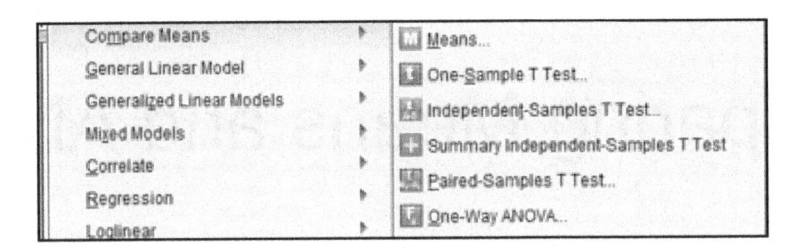

Starting with **Means** and progressing through **One-Way ANOVA** (the summary procedure will not be covered, since it is based on a Python add-on), the statistics available for evaluating mean differences become increasingly sophisticated. In addition, each of the techniques offers specialized statistics suited to the task they are designed to perform.

The Means procedure

The examples in this chapter will use the 33-variable subset of the General Social Survey data from 2016 that was the basis for the examples in Chapter 3, *Statistics for Individual Data Elements*, Chapter 4, *Dealing with Missing Data and Outliers*, and Chapter 10, *Crosstabulations Patterns for Categorical Data*. Open the SPSS data file you created earlier (or download and open the full GSS2016 following the steps in Chapter 3, *Statistics for Individual Data Elements*). Use the following to bring up the main dialog box:

Analyze | Compare Means | Means

Specify years of education as the dependent field and region as the layer field. Select **Options**, add the median to the cell statistics, and check the Anova table box at the bottom, then **Continue** and **OK**:

Comparing Means and ANOVA

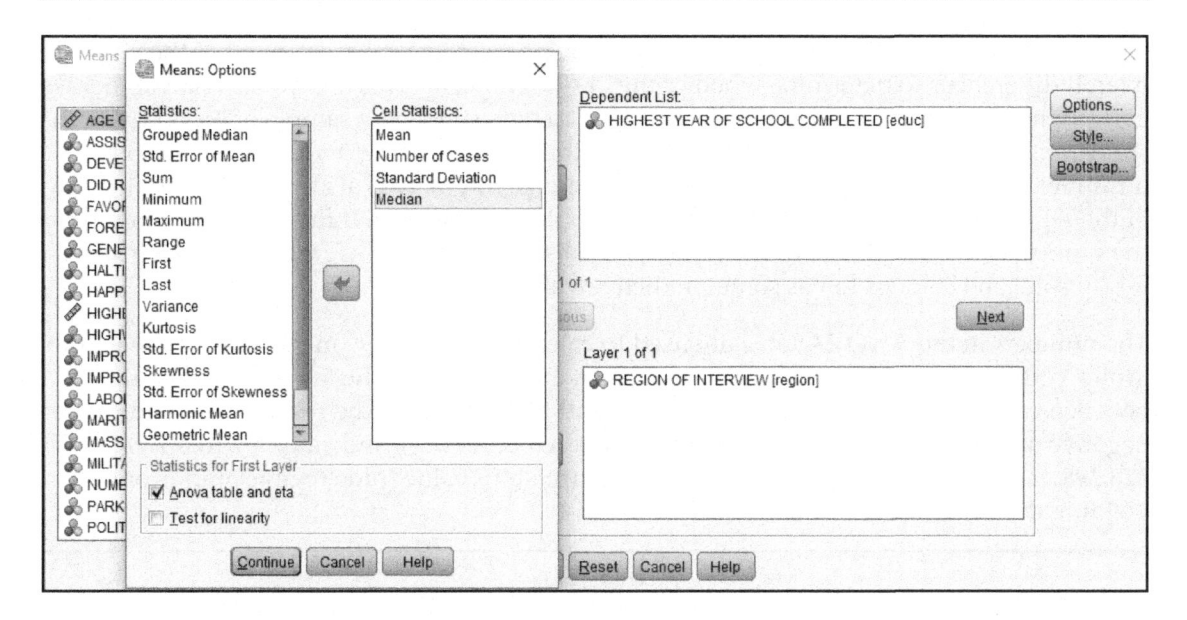

It is evident from the report in the following screenshot that the mean years of schooling varies somewhat across the nine regions from a high of **14.29** in New England to a low of **12.91** in the West South Central region. The number of cases also varies considerably among the regions, and their standard deviations, which, while not all that different, show some differences as well:

Report

HIGHEST YEAR OF SCHOOL COMPLETED

REGION OF INTERVIEW	Mean	N	Std. Deviation	Median
NEW ENGLAND	14.29	175	3.087	14.00
MIDDLE ATLANTIC	14.01	311	2.889	14.00
E. NOR. CENTRAL	13.85	499	2.836	13.00
W. NOR. CENTRAL	13.25	193	2.695	12.00
SOUTH ATLANTIC	13.83	548	2.756	14.00
E. SOU. CENTRAL	13.43	205	2.827	13.00
W. SOU. CENTRAL	12.91	297	3.054	12.00
MOUNTAIN	13.92	235	3.023	14.00
PACIFIC	13.91	395	3.337	14.00
Total	13.74	2858	2.964	13.00

Comparing Means and ANOVA

The analysis of results (the following figure) provides a statistical assessment of these overall differences to determine whether they are significant. This allows the analyst to gauge whether the observed variability is likely to persist if a new sample of individuals are surveyed. At a conceptual level, the analysis of the variance being performed is reasonably intuitive. There is variation between the nine regions, but there is also variation within each of the regions when it comes to the years of schooling completed. If the differences between the groups are large, relative to the differences observed within the groups, knowing what group someone belongs to has some predictive value.

The numbers in the ANOVA table are used to calculate the relative magnitude of the within group versus the between group's variability. In the first row of the table, the difference between each of the group Means and the overall mean is taken, the result is squared (so negative and positive differences do not cancel each other out), and summed to arrive at the **378.398** value. This is divided by the degrees of freedom value (nine regions minus one), yielding the mean square value of 47.3:

ANOVA Table

			Sum of Squares	df	Mean Square	F	Sig.
HIGHEST YEAR OF SCHOOL COMPLETED * REGION OF INTERVIEW	Between Groups	(Combined)	378.398	8	47.300	5.45	.000
	Within Groups		24719.261	2849	8.676		
	Total		25097.659	2857			

Similarly, for the within groups row, the difference between each respondent's years of education and the mean of their region is taken, the result is squared, and then summed across all the regions to arrive at the **24719.261** value, which, when divided by its associated degrees of freedom, yields the mean square of **8.676**. Dividing the between group mean square by the within group's mean square produces the **F** ratio of **5.45**. This value is compared with a table of **F** values for the corresponding degrees of freedom to find significance. Here, the value is highly significant, meaning it is not likely to find a ratio this large, even one time in a thousand, by chance.

The Eta statistic was introduced in the preceding chapter on the crosstabulation procedure in SPSS. It is appropriate when looking at the relationship between interval and nominal variables. The F ratio indicates that there is a statistically significant relationship between years of schooling completed and the region of the country where someone resides. Eta measures the strength of that relationship on a zero-to-one scale. In this instance, the relationship is present, but is not particularly strong. Eta squared can be thought of as an approximation of the portion of variability associated with the independent variable, region:

Comparing Means and ANOVA

Measures of Association

	Eta	Eta Squared
HIGHEST YEAR OF SCHOOL COMPLETED * REGION OF INTERVIEW	.123	.015

Adding a second variable

A breakdown of Means by a single grouping variable is often useful, but adding additional factors is frequently required to discover less obvious patterns, or to check for potentially confounding factors. The variation in educational attainment by region might be due to other influences, such as gender differences. It may also be of interest to examine the pattern of education by gender across the various regions as a topic. The **Means** procedure can be used for situations such as this by specifying additional factors to be included in the table.

In the following figure, the **Next** button is used to modify the previous **Means** request in order to add a second Layer variable; the sex of the respondent. The order of the variables is important since the first one, named region in this example, is the high-level split, and is the one used as the basis for the statistics that are calculated:

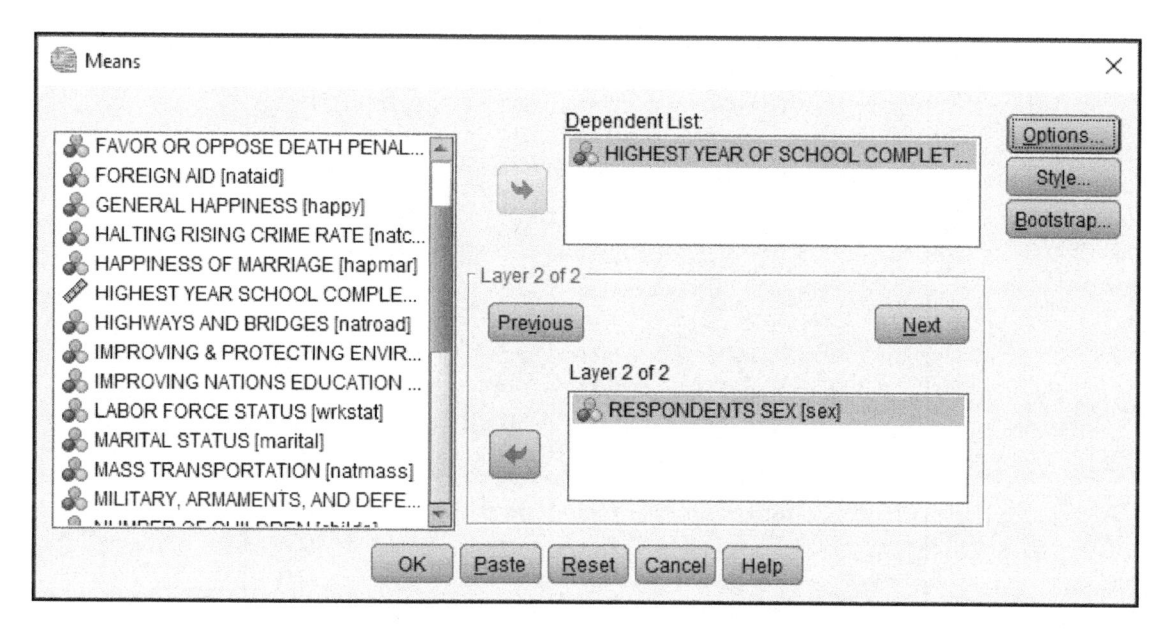

[239]

The results created by the **Means** request in the preceding figure are shown in the following table. By nesting gender within region, it is possible to compare the average years of schooling completed for males and females in each region. This greater degree of detail makes it possible to detect patterns that are not apparent when comparing the **Means** for each factor separately. For example, females have a slightly higher overall mean level of education (13.77 versus 13.70 for males). In five of the nine regions, however, the mean is higher for males than females:

Report

HIGHEST YEAR OF SCHOOL COMPLETED

REGION	Gender	Mean	N	Std. Deviation	Median
NEW ENGLAND	MALE	14.25	76	3.095	14.00
	FEMALE	14.32	99	3.097	14.00
	Total	14.29	175	3.087	14.00
MIDDLE ATLANTIC	MALE	14.25	128	2.721	14.00
	FEMALE	13.85	183	2.998	13.00
	Total	14.01	311	2.889	14.00
E. NOR. CENTRAL	MALE	13.99	245	2.938	14.00
	FEMALE	13.72	254	2.734	13.00
	Total	13.85	499	2.836	13.00
W. NOR. CENTRAL	MALE	13.36	90	2.675	12.00
	FEMALE	13.17	103	2.723	12.00
	Total	13.25	193	2.695	12.00
SOUTH ATLANTIC	MALE	13.57	233	2.897	13.00
	FEMALE	14.03	315	2.634	14.00
	Total	13.83	548	2.756	14.00
E. SOU. CENTRAL	MALE	13.51	87	2.945	13.00
	FEMALE	13.37	118	2.748	13.00
	Total	13.43	205	2.827	13.00
W. SOU. CENTRAL	MALE	12.89	137	2.902	12.00
	FEMALE	12.92	160	3.188	12.00
	Total	12.91	297	3.054	12.00
MOUNTAIN	MALE	13.82	94	3.246	14.00
	FEMALE	13.99	141	2.875	13.00
	Total	13.92	235	3.023	14.00
PACIFIC	MALE	13.65	183	3.047	14.00
	FEMALE	14.13	212	3.561	14.00
	Total	13.91	395	3.337	14.00
Total	MALE	13.70	1273	2.954	13.00
	FEMALE	13.77	1585	2.972	13.00
	Total	13.74	2858	2.964	13.00

Comparing Means and ANOVA

As the **Options** dialog box shown in the first example indicates, the statistics are for the first layer, so the ANOVA table and Eta statistics are the same as for the original **Means** procedure that only included the region field. One could run separate **Means** procedures for males and females using the techniques described in Chapter 6, *Sampling, Subsetting and Weighting*, and compare the results of the statistics. Later in this chapter, an example of this approach will be presented in the section covering T-test.

Test of linearity example

The region field used in the preceding two examples is coded numerically as one through nine, but the field is nominal in terms of the level of measurement. If the independent factor used as the basis for comparing Means is ordinal or interval, however, adding the test of linearity statistic provides useful additional information. The type of place the respondent lived in when they were growing up (the **RES16** field) is ordinal since larger values correspond to larger community sizes (see the following figure):

TYPE OF PLACE LIVED IN WHEN 16 YRS OLD

		Frequency	Percent	Valid Percent
Valid	1 COUNTRY,NONFARM	304	10.6	10.6
	2 FARM	234	8.2	8.2
	3 TOWN LT 50000	979	34.1	34.2
	4 50000 TO 250000	493	17.2	17.2
	5 BIG-CITY SUBURB	413	14.4	14.4
	6 CITY GT 250000	438	15.3	15.3
	Total	2861	99.8	100.0
Missing	8 DK	4	.1	
	9 NA	2	.1	
	Total	6	.2	
Total		2867	100.0	

Comparing Means and ANOVA

Return to the **Means** dialog and place the **RES16** field in the first layer of the independent list box at the lower right (remove the gender field from the second layer if it is still there from the previous request). In the **Options...** dialog, check the box at the lower left to add the **Test of linearity** statistic, as shown in the following figure:

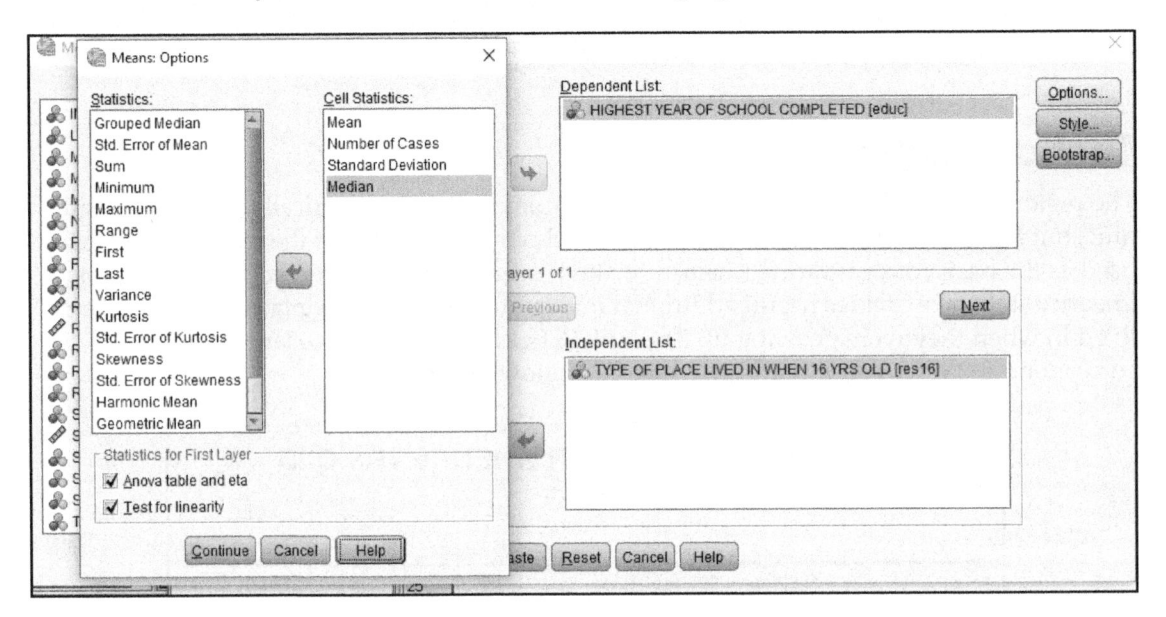

> **TIP**
>
> The Recall Dialog icon at the top of each SPSS window is a convenient way to go directly to a dialog you have used previously during an interactive session. All the settings from last use are preserved, so it is easy to make a minor change, such as adding the test of linearity statistic.

[242]

Comparing Means and ANOVA

The **Mean** in the following figure increase as the size of the community increases, except for the last row. This is generally consistent with what one would expect in a linear trend:

Report

HIGHEST YEAR OF SCHOOL COMPLETED

TYPE OF PLACE LIVED IN WHEN 16 YRS OLD	Mean	N	Std. Deviation	Median
COUNTRY,NONFARM	12.94	301	3.270	12.00
FARM	13.05	234	3.189	12.00
TOWN LT 50000	13.59	975	2.854	13.00
50000 TO 250000	13.95	492	2.753	14.00
BIG-CITY SUBURB	14.73	413	2.772	15.00
CITY GT 250000	13.82	438	2.988	13.00
Total	13.74	2853	2.964	13.00

The ANOVA table, shown next, contains results for the overall between groups and separate rows for the linearity and deviation from linearity components. Both the linear and deviation from linearity F-values are highly significant, which suggests that the linear relationship does not capture the complete pattern present in the data:

ANOVA Table

			Sum of Squares	df	Mean Square	F	Sig.
HIGHEST YEAR OF SCHOOL COMPLETED * TYPE OF PLACE LIVED IN WHEN 16 YRS OLD	Between Groups	(Combined)	755.47	5	151.09	17.70	.000
		Linearity	435.61	1	435.61	51.04	.000
		Deviation from Linearity	319.86	4	79.97	9.37	.000
	Within Groups		24298.6	2847	8.53		
	Total		25054.1	2852			

Comparing Means and ANOVA

The measures of association table (shown in the following figure) provides further evidence that the nonlinear component of the relationship is important. Since the Eta is larger than the R (.174 versus .132), there is support for the fact that the linear relationship between the size of the place one grew up in, and years of education, is not the full picture:

Measures of Association

	R	R Squared	Eta	Eta Squared
HIGHEST YEAR OF SCHOOL COMPLETED * TYPE OF PLACE LIVED IN WHEN 16 YRS OLD	.132	.017	.174	.030

Testing the strength of the nonlinear relationship

The test of linearity feature in the **Means** procedure can also be used when the mean comparisons themselves are not of interest. When examining the relationship between age and income, for example, it is generally the case that income increases with age up to a point, then levels off and eventually declines. The following figure depicts this pattern graphically using the midpoints for the income categories in the General Social Survey data (this RECODE was shown in Chapter 7, *Creating New Data Elements*):

```
RECODE RINCOM16
(1=750) (2=2000) (3=3500) (4=4500) (5=5500) (6=6500) (7=7500) (8=9000)
(9=11250) (10=13750) (11=16250) (12=18750) (13=21250) (14=23750) (15=27500) (16=32500)
(17=37500) (18=45000) (19=55000) (20=67500) (21=82500) (22=95500) (23=120000)
(24=140000) (25=160000) (26=200000) INTO RINCOME_MIDPT.
VARIABLE LABELS RINCOME_MIDPT Respondents income using midpoint of selected category.
```

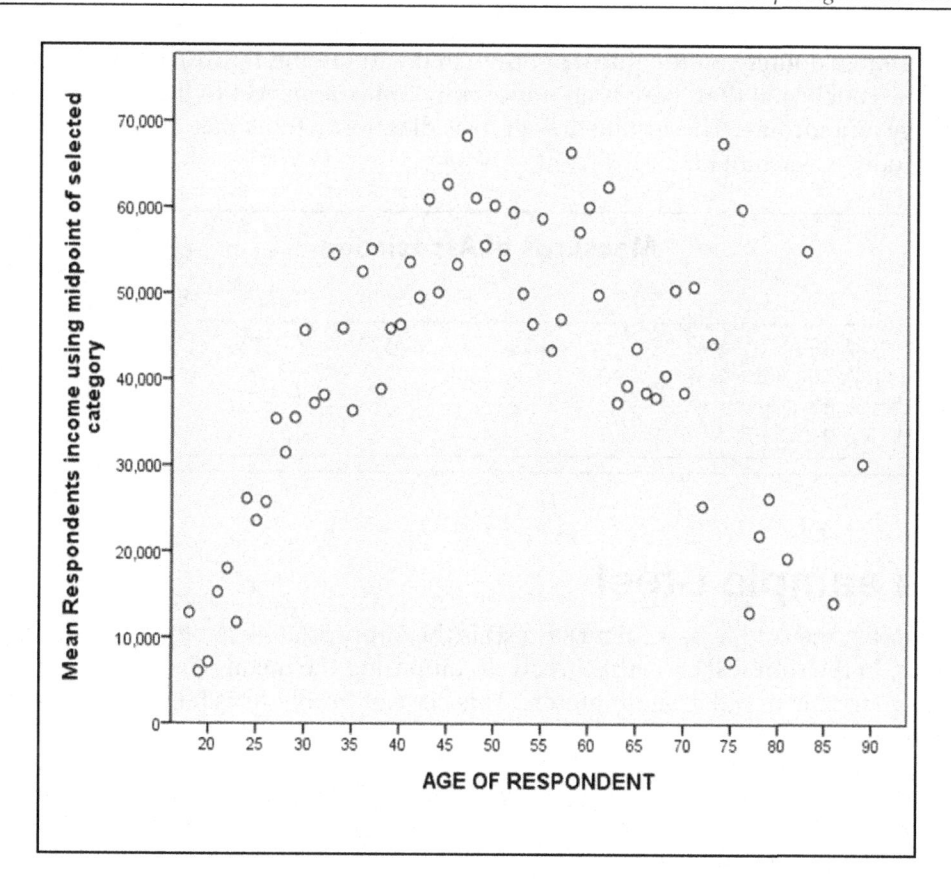

By specifying Age as the independent variable in **Means**, and income as the dependent variable, along with both statistics available in the Options dialog, information is required to evaluate the need to fit a nonlinear, as well as a linear, model. The **ANOVA table** (shown in the following figure) does indicate that both components yield significant F-values:

ANOVA Table

			Sum of Squares	df	Mean Square	F	Sig.
Respondents income using midpoint of selected category * AGE OF RESPONDENT	Between Groups	(Combined)	307729410100	65	4734298617	2.89	.000
		Linearity	76448522780	1	76448522780	46.68	.000
		Deviation from Linearity	231280887400	64	3613763865	2.21	.000
	Within Groups		2556216662000	1561	1637550712		
	Total		2863946072000	1626			

The Eta is almost double the **R** value (as shown in the following figure), which also supports the conclusion that there is an important nonlinear aspect to the relationship between age and income. These statistics serve as diagnostic tools that indicate a more complex model is warranted:

Measures of Association

	R	R Squared	Eta	Eta Squared
Respondents income using midpoint of selected category * AGE OF RESPONDENT	.163	.027	.328	.107

Single sample t-test

The t-test (often referred to as student's t-test) is the appropriate technique for comparing two **Means**. In the simplest case, this involves comparing the mean of a sample with a known mean for the population of interest. This class of problems is handled by one sample t-test procedure in SPSS.

One common use of this test is to check to see whether a sample is representative of the population with respect to a particular characteristic. The General Social Survey is a national sample of US adults and, as such, should have a mean of demographic attributes, such as age and income, that is very close to the average for all adults in the country. The representativeness of the GSS sample, with respect to income, can be checked by comparing the mean income of the respondents with the average income value provided by the Census Bureau. For 2015, the mean income reported by the Census Bureau was $46,120.

To perform a t-test comparing the income variable, based on the midpoints of the categories (the version of this field created by RECOCE and used in the preceding **Means** example), complete the **One-Sample T-Test** dialog as shown in the following figure. Enter the test value of 46120 to use it as the basis for the comparison:

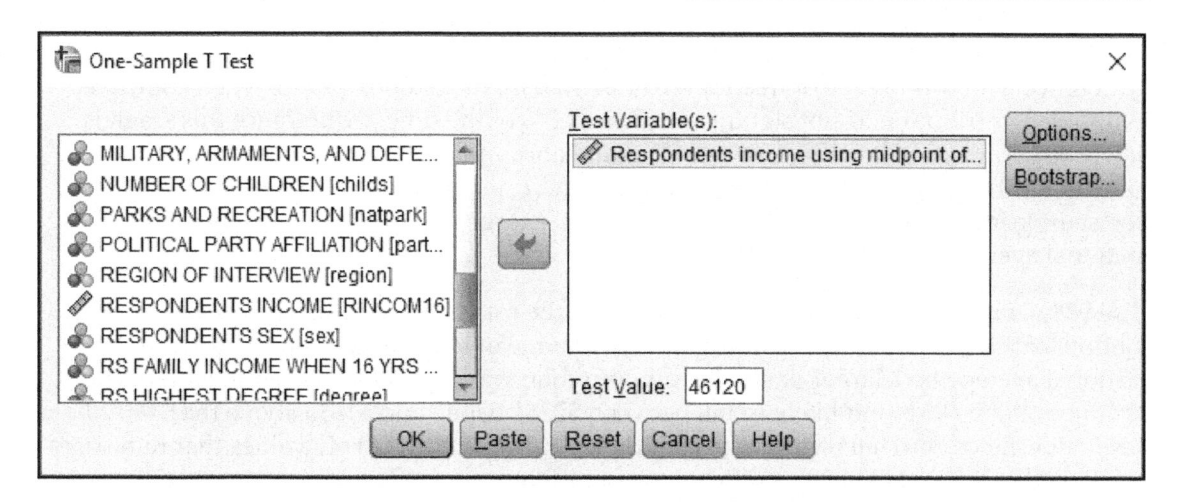

Comparing Means and ANOVA

[SPSS One-Sample T Test dialog box with Test Variable "Respondents income using midpoint of..." and Test Value: 46120]

The SPSS syntax for this same t-test is shown as follows:

```
T-TEST
 /TESTVAL=46120
 /MISSING=ANALYSIS
 /VARIABLES=RINCOME_MIDPT
 /CRITERIA=CI(.95).
```

The mean of the GSS sample is based on **1632** since this question is only asked of individuals that had income the previous year (2015). For the sample, the mean is slightly lower than the Census Bureau value, but the standard deviation is large at $42,187 (as shown in the following figure), which reflects the sizable variability in income among these individuals:

One-Sample Statistics

	N	Mean	Std. Deviation	Std. Error Mean
Respondents income using midpoint of selected category	1632	45886.7953	42187.15435	1044.28768

Comparing Means and ANOVA

The following figure shows the t-test results associated with the small (-233.2) mean difference with this degree of freedom (N-1 or 1631). The t-value of -.223, when compared with the t-distribution, is not significant since 82.3% of the time, a difference this small is likely to occur by chance. The two-tailed significance **Means** that a difference in either direction is being considered. This makes sense here, given that the interest is in whether the sample is representative of the population, so a large deviation above or below the national average would be important.

The 95% confidence interval provides a sense of the range of the mean difference. Another sample of this size would almost certainly yield a mean income value that differs from the national average by a larger or smaller amount than was found here. The range indicates that it would be 95% and likely to fall between $2281 below and $1815 above the $46,120 test value. Since zero falls within the confidence, it is one of the likely values that reinforces the idea that it is not likely a significant mean difference occuring:

One-Sample Test

Test Value = 46120

	t	df	Sig. (2-tailed)	Mean Difference	95% Confidence Interval of the Difference Lower	Upper
Respondents income using midpoint of selected category	-.223	1631	.823	-233.20466	-2281.4909	1815.0816

The confidence interval can be adjusted in the Options dialog. Using a more stringent setting, such as 99%, will result in a wider range. In the following figure, the 99% confidence interval range shown is almost $1300 wider than the 95% range shown in the preceding figure. To increase the level of confidence in the estimate, the band must be larger. Confidence intervals for estimates are provided in many places in SPSS, and this principle applies throughout:

One-Sample Test

Test Value = 46120

	t	df	Sig. (2-tailed)	Mean Difference	99% Confidence Interval of the Difference Lower	Upper
Respondents income using midpoint of selected category	-.223	1631	.823	-233.20466	-2926.2628	2459.8535

The independent samples t-test

Perhaps, the most common use of the t-test is to compare the Means of a measure for two groups, such as the difference between the income of males and females, or the difference in age between the supporters of two political candidates. Problems of this type fall into the category of the Independent Samples t-test, since all the observations can be put into two separate groups.

The independent samples t-test dialog shown in the following figure, specifies a comparison of males and females using the income measure in the previous examples. Groups are defined using the **Define Groups** dialog. For gender, the values are one for males and two for females, so these are the codes used to define the two groups:

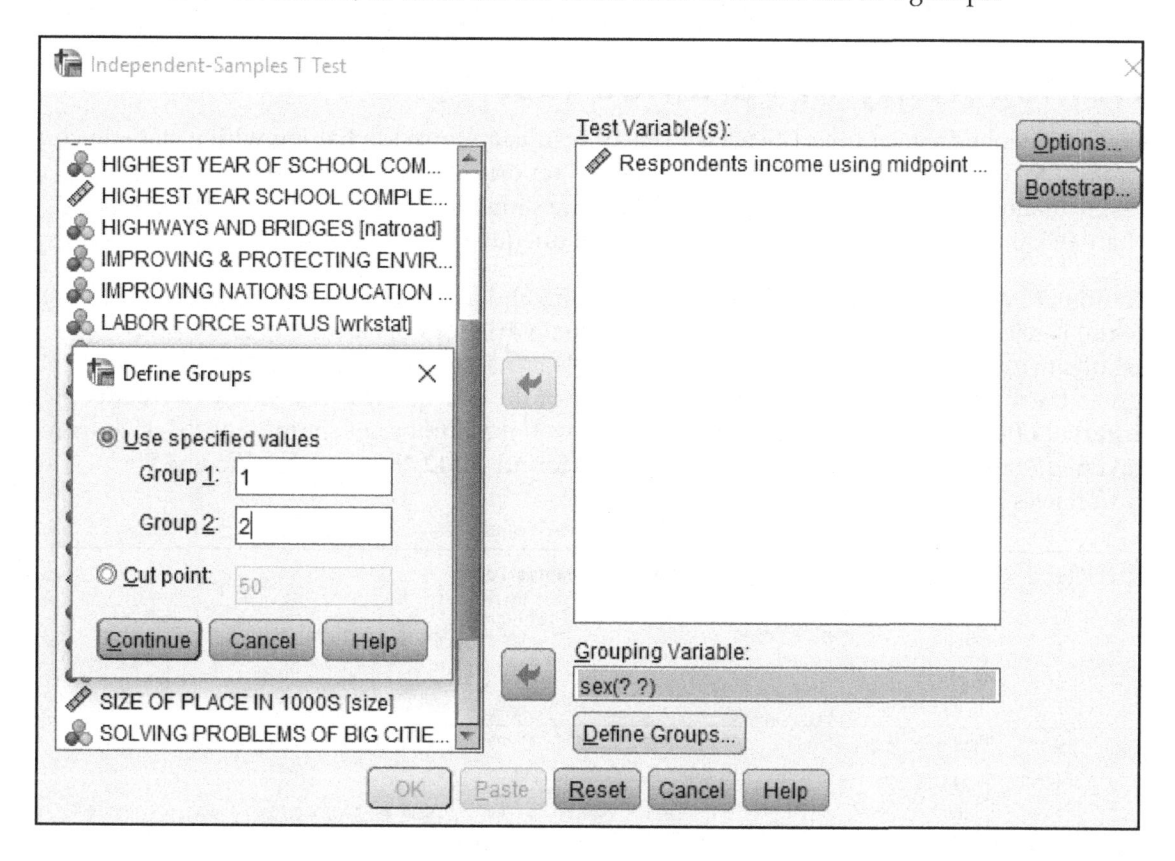

The statistics for the two groups (refer to the following figure) are close in size but have a large ($16,528) mean difference. Another important factor here is the large ($10,630) difference in the standard deviation for males and females with respect to income:

Group Statistics

	RESPONDENTS SEX	N	Mean	Std. Deviation	Std. Error Mean
Respondents income using midpoint of selected category	MALE	798	54333.33	46472.12	1645.10
	FEMALE	834	37804.86	35842.25	1241.12

Homogeneity of variance test

For an independent samples t-test, two sets of results are provided along with a statistic you can use to determine which set is appropriate to report. The null hypothesis for Levene's test is that the variances of the two groups are the same. If the F statistic is significant (less than .05), the null hypothesis is rejected and the unequal variances results should be used.

In this example, the F statistic is highly significant, and the hypothesis that the variances are equal is rejected. Therefore, the second row (equal variance not assumed) contains the results to evaluate and report. The t of 8.021 is clearly significant, which is not surprising, given the magnitude of the difference in income of the two groups. The **95% Confidence Interval of the Difference** values indicate that even if a number of samples of this size were taken, the smallest difference that is likely to be found is **$12,486,** and that income differences as high as **$20,570** may be observed:

Independent Samples Test

		Levene's Test for Equality of Variances		t-test for Equality of Means					95% Confidence Interval of the Difference	
		F	Sig.	t	df	Sig. (2-tailed)	Mean Difference	Std. Error Difference	Lower	Upper
Respondents income using midpoint of selected category	Equal variances assumed	42.757	.000	8.066	1630	.000	16528.48	2049.23	12509.07	20547.88
	Equal variances not assumed			8.021	1498.11	.000	16528.48	2060.75	12486.21	20570.75

Comparing subsets

While t-tests are generally used with variables that take on only two values, you can choose to compare just a pair of groups out of a larger set. The two values specified in the **Define Groups** dialog can be used to identify the groups you want to compare, leaving cases with other values out of the analysis.

In the example shown in the following figure, the income of married individuals is compared with that of individuals who have never been married. You can right-click on the variable name to see what the values for the field are, as shown here:

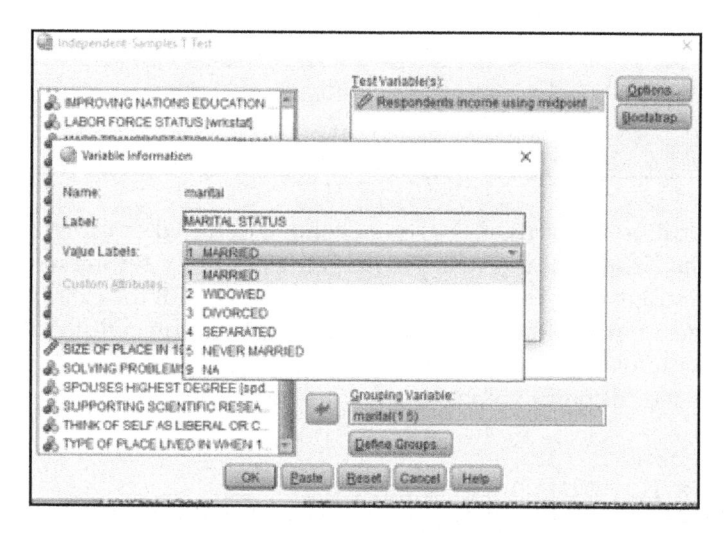

The summary statistics (as shown in the following figure) reflect the fact that only two of the marital status categories are being compared. As with the previous example, the mean difference is considerable (almost $26,500), and the standard deviations differs as well:

Group Statistics

	MARITAL STATUS	N	Mean	Std. Deviation	Std. Error Mean
Respondents income using midpoint of selected category	MARRIED	749	57722.6302	48837.46526	1784.48214
	NEVER MARRIED	495	31236.3636	27674.62391	1243.88184

Comparing Means and ANOVA

Since the F statistic for the Levene's test is significant, the *Equal variances not assumed* statistic in the following figure is used for the evaluation. Given the significance of the t statistic, this supports the conclusion that the difference in income for married and single individuals is real, and likely to be found in any sample of US adults:

Independent Samples Test

		Levene's Test for Equality of Variances		t-test for Equality of Means						
		F	Sig.	t	df	Sig. (2-tailed)	Mean Difference	Std. Error Difference	95% Confidence Interval of the Difference	
									Lower	Upper
Respondents income using midpoint of selected category	Equal variances assumed	84.72	.00	11.0	1242.0	.00	26486.27	2416.98	21744.44	31228.09
	Equal variances not assumed			12.2	1216.6	.00	26486.27	2175.23	22218.65	30753.88

> **TIP**
> In addition to comparing groups using a nominal or categorical field, the Define Groups dialog also provides the option of setting a cut point on a continuous field to create two groups. You could, for example, compare the mean income of individuals aged 40 and above with that of individuals under 40 years of age, using age as the grouping variable and 40 as the cut point value.

Paired t-test

Another use of the T Test is performing comparisons of two Means from a single sample. These paired T Tests are useful for situations in which the cases have attributes you wish to compare, such as blood pressure before and after participating in an exercise program.

The example shown in the following figure compares the highest year of schooling completed for the respondents and their spouses. Only those individuals with a value on both fields will be part of the analysis:

Comparing Means and ANOVA

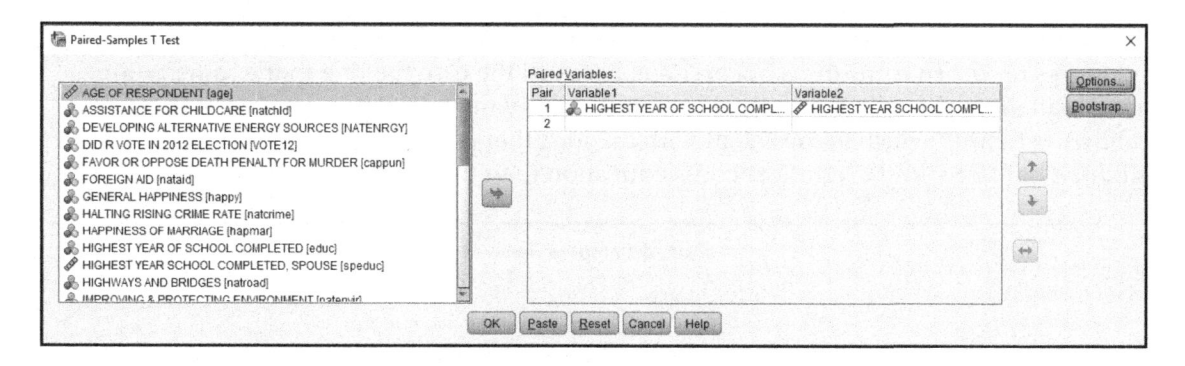

The `Paired Samples Statistics` table provided has the same N (1194) for each field, which reinforces the fact that only cases with both members of the pair are part of the t-test. There is a small difference (.27) in the mean years of schooling, but it may still be significant:

Paired Samples Statistics

		Mean	N	Std. Deviation	Std. Error Mean
Pair 1	HIGHEST YEAR OF SCHOOL COMPLETED	14.16	1194	3.028	.088
	HIGHEST YEAR SCHOOL COMPLETED, SPOUSE	13.89	1194	2.946	.085

Since both fields are at interval level, a correlation can be calculated. This is reported in the following table (shown in the following figure) as .552, with a significance level of at least .000. A correlation of this magnitude is consistent with a strong linear relationship, but a significant difference in the Means is still to be determined:

Paired Samples Correlations

		N	Correlation	Sig.
Pair 1	HIGHEST YEAR OF SCHOOL COMPLETED & HIGHEST YEAR SCHOOL COMPLETED, SPOUSE	1194	.552	.000

Comparing Means and ANOVA

For paired sample T Tests, only one set of results is provided, since the question of equal variances for the two groups is not an issue here--all the cases belong to the same group. The small mean difference does yield a significant T value of 3.306 (as shown in the following figure), which is consistent with the idea that people marry individuals with slightly, but statistically significant, less education than themselves:

Paired Samples Test

		Paired Differences						
					95% Confidence Interval of the Difference			
	Mean	Std. Deviation	Std. Error Mean	Lower	Upper	t	df	Sig. (2-tailed)
Pair 1 HIGHEST YEAR OF SCHOOL COMPLETED - HIGHEST YEAR SCHOOL COMPLETED, SPOUSE	.271	2.827	.082	.110	.431	3.306	1193	.001

Paired t-test split by gender

An interesting point to consider when interpreting the results from the paired t-test is gender. Respondents are both male and female, so the spouse's education is contextual. If one wants to know whether men marry women less or more educated than themselves, the preceding results are not sufficiently detailed enough to provide the answer.

SPSS provides a variety of methods to select subsets of a dataset for analysis (Chapter 6, *Sampling, Subsetting and Weighting*, describes these capabilities). One approach is to use the **SPLIT FILE** feature on the **Data** menu to identify the grouping field and decide how it is to be used. To obtain the information needed to compare males and females, with respect to the educational level of their spouses, use the specifications shown in the following figure:

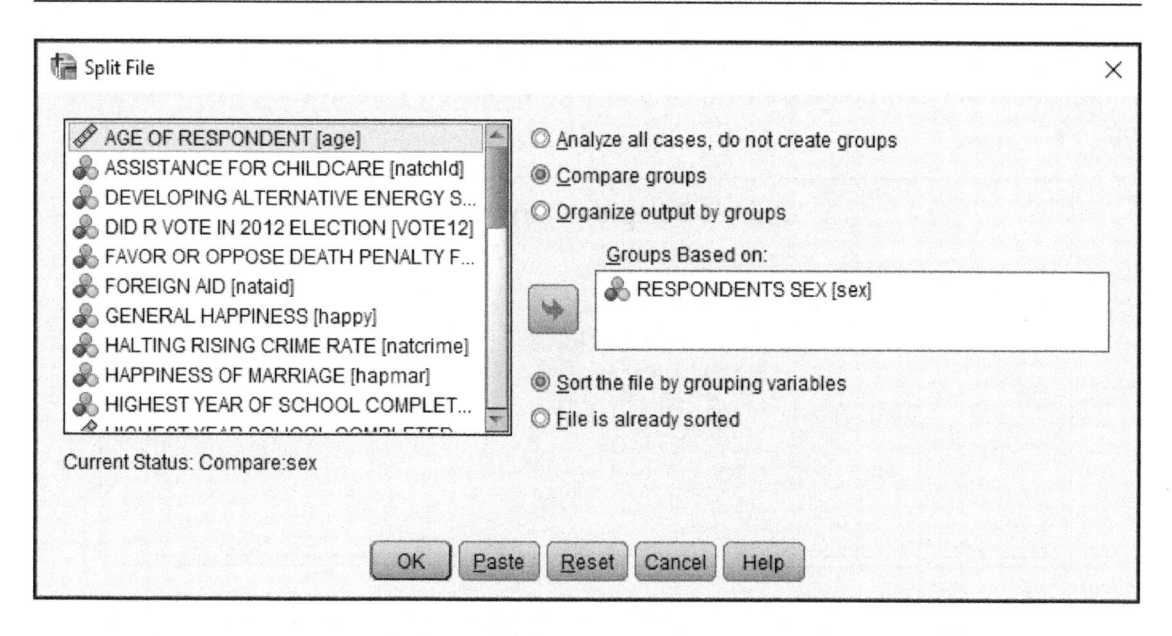

The paired t-test can be run again with the same settings to produce separate results for each group. As the Means in the following figure show, for men, the difference between their years of schooling and their spouse's is very small (14.09 versus 14.00), whereas for women, the difference is much larger 14.23 versus 13.79):

Paired Samples Statistics

RESPONDENTS SEX			Mean	N	Std. Deviation	Std. Error Mean
1 MALE	Pair 1	HIGHEST YEAR OF SCHOOL COMPLETED	14.09	558	3.098	.131
		HIGHEST YEAR SCHOOL COMPLETED, SPOUSE	14.00	558	2.856	.121
2 FEMALE	Pair 1	HIGHEST YEAR OF SCHOOL COMPLETED	14.23	636	2.967	.118
		HIGHEST YEAR SCHOOL COMPLETED, SPOUSE	13.79	636	3.022	.120

Comparing Means and ANOVA

The correlation between the educational attainment of individuals and that of their spouses is high for both males and females at .57 and .54 respectively (as shown in the following figure):

Paired Samples Correlations

RESPONDENTS SEX			N	Correlation	Sig.
1 MALE	Pair 1	HIGHEST YEAR OF SCHOOL COMPLETED & HIGHEST YEAR SCHOOL COMPLETED, SPOUSE	558	.571	.000
2 FEMALE	Pair 1	HIGHEST YEAR OF SCHOOL COMPLETED & HIGHEST YEAR SCHOOL COMPLETED, SPOUSE	636	.540	.000

The main value of splitting the file by gender and requesting that results be compared is seen in the following figure. For male respondents, there is no significant difference between the years of their education and those of their spouse. The t of .704 is not significant, and this is underscored by the fact that zero is within the confidence interval range, indicating that it is a potential value for the mean difference.

Female respondents, on the other hand, have significantly more education than their spouses. The t of 3.836 is highly significant, and the lower bound of the confidence interval is .212. This illustrates the benefits of combining the data handling capabilities of SPSS with the statistical capabilities of obtaining the results needed:

Paired Samples Test

Gender			Mean	Std. Deviation	Std. Error Mean	95% Confidence Interval of the Difference Lower	95% Confidence Interval of the Difference Upper	t	df	Sig. (2-tailed)
1 MALE	Pair 1	HIGHEST YEAR OF SCHOOL COMPLETED - HIGHEST YEAR SCHOOL COMPLETED, SPOUSE	.082	2.767	.117	-.148	.313	.704	557	.482
2 FEMALE	Pair 1	HIGHEST YEAR OF SCHOOL COMPLETED - HIGHEST YEAR SCHOOL COMPLETED, SPOUSE	.436	2.871	.114	.212	.659	3.826	635	.000

One-way analysis of variance

For a deeper investigation into mean differences involving a single independent factor, the one-way ANOVA procedure provides the broadest set of options. It is meant especially for comparisons involving more than two groups. While the **Means** procedure can identify whether there is a significant difference across a set of groups, identifying which groups differ significantly requires the use of one-way ANOVA.

To see the added information provided by one-way, we will repeat the comparison done at the beginning of the chapter. In the **One-Way ANOVA** dialog box, set education as the dependent variable and region as the factor. Use the Options dialog to select the options, as shown in the following figure:

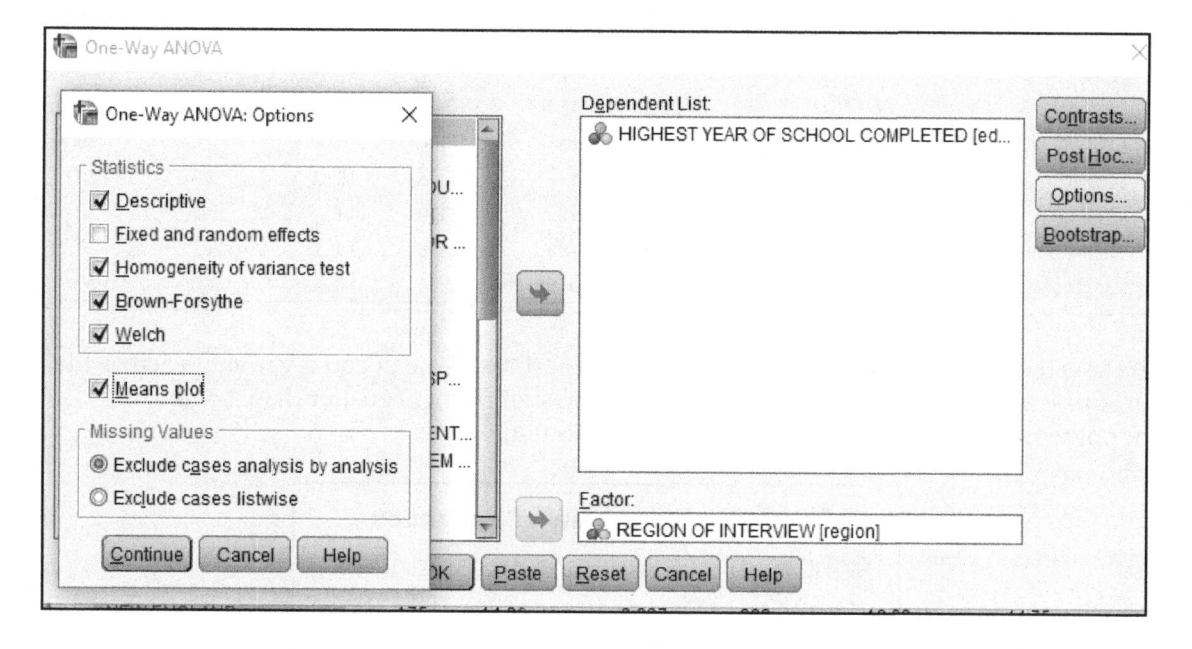

Comparing Means and ANOVA

The descriptive statistics provided (as shown in the following figure) include some of the same information as in the initial example at the beginning of the chapter, but with additional details, such as the confidence interval for each mean:

Descriptives

HIGHEST YEAR OF SCHOOL COMPLETED

	N	Mean	Std. Deviation	Std. Error	95% Confidence Interval for Mean Lower Bound	95% Confidence Interval for Mean Upper Bound	Minimum	Maximum
NEW ENGLAND	175	14.29	3.087	.233	13.83	14.75	0	20
MIDDLE ATLANTIC	311	14.01	2.889	.164	13.69	14.34	3	20
E. NOR. CENTRAL	499	13.85	2.836	.127	13.60	14.10	1	20
W. NOR. CENTRAL	193	13.25	2.695	.194	12.87	13.64	6	20
SOUTH ATLANTIC	548	13.83	2.756	.118	13.60	14.06	5	20
E. SOU. CENTRAL	205	13.43	2.827	.197	13.04	13.82	6	20
W. SOU. CENTRAL	297	12.91	3.054	.177	12.56	13.25	0	20
MOUNTAIN	235	13.92	3.023	.197	13.53	14.31	2	20
PACIFIC	395	13.91	3.337	.168	13.58	14.24	1	20
Total	2858	13.74	2.964	.055	13.63	13.85	0	20

As was the case with the independent samples t-test, the issue of equal variances across the groups is evaluated using Levene's test. Since the significant is greater than .05, the null hypothesis that the variances are equal is not rejected:

Test of Homogeneity of Variances

HIGHEST YEAR OF SCHOOL COMPLETED

Levene Statistic	df1	df2	Sig.
1.520	8	2849	.145

The **ANOVA** table produced by one-way is the same as in the first example (as would be expected):

[258]

ANOVA

HIGHEST YEAR OF SCHOOL COMPLETED

	Sum of Squares	df	Mean Square	F	Sig.
Between Groups	378.398	8	47.300	5.451	.000
Within Groups	24719.261	2849	8.676		
Total	25097.659	2857			

Brown-Forsythe and Welch statistics

Two additional statistics that can be used to test for a significant difference across the Means, when the equal variances test results in the rejection of the null hypothesis, are shown in the following figure:

Robust Tests of Equality of Means

HIGHEST YEAR OF SCHOOL COMPLETED

	Statistic[a]	df1	df2	Sig.
Welch	5.288	8	981.284	.000
Brown-Forsythe	5.429	8	2341.135	.000

a. Asymptotically F distributed.

To check out the meaning of these statistics, you can use the *What's This* help feature in the output to obtain information. If the equal variances assumption is not met, the Welch and Brown-Forsythe tests can be used instead of the ANOVA test, which relies on the F statistic to determine whether the Means are significantly different. This context-sensitive help makes this information available as you are reviewing the output, which is very convenient:

Dependent Variables HIGHEST YEAR OF SCHOOL COMPLETED

	Statistic[a]	df1	df2	Sig.
Welch	5.288	8	981.284	.000
		8	2341.135	.000

The Welch statistic tests for the equality of group means. This statistic is preferable to the F statistic when the assumption of equal variances does not hold.

Comparing Means and ANOVA

The optional Means plot available in one-way can be edited like other graphs to make it suitable for inclusion in a report. In the following figure, the overall mean was added as a reference line, so the regions that deviate the most (New England and West South Central in this example) stand out:

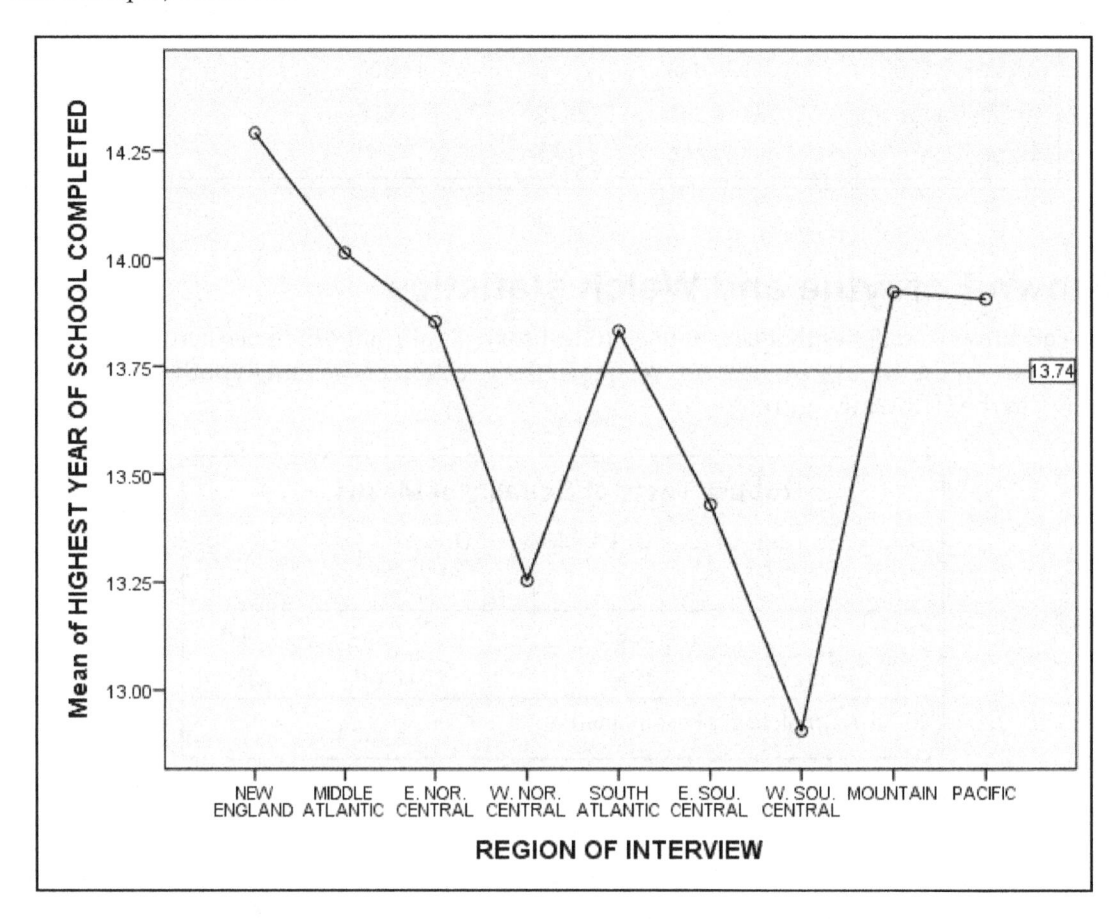

Planned comparisons

Both the Means procedure and one-way confirmed that there is a significant difference in education across the nine US regions. Often, however, there is a need to test whether two specific group's, out of the set of group's, differ significantly. Contrasts can be used to perform this test.

Comparing Means and ANOVA

The **Contrast** dialog (refer to the following figure) can be used to define a variety of contrasts to test for the Means, including polynomial and linear. Here, a simple contrast is defined by associating a contrast value with each of the six values of the RES16 field. Setting the values at one through four to zero indicates they are not part of this comparison. The fifth value, big-city suburb, is set to **1**, and the sixth value, big city, is set to **-1**, which indicates that these two groups are to be compared. A coefficient needs to be provided for each value of the factor in ascending order, and altogether, they must sum to zero. The coefficient total at the bottom of the dialog keeps track of the total as you add coefficients:

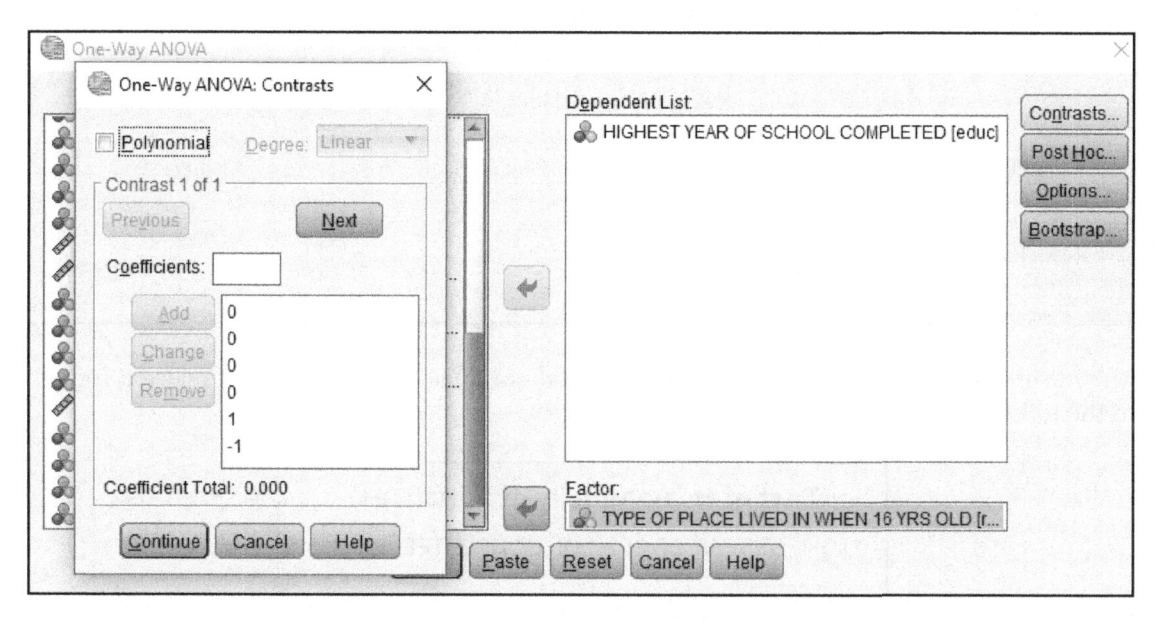

> If the objective was to compare two groups together with a third group, a contrast sequence, such as *(0,0,.5,.5,0,-1)*, could be used. This would result in groups three and four taken together, being compared with group six.

The Descriptives output (as shown in the following figure) shows both the Fixed and Random effects results. This is another example of how you can use context-sensitive help to provide more detail on a row or column in a table. According to, where someone lived at age 16, the independent factor is made up of six groups, but one can imagine other possibilities in terms of how many categories could be used to classify towns and cities by size. For this reason, it makes sense to think of the RES16 field as a random effect, since it can be thought of as representing a sample of the potential values:

[261]

Comparing Means and ANOVA

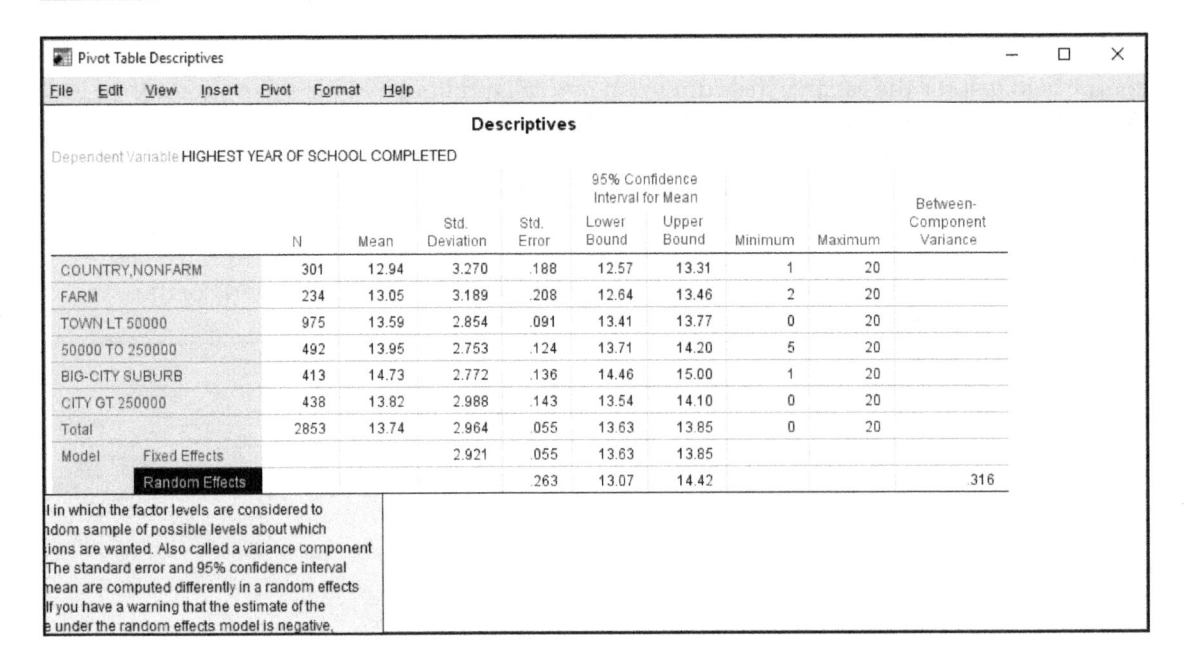

	Pivot Table Descriptives									
File Edit View Insert Pivot Format Help										

Descriptives

Dependent Variable HIGHEST YEAR OF SCHOOL COMPLETED

	N	Mean	Std. Deviation	Std. Error	95% Confidence Interval for Mean Lower Bound	95% Confidence Interval for Mean Upper Bound	Minimum	Maximum	Between-Component Variance
COUNTRY,NONFARM	301	12.94	3.270	.188	12.57	13.31	1	20	
FARM	234	13.05	3.189	.208	12.64	13.46	2	20	
TOWN LT 50000	975	13.59	2.854	.091	13.41	13.77	0	20	
50000 TO 250000	492	13.95	2.753	.124	13.71	14.20	5	20	
BIG-CITY SUBURB	413	14.73	2.772	.136	14.46	15.00	1	20	
CITY GT 250000	438	13.82	2.988	.143	13.54	14.10	0	20	
Total	2853	13.74	2.964	.055	13.63	13.85	0	20	
Model Fixed Effects			2.921	.055	13.63	13.85			
Random Effects				.263	13.07	14.42			.316

l in which the factor levels are considered to
ndom sample of possible levels about which
ions are wanted. Also called a variance component
The standard error and 95% confidence interval
mean are computed differently in a random effects
If you have a warning that the estimate of the
e under the random effects model is negative.

The Levene statistic is not significant, so the equal variance hypothesis is not rejected (refer to the following figure):

Test of Homogeneity of Variances

HIGHEST YEAR OF SCHOOL COMPLETED

Levene Statistic	df1	df2	Sig.
1.666	5	2847	.139

The **ANOVA** table in the following figure confirms that there is a significant mean difference across the six groups, and the F is meaningful, given that the equal variances test was met:

Comparing Means and ANOVA

ANOVA

HIGHEST YEAR OF SCHOOL COMPLETED

	Sum of Squares	df	Mean Square	F	Sig.
Between Groups	755.472	5	151.094	17.703	.000
Within Groups	24298.590	2847	8.535		
Total	25054.062	2852			

The contrast requested is described in the Contrast Coefficients table (refer to the following figure). Only one contrast test was asked for, but a set of separate contrasts can be done on a single one-way run:

Contrast Coefficients

TYPE OF PLACE LIVED IN WHEN 16 YRS OLD

Contrast	COUNTRY, NONFARM	FARM	TOWN LT 50000	50000 TO 250000	BIG-CITY SUBURB	CITY GT 250000
1	0	0	0	0	1	-1

Since it has already been established that the variances are equal based on the Levene's test results, the first row in the Contrast-tests table (refer to the following figure) can be used. The **t statistic** is highly significant, so the mean difference in education between big-city suburbs and big cities is likely to be present in any national sample:

Contrast Tests

		Contrast	Value of Contrast	Std. Error	t	df	Sig. (2-tailed)
HIGHEST YEAR OF SCHOOL COMPLETED	Assume equal variances	1	.91	.200	4.549	2847	.000
	Does not assume equal variances	1	.91	.197	4.617	848.78	.000

Comparing Means and ANOVA

The mean plot in the following figure depicts the difference between these two groups, as well as the fact that individuals that grew up in a big-city suburb have the highest level of education:

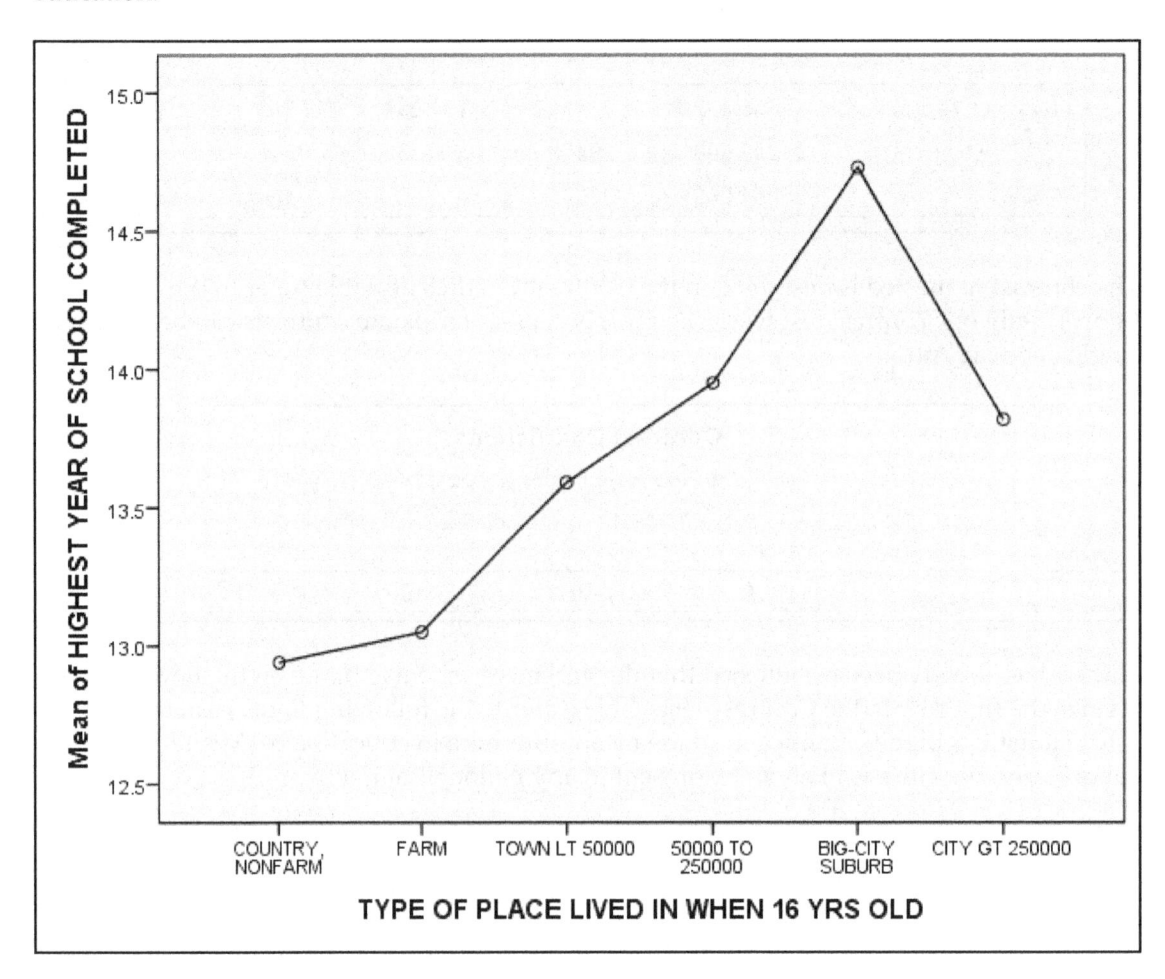

Post hoc comparisons

One of the features that makes one-way ANOVA a valuable procedure is the option to include post hoc multiple comparisons using a variety of statistical tests. These multiple comparisons make it possible to find the groups that differ from each other, and those that form homogenous subsets within a larger pool of groups.

Comparing Means and ANOVA

The post hoc dialog shown in the following figure has 14 choices associated with equal variances, and four for unequal variances. You can choose several and compare the results to check their agreement in terms of the differences they find significant. In this example, the **Scheffe**, **Tukey**, **Dunnett**, and **Tamhane's T2** tests are selected. By default, the Dunnett-test uses the **last** group of the independent factor as the control category, but you can change this using the dropdown:

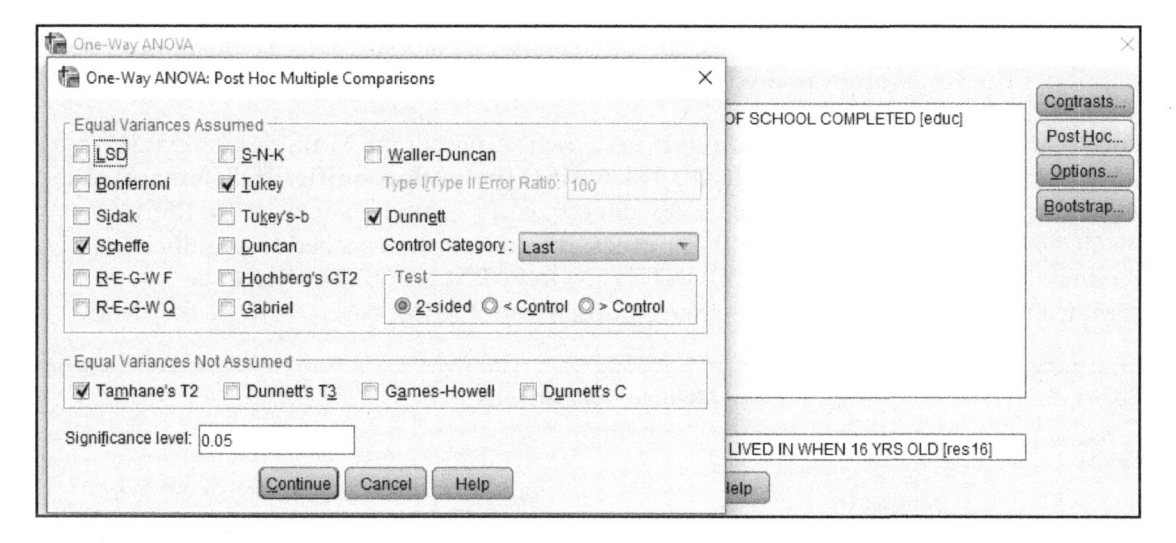

The **Help** option for one-way ANOVA is a quick way to get more details on the various tests. The following is the information for the four used in this example:

- **Scheffe**: This performs simultaneous joint pairwise comparisons for all possible pairwise combinations of Means. It uses the F sampling distribution and can be used to examine all possible linear combinations of group Means, not just pairwise comparisons.
- **Tukey**: This uses the studentized range statistic to make all of the pairwise comparisons between groups. It sets the experiment-wise error rate at the error rate for the collection for all pairwise comparisons.

Comparing Means and ANOVA

- **Dunnett**: This is a pairwise multiple comparison t-test that compares a set of treatments against a single control mean. The last category is the default control category but you can set the first category as the control if so desired. **2-sided** tests that the mean at any level (except the control category) of the factor is not equal to that of the control category. **< Control** tests if the mean at any level of the factor is smaller than that of the control category. **> Control** tests if the mean at any level of the factor is greater than that of the control category.
- **Tamhane's T2**: This is a conservative pairwise comparisons test based on a t-test. This test is appropriate when the variances are unequal.

Each of the statistical tests selected produces S own section in the Multiple Comparisons table. The first portion of the results for Tukey **HSD (honestly significant difference)** test is shown in the following figure. For the six categories of the independent factor, RES16, a mean comparison is performed with the other five groups and checked for significance. In the first portion of this table, the **COUNTRY, NONFARM** group is shown to be significantly different from all the other groups, except **FARM**, based on the Tukey test:

Multiple Comparisons

Dependent Variable: HIGHEST YEAR OF SCHOOL COMPLETED

	(I) TYPE OF PLACE LIVED IN WHEN 16 YRS OLD	(J) TYPE OF PLACE LIVED IN WHEN 16 YRS OLD	Mean Difference (I-J)	Std. Error	Sig.	95% Confidence Interval Lower Bound	95% Confidence Interval Upper Bound
Tukey HSD	COUNTRY, NONFARM	FARM	-.111	.255	.998	-.84	.61
		TOWN LT 50000	-.652*	.193	.009	-1.20	-.10
		50000 TO 250000	-1.011*	.214	.000	-1.62	-.40
		BIG-CITY SUBURB	-1.791*	.221	.000	-2.42	-1.16
		CITY GT 250000	-.879*	.219	.001	-1.50	-.26
	FARM	COUNTRY, NONFARM	.111	.255	.998	-.61	.84
		TOWN LT 50000	-.541	.213	.113	-1.15	.07
		50000 TO 250000	-.900*	.232	.001	-1.56	-.24
		BIG-CITY SUBURB	-1.680*	.239	.000	-2.36	-1.00
		CITY GT 250000	-.768*	.237	.015	-1.44	-.09
	TOWN LT 50000	COUNTRY, NONFARM	.652*	.193	.009	.10	1.20
		FARM	.541	.213	.113	-.07	1.15
		50000 TO 250000	-.359	.162	.227	-.82	.10
		BIG-CITY SUBURB	-1.139*	.172	.000	-1.63	-.65
		CITY GT 250000	-.228	.168	.753	-.71	.25

Comparing Means and ANOVA

The Dunnett-test (as shown in the following figure) results in the table using the last category, cities larger than 250,000, as the reference group, which is tested for the significance of the mean difference. Here, three of the groups--**COUNTRY/NONFARM**, **FARM**, and **BIG-CITY SUBURB**--differ significantly based on this test:

Dunnett t (2-sided)[b]							
	COUNTRY, NONFARM	CITY GT 250000	-.879*	.219	.000	-1.43	-.33
	FARM	CITY GT 250000	-.768*	.237	.005	-1.36	-.17
	TOWN LT 50000	CITY GT 250000	-.228	.168	.522	-.65	.19
	50000 TO 250000	CITY GT 250000	.132	.192	.939	-.35	.61
	BIG-CITY SUBURB	CITY GT 250000	.912*	.200	.000	.41	1.42

*. The mean difference is significant at the 0.05 level.
b. Dunnett t-tests treat one group as a control, and compare all other groups against it.

Homogenous subsets are calculated for the ten multiple comparison tests checked in the following figure. The other tests produce only multiple comparison results, such as the output shown in the previous two figures:

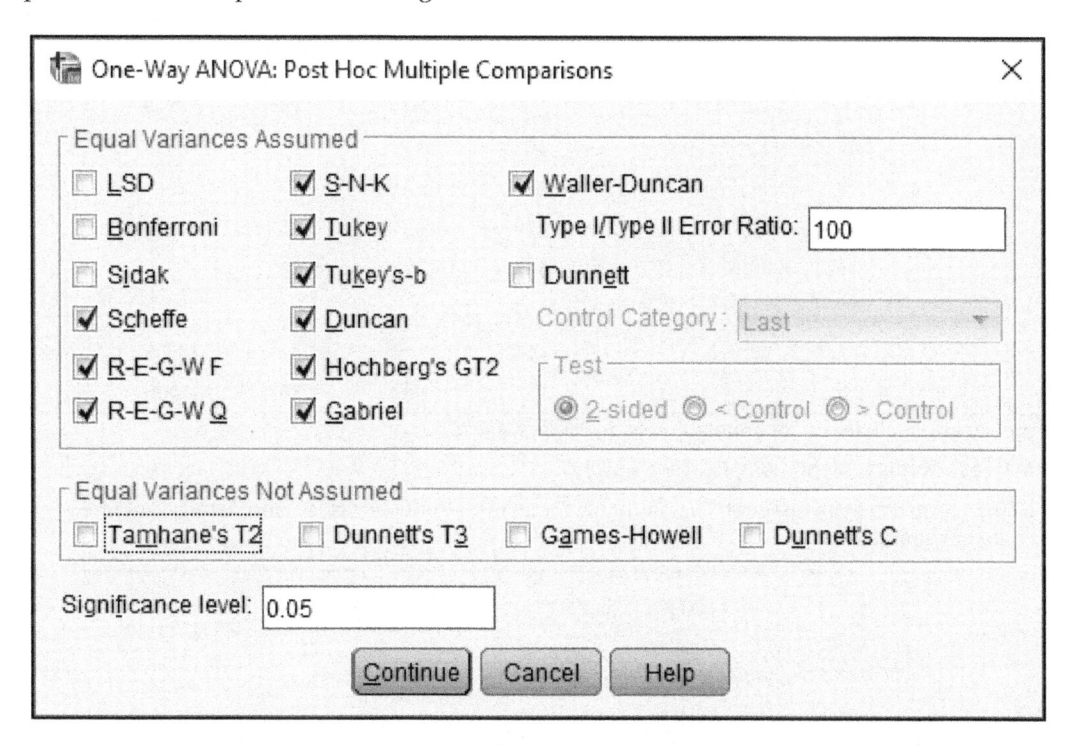

[267]

Comparing Means and ANOVA

The homogenous subsets results (see the following figure) separate the categories of the independent factors into subsets of groups that do not differ significantly from one another. In this example, the Tukey test identified four subsets, and Scheffe found three homogenous subsets. Both tests isolated big-city suburbs in its own subset and put towns less than 50,000, cities 50,000 to 250,000, and cities larger than 250,000 together in a subset, based on their similarities in education level.

These subsets can be very useful in terms of deciding how data can be grouped without masking important differences to outcome measures of interest, such as education in this instance:

HIGHEST YEAR OF SCHOOL COMPLETED

	TYPE OF PLACE LIVED IN WHEN 16 YRS OLD	N	Subset for alpha = 0.05 1	2	3	4
Tukey HSD[a,b]	COUNTRY,NONFARM	301	12.94			
	FARM	234	13.05	13.05		
	TOWN LT 50000	975		13.59	13.59	
	CITY GT 250000	438			13.82	
	50000 TO 250000	492			13.95	
	BIG-CITY SUBURB	413				14.73
	Sig.		.995	.101	.519	1.000
Scheffe[a,b]	COUNTRY,NONFARM	301	12.94			
	FARM	234	13.05			
	TOWN LT 50000	975	13.59	13.59		
	CITY GT 250000	438		13.82		
	50000 TO 250000	492		13.95		
	BIG-CITY SUBURB	413			14.73	
	Sig.		.084	.707	1.000	

Means for groups in homogeneous subsets are displayed.

a. Uses Harmonic Mean Sample Size = 390.667.

b. The group sizes are unequal. The harmonic mean of the group sizes is used. Type I error levels are not guaranteed.

The ANOVA procedure

One-way is a good place to start when it comes to comparing Means for a situation in which a single independent factor is being considered. For more complex mean comparisons involving a single dependent measure, but multiple factors and, potentially, covariates, the SPSS ANOVA procedure is the appropriate choice. Interaction terms among multiple factors can be tested, as well, using this ANOVA. This procedure is accessible only through command syntax.

> **TIP**: A series of IF statements can be used to combine two fields, such as gender and work status, into a single variable, so that one-way is an available option.

The following syntax requests a two-way ANOVA for the income measure used previously, with work status and gender as predictors. The range of independent factors must be specified in parentheses after the variable name. By default, all interaction terms up to five-way interactions are tested:

```
ANOVA variables = rincome_midpt by wrkstat(1,8) sex(1,2).
```

The eight values of interest for the `wrkstat` field are shown in the following figure:

```
0 = "IAP"
1 = "WORKING FULLTIME"
2 = "WORKING PARTTIME"
3 = "TEMP NOT WORKING"
4 = "UNEMPL, LAID OFF"
5 = "RETIRED"
6 = "SCHOOL"
7 = "KEEPING HOUSE"
8 = "OTHER"
9 = "NA"
```

The ANOVA results in the following figure confirm that mean income differs significantly across the categories of both labor force status and gender. They also indicate that there is no significant interaction between labor force status and gender. Identifying significant interactions, or verifying that suspected interactions do not exist, is an important aspect of any analysis undertaking, and ANOVA can be used to obtain this information.

ANOVA[a,b]

			Sum of Squares	df	Unique Method Mean Square	F	Sig.
Respondents income using midpoint of selected category	Main Effects	(Combined)	318556314800	8	39819539350	26.06	.000
		LABOR FORCE STATUS	301926653600	7	43132379080	28.23	.000
		RESPONDENTS SEX	8406713328	1	8406713328	5.50	.019
	2-Way Interactions	LABOR FORCE STATUS * RESPONDENTS SEX	13446722520	7	1920960360	1.26	.268
	Model		433566980000	15	28904465330	18.92	.000
	Residual		2469215043000	1616	1527979606		
	Total		2902782023000	1631	1779755992		

a. Respondents income using midpoint of selected category by LABOR FORCE STATUS, RESPONDENTS SEX
b. All effects entered simultaneously

To control other influences on an outcome measure, such as income, covariates can be included in the ANOVA specification. If, for example, it was deemed important to control the impact of education on the income of an individual, this could be done by declaring education as a covariate. The following ANOVA syntax accomplishes this by adding `with educ` to the right:

```
ANOVA variables = rincome_midpt by wrkstat(1,8) sex(1,2) with educ.
```

The first row of the following figure shows that education is significantly related to income (F=206.23). In the Main Effects section, you can see that the F values for work status and gender have changed a little, with the control for educational attainment introduced, and the F for the model is much larger (32.80 versus 18.92). The interaction term remains insignificant, which is a useful finding to report:

ANOVA[a,b]

Respondents income using midpoint of selected category

			Sum of Squares	df	Unique Method Mean Square	F	Sig.
Covariates		HIGHEST YEAR OF SCHOOL COMPLETED	279749359200	1	279749359200	206.23	.000
Main Effects		(Combined)	255519377000	8	31939922130	23.55	.000
		LABOR FORCE STATUS	238658904700	7	34094129240	25.13	.000
		RESPONDENTS SEX	10501977920	1	10501977920	7.74	.005
2-Way Interactions		LABOR FORCE STATUS * RESPONDENTS SEX	14899170930	7	2128452991	1.57	.140
Model			711878158600	16	44492384910	32.80	.000
Residual			2189429415000	1614	1356523801		
Total			2901307573000	1630	1779943297		

a. Respondents income using midpoint of selected category by LABOR FORCE STATUS, RESPONDENTS SEX with HIGHEST YEAR OF SCHOOL COMPLETED

b. All effects entered simultaneously

This brief introduction to ANOVA provides a sense of when you may need to use it to meet analysis requirements. The Help system includes examples and detailed information on the syntax for ANOVA, so make use of it as you explore this very powerful tool in SPSS.

Summary

This chapter focused on the variety of methods available in SPSS Statistics to conduct comparisons of Means. The basic analysis of variance and tests of linearity included in the **Means** procedure was explored in some detail. Two group comparisons, using t-test in the single sample, independent sample, and paired sample situations, were examined as well. One-way ANOVA, with its multiple comparisons and homogenous subset capabilities, based on 14 possible test statistics, was covered in-depth. Finally, the syntax-only ANOVA procedure was introduced as a method of handling multiple independent factors, and for detecting significant interactions among these factors.

The next chapter will look at correlational analysis, which is appropriate for analyses where both the independent and dependent variables are interval-level measures. ANOVA statistics will be seen again when regression techniques are discussed in a later chapter.

12
Correlations

Correlations form the foundation for some of the core statistical methods relied upon for detecting patterns in data. The word correlation can refer to the general idea that two things are related, but from a statistical perspective the term has a very specific meaning. Most frequently, it is the Pearson product moment correlation that is being referenced when the term is used, but there are other types of correlations that serve different purposes. This chapter explores the various types of correlations and ways in which they can be produced within SPSS Statistics.

In the previous chapters, correlations have been among the optional statistics that can be requested. Crosstabs, for instance, has Pearson and Kendall's Tau-b correlations available under statistics. The paired t-test example in the previous chapter included the Pearson correlation as part of the standard output generated. Interval level data is required for correlations although binary variables can also be used. It is also important to be aware that the Pearson correlation captures the strength of the linear relationship between two data fields. This is typically the first pattern one examines, but nonlinear relationships may be of interest as well.

> **TIP**
> The examples used in this chapter make use of data available from the Population Reference Bureau on various characteristics of nations around the world. To download the source data in CSV format, go to `http://www.worldpopdata.org/table`, select Countries under Geography, and then select the individual fields shown as follows.

Correlations

Only three fields can be selected for each CSV download, so the files need to be merged together in SPSS as described in Chapter 8, *Adding and Matching files*. The fields have been renamed in Excel before merging to make them better suited for analysis purposes. The column names used in the individual Excel files prior to merging them in SPSS resulted in the variable names shown in the following table. These are the variables that will be used in the examples throughout this chapter. The field names listed below are the renamed versions of the original column headings in the downloaded files.

Variable Names
Nation
Population_mid2017
Births_per_1K
Deaths_per_1K
Infant_Mortality_Rate
Life_Expectancy_Males
Life_Expectancy_Females
GNI_per_Capita_PPP_2016
Percent_Urban
Pop_per_Square_Kilometer_Arable_Land_thousands
Pop_Ages_15_24_millions
Secondary_School_Enroll_Ratio_Males
Secondary_School_Enroll_Ratio_Females
Tertiary_Educ_Enroll_Ratio_Males
Tertiary_Educ_Enroll_Ratio_Females

> **TIP**: For a description of the data, you can download the associated report at the following link: http://www.prb.org/pdf17/2017_World_Population.pdf.

The topics covered in this chapter are as follows:

- Choosing among several correlation measures: Pearson, Spearman, Kendall's Tau-b
- Testing the hypothesis that the correlation coefficient is 0 in the population
- Pairwise versus listwise deletion of missing cases
- Pivoting-table editing of the table of correlations
- Visualizing correlations using scatterplots
- Partial correlations

Pearson correlations

Linear regression uses a correlation matrix as its starting point, as does factor analysis. Before employing these statistical techniques, it is important to examine the underlying correlation matrix to understand the bivariate patterns that will serve as the foundation for multivariate data modeling. The Pearson correlation is embedded into linear regression and factor, so it is appropriate to discuss correlations before moving on to these topics. One useful property of correlation coefficients is that they are bounded by -1 and 1, so it is easy to compare their strength across a set of fields that may have very different means.

Under the **Analyze** menu in SPSS Statistics, the **Correlate** choice includes four options shown in the following screenshot:

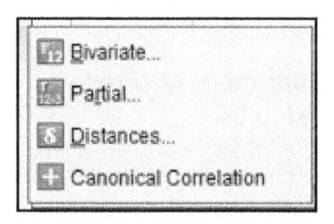

```
Bivariate...
Partial...
Distances...
Canonical Correlation
```

This chapter will cover the first two, **Bivariate...** and **Partial....** The **Distances...** and **Canonical Correlation** options are special topics that involve two different SPSS procedures. Distances are used with techniques such as clustering, while canonical correlation involves looking at links between two sets of variables. You can use the help for these two procedures to obtain more information on what they provide and when they may be appropriate methods to use.

Correlations

Bivariate is used to request a matrix of coefficients that capture the strength and direction of the relationship between each pair of fields. For the Pearson correlation, it is the linear relationship that is reflected in the coefficients. In the following screenshot, six variables have been selected, and the default settings of **Pearson** and **Two-tailed** significance have been left in place:

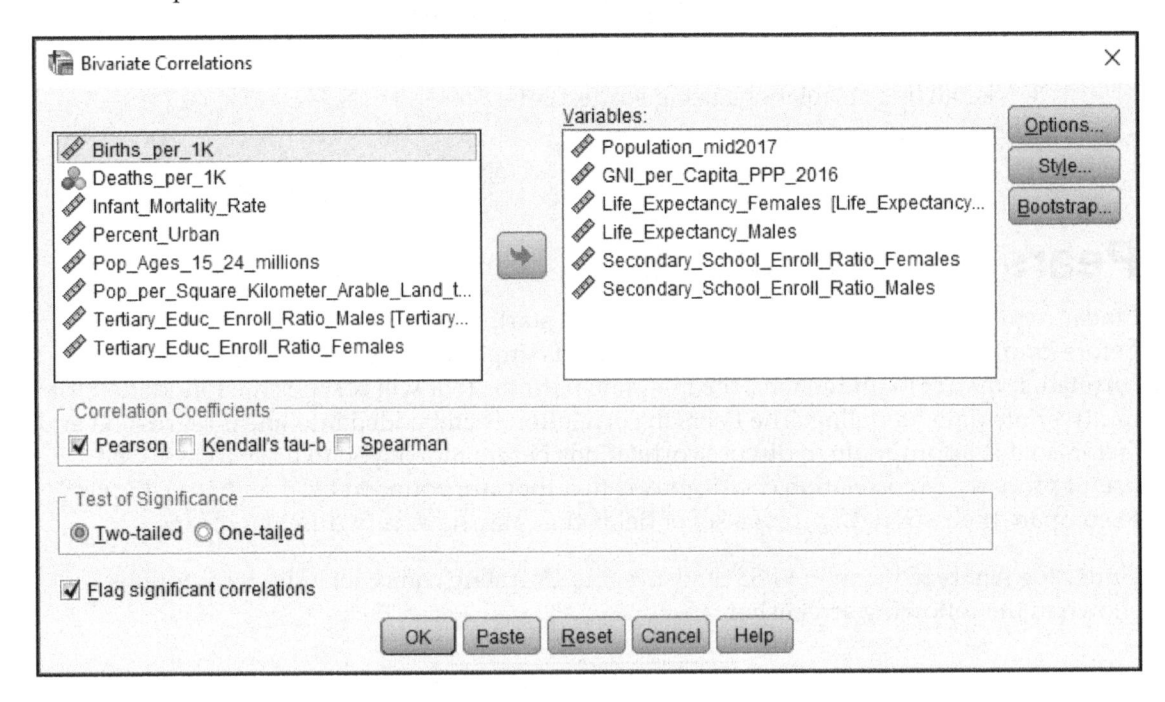

A **Two-tailed** test checks for a significant difference in either direction, positive or negative, and is generally the appropriate test to use.

The **Options** dialog shown in the following screenshot can be used to add descriptive statistics to the output produced:

Correlations

[Bivariate Correlations: Options dialog box with "Means and standard deviations" checked under Statistics, and "Exclude cases pairwise" selected under Missing Values.]

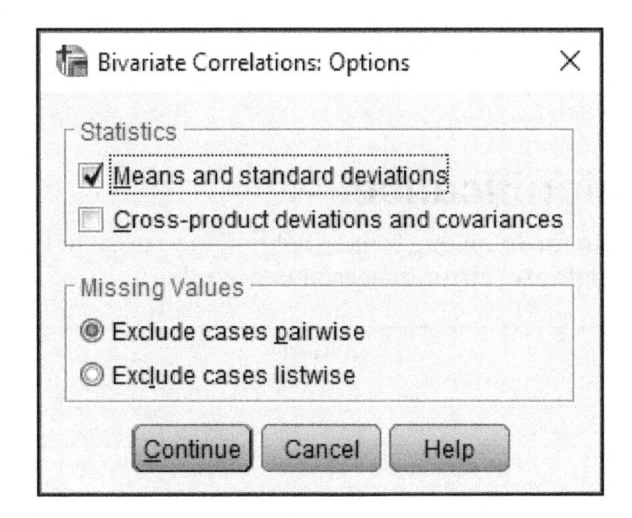

> Note that the missing values are handled in a pairwise fashion by default. Pairwise versus listwise handling of missing values will be discussed in more detail later in the chapter.

Basic descriptive statistics for the six variables provide a general context for this data. There are **201** nations in the dataset, but not all of them have information about all the fields. Population is in millions, and the average is **37.4** for the world, but the standard deviation indicates the wide variation that exists:

Descriptive Statistics	Mean	Std. Deviation	N
Population_mid2017	37.41	141.21	201
GNI_per_Capita_PPP_2016	17957.85	19801.66	191
Life_Expectancy_Females	74.31	8.21	199
Life_Expectancy_Males	69.52	7.62	199
Secondary_School_Enroll_Ratio_Females	83.57	30.64	172
Secondary_School_Enroll_Ratio_Males	83.44	27.66	172

Correlations

GNI_per_Capita_PPP_2016 is a means of comparing nations economically. It uses gross national income per capita adjusted for **purchasing power parity** (PPP).

Testing for significance

The correlation matrix in the following screenshot is symmetrical in the sense that the upper triangle and lower triangle are mirror images of one another:

Correlations

		Population_mid2017	GNI_per_Capita_PPP_2016	Life_Expectancy_Females	Life_Expectancy_Males	Secondary_School_Enroll_Ratio_Females	Secondary_School_Enroll_Ratio_Males
Population_mid2017	Correlation	1	-.030	-.010	.014	-.008	-.006
	Sig. (2-tailed)		.681	.890	.844	.920	.936
	N	201	191	199	199	172	172
GNI_per_Capita_PPP_2016	Correlation	-.030	1	.595**	.640**	.606**	.607**
	Sig. (2-tailed)	.681		.000	.000	.000	.000
	N	191	191	191	191	169	169
Life_Expectancy_Females	Correlation	-.010	.595**	1	.967**	.831**	.817**
	Sig. (2-tailed)	.890	.000		.000	.000	.000
	N	199	191	199	199	172	172
Life_Expectancy_Males	Correlation	.014	.640**	.967**	1	.794**	.785**
	Sig. (2-tailed)	.844	.000	.000		.000	.000
	N	199	191	199	199	172	172
Secondary_School_Enroll_Ratio_Females	Correlation	-.008	.606**	.831**	.794**	1	.965**
	Sig. (2-tailed)	.920	.000	.000	.000		.000
	N	172	169	172	172	172	172
Secondary_School_Enroll_Ratio_Males	Correlation	-.006	.607**	.817**	.785**	.965**	1
	Sig. (2-tailed)	.936	.000	.000	.000	.000	
	N	172	169	172	172	172	172

**. Correlation is significant at the 0.01 level (2-tailed).

There is a diagonal of 1s that separates the two sections of the matrix, and these represent the correlation of each field with itself. Each cell of the matrix includes the coefficient, followed by a pair of asterisks if it meets the **.01** significance level, the exact significance level, and the N that the correlation is based upon. The default approach is to test for significance from zero in either direction, so the Two-tailed result is the value shown in the table. This is noted as well in the footnote at the bottom of the table.

Some pairs, such as the two life expectancy variables, are almost perfectly correlated at **.967**, while the population variable is not correlated with any of the other fields. The high coefficient between male and female life expectancy is a good opportunity to reinforce the idea that correlation and causation are not the same. It is likely that a range of factors, such as access to healthcare, result in higher (or lower) than average life expectancy for both males and females, which leads to them moving up or down in unison across the nations:

Another point to note about this matrix is that some coefficients are based on 199 of the 201 nations, while others, such as the two secondary school fields, are based on only 172 nations. This means that the subset of nations for which education information was unavailable are not contributing to the coefficient. How the correlation would change if data for these 27 nations became available is unknown, but it is important to understand whether the missing data is concentrated in certain geographic regions or is associated with other variables such as population or the GNI measure. These factors would limit the ability to generalize the relationship to all nations since there would be the possibility of a biased estimate.

Mean differences versus correlations

The previous chapter focused on comparing means, while here, the focus is on correlations. There are two different analysis objectives that can be seen by contrasting the two sets of results using a paired t-test. The following screenshot shows the correlations for both the two life expectancy variables and the two secondary education variables:

		N	Correlation	Sig.
Pair 1	Life_Expectancy_Females & Life_Expectancy_Males	199	.967	.000
Pair 2	Secondary_School_Enroll_Ratio_Females & Secondary_School_Enroll_Ratio_Males	172	.965	.000

Paired Samples Correlations

For both pairs, there is a very strong, positive correlation between the values for males and females.

Correlations

The mean comparison for these two pairs in the following screenshot, however, indicates that for one pair life expectancy is significantly higher for females compared to males, while for the other it is not:

Paired Samples Test

		Paired Differences							
		Mean	Std. Deviation	Std. Error Mean	95% Confidence Interval of the Difference Lower	Upper	t	df	Sig. (2-tailed)
Pair 1	Life_Expectancy_Females - Life_Expectancy_Males	4.784	2.108	.149	4.489	5.079	32.02	198	.000
Pair 2	Secondary_School_Enroll_Ratio_Females - Secondary_School_Enroll_Ratio_Males	.128	8.274	.631	-1.117	1.373	.203	171	.840

Both the correlation and t-test results are valid of course, but they are designed to answer different questions, and it is important to keep that in mind when reviewing them.

Listwise versus pairwise missing values

As was shown in the first correlation matrix earlier in the chapter, missing values are, by default, handled in a pairwise manner in the correlation procedure. In linear regression, the default is to exclude cases on a listwise basis. While the default setting can be changed in each of these procedures, it is important to appreciate the differences and decide how to best handle this aspect of the analysis process.

> The pairwise approach makes use of all the available information, so it provides the most complete picture of the linear relationship between a pair of variables. Listwise handling of missing values creates a matrix in which each coefficient is based on the same set of observations, which provides consistency.

Comparing pairwise and listwise correlation matrices

When a set of variables is going to be used in a regression analysis, it is a good idea to use correlations to assess all the bivariate patterns, and part of this evaluation involves comparing the correlations with both the pairwise and listwise missing value treatment.

The following screenshot contains the coefficients for the same six variables as the first matrix shown in the preceding section, but now, the N is the equivalent (169) for all of them due to the listwise handling of missing values:

		Population _mid2017	GNI_per_Capit a_PPP_2016	Life_Expectancy _Females	Life_Expectanc y_Males	Secondary_Sc hool_Enroll_R atio_Females	Secondary_S chool_Enroll_ Ratio_Males
Population_mid 2017	Correlation	1	-.033	-.018	.011	-.008	-.005
	Sig. (2-tailed)		.673	.813	.891	.916	.953
GNI_per_Capita _PPP_2016	Correlation	-.033	1	.612**	.657**	.606**	.607**
	Sig. (2-tailed)	.673		.000	.000	.000	.000
Life_Expectancy _Females	Correlation	-.018	.612**	1	.964**	.833**	.819**
	Sig. (2-tailed)	.813	.000		.000	.000	.000
Life_Expectancy _Males	Correlation	.011	.657**	.964**	1	.798**	.786**
	Sig. (2-tailed)	.891	.000	.000		.000	.000
Secondary_Sch ool_Enroll_Rati o_Females	Correlation	-.008	.606**	.833**	.798**	1	.968**
	Sig. (2-tailed)	.916	.000	.000	.000		.000
Secondary_Sch ool_Enroll_Rati o_Males	Correlation	-.005	.607**	.819**	.786**	.968**	1
	Sig. (2-tailed)	.953	.000	.000	.000	.000	

Pearson Correlations[b]

**. Correlation is significant at the 0.01 level (2-tailed).

b. Listwise N=169

Some of the coefficients increase slightly, such as **Life_Expectancy_Females** with **GNI_per_Capita** (.612 versus .595), because of the smaller number of nations included in the calculation.

Using a correlation matrix with the pairwise treatment of missing values as the foundation for regression means that the coefficients are not based on the same subset of observations. In most situations, this is not the recommended approach. If there are noticeable differences in the size of the correlations when the pairwise and listwise matrices are compared, it is a good idea to consider some of the missing value replacement strategies described in `Chapter 4`, *Dealing with Missing Data and Outliers*. At a minimum, when listwise handling is used, it is essential to determine the subset of observations that are being excluded and to identify the variables that are most responsible for any sizeable reduction in the N.

Pivoting table editing to enhance correlation matrices

A correlation matrix includes a lot of important information, but it can be challenging to make key patterns clearly evident. Editing the original table is often necessary to make it presentation-ready. The results shown previously in this chapter were edited using the pivot table editing techniques covered in `Chapter 7`, *Creating New Data Elements*.

Following are some additional editing capabilities that are particularly relevant to correlation matrices. In addition to resizing the variable names (or labels) to make them more compact and editing the row labels so they require less space, it is useful to modify the cell properties.

Correlations

In the following screenshot, the rows labeled **correlations** are highlighted and then **Select | Data and Label Cells** is selected:

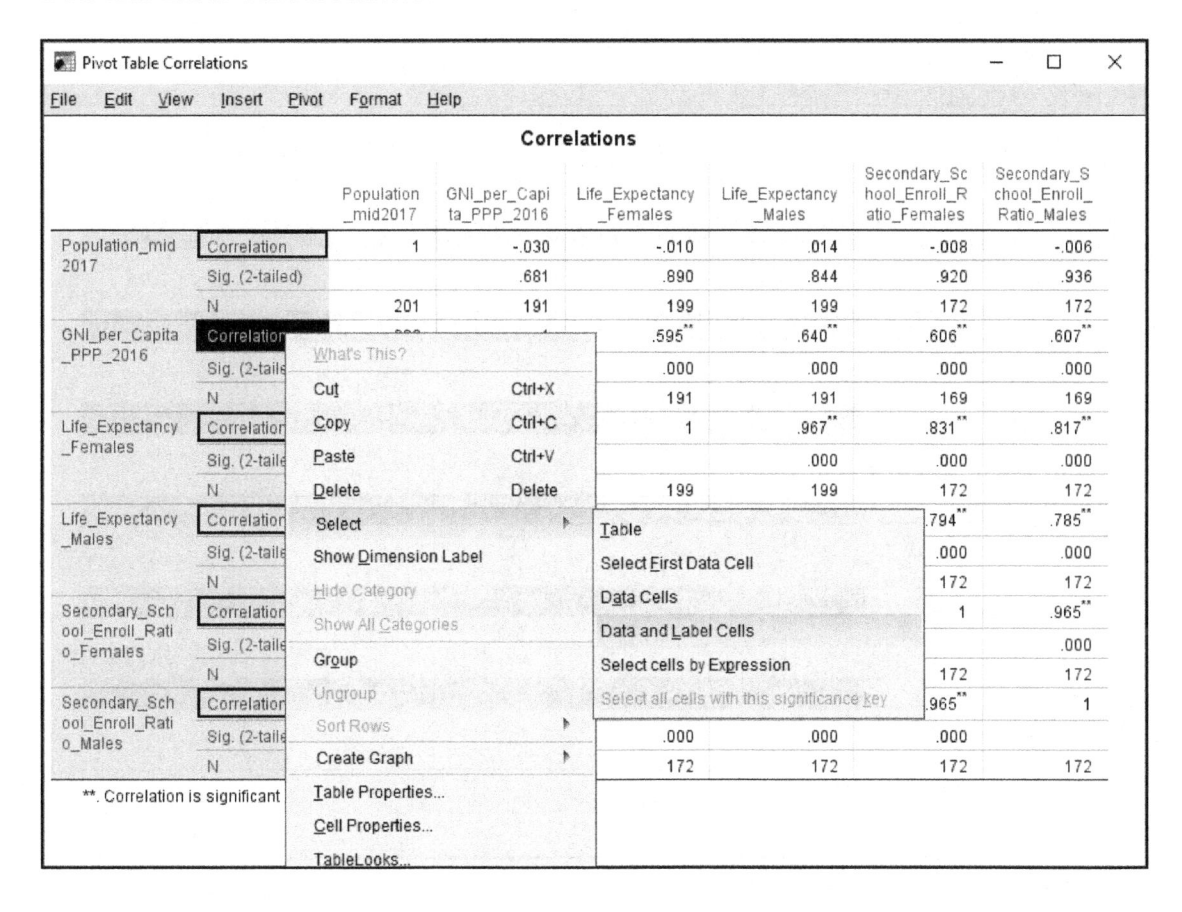

Correlations

This results in just the rows containing correlations being selected, as shown in the following screenshot:

		Population_mid2017	GNI_per_Capita_PPP_2016	Life_Expectancy_Females	Life_Expectancy_Males	Secondary_School_Enroll_Ratio_Females	Secondary_School_Enroll_Ratio_Males
Population_mid2017	Correlation	1	-.030	-.010	.014	-.008	-.006
	Sig. (2-tailed)		.681	.890	.844	.920	.936
	N	201	191	199	199	172	172
GNI_per_Capita_PPP_2016	Correlation	-.030	1	.595**	.640**	.606**	.607**
	Sig. (2-tailed)	.681		.000	.000	.000	.000
	N	191	191	191	191	169	169
Life_Expectancy_Females	Correlation	-.010	.595**	1	.967**	.831**	.817**
	Sig. (2-tailed)	.890	.000		.000	.000	.000
	N	199	191	199	199	172	172
Life_Expectancy_Males	Correlation	.014	.640**	.967**	1	.794**	.785**
	Sig. (2-tailed)	.844	.000	.000		.000	.000
	N	199	191	199	199	172	172
Secondary_School_Enroll_Ratio_Females	Correlation	-.008	.606**	.831**	.794**	1	.965**
	Sig. (2-tailed)	.920	.000	.000	.000		.000
	N	172	169	172	172	172	172
Secondary_School_Enroll_Ratio_Males	Correlation	-.006	.607**	.817**	.785**	.965**	1
	Sig. (2-tailed)	.936	.000	.000	.000	.000	
	N	172	169	172	172	172	172

**. Correlation is significant at the 0.01 level (2-tailed).

Under **Cell Properties...**, the number format was changed to show two decimal places for just the correlations. Next, the Two-tailed significance rows are selected using the same approach and then deleted since the ** symbol indicates those that are significant.

The diagonal of 1s is selected individually (*Ctrl* + click does this) and made bold to emphasize the diagonal values in the matrix. These modifications produce the matrix displayed in the following screenshot:

Correlations

		Population_mid2017	GNI_per_Capita_PPP_2016	Life_Expectancy_Females	Life_Expectancy_Males	Secondary_School_Enroll_Ratio_Females	Secondary_School_Enroll_Ratio_Males
Population_mid 2017	Correlation	**1.00**	-.03	-.01	.01	-.01	-.01
	N	201	191	199	199	172	172
GNI_per_Capita _PPP_2016	Correlation	-.03	**1.00**	.60**	.64**	.61**	.61**
	N	191	191	191	191	169	169
Life_Expectancy _Females	Correlation	-.01	.60**	**1.00**	.97**	.83**	.82**
	N	199	191	199	199	172	172
Life_Expectancy _Males	Correlation	.01	.64**	.97**	**1.00**	.79**	.79**
	N	199	191	199	199	172	172
Secondary_School_Enroll_Ratio_Females	Correlation	-.01	.61**	.83**	.79**	**1.00**	.96**
	N	172	169	172	172	172	172
Secondary_School_Enroll_Ratio_Males	Correlation	-.01	.61**	.82**	.79**	.96**	**1.00**
	N	172	169	172	172	172	172

**. Correlation is significant at the 0.01 level (2-tailed).

Creating a very trimmed matrix

This process can be carried a step further in terms of reducing the amount of content in the matrix by selecting each column in the lower triangle and changing the font to white so it becomes invisible. Finally, individual coefficients can be emphasized by changing their size and color. The following screenshot provides a sense of what such a cleaned up matrix looks like:

Pearson Correlations

		Population_mid2017	GNI_per_Capita_PPP_2016	Life_Expectancy_Females	Life_Expectancy_Males	Secondary_School_Enroll_Ratio_Females	Secondary_School_Enroll_Ratio_Males
Population_mid2017	Correlation	1.00	-.03	-.01	.01	-.01	-.01
	N		191	199	199	172	172
GNI_per_Capita_PPP_2016	Correlation		1.00	.60**	.64**	.61**	.61**
	N			191	191	169	169
Life_Expectancy_Females	Correlation			1.00	.97**	.83**	.82**
	N				199	172	172
Life_Expectancy_Males	Correlation				1.00	.79**	.79**
	N					172	172
Secondary_School_Enroll_Ratio_Females	Correlation					1.00	.96**
	N						172
Secondary_School_Enroll_Ratio_Males	Correlation						1.00
	N						

**. Correlation is significant at the 0.01 level (2-tailed).

If the matrix was generated with listwise missing values, the rows of Ns would not be present, which would result in a very compact and easy-to-read matrix. Since these coefficients are based on a pairwise handling of missing values, the Ns are retained so any differences can be seen.

Visualizing correlations with scatterplots

Pearson correlations summarize the linear pattern between two variables into a single number. This is very valuable, but it is useful to *see* the actual details of the pattern, and this can be done using a scatterplot. In `Chapter 5`, *Visually Exploring the Data*, one of the graphs described was a scatterplot, and once this type of plot is generated, it can be edited to add a fit line using the following dialog:

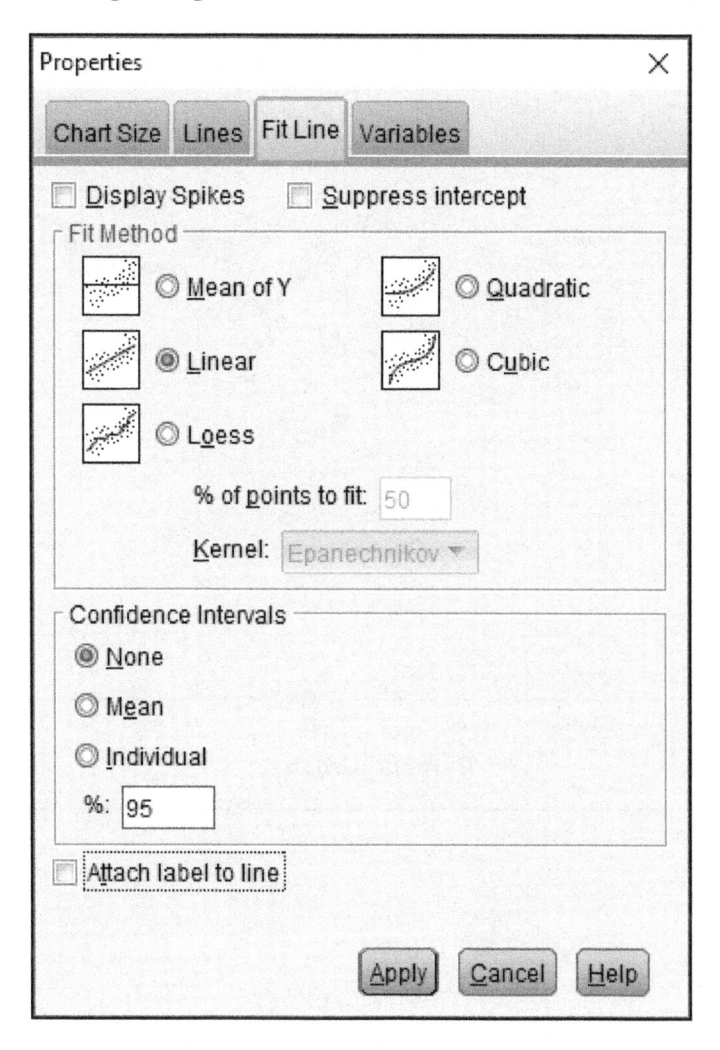

Correlations

The default setting is to add a line for the linear fit, but other types of patterns can be fit as well if the pattern suggests they are more suited to the data. In the following chart, the linear fit line has been added along with the R^2 value at the upper right:

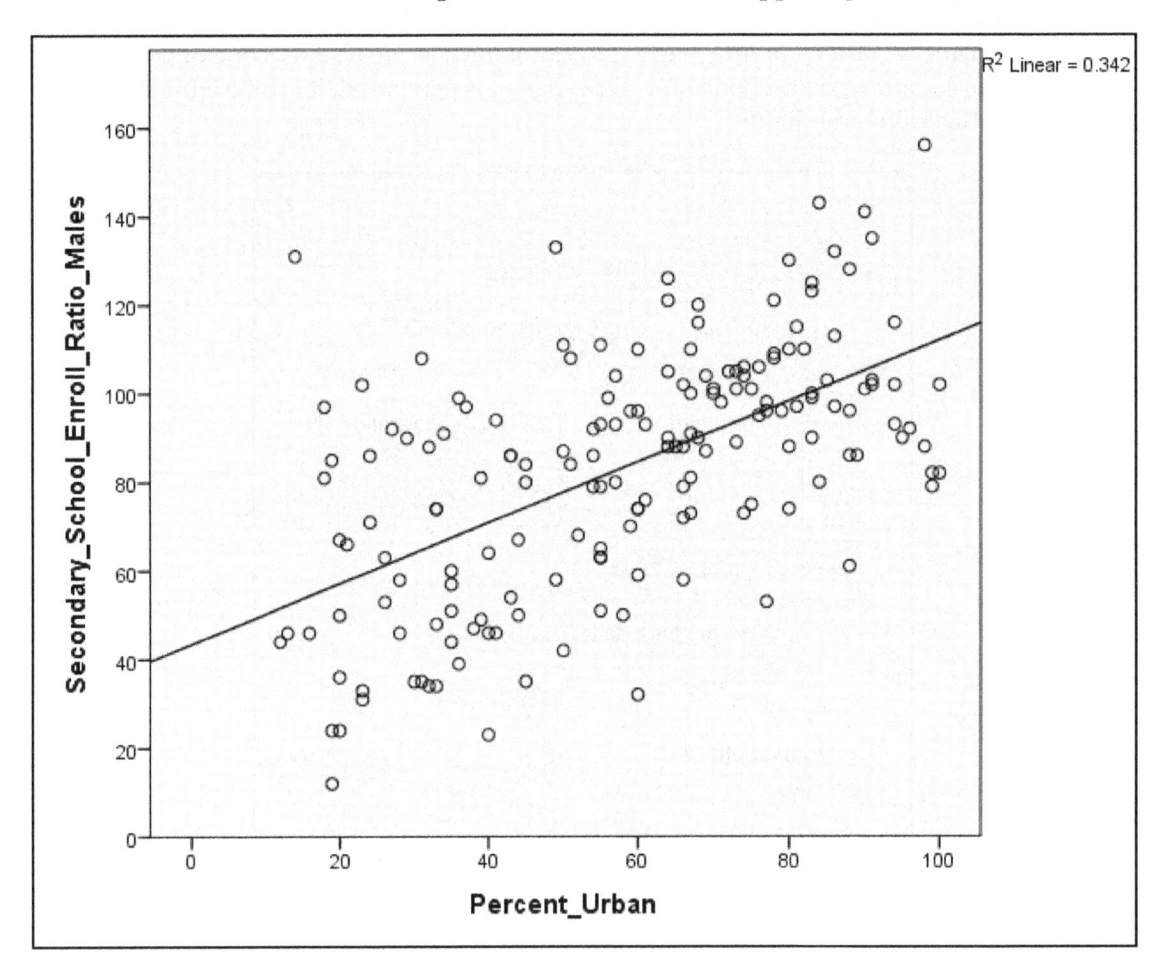

The R² value is equal to the square of the Pearson correlation. For these two fields, **Percent_Urban** and **Secondary_School_Enrollment_Ratio_Males**, the correlation is shown in the following screenshot. This underscores the direct link between correlations and more sophisticated analytical methods they support, such as linear regression:

Correlations

		Percent_Urban	Life_Expectancy_Males
Percent_Urban	Pearson Correlation	1	.578**
	Sig. (2-tailed)		.000
	N	201	199
Life_Expectancy_Males	Pearson Correlation	.578**	1
	Sig. (2-tailed)	.000	
	N	199	199

**. Correlation is significant at the 0.01 level (2-tailed).

Rank order correlations

Although Pearson correlations are central statistical analyses, correlations based on ranking values require fewer assumptions and can capture patterns that are not linear. Bivariate correlations in SPSS include Spearman's Rho and Kendall's Tau-b. Tau-b was introduced as one of the ordinal measures of association in the Crosstabulation discussion (Chapter 10, *Crosstabulation Patterns for Categorical Data*). Spearman's Rho works well with values that can be ranked, such as the data for the 201 nations used in this chapter.

Correlations

The following table contains these two sets of coefficients for the two life expectancy variables and the **Percent_Urban** field:

Correlations

			GNI_per_Capita_PPP_2016	Life_Expectancy_Females	Life_Expectancy_Males
Kendall's tau_b	GNI_per_Capita_PPP_2016	Coefficient	1.000	.622**	.597**
		Sig. (2-tailed)	.	.000	.000
		N	191	191	191
	Life_Expectancy_Females	Coefficient	.622**	1.000	.860**
		Sig. (2-tailed)	.000	.	.000
		N	191	199	199
	Life_Expectancy_Males	Coefficient	.597**	.860**	1.000
		Sig. (2-tailed)	.000	.000	.
		N	191	199	199
Spearman's rho	GNI_per_Capita_PPP_2016	Coefficient	1.000	.782**	.767**
		Sig. (2-tailed)	.	.000	.000
		N	191	191	191
	Life_Expectancy_Females	Coefficient	.782**	1.000	.955**
		Sig. (2-tailed)	.000	.	.000
		N	191	199	199
	Life_Expectancy_Males	Coefficient	.767**	.955**	1.000
		Sig. (2-tailed)	.000	.000	.
		N	191	199	199

**. Correlation is significant at the 0.01 level (2-tailed).

The Tau-b coefficients differ only slightly from the Pearson correlations shown earlier, while the Spearman coefficients are noticeably higher. This suggests that while **GNI_per_Capita** and life expectancy move in tandem to a large degree, the pattern is not captured fully by a linear trend. Creating new versions of these fields in which the original values are converted to ranks, results in Pearson correlations equal that are the same as the Spearman correlation for this example. The **Transform | Rank Cases** function can be used to build these fields.

Partial correlations

One of the principal objectives of analytics is to discover underlying factors that account for observed patterns in data. Identifying these intervening factors often leads to an understanding of what drives a process or outcome of interest. Partial correlation is a technique that makes it possible to examine the correlation between two variables while controlling a third variable. Control variables are selected based on a hypothesis (or, at least, a hunch) that they influence the correlation between the two variables of interest.

For this example, we will look at the relationship between the birth rate, the infant mortality rate, and the secondary school enrollment ratio for females across nations. The hypothesis is that the educational level influences both the number of children born and the likelihood of a child surviving infancy.

The partial procedure under **Analyze** | **Correlate** brings up the dialog shown in the following screenshot. At the lower right, the control variable is specified:

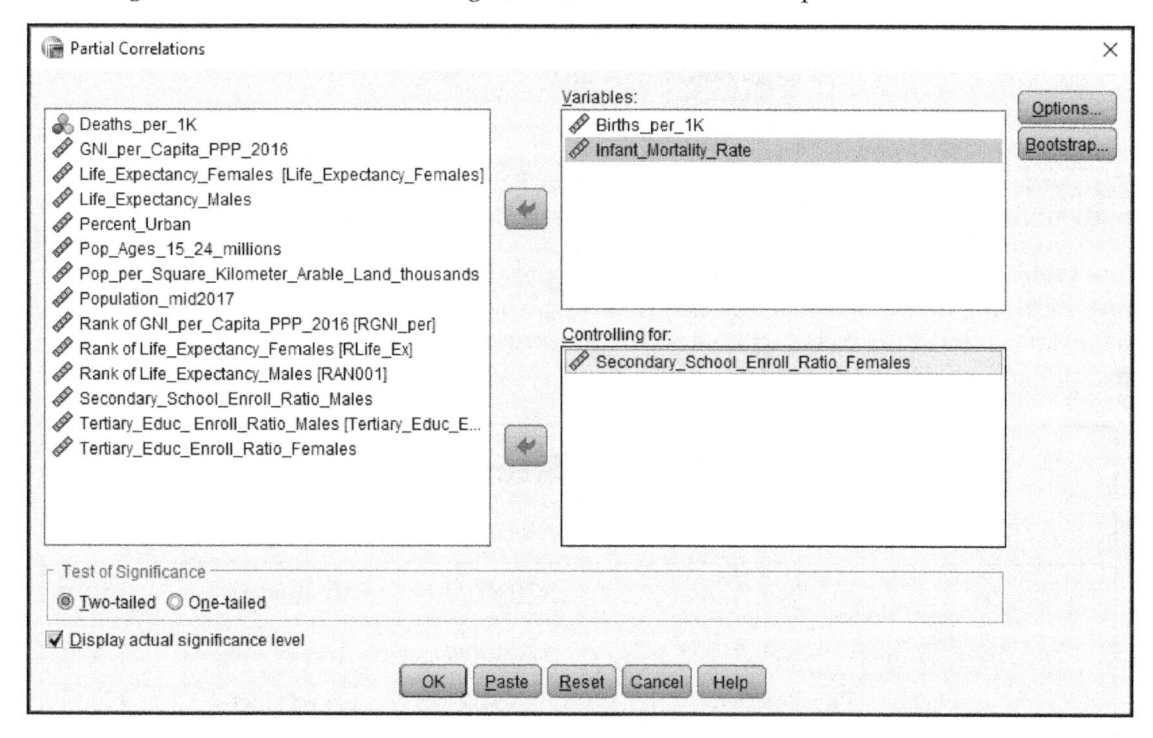

[291]

Correlations

Descriptive statistics and zero-order correlations are requested via the Options dialog as shown in the following image:

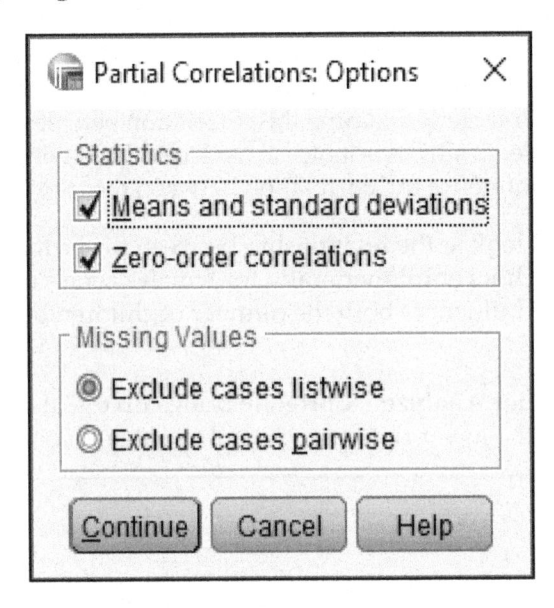

Zero-order correlations refer to the matrix of bivariate coefficients for all the variables without controls. These serve as a baseline for assessing the impact of the control variable.

The standard descriptive statistics for each field provide background information on each one, including the N, which in this case reflects the fact that only 172 of the 201 countries have data on these three characteristics. The following screenshot displays the statistics mean, standard deviation and N:

Descriptive Statistics

	Mean	Std. Deviation	N
Births_per_1K	20.87209	10.406697	172
Infant_Mortality_Rate	22.80581	21.190533	172
Secondary_School_Enroll_Ratio_Females	83.56977	30.641691	172

The upper section of the following screenshot contains the zero-order correlations:

Correlations

Control Variables			Births_per _1K	Infant_ Mortality _Rate	Secondary_Sch ool_Enroll_Ratio _Females
-none-[a]	Births_per_1K	Correlation	1.000	.865	-.818
		Significance (2-tailed)	.	.000	.000
		df	0	170	170
	Infant_Mortality_Rate	Correlation	.865	1.000	-.846
		Significance (2-tailed)	.000	.	.000
		df	170	0	170
	Secondary_School_Enroll _Ratio_Females	Correlation	-.818	-.846	1.000
		Significance (2-tailed)	.000	.000	.
		df	170	170	0
Secondary_Scho ol_Enroll_Ratio_ Females	Births_per_1K	Correlation	1.000	.564	
		Significance (2-tailed)	.	.000	
		df	0	169	
	Infant_Mortality_Rate	Correlation	.564	1.000	
		Significance (2-tailed)	.000	.	
		df	169	0	

a. Cells contain zero-order (Pearson) correlations.

The education field has a very high negative correlation with both the birth rate and infant mortality as was anticipated. In the lower portion of the matrix, the correlation between birth rate and infant mortality is **.564** versus the zero-order coefficient of **.865**. A decrease of this magnitude confirms that part of the linear relationship between these two characteristics is associated with the education attainment of females.

Correlations

Adding a second control variable

The process of exploring the influence of other factors on a correlation pattern can be extended by introducing more control variables. In the following screenshot, the results produced when the **GNI_per_Capita** field is added as another control are shown:

Correlations

Control Variables			Births_per_1K	Infant_Mortality_Rate	Secondary_School_Enroll_Ratio_Females	GNI_per_Capita_PPP_2016
-none-[a]	Births_per_1K	Correlation	1.000	.867	-.822	-.585
		Sig (2-tailed)	.	.000	.000	.000
		df	0	167	167	167
	Infant_Mortality_Rate	Correlation	.867	1.000	-.844	-.591
		Sig (2-tailed)	.000	.	.000	.000
		df	167	0	167	167
	Secondary_School_Enroll_Ratio_Females	Correlation	-.822	-.844	1.000	.606
		Sig (2-tailed)	.000	.000	.	.000
		df	167	167	0	167
	GNI_per_Capita_PPP_2016	Correlation	-.585	-.591	.606	1.000
		Sig (2-tailed)	.000	.000	.000	.
		df	167	167	167	0
Secondary_School_Enroll_Ratio_Females & GNI_per_Capita_PPP_2016	Births_per_1K	Correlation	1.000	.551		
		Sig (2-tailed)	.	.000		
		df	0	165		
	Infant_Mortality_Rate	Correlation	.551	1.000		
		Sig (2-tailed)	.000	.		
		df	165	0		

a. Cells contain zero-order (Pearson) correlations.

The addition of this second control reduces the correlation between birth rate and infant mortality a little more (from .564 to .551), which is a much smaller reduction than the initial one but potentially important in terms of identifying key drivers of these metrics.

[294]

Summary

This chapter addressed the general topic of summarizing the relationship between a pair of interval level fields using a correlation coefficient. The most prominent of these, the Pearson product moment correlation, was the primary focus of the examples since it serves as the basis for regression models. Making correlation matrices readable using various pivot table editing techniques was demonstrated since it is often necessary to include such matrices in reports and presentations.

Rank order correlations, Spearman and Tau-b, were discussed as alternatives to the linear Pearson correlation, and partial correlations were explored as well. At this point, the foundation has been laid for moving on to the next chapter, which focuses on what is perhaps the most central statistical technique--regression.

13
Linear Regression

Multiple regression is an important statistical procedure for estimating the relationship between a numeric target and one or more numeric predictors. It is used for **prediction**--to predict the response variable based on the predictor variable's values -- or for **explanation**--learning the relationship between the response variable and the predictor variables. Since its results include an equation with coefficients, multiple regression produces a transparent model that lends itself to interpretation and also makes it easy to predict new cases.

Through the use of various types of coding and transformation, multiple regression is actually very general in its applicability. For this reason, multiple regression is popular in areas such as the physical and social sciences, policy studies, and classic business applications. Regression has been so successful and popular that it has been extended to other situations beyond its original form, for example, in generalized linear models. In this chapter, we consider the **classical linear regression model**.

We will be discussing the following topics:

- Assumptions underlying the use of linear regression
- Exploring associations between the target and predictors
- Fitting and interpreting a simple regression model
- Residual analysis for a simple regression model
- Saving and interpreting casewise diagnostics
- Multiple regression: Model-building strategies

Assumptions of the classical linear regression model

Multiple regression fits a linear model by relating the predictors to the target variable. The model has the following form:

$$Y = B0 + B1 * X1 + B2 * X2 + \ldots + Bp * Xp + e$$

Here, Y is the target variable, the Xs are the predictors, and the e term is the random disturbance. The Bs are capitalized to indicate that the are population parameters. Estimates of the Bs are found from the sample such that the sum of squares of the sample errors is minimized. The term **ordinary least squares regression** captures this feature.

The assumptions of the classical linear regression model are as follows:

- The target variable can be calculated as a linear function of a specific set of predictor variables plus a disturbance term. The coefficients in this linear function are constant.
- The expected value of the disturbance term is zero.
- The disturbance terms have a constant variance.
- The disturbance terms are uncorrelated across cases.
- The observations on the independent variables can be considered fixed in repeated samples.
- The number of observations is greater than the number of predictor variables.
- There are no exact linear relationships between the predictors.
- If you make the assumption that the residuals are normally distributed, then regression provides a statistical hypothesis testing framework.

Note that many of the assumptions are about the disturbances in e. The above model is a population model. When you obtain and estimate the model, you also obtain sample estimates of the disturbances, which are the regression **residuals**.

Multiple regression is the topic of many textbook treatments. In the following discussion, we assume a basic knowledge of statistics and multiple regression and focus on an applied example showing the use of SPSS Statistics to estimate and assess regression models for data.

Example - motor trend car data

Data was obtained from the 1974 *Motor Trend* magazine and consists of fuel consumption in **miles per gallon** (**mpg**) and 10 variables measuring various aspects of automobile design and performance for 32 automobiles from the 1973-74 model year. The data is publicly available in the R statistical software package and is widely featured in discussions on regression.

> Our presentation draws upon the discussion by Henderson and Velleman: Henderson and Velleman (1981), Building multiple regression models interactively. *Biometrics*, **37**, 391–411.

Here are the variables in the original source file:

Model	Model of vehicle (descriptor field)
mpg	Miles/(US) gallon
cyl	Number of cylinders
disp	Displacement (cu.in.)
hp	Gross horsepower
drat	Rear axle ratio
wt	Weight (1000 lbs)
qsec	1/4 mile time
vs	Engine cylinder configuration
am	Transmission (0 = automatic, 1 = manual)
gear	Number of forward gears
carb	Number of carburetors

Linear Regression

In addition, there is an added field named **code**, enabling simple point labeling in plots. You could use the **model** to label points, but **code** has the benefit of using compact code of 1-2 letters.

The analytic goal is to predict the gasoline mileage from a set of the other variables (excluding case descriptors such as **model** or **code**). Analysts have noted that the particular sample of 32 automobiles includes such automobiles as Mercedes, Porsche, Ferrari, and Maserati, so there is some question regarding the generalization of any model obtained on these data to automobiles in general.

In addition, the data present modeling challenges for the following reasons:

- The overall sample is not large
- The ratio of variables to cases is large
- There are large correlations between some pairs of variables
- Associations between some variables appear to be non-linear

Our goal here is not to show every feature of SPSS regression or to find the *best* model, but instead to show useful analyses that you can do with SPSS statistics using regression and other SPSS statistics facilities. We will demonstrate SPSS regression via a single-variable model and a multiple-variable model.

Exploring associations between the target and predictors

One task awaiting the researcher is to explore the association between **mpg** and potential predictors via plots. For example, here is the plot of **mpg** versus **disp**:

Linear Regression

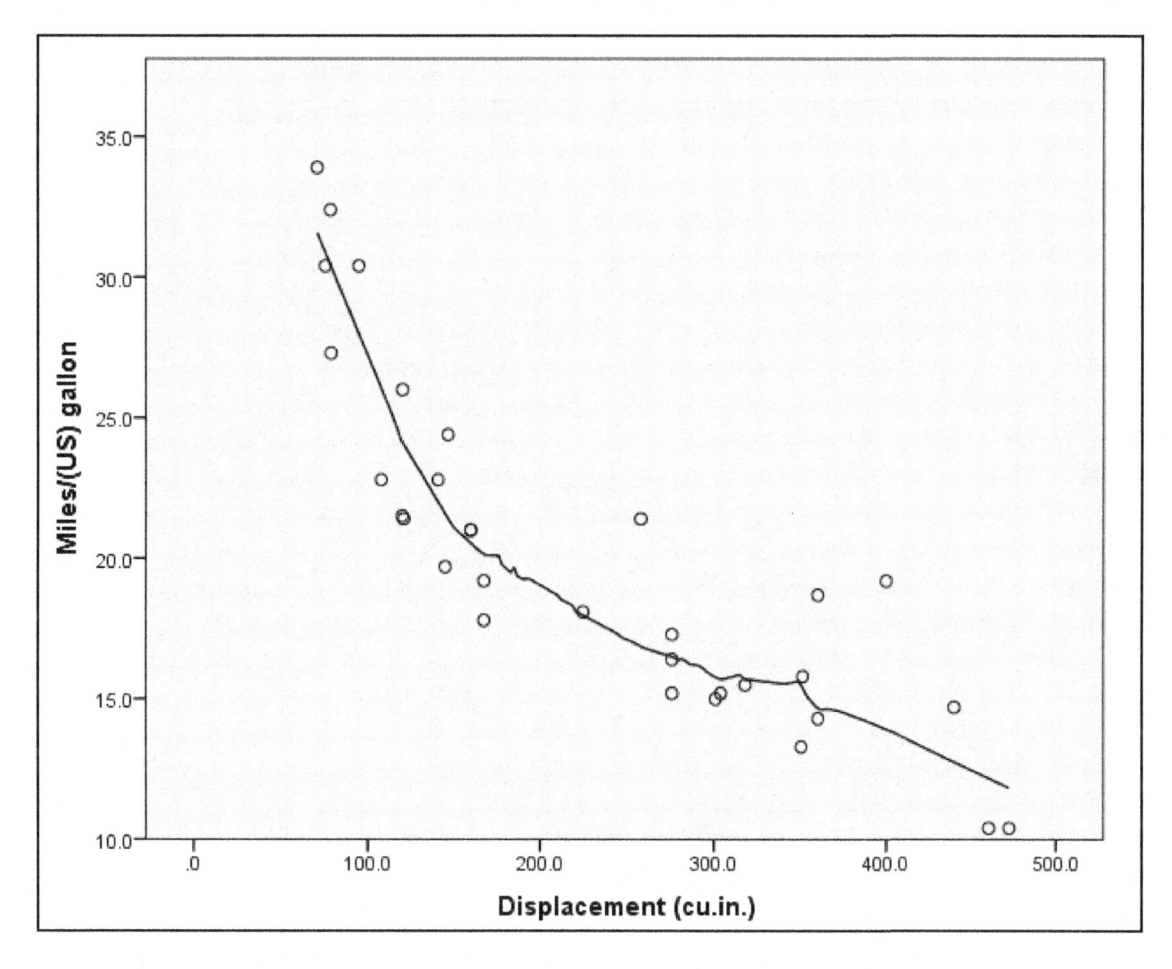

The plot reveals what we would expect: automobiles with larger displacement get lower mileage. The superimposed line is a loess fit line, which fits points locally. Recall that you can add the loess fit line via the chart editor. The pattern of points along with the loess fit line suggests nonlinearity in the association between **mpg** and **disp**. It would seem that linear regression is not suited to this data.

However, in similar analysis situations, statisticians have noted that it is worth considering the inverse transformation of **mpg**, that is, working with **gallons per mile** or some convenient scaling of it such as **gallons per 100 miles**.

Here are the COMPUTE statements for these:

```
COMPUTE gpm=1 / mpg.
COMPUTE gpm100=100*gpm.
EXECUTE.
```

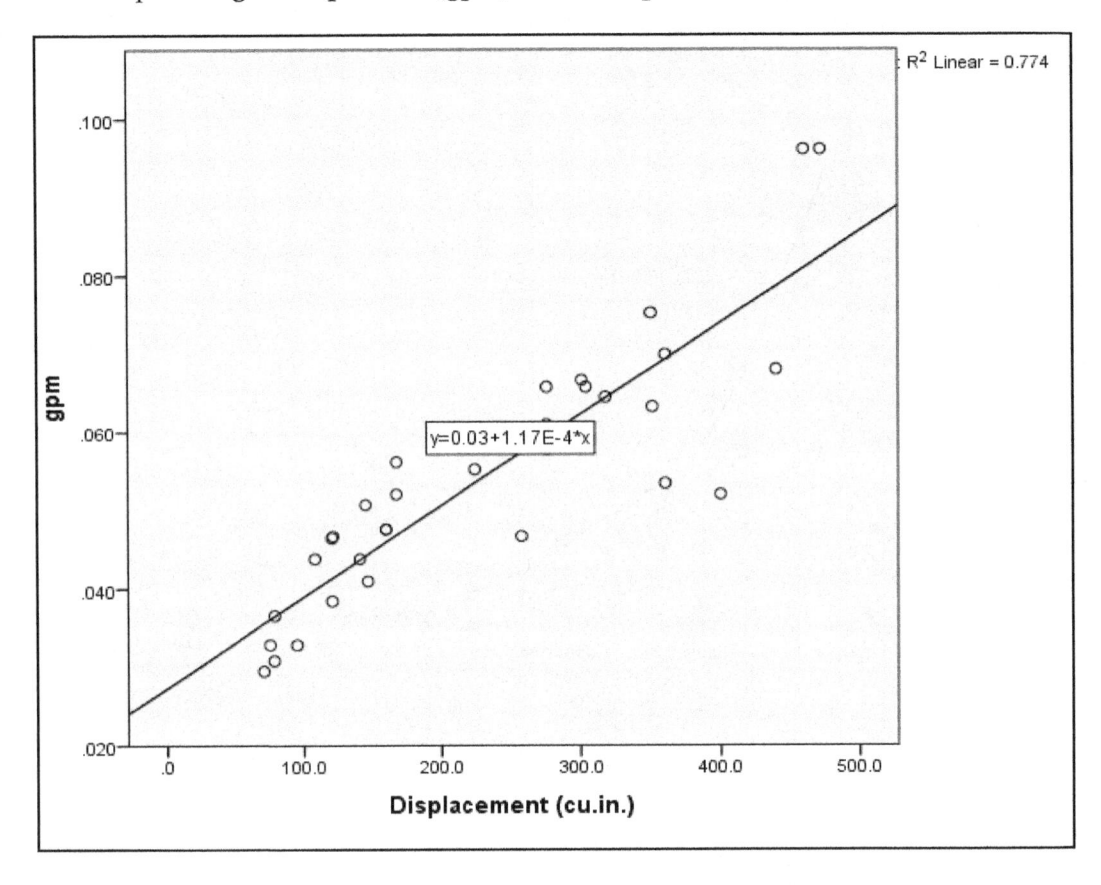

Linear Regression

Here is the plot for **gallons per mile (gpm)** versus **disp**:

[Scatter plot of gpm vs Displacement (cu.in.) with least squares line $y = 0.03 + 1.17E\text{-}4 \cdot x$ and R^2 Linear = 0.774]

The plot reveals what we would expect: automobiles with larger displacement have a higher gallons per mile measure. The superimposed line is a **least squares** fit line--the loess fit line (not shown) in this instance looks similar. The pattern of points now looks broadly linear.

Next, consider the correlations of **gpm** with the potential predictors.

Here are the commands:

```
CORRELATIONS
  /VARIABLES=gpm cyl disp hp drat wt qsec vs am gear carb
  /PRINT=TWOTAIL NOSIG
  /MISSING=PAIRWISE.
```

By default, the commands produce a square correlation matrix showing correlations, significance levels, and numbers of cases. In the following screenshot, we isolate the column that shows the correlations of the target variable with each predictor. Note that you should also inspect the correlations between the predictors.

	gpm
gpm	1
Number of cylinders	.814**
Displacement (cu.in.)	.880**
Gross horsepower	.763**
Rear axle ratio	-.638**
Weight (1000 lbs)	.890**
1/4 mile time	-.386*
Engine cylinder configuration	-.640**
Transmission (0 = automatic, 1 = manual)	-.540**
Number of forward gears	-.479**
Number of carburetors	.526**

The correlation of gpm with disp is .880, but the correlation of gpm with **weight** (**wt**) is a bit larger at .890. In fact, wt is the best single predictor of gpm. Other variables that correlate highly with gpm include hp and cyl. If you are interested in the best single predictor of gpm, you would choose wt as the predictor. Almost as good as a predictor is disp, but inspection of the correlations shows wt and disp to be highly correlated, so both are likely not needed in the model. Since hp and cyl have a lower correlation with gpm, neither one is the best single predictor. They might have additional explanatory power, which you can explore by moving beyond single-predictor regression to multiple regression.

Next, we will take a look at the scatterplot of gpm100--rather than gpm--with wt. Recall that gpm100 is just a rescaling of gpm. The overall correlation is the same, but the units of gpm100 are more convenient and interpretable.

Linear Regression

Here is the scatterplot:

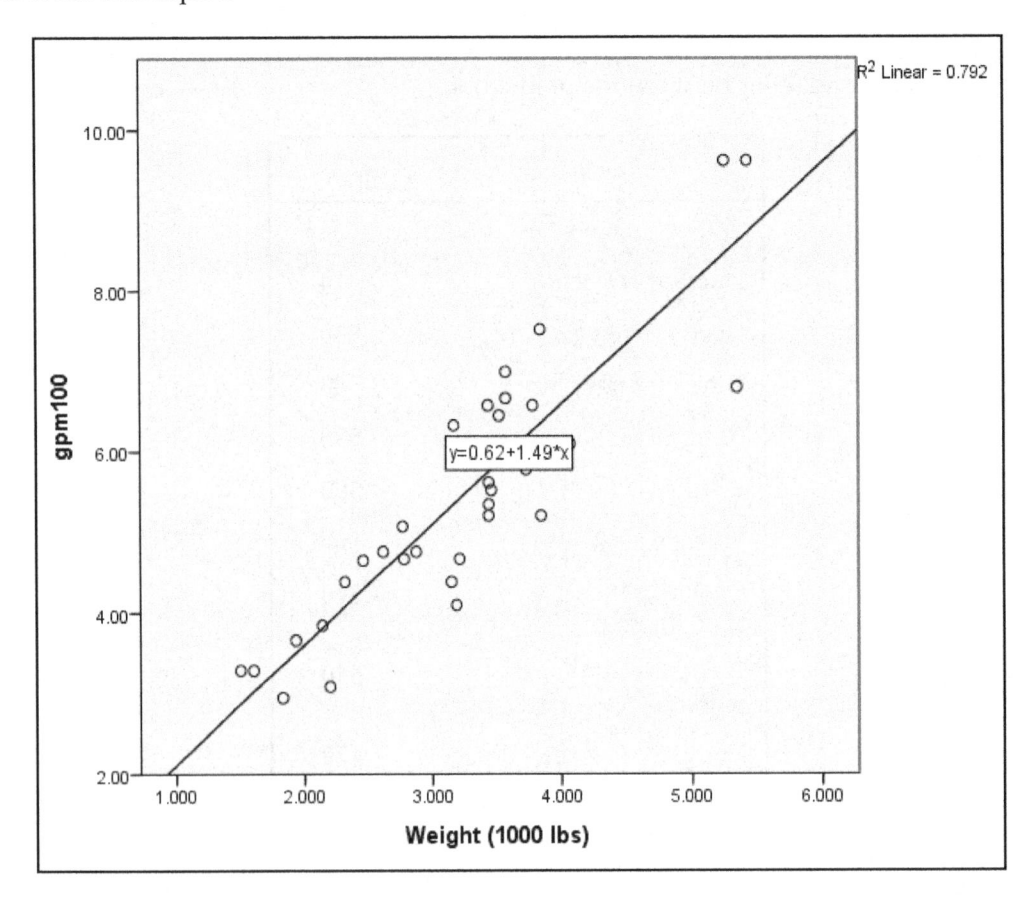

[Scatterplot of gpm100 vs Weight (1000 lbs), with fit line y=0.62+1.49*x and R² Linear = 0.792]

Note that the plot of `gpm100` with `wt` looks linear, which suggests that the inverse transformation of `mpg` was a good idea. As in the last plot, we superimposed the linear fit line.

Fitting and interpreting a simple regression model

Simple regression involves regression with a single predictor. Here, we run an analysis of `gpm100` and `wt` in SPSS Statistics regression. We will run it with the default settings.

To run **Regression** from the menus, specify:

Analyze | Regression | Linear

This brings up the **Linear Regression** dialog box:

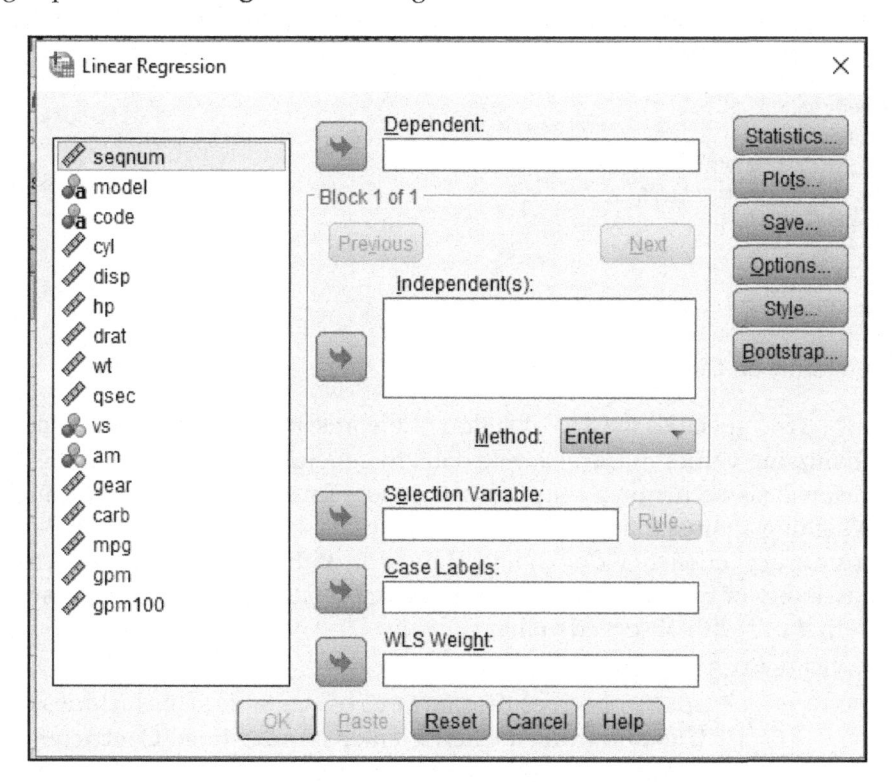

Here are some comments on the **Linear Regression** dialog box:

- The target variable goes in the **Dependent** list.
- The predictor or predictors goes in the **Independent(s)** list.
- The **Selection Variable** entry specifies a variable used to limit the analysis to a subset of cases having a particular value(s) for this variable.
- The **Case Labels** entry specifies a case identification variable for identifying points on plots.
- The **WLS Weight** entry specifies a weight variable for weighted least squares analysis.

Linear Regression

Note that only the target variable and one predictor are required.

The buttons along the right side contain many additional features of Regression that we skip in this run.

Specify **gpm100** as a **dependent** variable and **wt** as an **independent** variable in the dialog box, and then **paste** the commands.

Here are the commands.
```
REGRESSION
  /MISSING LISTWISE
  /STATISTICS COEFF OUTS R ANOVA
  /CRITERIA=PIN(.05) POUT(.10)
  /NOORIGIN
  /DEPENDENT gpm100
  /METHOD=ENTER wt.
```

Here are comments on the SPSS code:

- `/MISSING` specifies listwise deletion of the missing data. In point of fact, there are no missing values in the example data. In general, listwise deletion insures that the analysis occurs on a common set of cases for the variables in the analysis. Weighing against that are the following points: listwise deletion can lead to loss of statistical efficiency due to loss of records with information; plus it raises the possibility of bias if those who are missing on one or more variables are different from those with observed values.
- `/STATISTICS` has four keywords:
    - `COEFF` specifies the `Coefficients` table. This includes the **Unstandardized Coefficients**, **Standardized Coefficients**, **t** statistics, and the two-tailed probability of *t* (**Sig.**).
    - `OUTS` specifies the statistics for variables not yet in the equation that have been named on `METHOD` subcommands for the equation. In this instance, this keyword is not relevant.
    - `R` specifies the `Model Summary` table, which shows **R**, **R square**, **Adjusted R Square**, and **Std Error of the Estimate**.
    - `ANOVA` specifies the **Analysis of variance** table, which includes the **Regression Sum of Squares**, degrees of freedom (**df**), **Residual Sum of Squares**, **Mean Square**, **F**, and the probability of *F* (**Sig.**) displayed in the **ANOVA** table.
- `/CRITERIA` specifies `Probability of F-to-enter` and `Probability of F-to-remove`, which are relevant for variable selection methods such as backward, forward, or stepwise.

- /NOORIGIN specifies that a constant term be included in the regression model.
- /DEPENDENT specifies that gpm100 is the dependent variable in the regression.
- /METHOD specifies the direct entry of wt into the regression equation.

Here is the output from regression. The output appears in a sequence of tables.

Here is the `Variables Entered/Removed` table:

Variables Entered/Removed[a]

Model	Variables Entered	Variables Removed	Method
1	Weight (1000 lbs)[b]	.	Enter

a. Dependent Variable: gpm100
b. All requested variables entered.

The table shows that wt was entered via direct entry.

Here is the `Model Summary` table:

Model Summary

Model	R	R Square	Adjusted R Square	Std. Error of the Estimate
1	.890[a]	.792	.785	.76161

a. Predictors: (Constant), Weight (1000 lbs)

The **Model Summary** table shows four statistics: the multiple **R**, the **R Square**, the **Adjusted R Square**, and the **Standard Error of the Estimate**. The **R Square** value has the usual interpretation as the proportion of variation in the target variable is accounted for by the variation in the predictor. Here, roughly 79% of the variance in **gpm100** is explained by the variance in **wt**. It has long been observed that **R** and **R Square** evaluated on the training data has a built-in optimism, meaning that they are upward-biased toward 1 when sample sizes are small and/or the number of predictors approaches the number of cases. For this reason, SPSS Statistics also reports the **Adjusted R Square**, which attempts to correct R Square for this bias. The **Std. Error of the Estimate** is in the same metric as the dependent variable and represents variability not accounted for by the model.

Linear Regression

Here is the **ANOVA** table for the regression:

ANOVA[a]

Model		Sum of Squares	df	Mean Square	F	Sig.
1	Regression	66.224	1	66.224	114.168	.000[b]
	Residual	17.402	30	.580		
	Total	83.625	31			

a. Dependent Variable: gpm100
b. Predictors: (Constant), Weight (1000 lbs)

The **F** statistic, and its associated **Sig.** level, tests the null hypothesis that the regression coefficients in the regression equation are 0 in the population. Here, since the significance level is small relative to .05, we reject the null hypothesis.

Finally, the coefficients table presents the coefficients for the regression equation relating gpm100 to wt:

Coefficients[a]

Model		Unstandardized Coefficients B	Std. Error	Standardized Coefficients Beta	t	Sig.
1	(Constant)	.617	.469		1.314	.199
	Weight (1000 lbs)	1.494	.140	.890	10.685	.000

a. Dependent Variable: gpm100

The regression equation should be understood in the units of the variables. **wt** is in units of 1000 pounds, while gpm100 is in units of gallons per 100 miles. The estimated regression coefficient for wt is 1.494, which indicates that for every 1000-pound increment in vehicle weight, gallons-per-100 miles goes up by about 1.5.

The t statistic for wt is 10.685 with an associated significance level of < .0005 (which is how you should report **.000**). For this reason, we reject the null hypothesis that, the regression coefficient for wt is 0 in the population. The coefficient for the constant term represents the expected value of gpm100 when wt is 0. In this instance, there is no meaningful interpretation of the constant since the meaningful range of wt does not include 0. In addition, the value of the constant is estimated from the sample data, and the accompanying significance level indicates that the constant term could be 0.

On a side note, in the special case of simple regression with a single predictor, the t statistic for the regressor and the F statistic from the ANOVA table are related: 10.685**2 equals 114.168.

Residual analysis for the simple regression model

In regression analysis, you make the assumption that the disturbances are normally distributed. To assess this assumption, you can produce either a histogram or a normal probability plot of the residuals. In addition, the plot of the residuals versus the predicted values is a useful diagnostic plot for assessing whether the regression assumptions are met.

To produce the added plots, recall the **Linear Regression** dialog box.

Press the **Plots** button.

Linear Regression

This brings up the **Linear Regression Plots** dialog box.

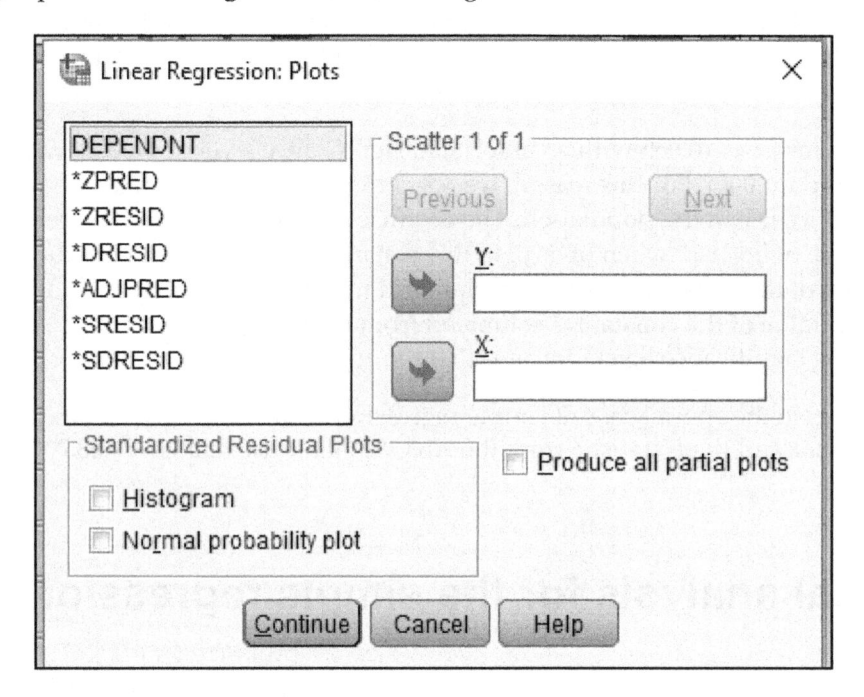

The **Linear Regression Plots** dialog box makes available a list of variables with default internal names:

- **DEPENDNT**-the dependent variable,
- ***ZPRED**-standardized predicted values,
- ***ZRESID**-standardized residuals,
- ***DRESID**-deleted residuals,
- ***ADJPRED**-adjusted predicted values,
- ***SRESID**-Studentized residuals,
- ***SDRESID**-Studentized deleted residuals.

You can produce a scatterplot of any two of these variables by specifying one of them as the **Y** variable and the other as the **X** variable in the dialog box entries.

Place ***ZRESID** and ***ZPRED** in the **Y** and **X** lists. Then, check the check boxes for **Histogram** and **Normal probability plot** and press **Continue**. This puts you back at the main Linear Regression dialog box. Press **Paste**.

Here is the pasted syntax, which is similar to the previous syntax, except that now there are two additional lines.

```
REGRESSION
  /MISSING LISTWISE
  /STATISTICS COEFF OUTS R ANOVA
  /CRITERIA=PIN(.05) POUT(.10)
  /NOORIGIN
  /DEPENDENT gpm100
  /METHOD=ENTER wt
  /SCATTERPLOT=(*ZRESID ,*ZPRED)
  /RESIDUALS HISTOGRAM(ZRESID) NORMPROB(ZRESID).
```

The /SCATTERPLOT subcommand specifies the plot of the standardized residuals versus the standardized predicted values, while the /RESIDUALS subcommand specifies the histogram and normal probability plot of the residuals.

Here is the histogram of the residuals:

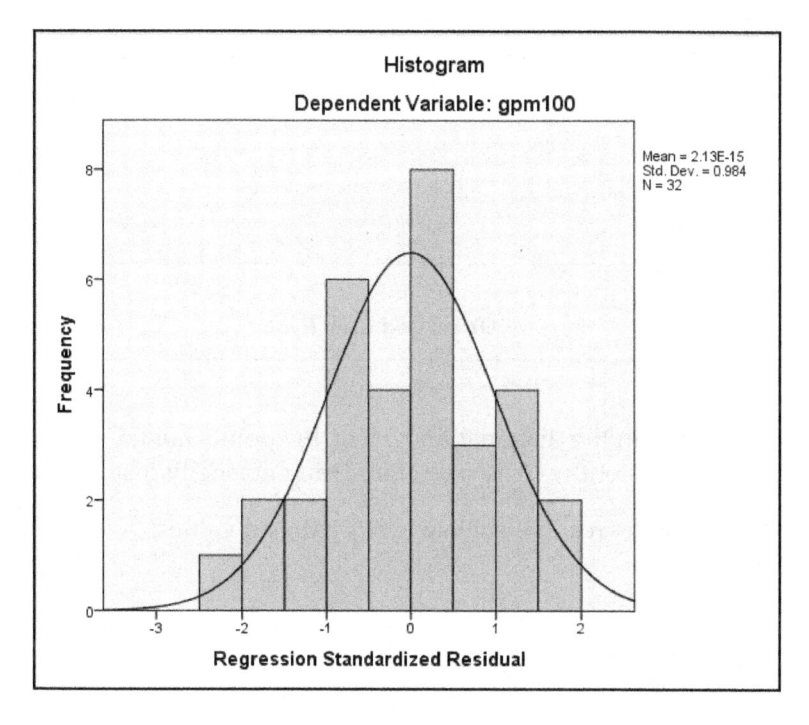

Histogram
Dependent Variable: gpm100

Mean = 2.13E-15
Std. Dev. = 0.984
N = 32

With an overall sample size of 32, the histogram is somewhat coarsely filled in but is overall consistent with normality.

Linear Regression

Here is the normal p-p plot of the residuals:

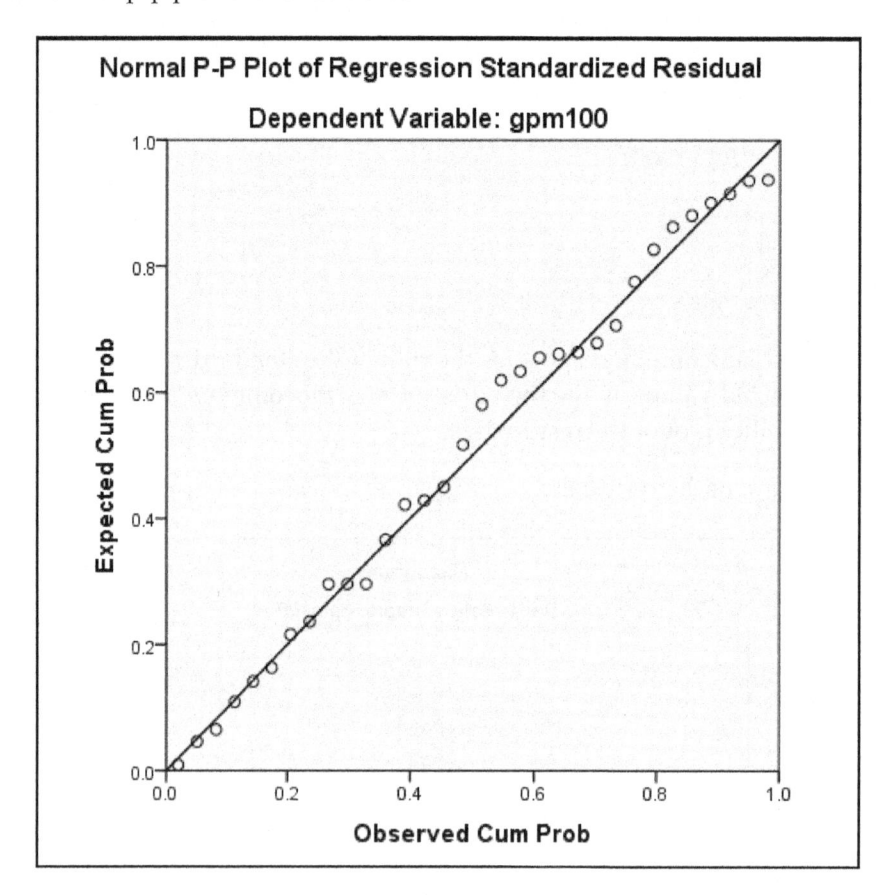

Normal P-P Plot of Regression Standardized Residual
Dependent Variable: gpm100

Ideally, the points align with the diagonal line. Here, the points fall fairly close to the line overall. Again, this is consistent with the residuals being normally distributed.

Finally, here is the plot of the residuals versus the predicted values:

Scatterplot
Dependent Variable: gpm100

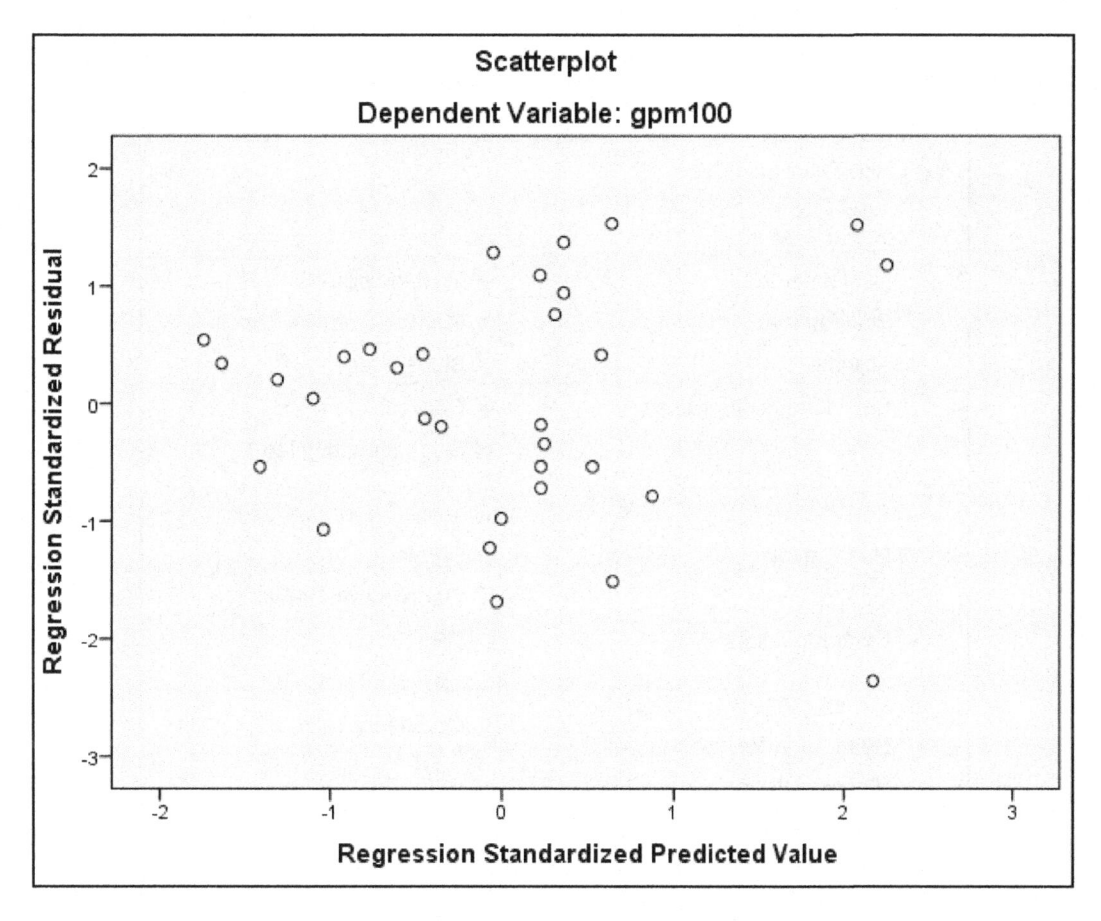

Ideally, the plot is without pattern, which appears to be the case here. Regression textbooks present common patterns such as the following: A funnel-shaped pattern suggests that the residuals do not have a constant variance across the predictors; a horseshoe-shaped pattern suggests an underlying nonlinearity not captured by the model; and so on.

Saving and interpreting casewise diagnostics

Especially, in small samples, you might want to explore whether individual data points in the regression model are **influential points**, that is, points whose presence or absence leads to a notably different estimated model or is poorly predicted by the overall model. SPSS Statistics Regression offers an extensive list of diagnostic statistics for this, which we illustrate using the example data.

Linear Regression

To see the casewise statistics that you can save, press the **Save** button on the main **Linear Regression** dialog box. This brings up the **Linear Regression: Save** dialog box.

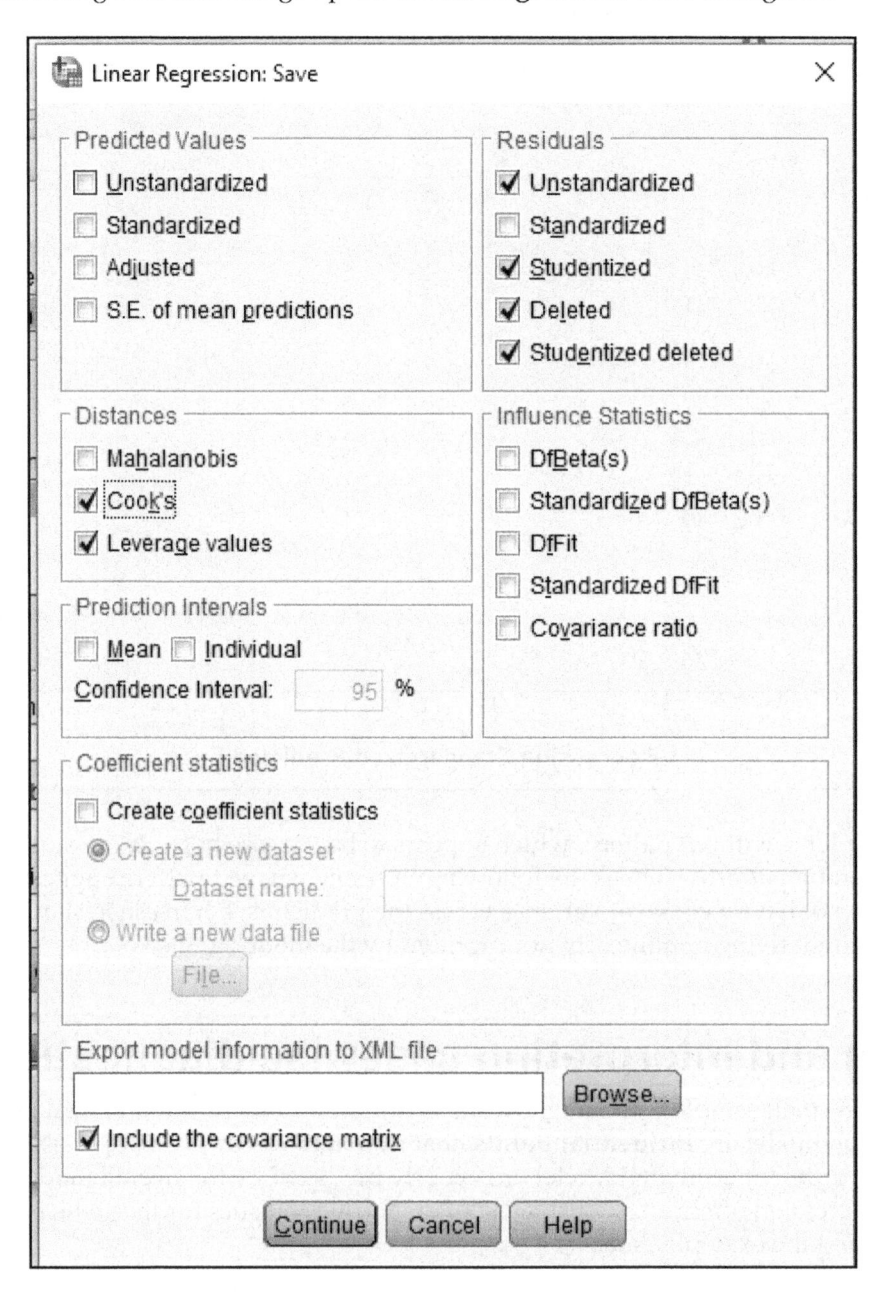

This dialog box presents all the variables that you can save to the active file. Here we check a handful of variables in the **Residuals** and **Distances** check box areas. The **Residuals** items checked produce the usual regression residuals plus scaled forms of the residuals. The **Distances** items checked produce saved variables that indicate how far a case is from the center of the predictors (**Mahalanobis**) and a measure of how much the residuals of all cases would change if a particular case were excluded from the calculation of the regression coefficients (**Cook's**).

With the check boxes checked, press **Continue** and the press **Paste**. Here is the resulting REGRESSION code:

```
REGRESSION
 /MISSING LISTWISE
 /STATISTICS COEFF OUTS R ANOVA
 /CRITERIA=PIN(.05) POUT(.10)
 /NOORIGIN
 /DEPENDENT gpm100
 /METHOD=ENTER wt
 /SAVE RESID SRESID DRESID SDRESID LEVER COOK.
```

The /SAVE subcommand saves a number of new fields based on the regression analysis:

- RESID is the usual **unstandardized** residual, defined as the difference between the observed target value and the predicted value from the model for that case.
- SRESID is the **studentized** residual, which is the residual scaled by an estimate of its standard deviation that varies from case to case.
- DRESID is the **deleted** residual, defined as the residual for a case when the case is excluded from the calculation of the regression coefficients.
- SDRESID is the **studentized deleted** residual, defined as the deleted residual for a case divided by its standard error.
- LEVER is the **centered leverage** value, a measure of influence of a point on the fit of the regression line. It will range in value from 0 to (N-1)/N, where N is the sample size. Larger values of the leverage are associated with points far from the center value of the predictor or predictors.
- COOK is Cook's distance, a measure of how much the residuals of all cases would change if a particular case were excluded from the calculation of the regression coefficients.

Linear Regression

Here is a table showing the observation that most stands out on these diagnostic measures:

Model of vehicle	gpm100	Weight (1000 lbs)	Unstandardized Residual	Studentized Residual	Studentized Deleted Residual	Centered Leverage Value	Cook's Distance
Chrysler Imperial	6.80	5.345	-1.79837	-2.61363	-2.92409	.15254	.76912

First, consider the various residual values. In a relative sense, the Chrysler Imperial is the most poorly predicted observation. As a rule of thumb, studentized residuals that exceed 3 in absolute value could be viewed as outliers, and the **studentized residual** and **studentized deleted residual** values for the Chrysler Imperial approach that cutoff. You should inspect these residuals for some of the other cases to get a sense of their values and range.

To assess the leverage values, consider that the mean of the centered leverage values is p/N, where p is the number of predictors and N is the sample size. Here, this is 1/32, which equals 0.031. A rule of thumb for the leverage is that values of the leverage that exceed twice this value merit a closer look. The **centered leverage value** for the Chrysler Imperial is .15254, which exceeds this value, and, in fact, this case has the second largest wt value, which places it at some distance from the mean wt. Leverage indicates a potential for influence; other things equal, points far from the center of the predictor values have a potential for influence.

Regarding Cook's distance, one rule of thumb says that values of Cook's distance that exceed 1 indicate an influential point. Another rule of thumb suggests looking closer at cases for which Cook's distance exceeds 4/N. For the point in question, the **Cook's distance** value is .769, which is the largest value but less than the cutoff of 1. The Cook's distance value for this point reflects both its leverage and the relative magnitude of its scaled residual. You might also assess this Cook's distance value against the mean value of Cook's distance, which is .054 for these data.

Here is the plot of gpm100 versus wt, with the case identifier **17** labeling the point in question:

Linear Regression

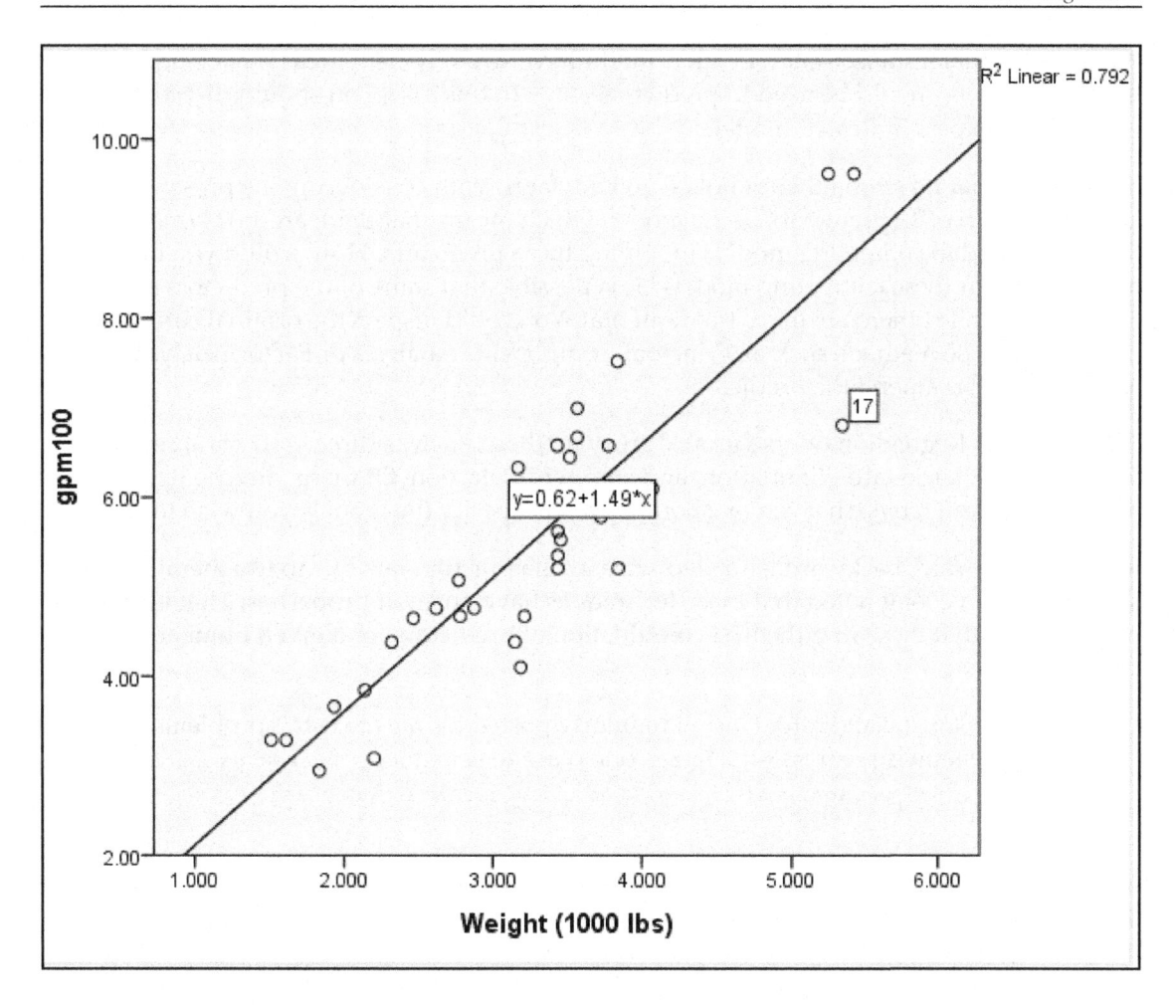

[Scatterplot of gpm100 vs Weight (1000 lbs) with regression line y=0.62+1.49*x, R² Linear = 0.792, case 17 labeled]

Having identified case number 17 as the most influential point, what should you do? In point of fact, every data situation will have a most influential point, and the naive removal of the point is not in itself justified. Here, we choose to retain all the data.

Multiple regression - Model-building strategies

Let's consider again the motor trends car data with target variable gpm100 and 10 predictors.

Linear Regression

It is possible that a subject-matter expert might have strongly-held ideas regarding which of the 10 predictors should be used to predict gpm100. In this case, you should directly estimate the expert-indicated model.

In the event that no strong theory holds, you are faced with considering the presence or absence of each of 10 predictors in the model, which means that there are 1,024 (including the empty model) competing models involving these predictors. How would you even begin to look at these competing models? It is possible that some of the predictors are redundant, while others are more fundamental. You could inspect the original correlations, or you could use methods such as Principal Components Analysis or Factor Analysis to look for patterns among the predictors.

SPSS Statistics Regression offers variable entry methods such as direct entry and removal, forward entry, backward elimination, and step-wise selection. Of these, direct entry and removal are preferable. That is, you should directly specify the models you wish to see.

Regarding forward, backward, and step-wise, while practitioners like to use them, statisticians have long noted that these techniques have no good properties. That is, there is no guarantee that these find the best combination of predictors for a given number of predictors.

> Statistician Frank Harrell regularly posted his *top ten* list of problems with stepwise regression. Here is one place to find it: http://www.stata.com/support/faqs/statistics/stepwise-regression-problems/.

In choosing between 1,024 possible equations, you cannot use R or R-square for model selection since these increase as variables are added to the equation and would favor the full model with 10 predictors. Instead, statisticians have developed various measures that attempt to balance model goodness of fit with model complexity/parsimony. These measures include the Akaike information criterion and the adjusted R-square.

In addition, statisticians have also found fast ways to do all possible subsets regression for problems of up to several dozen predictors. You can accomplish this in the SPSS Statistics Linear procedure. In an analysis that isn't shown here, the equation with **wt** and **hp** produces the *best* AIC value and one of the best adjusted R-square values.

Suppose instead that you consider **feature engineering**, that is, creating new variables that are some transformation of the existing ones. Henderson and Velleman suggested that some measure of how overpowered a car is might be a useful measure, and they used the ratio of horsepower to weight, hp/wt.

Here is the SPSS code for deriving this new variable as well as looking at its correlation with the target variable and the predictor already considered, `wt`:

```
COMPUTE hp_wt=hp / wt.
CORRELATIONS
  /VARIABLES=gpm100 wt hp_wt
  /PRINT=TWOTAIL NOSIG
  /MISSING=PAIRWISE.
```

Here is the correlation table for `gpm100`, `wt`, and `hp_wt`:

Correlations

Pearson Correlation

	Gallons per 100 miles	Weight (1000 lbs)	hp_wt
Gallons per 100 miles	1	.890**	.285
Weight (1000 lbs)	.890**	1	.054
hp_wt	.285	.054	1

**. Correlation is significant at the 0.01 level (2-tailed).

Note that `hp_wt` is both moderately correlated with the target, `gpm100`, and almost uncorrelated with the other predictor, `wt`. This is a good sign as it suggests that each of these predictors will be useful in predicting `gpm100`.

Now, run the regression of `gpm100` on `wt` and `hp_wt`:

```
REGRESSION
  /MISSING LISTWISE
  /STATISTICS COEFF OUTS R ANOVA
  /CRITERIA=PIN(.05) POUT(.10)
  /NOORIGIN
  /DEPENDENT gpm100
  /METHOD=ENTER wt hp_wt
  /PARTIALPLOT ALL
  /SCATTERPLOT=(*ZRESID ,*ZPRED)
  /RESIDUALS HISTOGRAM(ZRESID) NORMPROB(ZRESID).
```

This regression specification is similar to the previous ones. Here, we enter two predictors, `wt` and `hp_wt`. One new subcommand is `/PARTIALPLOT`, which displays partial regression plots.

Linear Regression

Now, let's review the regression results for this model.

Here is the **Variables Entered/Removed** table:

Variables Entered/Removed[a]

Model	Variables Entered	Variables Removed	Method
1	hp_wt, Weight (1000 lbs)[b]	.	Enter

a. Dependent Variable: Gallons per 100 miles
b. All requested variables entered.

Two predictors are directly entered: wt and hp_wt.

Here is the **Model Summary** table:

Model Summary[b]

Model	R	R Square	Adjusted R Square	Std. Error of the Estimate
1	.921[a]	.848	.838	.66123

a. Predictors: (Constant), hp_wt, Weight (1000 lbs)
b. Dependent Variable: Gallons per 100 miles

Note the improvement in the multiple R relative to our first model: from **.890** to **.921**.

Here is the ANOVA table for the regression:

ANOVA[a]

Model		Sum of Squares	df	Mean Square	F	Sig.
1	Regression	70.946	2	35.473	81.131	.000[b]
	Residual	12.680	29	.437		
	Total	83.625	31			

a. Dependent Variable: Gallons per 100 miles
b. Predictors: (Constant), hp_wt, Weight (1000 lbs)

The **F** statistic is **81.131** on **2** and **29** degrees of freedom, and it is statistically significant at the .05 level.

Here is the regression `coefficients` table:

Coefficients[a]

Model		Unstandardized Coefficients B	Std. Error	Standardized Coefficients Beta	t	Sig.
1	(Constant)	-.402	.512		-.784	.439
	Weight (1000 lbs)	1.472	.122	.877	12.111	.000
	hp_wt	.024	.007	.238	3.286	.003

a. Dependent Variable: Gallons per 100 miles

The individual coefficients associated with `wt` and `hp_wt` are both statistically significant.

Linear Regression

Here is the partial regression plot for `gpm100.wt` versus `hp_wt.wt`, where the *dot* notation denotes that `wt` is partialed out of the plot as explained in the following screenshot:

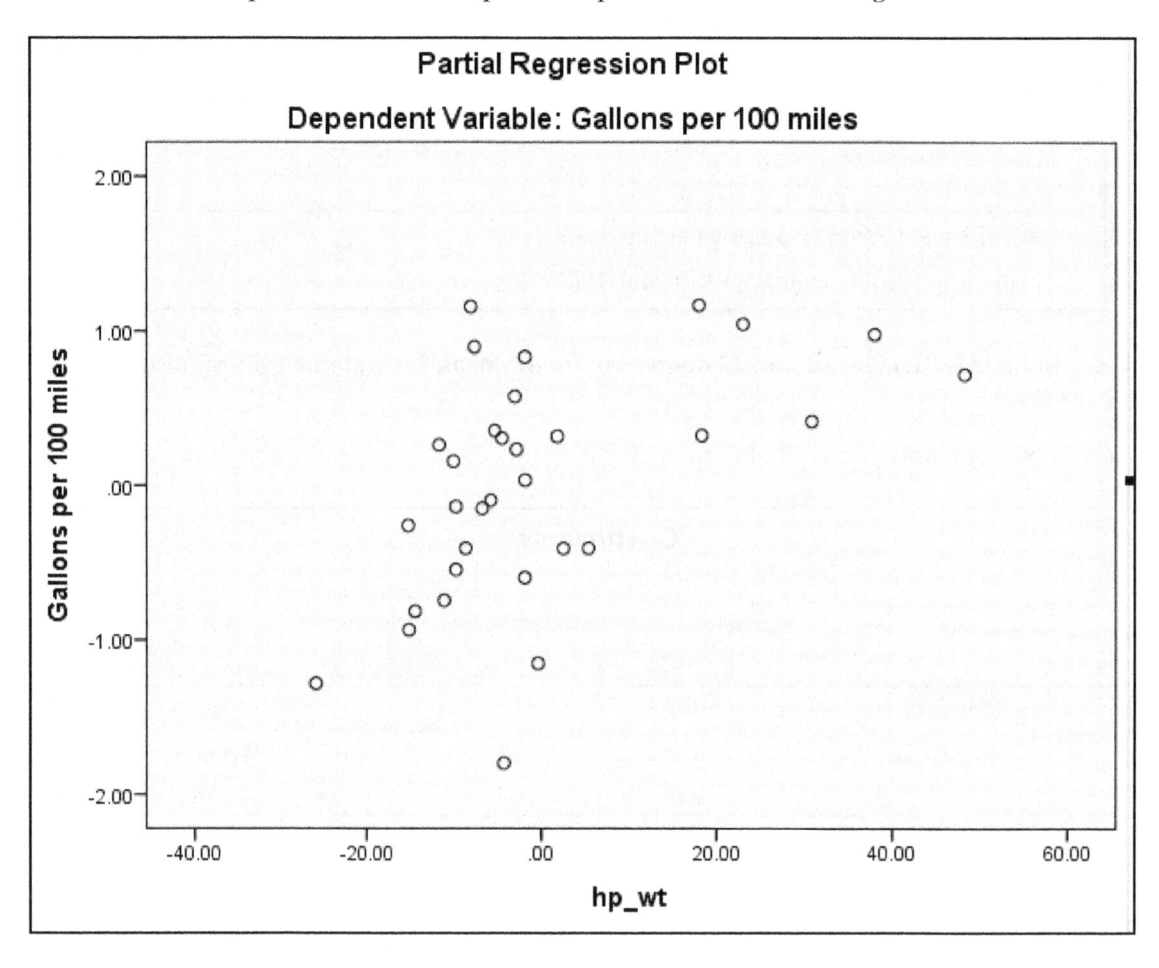

Partial Regression Plot

Dependent Variable: Gallons per 100 miles

[Scatter plot with x-axis labeled "hp_wt" ranging from -40.00 to 60.00, and y-axis labeled "Gallons per 100 miles" ranging from -2.00 to 2.00]

In general, the partial regression plot attempts to show the effect of adding a variable to the model, given that one or more predictors are already in the model. In this situation, we see the effect of adding `hp_wt` to the model containing `wt`. For this particular plot, Henderson and Velleman note that most of the high-performance cars are in a *band* to the right.

At this point, you have a parsimonious model that fits the data well and accounts for patterns in the data. Also, it turns out that the remaining predictors do not significantly improve the model. You can learn this by adding each predictor in turn to the current model.

Summary

The example used a *classic* dataset to explore models relating car mileage to a set of design and performance features. One key insight was to work with a scaled version of the reciprocal of **mpg** rather than **mpg** itself. Another insight was to develop a parsimonious model, given the relatively small sample size and high ratio of variables to cases. A final insight was to create a predictor by taking the ratio of two predictors--`hp` and `wt`--rather than working with the manifest predictors.

Indeed, this was one of the points of the article by Henderson and Velleman, who cautioned against *automated* multiple regression model-building back in 1981! The model we ended up with is parsimonious, interpretable, and fits the data well.

In the next chapter, we turn to two important exploratory techniques: Principal Components Analysis and Factor Analysis.

14
Principal Components and Factor Analysis

The SPSS Statistics **FACTOR** procedure provides a comprehensive procedure for doing principal components analysis and factor analysis. The underlying computations for these two techniques are similar, which is why SPSS Statistics bundles them in the same procedure. However, they are sufficiently distinct, so you should consider what your research goals are and choose the appropriate method for your goals.

Principal components analysis (PCA) finds weighted combinations of the original variables that account for the total variance in the original variables. The first principal component finds the linear combination of variables that accounts for as much variance as possible. The second principal component finds the linear combination of variables that accounts for as much of the remaining variance as possible, and also has the property that it is orthogonal (independent) to the first component, and so on.

PCA is employed as a dimension reduction technique. Your data might contain a large number of correlated variables, and it can be a challenge to understand the patterns and relationships among them. While there are as many components as there are original variables in the analysis, you can often account for a sufficient fraction of the total variance in the original variables using a smaller set of principal components.

Factor analysis (FA) finds one or more common factors--that is, latent variables (variables that are not directly observed)--that account for the correlations between the observed variables. There are necessarily fewer factors than variables in the analysis. Typically, the researcher employs factor rotation to aid interpretation.

Principal Components and Factor Analysis

Both of these techniques are exploratory techniques. The researcher is often unsure at the outset of the analysis what number of components or factors might be adequate or right. The SPSS Statistics FACTOR program offers statistics and plots both for assessing the suitability of the data for analysis as well as for assessing the quality of the tentative PCA or FA solution.

This chapter covers the following topics:

- Choosing between PCA and FA
- Description of PCA example data
- SPSS Code for initial PCA analysis of example data
- Assessing factorability of the data
- Principal components analysis--two-component run
- Description of factor analysis example data
- The reduced correlation matrix and its eigenvalues
- Factor analysis code
- Factor analysis results

Choosing between principal components analysis and factor analysis

How does FA differ from PCA? Overall, as indicated in the chapter introduction, PCA accounts for the total variance of the variables in terms of the linear combinations of the original variables, while FA accounts for the correlations of the observed variables by positing latent factors. Here are some contrasts on how you would approach the respective analyses in SPSS Statistics FACTOR.

> **TIP**
> You can employ PCA on either covariances or correlations. Likewise, you can employ FA on either covariances (for extraction methods `PAF` or `IMAGE`) or correlations. The analysis in this chapter analyzes correlation matrices because correlations implicitly put variables on a common scale, and that is often needed for the data with which we work.

Principal Components and Factor Analysis

Following are a few of the important parameters in the discussion of PCA and FA:

- Regarding **methods**: If you wish to run PCA, there is one method--`PCA`. If you wish to run factor analysis, the most commonly used methods are **principal axis factoring (PAF)** and **maximum likelihood (ML)**. Other methods are available in FACTOR, and you should consult a textbook or the following references for more information. Because the default method is `PCA`, you must explicitly specify a factor method if you intend to do factor analysis and not principal components analysis.
- Regarding **communality estimates**: The **communality**, or common variance, of a variable is the amount of variance that is shared among a set of variables that can be explained by a set of common factors. The goal of PCA is to explain the **total variance** among the set of variables, or at least some fraction of it, while the goal of FA is to explain the **common variance** among a set of variables.

  As indicated in the following PCA example, the initial communality estimates for the variables are ones, while the final communality estimates depends on the order of the solution. If you specify as many components as there are factors, then the final communalities are one, while if you specify fewer components than there are factors, the final communalities are typically less than one.

  In FA, SPSS Statistics FACTOR supplies initial communality estimates automatically. Typically, these are squared multiple correlations when the variable in question is regressed on the rest of the variables in the analysis. Final communalities are a byproduct of analysis elements, such as the extraction method used and the specified number of factors.
- Regarding **the number of components or factors:** In PCA, you can extract as many components as there are variables, while in FA, the number of factors is necessarily less than the number of variables. In FA, but not PCA, the closeness of the reproduced correlations (off the main diagonal) to the observed correlations guides the choice of the number of factors to retain.
- Regarding **rotation:** Principal components have the geometric interpretation of being uncorrelated directions of maximum variations in the data. This interpretation holds only for the unrotated component loadings, so if you do perform rotation on component loadings, you lose this interpretation.

  In the case of factor analysis, rotation is often done to aid **interpretability**. Ideally, after rotation, you can identify sets of variables that go together, as indicated by high loadings on a given factor. Presumably, these sets represent variables that are correlated more with each other than with the rest of the variables.

  SPSS Statistics FACTOR provides a number of popular orthogonal and oblique rotation methods. Orthogonal rotations lead to uncorrelated factors, but there is no reason to think **a priori** that the factors are uncorrelated, so in general, you should consider oblique rotation methods which allow factors to correlate.

- Regarding **scores:** When using PCA, you can compute component scores, and when using FA, you can compute factor scores. When computing component scores, you are mathematically projecting the observations into the space of components. We demonstrate this in the following PCA example. When computing factor scores, technical literature draws attention to the problem of factor indeterminacy (see the Mulaik reference for a discussion). For this reason, some researchers caution against computing and using factor scores.

> Often, the reason the analyst computes factor scores is to use the derived variable as either a predictor or a target in an analysis. In this case, you might avoid computing factor scores altogether, and instead consider the framework of Structural Equation Models (not covered in this book).

This chapter focuses on using SPSS Statistics FACTOR for PCA and FA. For background, and more information on these methods, here are two recommended books.

> Here is a readable modern treatment: Fabrigar, Leandre and Wegener, Duane. (2012). *Exploratory Factor Analysis*. New York: Oxford University Press. Here is a technical reference: Mulaik, Stanley. (2010). *Foundations of Factor Analysis, 2nd edition*. Boca Raton: Chapman & Hall/CRC Press.

PCA example - violent crimes

The data consists of state-level data for the 50 states of the USA and also the District of Columbia. It comes from the year 2014, the most recent year available on our source website.

> The data was obtained from the website: https://www.ucrdatatool.gov. This website is maintained by the Federal Bureau of Investigation.

The measures consist of estimated crime counts and crime rates per 100,000 for the following violent crimes:

- Murder and non-negligent manslaughter
- Rape
- Robbery
- Aggravated assault

Following are the property crimes:

- Burglary
- Larceny-theft
- Motor vehicle theft

Here is a description of the **Uniform Crime Reporting (UCR)** program from the website:

> "The FBI has gathered crime statistics from law enforcement agencies across the nation that have voluntarily participated in the UCR program since 1930. These data have been published each year, and since 1958, have been available in the publication Crime in the United States (CIUS). As a supplement to CIUS, the FBI, in cooperation with the Bureau of Justice Statistics, provides this site that allows users to build their own customized data tables. The UCR Program collects statistics on violent crime (murder and nonnegligent manslaughter, rape, robbery, and aggravated assault) and property crime (burglary, larceny-theft, and motor vehicle theft)".

For more information on the data, including definitions of the offenses, take a look at the website.

In particular, we will work with the following fields measuring state crime rates per 100,000:

- MurderandManslaughterRate
- RevisedRapeRate
- RobberyRate
- AggravatedAssaultRate
- BurglaryRate
- Larceny_TheftRate
- MotorVehicleRate

The first four crimes are violent crimes against people, while the last three crimes are crimes against property.

We work with rates here, because the rates put the measures on a common scale. If instead we work with raw numbers, then states with large populations will tend to have large numbers of crimes, and that will likely dominate the PCA solution.

The sample size of 51 is a given--50 states plus DC.

Simple descriptive analysis

As shown throughout the examples in this book, you should begin with simple descriptive statistics and charts.

Here are the **Descriptive Statistics** obtained from running the DESCRIPTIVES procedure:

Descriptive Statistics	N	Minimum	Maximum	Mean	Std. Deviation
MurderandManslaughterRate	51	.9	15.9	4.298	2.5185
RevisedRapeRate	51	14.3	104.7	40.506	15.2707
RobberyRate	51	9.1	530.7	88.965	75.2287
AggravatedAssaultRate	51	66.9	626.1	230.635	110.3125
BurglaryRate	51	257.2	887.3	527.284	181.6954
Larceny_TheftRate	51	1160.8	4082.3	1876.239	485.9266
MotorVehicleTheftRate	51	38.9	574.1	199.976	98.2804
Valid N (listwise)	51				

Murder and manslaughter crimes have the lowest mean rate of 4.298 per 100,000, while at the other extreme, larceny-theft has a mean rate of about 1,876 per 100,000.

Here are the **Correlations** for all pairs of variables:

Pearson Correlation	MurderandManslaughterRate	RevisedRapeRate	RobberyRate	AggravatedAssaultRate	BurglaryRate	Larceny_TheftRate	MotorVehicleTheftRate
MurderandManslaughterRate	1	.272	.800**	.743**	.489**	.685**	.532**
RevisedRapeRate	.272	1	.209	.586**	.169	.445**	.420**
RobberyRate	.800**	.209	1	.650**	.252	.648**	.647**
AggravatedAssaultRate	.743**	.586**	.650**	1	.476**	.644**	.579**
BurglaryRate	.489**	.169	.252	.476**	1	.546**	.458**
Larceny_TheftRate	.685**	.445**	.648**	.644**	.546**	1	.720**
MotorVehicleTheftRate	.532**	.420**	.647**	.579**	.458**	.720**	1

**. Correlation is significant at the 0.01 level (2-tailed).

The first thing to notice is that all of the correlations are the same sign. Large correlations include those between the `MurderandManslaughterRate` and the `Robbery` and `AggravatedAssaultrates`, as well as the one between `Larceny_TheftRate` and `MotorVehicleTheftRate`.

SPSS code - principal components analysis

Here is the `FACTOR` command for running PCA on the crime data:

```
FACTOR
  /VARIABLES MurderandManslaughterRate RevisedRapeRate RobberyRate
  AggravatedAssaultRate BurglaryRate Larceny_TheftRate
MotorVehicleTheftRate
  /MISSING LISTWISE
  /ANALYSIS MurderandManslaughterRate RevisedRapeRate RobberyRate
AggravatedAssaultRate
  BurglaryRate Larceny_TheftRate MotorVehicleTheftRate
  /PRINT INITIAL DET KMO INV AIC EXTRACTION
  /PLOT EIGEN
  /CRITERIA FACTORS(7) ITERATE(25)
  /EXTRACTION PC
  /ROTATION NOROTATE
  /METHOD=CORRELATION.
```

The key elements of the preceding code are as follows:

- The extraction method is `PC`
- The rotation method is `Norotate`
- The analysis is based on `correlations`

Here are comments on the `FACTOR` syntax:

- The `/VARIABLES` subcommand specifies all of the variables to be used in the principal components analysis.
- The `/MISSING` subcommand controls the treatment of cases with missing values. By default, the `/MISSING` subcommand specifies listwise deletion. In fact, there are no missing values in this data.
- The `/ANALYSIS` subcommand specifies a subset of the variables named on the `/VARIABLES` subcommand for use in the analysis. Here, the variables specified are the same as those specified in `/VARIABLES`.

- The /PRINT subcommand controls the statistical display in the output. Here, we specify some additional non-default commands. INITIAL specifies the initial communalities for each variable, the eigenvalues of the unreduced correlation matrix, and the percentage of variance for each factor or component. DET specifies the determinant of the correlation matrix. KMO specifies the Kaiser-Meyer-Olkin measure of sampling adequacy and Bartlett's test of sphericity. INV specifies the inverse of the correlation matrix. AIC specifies the anti-image covariance and correlation matrices. The measure of sampling adequacy for the individual variables is displayed on the diagonal of the anti-image correlation matrix.
- The /PLOT subcommand specifies the EIGEN keyword, which instructs SPSS Statistics to print the **scree plot**. The **scree plot** displays the eigenvalues versus their order.
- The /CRITERIA subcommand controls extraction and rotation criteria. FACTORS controls the number of factors or components extracted. Here, we request all seven components. ITERATE specifies 25 as the maximum number of iterations for extraction and rotation.
- The /EXTRACTION subcommand specifies the factor extraction technique. Here, the keyword PC specifies principal components analysis.
- The /ROTATION subcommand specifies the factor rotation method. Here, NOROTATE specifies no rotation.
- The /METHOD subcommand specifies whether factor analysis is performed on a correlation matrix or a covariance matrix. Here, the CORRELATION keyword specifies that the principal components analysis be performed on the correlation matrix.

Assessing factorability of the data

In the case of either principal components analysis or factor analysis, you should first examine a number of factorability statistics and tests.

Essentially, you wish to ascertain whether it makes sense to proceed with the principal components analysis or factor analysis. Essentially, you wish to establish that the variables are mutually correlated to some extent. At one extreme, if the variables in the analysis are unrelated, then it makes no sense to proceed with an analysis. At the other extreme, one or more variables might be redundant given other variables in the analysis. In this situation, you might proceed by removing redundant variables from the analysis.

In this section, we consider the following factorability statistics:

- Determinant of the correlation matrix
- Inverse of the correlation matrix
- Kaiser-Meyer-Olkin measure of sampling adequacy
- Bartlett's test of sphericity
- Anti-image correlation matrix

Here is the determinant of the correlation matrix:

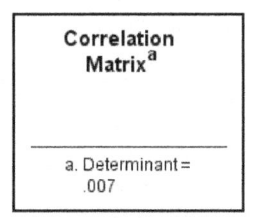

Correlation Matrix[a]

a. Determinant = .007

In general, two conditions should hold for the correlation matrix:

- The correlation matrix should be based on a common set of observations (either listwise deletion of missing data or no missing data on the variables being analyzed). If the correlation matrix is not based on a common set of observations, which could happen with pairwise deletion of missing values, the resulting correlation matrix could lack the properties necessary for PCA, in particular, that all of the eigenvalues of the correlation matrix are nonnegative.
- The correlation matrix should be obtained in a situation where the number of observations exceeds the number of variables. If the number of variables exceeds the number of observations, then the determinant of the correlation matrix is necessarily zero.

Given that we meet the preceding two conditions, the determinant of the correlation matrix is non-negative and ranges between zero and one. If the determinant is exactly zero, then at least one of the variables in the analysis is perfectly predicted by a linear combination of other variables. If the determinant is near-zero, then at least one of the variables in the analysis is almost perfectly predicted by a linear combination of other variables. Near-zero means very small, and a determinant of .007 is not extremely small. While there is no ironclad rule, some researchers recommend that the determinant be larger than .00001.

The determinant is a useful measure because it goes beyond the bivariate view of things seen in the preceding correlation matrix. In the event that you identify a redundancy, you might consider dropping one or more of the highly correlated items from the analysis.

Here is the **Inverse of Correlation Matrix**:

Inverse of Correlation Matrix

	MurderandManslaughterRate	RevisedRapeRate	RobberyRate	AggravatedAssaultRate	BurglaryRate	Larceny_TheftRate	MotorVehicleTheftRate
MurderandManslaughterRate	4.736	.216	-2.819	-1.432	-1.007	-.836	1.103
RevisedRapeRate	.216	2.145	1.153	-1.706	.713	-.726	-.576
RobberyRate	-2.819	1.153	4.896	-1.082	1.650	-.666	-1.797
AggravatedAssaultRate	-1.432	-1.706	-1.082	3.912	-.801	.334	.038
BurglaryRate	-1.007	.713	1.650	-.801	2.118	-.782	-.772
Larceny_TheftRate	-.836	-.726	-.666	.334	-.782	3.265	-1.007
MotorVehicleTheftRate	1.103	-.576	-1.797	.038	-.772	-1.007	2.874

The diagonal elements are probably the most informative elements of the **Inverse of Correlation Matrix**. They are **Variance Inflation Factors** for the variables in question, and they measure the extent to which a variable is predicted by a linear combination of the other variables. The *j*th diagonal element of the inverse correlation matrix is $1/(1 - R^2_j)$, where R^2_j is the squared multiple correlation of the *j*th variable with the others. A large diagonal element indicates that the variable shares a lot of variances with the rest of the set. There is no firm rule for how large these numbers need to be before you should take action, although some researchers use a cutpoint of 10 or more. By that standard, these numbers are not large.

The **KMO and Bartlett's Test** table displays two statistics:

- The **Kaiser-Meyer-Olkin (KMO) measure of sampling adequacy**
- **Bartlett's test of sphericity**

KMO and Bartlett's Test

Kaiser-Meyer-Olkin Measure of Sampling Adequacy.		.729
Bartlett's Test of Sphericity	Approx. Chi-Square	230.555
	df	21
	Sig.	.000

The **KMO measure of Sampling Adequacy** is a measure of how suited the data is to principal components analysis or factor analysis. The measure takes into account the magnitudes of the original bivariate correlations of the variables, as well as the partial correlations of each pair when the other variables in the set are accounted for.

The measure takes the following form:

$$sum(correlations)^2 / (sum(correlations)^2 + sum(partials)^2)$$

In the event that the variables are related, the partials will be small, and the overall expression will be close to one. In the event that relationships between variables are weak, the partials will be large and the overall expression will be relatively small.

The measure ranges between zero and one, with larger values indicating suitability for further analysis. While it is difficult to give firm recommendations, research literature suggests the following rules of thumb (with adjectives supplied by Kaiser):

- A KMO value of 0.8 or higher indicates that the sampling is meritorious
- A KMO value of 0.7-0.8 indicates that the sampling is middling
- A KMO value of less than 0.6 is mediocre or unacceptable

In our situation, the KMO value is about .73, indicating the suitability of the data for further analysis by Kaiser's standard.

Bartlett's test of sphericity tests the null hypothesis that the correlation matrix is an identity matrix--the off-diagonal correlations are not statistically different from zero. In the event that we cannot reject the null hypothesis, there would be no justification for further analysis, since the set of variables would lack association. With seven variables, there are 21 unique correlations. The Bartlett value here is 230.555, which is large and leads us to reject the null hypothesis. Thus, the Bartlett test also indicates the suitability of the data for further analysis.

Here is the **Anti-image Correlation** matrix:

Anti-image Correlation	MurderandManslaughterRate	RevisedRapeRate	RobberyRate	AggravatedAssaultRate	BurglaryRate	Larceny_TheftRate	MotorVehicleTheftRate
MurderandManslaughterRate	.765[a]	.068	-.585	-.333	-.318	-.212	.299
RevisedRapeRate	.068	.546[a]	.356	-.589	.335	-.274	-.232
RobberyRate	-.585	.356	.657[a]	-.247	.512	-.167	-.479
AggravatedAssaultRate	-.333	-.589	-.247	.791[a]	-.278	.093	.011
BurglaryRate	-.318	.335	.512	-.278	.590[a]	-.297	-.313
Larceny_TheftRate	-.212	-.274	-.167	.093	-.297	.868[a]	-.329
MotorVehicleTheftRate	.299	-.232	-.479	.011	-.313	-.329	.770[a]

a. Measures of Sampling Adequacy(MSA)

Off diagonal, this matrix contains the negatives of the partial correlation coefficients. On the main diagonal, this matrix contains individual measures of sampling adequacy. Again, we would like to see values of about 0.7 or higher. Given the adjectives proposed by Kaiser, the measures of sampling adequacy for **RevisedRapeRate** and **BurglaryRate** are somewhat low.

> In sum, the concluded review of factorability measures suggests that we are justified in proceeding with principal components analysis on the violent crime rate variables.

Principal components analysis of the crime variables

Now we turn to the principal components analysis of the crime variables. The tables and chart that we cover here are as follows:

- The Communalities table
- The Total Variance Explained table
- The **Scree Plot**
- The Component Matrix table

Here is the Communalities table:

Communalities	Initial	Extraction
MurderandManslaughterRate	1.000	1.000
RevisedRapeRate	1.000	1.000
RobberyRate	1.000	1.000
AggravatedAssaultRate	1.000	1.000
BurglaryRate	1.000	1.000
Larceny_TheftRate	1.000	1.000
MotorVehicleTheftRate	1.000	1.000

Extraction Method: Principal Component Analysis.

The **Initial** communalities are one. This will always be the case in PCA when the correlation matrix is being analyzed, since PCA attempts to account for the total variance of the variables.

The **Extraction** communalities are the communalities of the variables, given the specified unrotated PCA solution. Since the PCA solution is the full solution with seven components, which is the same as the number of variables in the analysis, the PCA solution accounts for all the variance in the variables.

Here is the `Total Variance Explained` table:

Total Variance Explained

	Initial Eigenvalues			Extraction Sums of Squared Loadings		
Component	Total	% of Variance	Cumulative %	Total	% of Variance	Cumulative %
1	4.230	60.430	60.430	4.230	60.430	60.430
2	.924	13.200	73.629	.924	13.200	73.629
3	.786	11.231	84.860	.786	11.231	84.860
4	.527	7.532	92.392	.527	7.532	92.392
5	.272	3.880	96.272	.272	3.880	96.272
6	.152	2.177	98.450	.152	2.177	98.450
7	.109	1.550	100.000	.109	1.550	100.000

Extraction Method: Principal Component Analysis.

This table has two halves:

- Left side: **Initial Eigenvalues-Component, Total, % of Variance, Cumulative %**
- Right side: **Extraction Sums of Squared Loadings-Total, % of Variance, Cumulative %**

In the special case where the number of components is the same as the number of original variables, the two halves are identical.

Regarding the **Initial Eigenvalues** side, these statistics pertain to the original correlation matrix.

The **Total** column contains the eigenvalues of the correlation matrix. The eigenvalues are the variances of the principal components. When you analyze a correlation matrix, each variable has a variance of one. The eigenvalues sum up to the total variance, which is seven, the number of variables in the analysis. At one extreme, if the variables in the analysis are completely uncorrelated, the individual eigenvalues will all be one.

Principal Components and Factor Analysis

At the other extreme, if the variables in the analysis are completely redundant, the first eigenvalue will be seven and the others will all be zero. In between, as is the case here, the first eigenvalue is substantial and accounts for the largest portion of variance, while the other eigenvalues trail off in magnitude.

As an aside, researchers have long proposed a rule of thumb that suggests retaining the components, or factors, for which eigenvalues are greater than one. While this rule is well known, the modern consensus is that there is nothing to recommend this rule of thumb. See the two recommended references for details.

The **% of variance** column contains the percent of variance accounted for by each principal component.

The **Cumulative %** column contains the cumulative percentage of variance accounted for by the current and preceding principal components.

Regarding the **Extraction Sums of Squared Loadings** side, the full seven-component solution reproduces the **Initial Eigenvalues** analysis.

Here is the **Scree Plot**:

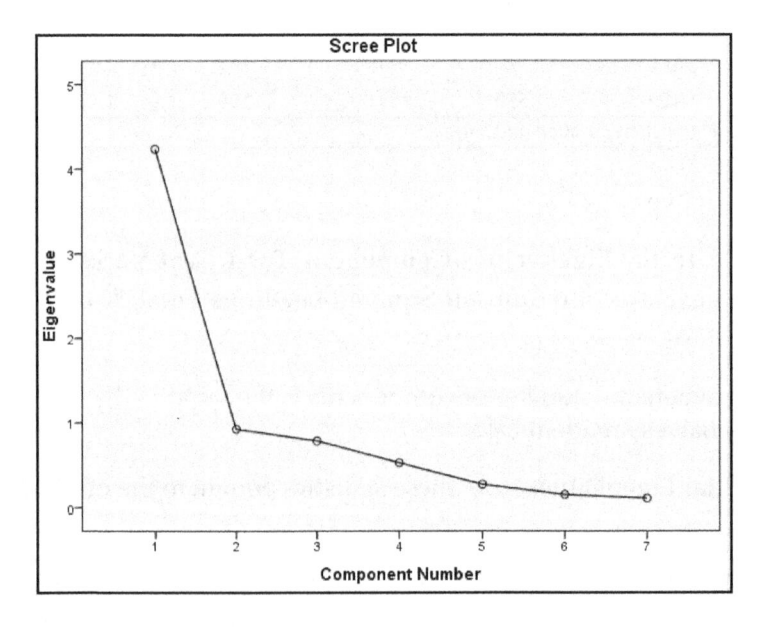

The **Scree Plot** plots the eigenvalues versus their order. The idea is to look for an *elbow* in the plot. Here, we see one substantial eigenvalue plus an *elbow* in the plot at component two. The plot suggests one important component, but you should explore neighboring solutions, such as two components.

Finally, here is the **Component Matrix** of component loadings:

Component Matrix[a]

	Component 1	2	3	4	5	6	7
MurderandManslaughterRate	.857	-.285	-.150	.298	-.083	.186	-.177
RevisedRapeRate	.540	.822	-.026	.060	-.048	.153	.059
RobberyRate	.808	-.310	-.440	-.041	.054	.051	.224
AggravatedAssaultRate	.868	.178	-.065	.327	.190	-.258	-.033
BurglaryRate	.612	-.195	.745	.107	.074	.068	.099
Larceny_TheftRate	.876	-.012	.094	-.208	-.401	-.142	-.003
MotorVehicleTheftRate	.811	.033	.020	-.521	.238	.029	-.111

Extraction Method: Principal Component Analysis.
a. 7 components extracted.

Overall, the component loadings reveal the following pattern: the first component's loadings are all positive, while the component loadings for components two through seven have a mix of positive and negative signs.

The component loadings indicate patterns in the original data. The first component is a general component. Since the original variables are all positively correlated, the component indicates a dimension of high-to-low crime rates across the states, and since the original variables were positively correlated, states that have a higher rate of one crime are likely to have a higher rate of another crime. Components two through seven are *contrast* components. For example, component two appears to contrast **RevisedRapeRates** and **AggravatedAssaultRates** versus **RobberyRate, MurderandManslaughterRate, BurglaryRate,** and so on.

What is the next step?

Since PCA is a method used in dimension reduction, you could explore low-dimensional representations of the crime data. In this analysis, you should be guided by the following:

- Relative magnitudes of successive eigenvalues
- The cumulative % of variance explained
- The pattern in the scree plot
- Meaningfulness

Principal Components and Factor Analysis

To show that these criteria can be used here, suppose we consider the two-component solution. As we have seen, the first eigenvalue is sizeable, while the second eigenvalue is relatively much smaller--.924 versus 4.23. A one-component solution accounts for about 60% of the variability in the data, while a two-component solution accounts for about 74% of the variability in the data. Largely for this reason, we will look at the two-component solution.

Principal component analysis – two-component solution

Here is the revised syntax for a two-component analysis of the crime data:

```
FACTOR
 /VARIABLES MurderandManslaughterRate RevisedRapeRate RobberyRate AggravatedAssaultRate
 BurglaryRate Larceny_TheftRate MotorVehicleTheftRate
 /MISSING LISTWISE
 /ANALYSIS MurderandManslaughterRate RevisedRapeRate RobberyRate AggravatedAssaultRate
 BurglaryRate Larceny_TheftRate MotorVehicleTheftRate
 /PRINT INITIAL EXTRACTION
 /PLOT ROTATION
 /CRITERIA FACTORS(2) ITERATE(25)
 /EXTRACTION PC
 /ROTATION NOROTATE
 /SAVE REG(ALL)
 /METHOD=CORRELATION.
```

The key differences from the previous code are as follows:

- `/PRINT` now specifies only the default output, since the added factorability output does not change and we have already done a factorability assessment
- `/PLOT` plots the rotated loading plot, but since no rotation is in effect, this is an unrotated loading plot
- `/CRITERIA` specifies a two-component solution
- `/SAVE` specifies that FACTOR should save component scores as added variables to the SPSS Statistics **Data Editor** window

[340]

Here is the `Communalities` table from the two-component solution:

Communalities

	Initial	Extraction
MurderandManslaughterRate	1.000	.816
RevisedRapeRate	1.000	.967
RobberyRate	1.000	.749
AggravatedAssaultRate	1.000	.785
BurglaryRate	1.000	.413
Larceny_TheftRate	1.000	.767
MotorVehicleTheftRate	1.000	.659

Extraction Method: Principal Component Analysis.

As before, the **Initial** communalities are one. The **Extraction** communalities are the squared multiple correlations for each variable using the components as predictors. If the extraction communality for a variable is small, the chosen dimensionality does not represent that variable well. In this instance, the **Extraction** communalities range between .65 and .96, with the exception of **BurglaryRate**, which has an extraction communality of about 0.41.

Here is the **Total Variance Explained** table for the two-component solution:

Total Variance Explained

Component	Initial Eigenvalues			Extraction Sums of Squared Loadings		
	Total	% of Variance	Cumulative %	Total	% of Variance	Cumulative %
1	4.230	60.430	60.430	4.230	60.430	60.430
2	.924	13.200	73.629	.924	13.200	73.629
3	.786	11.231	84.860			
4	.527	7.532	92.392			
5	.272	3.880	96.272			
6	.152	2.177	98.450			
7	.109	1.550	100.000			

Extraction Method: Principal Component Analysis.

The **Initial Eigenvalues** output is identical to the **Initial Eigenvalues** output of the preceding seven-component analysis, while the **Extraction Sums of Squared Loading** output is identical to the first two rows of the **Extraction Sums of Squared Loading** output of the preceding seven-component analysis. The two-component solution accounts for 73.6% of the variance in the original variables.

Principal Components and Factor Analysis

Looking at the one-component versus two-component solution, the variance explained is 60% with one component and almost 74% with two components. The eigenvalue for the second component is .924, which is less than one. Some researchers argue that you should consider retaining a component when its eigenvalue is greater than one. However, here, we chose to retain the second component for the added variance explained in order to see the two-dimensional representation of both the variables and the observations in the component space.

Here is the **Component Matrix** for the two-component solution:

Component Matrix[a]

	Component 1	Component 2
MurderandManslaughterRate	.857	-.285
RevisedRapeRate	.540	.822
RobberyRate	.808	-.310
AggravatedAssaultRate	.868	.178
BurglaryRate	.612	-.195
Larceny_TheftRate	.876	-.012
MotorVehicleTheftRate	.811	.033

Extraction Method: Principal Component Analysis.
a. 2 components extracted.

The component matrix table for the two-component solution is the same as the first two columns of the component matrix table for the seven-component solution. The first component loadings represent a *general* component, while the second component loadings represent a contrast between **RevisedRapeRate** and **AggravatedAssaultRate** versus **RobberyRate**, **MurderandManslaugherRate**, and **BurglaryRate**.

Here is the **Component Plot** for the two-component solution:

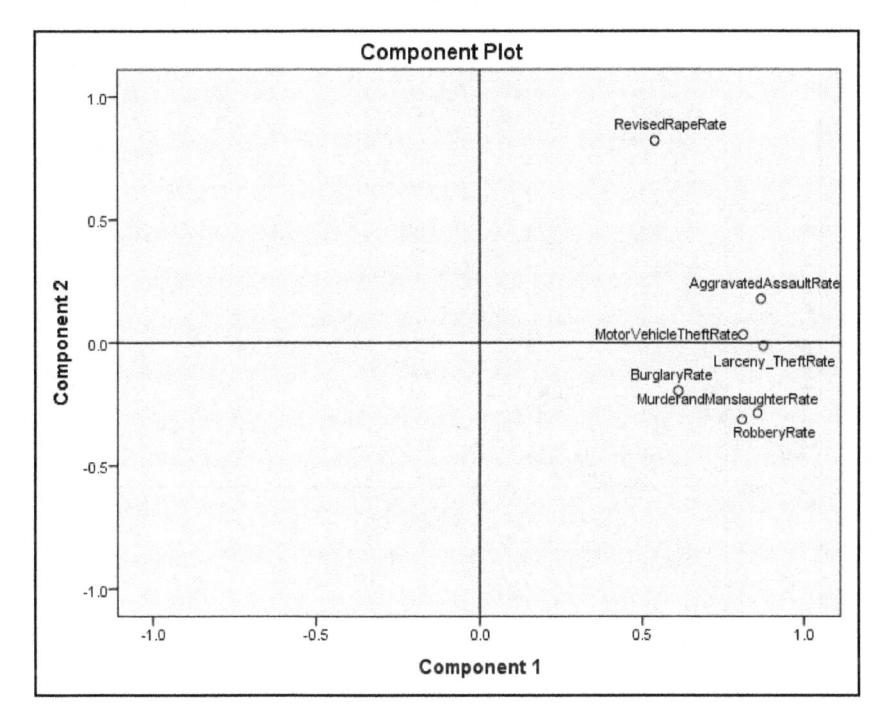

Component Plot showing Component 1 (x-axis) vs Component 2 (y-axis) with the following variables plotted:
- *RevisedRapeRate (upper right, ~0.75 on Component 2)*
- *AggravatedAssaultRate (right, ~0.1 on Component 2)*
- *MotorVehicleTheftRate (right, ~0.0)*
- *Larceny_TheftRate (right, ~0.0)*
- *BurglaryRate (right, slightly below 0)*
- *MurderandManslaughterRate (lower right)*
- *RobberyRate (lower right)*

This chart graphically portrays the component loadings in a two-dimensional space. If you picture each variable point as the endpoint of a vector from the origin, the angles between the point-vectors approximate the correlations of the variables. The overall positive correlation among the items accounts for the V shape of the points, fanning to the right from the origin. As particular examples, note that **RobberyRate** and **MurderandManslaugherRate** have a narrow angle between them, while **RobberyRate** and **RevisedRapeRate** have a larger angle between them. Check the correlations to confirm that the correlation is higher for the first pair than the second.

Here is a plot of Component 1 scores versus Component 2 scores, saved by default in the names FAC1_1 and FAC2_1:

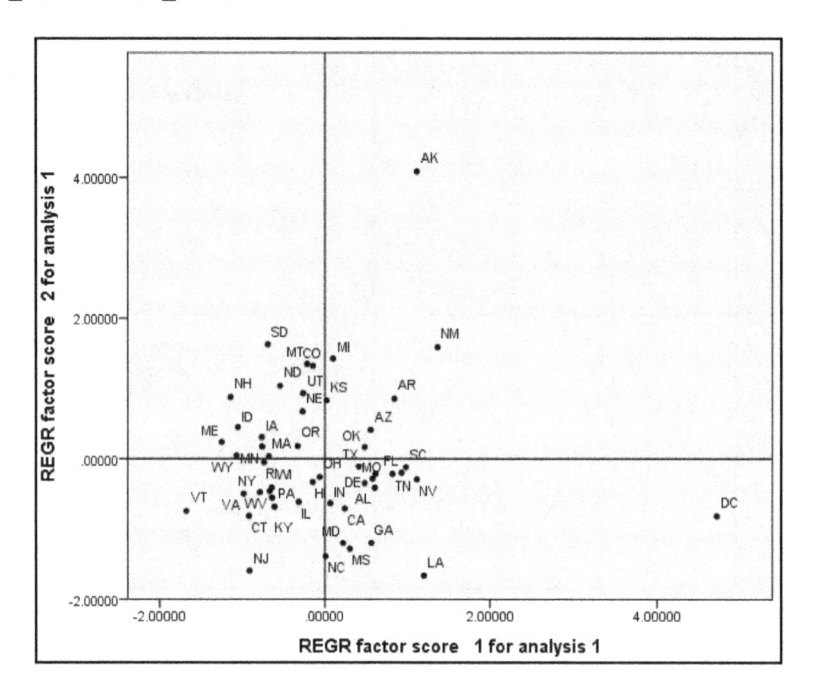

How do you interpret this plot?

If you project the points to the horizontal axis, this axis orders the observations by *overall* crime rate across the seven crimes. DC falls at the extreme right of the plot, while VT falls at the extreme left.

Here is individual case-level data for the two observations, with the extreme values on the first component score:

State	MurderandManslaughterRate	RevisedRape Rate	RobberyRate	AggravatedAssaultRate	BurglaryRate	Larceny_Theft Rate	MotorVehicleTheftRate	REGR factor score 1 for analysis 1
District of Columbia	15.9	71.6	530.7	626.1	526.0	4082.3	574.1	4.71816
Vermont	1.6	17.6	11.2	68.9	324.6	1160.8	38.9	-1.68698

[344]

Inspecting the data, at one extreme the District of Columbia has the maximum value on five of the original variables--**MurderandManslaughterRate**, **RobberyRate**, **AggravatedAssaultRate**, **LarcenyTheftRate**, and **MotorVehicleTheftRate**, while Alaska has a higher **RevisedRapeRate** and many states have higher **BurglaryRate** values. At the other extreme, Vermont has the minimum values for **LarcenyTheftRate** and **MotorVehicleTheftRate,** and near-minimum values for the other crime rates.

Here is individual case-level data for the two observations, with the extreme values on the second component score--AK and LA:

State	MurderandManslaughterRate	RevisedRapeRate	RobberyRate	AggravatedAssaultRate	BurglaryRate	Larceny_TheftRate	MotorVehicleTheftRate	REGR factor score 2 for analysis 1
Alaska	5.6	104.7	85.4	440.2	427.6	2096.4	236.0	4.08453
Louisiana	10.3	29.6	122.5	352.4	824.5	2421.6	212.7	-1.66353

Again, the component scores for these extreme cases are best understood in conjunction with the component loadings, or the loading plot. Alaska has an extreme **RevisedRapeRate** and relatively low-to-middle values on **MurderManslaughterRate** and **RobberyRate**, while **Lousiana** has among the highest values on **MurderManslaughterRate** and **RobberyRate,** and one of the lowest **RevisedRapeRate** values.

Summarizing this example, the factorability assessment shows that the data was suited to PCA. The first principal component analysis shows one substantial eigenvalue with the others trailing off. In the comparison of the one-component and two-component solution, we favored the two-component solution for the additional variance explained.

Factor analysis - abilities

This example starts with the premise that you do not have the original observational data, but instead have the published correlations of the variables. In this instance, you can read the correlations into SPSS Statistics. You can conduct a factor analysis as if you had the raw data, except that you are not able to calculate factor scores (or component scores, if you were conducting PCA). Note that you can perform Factor Analysis with a flat file of observations, much as we showed with the PCA example that begins with a flat file of observations.

Suppose that the researcher has administered six psychological tests to 112 respondents. The variables are as follows:

- General: A nonverbal measure of general intelligence

- Picture: A picture completion test
- Blocks: A block design test
- Maze: A maze test
- Reading: A reading comprehension test
- Vocab: A vocabulary test

The research question is: can you account for the observed correlations between these tests, in terms of some small numbers of factors?

> The source for this data is the psych contributed package available for R. For example, see https://cran.r-project.org/web/packages/psych/index.html

Here is code for defining the correlation matrix to SPSS Statistics:

```
matrix data variables=rowtype_
  general picture blocks maze reading vocab.
begin data.
mean 0 0 0 0 0 0
stddev 1 1 1 1 1 1
n 112 112 112 112 112 112
corr 1
corr .47 1
corr .55 .57 1
corr .34 .19 .45 1
corr .58 .26 .35 .18 1
corr .51 .24 .36 .22 .79 1
end data.
*variable labels
  general 'nonverbal measure of general intelligence'
  picture 'picture completion test'
  blocks 'block design test'
  maze 'maze test'
  reading 'reading comprehension test'
  vocab 'vocabulary test'.
```

Here are comments on the commands:

- `matrix data` reads raw matrix materials and converts them to a matrix data file that you can read using procedures that accept matrix materials. The matrix data command specifies variable names for variables found in the data.
- `begin data` signals the beginning of data rows or matrix data rows.

- Following `begin data` are matrix data rows. The first element of the matrix data row is the row type, with possible values being `mean`, `stddev`, `n`, `corr`. Note that for correlations, you need to specify only the lower triangle plus the diagonal of ones.
- `end data` signals the end of data rows or matrix data rows.
- The `variable labels` command is commented out. The variable labels are useful descriptors for the variables. Since we turn the variable labels into a comment, SPSS Statistics will use the shorter variable names in the output.

Run the preceding commands. Here is the **SPSS Statistics Data Editor** window:

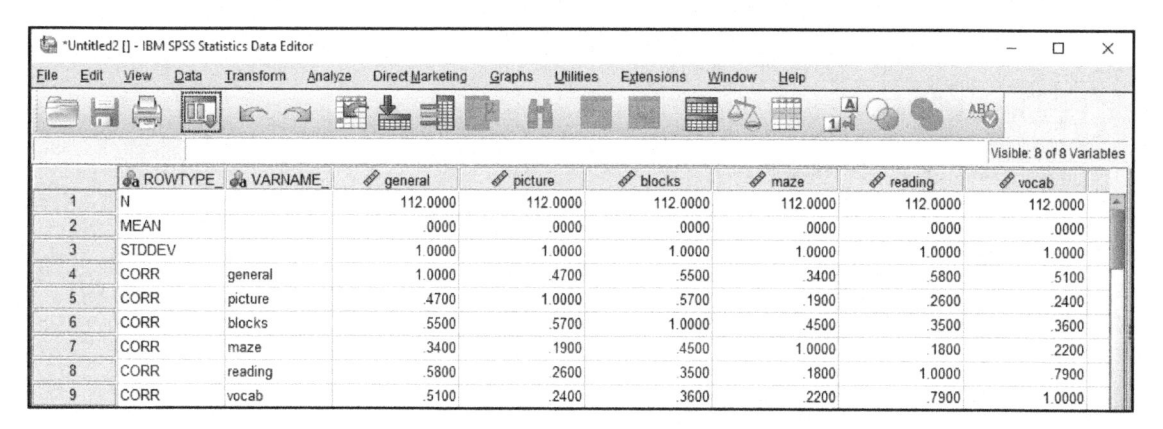

ROWTYPE_	VARNAME_	general	picture	blocks	maze	reading	vocab
N		112.0000	112.0000	112.0000	112.0000	112.0000	112.0000
MEAN		.0000	.0000	.0000	.0000	.0000	.0000
STDDEV		1.0000	1.0000	1.0000	1.0000	1.0000	1.0000
CORR	general	1.0000	.4700	.5500	.3400	.5800	.5100
CORR	picture	.4700	1.0000	.5700	.1900	.2600	.2400
CORR	blocks	.5500	.5700	1.0000	.4500	.3500	.3600
CORR	maze	.3400	.1900	.4500	1.0000	.1800	.2200
CORR	reading	.5800	.2600	.3500	.1800	1.0000	.7900
CORR	vocab	.5100	.2400	.3600	.2200	.7900	1.0000

Notice that the **SPSS Statistics Data Editor** window does not contain the usual tidy data, or a flat file of individual observations by variables, but instead has a special structure. It contains one row each of counts, means, and standard deviations, and it also includes a square correlation matrix.

The reduced correlation matrix and its eigenvalues

In PCA, the starting point for analysis is the original correlation matrix of the variables in the analysis. In FA, the starting point for the analysis is the *reduced correlation matrix*, which consists of the correlations of the measures off the main diagonal, and communalities on the main diagonal.

The fundamental equation underlying factor analysis is as follows:

original_correlation_matrix= reduced_correlation_matrix + uniquenesses

Principal Components and Factor Analysis

SPSS Statistics FACTOR does not report the reduced correlation matrix, but you can obtain it via the SPSS code. In truth, the communalities are not known at the start of the analysis, nor is the uniqueness. For initial estimates of the communalities, we can insert squared multiple correlations of each variable, regressed on the rest of the set excluding that variable. You do not have to perform the regressions; instead, the R-squared values are obtained analytically.

Here is an SPSS code to produce the reduced correlation matrix and its eigenvalues:

```
MATRIX.
MGET /FILE=* /TYPE=CORR.
COMPUTE RINV=INV(CR).
COMPUTE SDIAG = DIAG(RINV).
COMPUTE S2=INV(MDIAG(SDIAG)).
COMPUTE RMS2=CR-S2.
CALL EIGEN(RMS2,VECTORS,VALUES).
PRINT CR/FORMAT F6.3/TITLE 'CR'.
PRINT RINV/FORMAT F6.3/TITLE 'RINV'.
PRINT SDIAG/FORMAT F6.3/TITLE 'SDIAG'.
PRINT S2/FORMAT F6.3/TITLE 'S2'.
PRINT RMS2 /FORMAT F5.3 /TITLE 'R - S2 MATRIX'.
PRINT VALUES /FORMAT=F6.3 /TITLE='EIGENVALUES'.
PRINT VECTORS /FORMAT=F5.3 /TITLE='EIGENVECTORS'.
END MATRIX.
```

Here are some comments on the SPSS code:

- `MATRIX` and `END MATRIX` bracket the beginning and end of the SPSS matrix code block.
- `MGET` reads a matrix-format data file. The asterisk (*) represents the active file. `/TYPE` tells SPSS Statistics to read the correlation row type. `MGET` automatically puts the correlation matrix into the matrix variable name **CR**.
- The `INV` function finds the inverse of **CR** and puts it in the matrix variable **RINV**.
- The `DIAG` function extracts the diagonal elements of **RINV** and puts them in the matrix variable **SDIAG**. **SDIAG** is a column vector.
- `MDIAG` makes a matrix with the diagonal given by the values in **SDIAG**. Take the inverse of the matrix and put that result in **S2**. **S2** contains the uniqueness for each variable. **RMS2** is the reduced correlation matrix.
- `CALL EIGEN` gets the eigenvectors and eigenvalues of the reduced matrix.
- The `PRINT` command prints and titles the various results.
- The `MATRIX` command prints simple results in unformatted "text" output style.

Here is the original correlation matrix:

```
cr
 1.000   .470   .550   .340   .580   .510
  .470  1.000   .570   .190   .260   .240
  .550   .570  1.000   .450   .350   .360
  .340   .190   .450  1.000   .180   .220
  .580   .260   .350   .180  1.000   .790
  .510   .240   .360   .220   .790  1.000
```

Here is the reduced correlation matrix, named **R-S2**:

```
R - S2 MATRIX
 .511   .470   .550   .340   .580   .510
 .470   .371   .570   .190   .260   .240
 .550   .570   .504   .450   .350   .360
 .340   .190   .450   .232   .180   .220
 .580   .260   .350   .180   .669   .790
 .510   .240   .360   .220   .790   .635
```

Off the main diagonal, the numbers agree with the original correlations. On the diagonal are the squared multiple correlations when a given variable is regressed on the rest of the set.

Finally, here are the **eigenvalues**:

```
EIGENVALUES
 2.605
  .665
  .107
 -.063
 -.161
 -.230
```

The eigenvalues of the original correlation matrix are all non-negative and have an expected value of one for uncorrelated data. The eigenvalues of the reduced correlation matrix can be positive or negative and have an expected value of zero for uncorrelated data. You could produce a scree plot by plotting the eigenvalues versus their order.

Principal Components and Factor Analysis

As an extension of eigenvalue analysis, Brian O'Connor has written SPSS Statistics code that can perform a so-called **parallel analysis**. See the discussion and download links at the following URL:

`https://people.ok.ubc.ca/brioconn/nfactors/nfactors.html`

The idea is to assess the observed eigenvalues against eigenvalues that would be obtained on uncorrelated random variables for the same size problem--for example, where the number of cases equals 112 and the number of variables equals six. To use O'Connor's code, open it in an SPSS syntax window and specify the parameters of the problem.

Here are the results of running O'Connor's code:

```
PARALLEL ANALYSIS:

Principal Axis / Common Factor Analysis

Specifications for this Run:
Ncases      112
Nvars         6
Ndatsets   1000
Percent      95

Random Data Eigenvalues
       Root          Means        Prcntyle
    1.000000       .381272        .533762
    2.000000       .207757        .323545
    3.000000       .080258        .168908
    4.000000      -.029298        .037865
    5.000000      -.131729       -.073888
    6.000000      -.235834       -.167212
```

The specifications indicate 1,000 simulations. The **Means** column contains the middle values of the six eigenvalues from the 1,000 simulations, while the **Prcntyle** column contains the 95th percentile values of the six eigenvalues from the 1,000 simulations. Compare the six obtained eigenvalues of the reduced correlation matrix to their respective **Prcntyle** value under simulation from random data. The first two eigenvalues--2.605 and .665--exceed their respective **Prcntyle** values, suggesting that we should consider a two-factor solution.

[350]

Principal Components and Factor Analysis

In fact, we will look at both the one-factor and two-factor solutions. Comparing tables such as the communalities and the reproduced correlation matrix from these respective solutions shows the relative performance of the one-factor versus two-factor solution.

Factor analysis code

Here is the SPSS code for the factor analysis runs:

```
FACTOR /MATRIX=IN(COR=*)
 /MISSING LISTWISE
 /ANALYSIS=GENERAL PICTURE BLOCKS MAZE READING VOCAB
 /PRINT UNI COR INITIAL EXTRACTION REP KMO
 /CRI=FACTORS(1) ITERATE(99) ECONVERGE(.0001)
 /EXT PAF
 /ROT NOROTATE
 /METHOD=CORRELATION.
FACTOR /MATRIX=IN(COR=*)
 /MISSING LISTWISE
 /ANALYSIS=GENERAL PICTURE BLOCKS MAZE READING VOCAB
 /PRINT INITIAL EXTRACTION ROTATION REP
 /CRI=FACTORS(2) ITERATE(99) ECONVERGE(.0001)
 /EXT PAF
 /ROT PROMAX
 /METHOD=CORRELATION.
```

Here are the comments on key elements of the SPSS code:

- There are two FACTOR commands. The first specifies a one-factor solution, while the second specifies a two-factor solution.
- The first /PRINT subcommand specifies default and non-default keywords. UNI and COR print simple univariate statistics and the correlations. INITIAL prints the initial communalities for each variable, the eigenvalues of the unreduced correlation matrix, and the percentage of variance for each factor. EXTRACTION prints the factor pattern matrix, revised communalities, eigenvalue for each factor retained, and the percentage of variance each eigenvalue represents. REP prints the reproduced correlation matrix and the residual correlation matrix. KMO prints the Kaiser-Meyer-Olkin measure of sampling adequacy, along with Bartlett's test of sphericity. The second /PRINT subcommand omits UNI and COR, since their results will not change across FACTOR specifications.

- The first /CRITERIA subcommand (abbreviated in the preceding part) specifies that FACTOR should extract one factor, and also shows how to set algorithm criteria such as the number of iterations and the convergence criterion. The second /CRITERIA subcommand specifies that FACTOR should extract two factors.
- The /EXTRACT subcommand specifies the PAF extraction method. Note that FACTOR employs PCA by default, so you need to explicitly override this if you want to perform factor analysis.
- The first /ROTATE subcommand specifies no rotation. With one factor, rotation cannot happen. The second /ROTATE subcommand specifies promax rotation, which is a form of oblique rotation.
- The /METHOD subcommand specifies that the factor analysis should be based on correlations.

Factor analysis results

Here is the **KMO and Bartlett's Test** table:

KMO and Bartlett's Test		
Kaiser-Meyer-Olkin Measure of Sampling Adequacy.		.728
Bartlett's Test of Sphericity	Approx. Chi-Square	268.977
	df	15
	Sig.	.000

Recall that for the **KMO Measure of Sampling Adequacy** statistic, bigger is better. A value of 0.728 is sufficiently high enough to proceed. In addition, **Bartlett's Test of Sphericity** has an associated p-value of < .0005, so we reject the null hypothesis that the six items are mutually uncorrelated.

Here is the `Communalities` table for the one-factor model:

Communalities	Initial	Extraction
general	.511	.645
picture	.371	.277
blocks	.504	.467
maze	.232	.162
reading	.669	.517
vocab	.635	.484

Extraction Method: Principal Axis Factoring.

As already mentioned, the **Initial** communalities denotes the squared multiple correlations of the given variable, along with the others. The **Extraction** communalities are the proportions of each variable's variance that can be explained by the one factor. Variables with high values are well represented in the factor space, while variables with low values are not. Here, the **Extraction** communalities range between .162 and .645; some are larger than the respective **Initial** communality, while some are not.

Here is the `Total Variance Explained` table for the one-factor solution:

Total Variance Explained

	Initial Eigenvalues			Extraction Sums of Squared Loadings		
Factor	Total	% of Variance	Cumulative %	Total	% of Variance	Cumulative %
1	3.075	51.244	51.244	2.553	42.542	42.542
2	1.141	19.018	70.263			
3	.820	13.665	83.928			
4	.413	6.879	90.806			
5	.353	5.889	96.695			
6	.198	3.305	100.000			

Extraction Method: Principal Axis Factoring.

Principal Components and Factor Analysis

The left-hand side of the table--**Initial Eigenvalues**--is based on the original correlations. The right-hand side is based on the factor analysis. Notice that unlike PCA, in FA the right-hand row one is not identical to the left-hand row one. The one-factor solution explains about 43% of the variance in the six psychological tests.

Here is the `Factor Matrix` table:

Factor Matrix[a]

	Factor 1
general	.803
picture	.526
blocks	.683
maze	.403
reading	.719
vocab	.696

Extraction Method: Principal Axis Factoring.

a. 1 factors extracted. 11 iterations required.

Much as we saw in the PCA analysis of crime data, the loadings are all positively signed. If you inspect the original correlations, you will see that all correlations are positive. So, it could be that these six tests are tapping into some general underlying ability, to a greater or less extent. However, before we make too much of the one-factor solution, it is very important that we inspect the reproduced correlation table.

Here is the `Reproduced Correlations` table:

Reproduced Correlations

		general	picture	blocks	maze	reading	vocab
Reproduced Correlation	general	.645[a]	.423	.549	.324	.578	.559
	picture	.423	.277[a]	.360	.212	.379	.366
	blocks	.549	.360	.467[a]	.275	.492	.475
	maze	.324	.212	.275	.162[a]	.290	.280
	reading	.578	.379	.492	.290	.517[a]	.500
	vocab	.559	.366	.475	.280	.500	.484[a]
Residual[b]	general		.047	.001	.016	.002	-.049
	picture	.047		.210	-.022	-.119	-.126
	blocks	.001	.210		.175	-.142	-.115
	maze	.016	-.022	.175		-.110	-.060
	reading	.002	-.119	-.142	-.110		.290
	vocab	-.049	-.126	-.115	-.060	.290	

Extraction Method: Principal Axis Factoring.
a. Reproduced communalities
b. Residuals are computed between observed and reproduced correlations. There are 9 (60.0%) nonredundant residuals with absolute values greater than 0.05.

This table has two halves. The top half is the actual reproduced correlations. On the diagonal are the estimated communalities, while off the diagonal are the *implied* correlations if the one-factor model holds. If you compare these implied correlations with the actual ones in the original correlation matrix, you will find some substantial discrepancies. The lower half of the table, labeled **Residual**, contains the discrepancies between the observed and implied correlations. You can see some large ones, for example, .290 and .210. For this reason, we conclude that the data is not consistent with the one-factor model.

In sum, the one-factor model has some low **Extraction** communalities, accounts for about 43% of the variance in the variables, and does not adequately account for the observed correlations in the items. For this reason, we next consider the two-factor model.

Here is the `Communalities` table for the two-factor model:

Communalities		
	Initial	Extraction
general	.511	.567
picture	.371	.373
blocks	.504	.834
maze	.232	.205
reading	.669	.972
vocab	.635	.648

Extraction Method: Principal Axis Factoring.

The **Extraction** communalities are generally larger in value now.

Here is the `Total Variance Explained` table for the two-factor solution:

Total Variance Explained

Factor	Initial Eigenvalues Total	% of Variance	Cumulative %	Extraction Sums of Squared Loadings Total	% of Variance	Cumulative %	Rotation Sums of Squared Loadings[a] Total
1	3.075	51.244	51.244	2.752	45.864	45.864	2.312
2	1.141	19.018	70.263	.848	14.127	59.992	2.253
3	.820	13.665	83.928				
4	.413	6.879	90.806				
5	.353	5.889	96.695				
6	.198	3.305	100.000				

Extraction Method: Principal Axis Factoring.
a. When factors are correlated, sums of squared loadings cannot be added to obtain a total variance.

The two factors account for about 60% of the variance in the six psychological tests.

Here is the unrotated `Factor Matrix` table:

Factor Matrix[a]

	Factor	
	1	2
general	.750	.074
picture	.522	.318
blocks	.748	.523
maze	.392	.227
reading	.827	-.536
vocab	.721	-.358

Extraction Method: Principal Axis Factoring.

a. 2 factors extracted. 71 iterations required.

The first factor is a *general* factor, with all positive loadings, while the second factor has a mix of positive and negative loadings. Since it can be difficult to discern the overall pattern in the initial **Factor Matrix**, researchers often rely on rotation to produce a more interpretable result.

Here is the `Reproduced Correlations` table:

Reproduced Correlations

		general	picture	blocks	maze	reading	vocab
Reproduced Correlation	general	.567[a]	.415	.600	.311	.581	.514
	picture	.415	.373[a]	.557	.277	.261	.262
	blocks	.600	.557	.834[a]	.412	.338	.352
	maze	.311	.277	.412	.205[a]	.203	.201
	reading	.581	.261	.338	.203	.972[a]	.788
	vocab	.514	.262	.352	.201	.788	.648[a]
Residual[b]	general		.055	-.050	.029	-.001	-.004
	picture	.055		.013	-.087	-.001	-.022
	blocks	-.050	.013		.038	.012	.008
	maze	.029	-.087	.038		-.023	.019
	reading	-.001	-.001	.012	-.023		.002
	vocab	-.004	-.022	.008	.019	.002	

Extraction Method: Principal Axis Factoring.

a. Reproduced communalities

b. Residuals are computed between observed and reproduced correlations. There are 2 (13.0%) nonredundant residuals with absolute values greater than 0.05.

Principal Components and Factor Analysis

For the two-factor solution, the implied correlations are closer to the observed correlations, and the residual correlations are, in general, smaller.

To aid interpretation, we use oblique rotation. This produces three tables of coefficients.

Here is the **Pattern Matrix**:

Pattern Matrix[a]

	Factor 1	Factor 2
general	.372	.493
picture	-.007	.615
blocks	-.077	.950
maze	.007	.449
reading	1.026	-.084
vocab	.785	.038

Extraction Method: Principal Axis Factoring.
Rotation Method: Promax with Kaiser Normalization.[a]

a. Rotation converged in 3 iterations.

The pattern matrix contains coefficients that give the direct impact from the factor to the variable. Interpreting these, factor one appears to be a **verbal** factor, while factor two appears to be a **nonverbal** (or **visual** or **spatial**) factor, with the general item loading on both factors. The naming of these factors is part science and part art, and you should work with the subject-matter expert to come up reasonable terms that characterize the factors.

Here is the **Structure Matrix**:

Structure Matrix

	Factor 1	Factor 2
general	.622	.682
picture	.305	.611
blocks	.404	.911
maze	.235	.453
reading	.983	.436
vocab	.804	.436

Extraction Method: Principal Axis Factoring.
Rotation Method: Promax with Kaiser Normalization.

[358]

Principal Components and Factor Analysis

The structure matrix is a matrix of correlations between the variables and the factors. The magnitudes of these can be higher than the coefficients of the pattern matrix, since we allowed the two factors to correlate.

Finally, here is the `Factor Correlation` table:

Factor Correlation Matrix

Factor	1	2
1	1.000	.507
2	.507	1.000

Extraction Method: Principal Axis Factoring.
Rotation Method: Promax with Kaiser Normalization.

The two factors are correlated at 0.5. If the correlation is negligible, we might run an orthogonal rotation method, such as VARIMAX, instead. If the correlation is too close to one, that would raise the question of whether the factors are distinct. As it stands, it appears that the two factors are correlated but distinct.

In sum, the two-factor model has larger **Extraction** communalities than the one-factor model, accounts for about 60% of the variance in the variables rather than 43%, and does a good job of accounting for the observed correlations in the items.

Summary

This chapter presented extensive examples of principal components analysis and factor analysis. The PCA analysis began with a flat file of individual observations and produced a two-component solution for aggregate state-level (plus DC) crime rates for seven violent crimes. This analysis led to insights into both the variables and the observations in the analysis. The FA analysis began with a correlation matrix, of various ability tests, on 112 individuals, and produced a two-factor solution that showed evidence of two subsets of tests, along with a general item that loaded on both factors.

In the next chapter, we will look at cluster analysis, which is a technique for grouping observations into clusters that are hopefully homogeneous and well separated.

15
Clustering

Cluster analysis is a family of classification techniques for finding groups in data when both the number of groups, and which object falls in which group, are not observed at the start. The object is typically a case (data row), although it can be a variable. This makes cluster analysis a type of **unsupervised learning**, meaning that the data consists of inputs with no target variable. Since you are not aiming to predict or explain a target variable, you cannot turn to measures of model performance used in predictive modeling, such as classification accuracy or percent of variance explained.

Some researchers have contended that the idea of a cluster is ill-defined. However, most sources suggest that clusters are groupings of objects that can be understood in terms of internal cohesion (**homogeneity**) and external separation. Cluster analysis has been used in market research, the physical sciences, psychiatry, archaeology, and bioinformatics, among other areas.

This chapter covers the following major topics:

- Overview of cluster analysis
- Overview of SPSS Statistics cluster analysis procedures
- Hierarchical cluster analysis example
- K-means cluster analysis example
- Two-step cluster analysis example

Overview of cluster analysis

Cluster analysis is generally done in a series of steps. Here are things to consider in a typical cluster analysis:

- **Objects to cluster**: What are the objects? Typically, they should be representative of the cluster structure to be present. Also, they should be randomly sampled if generalization of a population is required.
- **Variables to be used**: The input variables are the basis on which clusters are formed. Popular clustering techniques assume that the variables are numeric in scale, although you might work with binary data or a mix of numeric and categorical data.
- **Missing values**: Typically, you begin with the flat file of objects in rows and variables in columns. In the presence of missing data, you might either delete the case or input the missing value, while special clustering methods might allow other handling of missing data.
- **Scale the data**: Popular clustering methods are not invariant to changes in scale of the variables. When variables differ in scale, the variable with the largest variance can dominate the clustering. Therefore, researchers sometimes employ any of a number of standardizations, including z-score standardizing and range standardizing.
- **Proximity measure**: There are dozens of proximity measures from which to choose. SPSS Statistics offers measures for three types of data: interval data, frequency-count data, and binary data.
- **Method**: Researchers have studied the abilities of methods to recover structure, as well as sensitivities to error or unusual values. The issue is that you are not always in a position to know which method would be best in your situation. In addition, if you know something about the process that generated the data, you might be able to apply model-based clustering methods (not discussed in this chapter).
- **Number of clusters**: It can be difficult to decide what number of clusters to use. In the sciences, the number of clusters might have a conceptual basis, such as a correspondence to species. In business, the choice of the number of clusters might in part be a matter of convenience or usefulness.
- **Replication**: This includes techniques such as splitting the sample, running multiple methods, perturbing the sample, and the like.
- **Interpretation**: This relies on descriptive statistics and graphical techniques that aid understanding.

This chapter necessarily has a tutorial flavor and is not a comprehensive look at cluster analysis. A useful reference is the book by Everitt and his co-authors.

> For a comprehensive reference, see *Cluster Analysis: 5th Edition*. Brian S. Everitt, Sabine Landau, Morven Leese, and Daniel Stahl. Copyright 2011, John Wiley and Sons.

In addition, cluster analysis is not a purely statistical activity. For a good discussion of some useful criteria for evaluating clusters in business settings, see the reference by Wedel and Kamakura.

> *Market Segmentation*. Michel Wedel and Wagner Kamakura. Copyright 1998, Kluwer Academic Publishers.

Overview of SPSS Statistics cluster analysis procedures

SPSS Statistics offers three clustering procedures: CLUSTER, QUICK CLUSTER, and TWOSTEP CLUSTER.

CLUSTER produces hierarchical clusters of items based on distance measures of dissimilarity or similarity. The items being clustered are usually rows in the active dataset, and the distance measures are computed from the row values for the input variables. Hierarchical clustering produces a set of cluster solutions from a starting situation where each case is its own cluster of size one, to an ending situation where all cases are in one cluster. Case-to-case distance is unambiguous, but case-to-cluster and cluster-to-cluster distance can be defined in different ways, so there are multiple methods for **agglomeration**, which is the bring together of objects or clusters.

This form of clustering is called hierarchical because cluster solutions are nested. For example, the difference between, say, a five-cluster solution and a four-cluster solution is that two of the clusters in the five-cluster solution are fused to produce the four-cluster solution. Hierarchical clustering begins with the square proximity matrix of distances between all pairs of objects, and this can grow prohibitively large as the number of rows gets large. Finally, with many rows, you end up performing a lot of agglomeration to get to the point in which you are really interested, namely, a relative handful of clusters.

Clustering

QUICK CLUSTER performs K-means clustering. A key element of K-means clustering is that it does not need to form the square proximity matrix for all the cases. For this reason, it can be used on data with a large number of rows. K-means clustering forms K initial cluster centers, assigns the cases to the clusters, updates the centers, and repeats the assignment, until it converges or reaches some maximum number of iterations. To run it, you must specify an explicit K, and if you are uncertain what to use, you might try a range of values. Or, you might instead turn to hierarchical clustering, either as an alternative, or to decide on a tentative number of clusters.

K-means clustering is popular, but it has several features that you should consider when using it. It needs K initial cluster centers at the start, and a poor choice of these can lead to poor final clusters. Its solution is not invariant to scaling of the inputs. As with hierarchical clustering, you might consider standardizing the variables if they have different scales. If not, then the variable with the large standard deviation can dominate the cluster solution. With otherwise identical runs but two different sort orders of the records, K-means clustering can arrive at different cluster solutions. K-means clustering tends to find spherical clusters in the given metrics of the input variables, which can sometimes be appropriate. However, if the inputs are correlated, K-means cluster might not recover the structure.

TWOSTEP CLUSTER performs a form of agglomerative clustering in two data passes. The algorithm is designed to cluster large numbers of cases, and for this reason, avoids building the proximity matrix of inter-case distances. In the first pass, TWOSTEP finds candidate cluster centers and assigns the cases to the candidate centers, while in the second pass, TWOSTEP combines the clusters. TWOSTEP has two distance algorithms: Euclidean and Likelihood. The Likelihood distance is the only one available when categorical inputs are present, but could also be used when only continuous inputs are present. You can specify an explicit number of desired clusters, or you can rely on some built-in heuristics for automatic selection of the number of clusters. TWOSTEP can produce a useful summary and visuals in model viewer-style output. TWOSTEP CLUSTER assumes that the inputs are uncorrelated, and can fail to recover structure when the inputs are correlated.

> **TIP** For comprehensive coverage of cluster analysis, see the Everitt et al. reference. Our purpose in this chapter is to show how to do cluster analysis in SPSS Statistics via examples.

Hierarchical cluster analysis example

The example data is the USA violent crime data previously analyzed via the *Principal components analysis* section in `Chapter 14`, *Principal Components and Factor Analysis*. Recall that the data consists of state-level data for the 50 states of the USA and also the District of Columbia. The data came from the year 2014, the most recent year available on our source website. For a full description of the data, see `Chapter 14`, *Principal Components and Factor Analysis*.

The goal is to use the seven crime rate variables as inputs in a hierarchical cluster analysis. The variables are:

- `MurderandManslaughterRate`
- `RevisedRapeRate`
- `RobberyRate`
- `AggravatedAssaultRate`
- `BurglaryRate`
- `Larceny_TheftRate`
- `MotorVehicleTheftRate`

The overall problem size is small. The data is complete; there is no missing data. We are primarily interested in description, and there is no need to generalize to a larger set of objects.

The analysis proceeds as follows:

1. Perform simple descriptive analysis for data understanding.
2. Perform hierarchical cluster analysis for the purpose of identifying a tentative number of clusters.
3. Perform a second hierarchical cluster analysis for the purpose of obtaining the cluster solution identified in step 2.
4. Seek to understand the cluster solution obtained in step 3. This includes cluster profiling.

Descriptive analysis

First, let's look at simple descriptive statistics. Here is SPSS Statistics code for default `DESCRIPTIVES` analysis:

```
DESCRIPTIVES
 VARIABLES=MurderandManslaughterRate RevisedRapeRate RobberyRate
AggravatedAssaultRate
 BurglaryRate Larceny_TheftRate MotorVehicleTheftRate
 /STATISTICS=MEAN STDDEV MIN MAX.
```

Here is the `Descriptive Statistics` table:

Descriptive Statistics

	N	Minimum	Maximum	Mean	Std. Deviation
MurderandManslaughterRate	51	.9	15.9	4.298	2.5185
RevisedRapeRate	51	14.3	104.7	40.506	15.2707
RobberyRate	51	9.1	530.7	88.965	75.2287
AggravatedAssaultRate	51	66.9	626.1	230.635	110.3125
BurglaryRate	51	257.2	887.3	527.284	181.6954
Larceny_TheftRate	51	1160.8	4082.3	1876.239	485.9266
MotorVehicleTheftRate	51	38.9	574.1	199.976	98.2804
Valid N (listwise)	51				

> Note particularly the wide range in the values of the standard deviations. If the variables are analyzed as-is, the variables with the larger standard deviations could dominate the cluster solution. For this reason, you should consider standardizing the inputs.

Cluster analysis - first attempt

Here is the SPSS statistics code for running a hierarchical cluster analysis:

```
DATASET DECLARE D0.5999347690493206.
PROXIMITIES
 MurderandManslaughterRate RevisedRapeRate RobberyRate
AggravatedAssaultRate
 BurglaryRate Larceny_TheftRate MotorVehicleTheftRate
```

Clustering

```
  /MATRIX OUT(D0.5999347690493206)
  /VIEW=CASE
  /MEASURE=SEUCLID
  /PRINT NONE
  /STANDARDIZE=VARIABLE Z.
CLUSTER
  /MATRIX IN(D0.5999347690493206)
  /METHOD WARD
  /PRINT SCHEDULE
  /PLOT DENDROGRAM.
DATASET CLOSE D0.5999347690493206.
```

Following are the comments in the SPSS Statistics code.

`DATASET DECLARE` creates a new dataset name that is not associated with any open dataset. The purpose of this command is to declare a name for the anticipated proximities matrix produced by the subsequent `PROXIMITIES` command.

Regarding the `PROXIMITIES` command:

- `PROXIMITIES` specifies the seven violent crime rate variables as inputs.
- `PROXIMITIES` calculates the square matrix of distances between all cases.
- `/MATRIX` specifies the dataset name specified on `DATASET DECLARE` as the dataset to which SPSS Statistics should write the proximity matrix.
- `/VIEW` specifies that proximities are calculated between cases.
- `/MEASURE` specifies squared Euclidean distances. Since the input variables are numeric, either the Euclidean distance or squared Euclidean distance is a natural choice. Here, we use the squared Euclidean distance because we intend to use the `WARD` method for clustering.
- `/STANDARDIZE` specifies standardization by variable using Z-score standardizing. Recall that you should consider standardizing the inputs when they have widely different scales.

Regarding the `CLUSTER` command:

- `CLUSTER` reads the proximities matrix produced by `PROXIMITIES`.
- `/MATRIX` specifies the dataset name of the proximities matrix to read.

Clustering

- /METHOD specifies the WARD clustering method, which is not the default. The WARD method is used here because it is an agglomerative method that brings two clusters together in a way that minimizes the increase in the total within-cluster sum of squares.
- /PRINT specifies the agglomeration Schedule.
- /PLOT specifies the Dendogram plot.

DATASET CLOSE closes the **SPSS Statistics Data Editor** window that holds the proximities matrix.

Note that you should consult the SPSS Statistics documentation on PROXIMITIES and CLUSTER to see the full range of their capabilities.

When you perform hierarchical clustering, the Schedule shows the order in which cases combine into clusters, and then clusters into clusters, from one extreme in which each case is its own cluster of size one, to all cases being in one cluster.

Since the Agglomeration Schedule table can be lengthy, here we show only the beginning and ending stages of Agglomeration Schedule:

Ward Linkage

Agglomeration Schedule

Stage	Cluster Combined Cluster 1	Cluster Combined Cluster 2	Coefficients	Stage Cluster First Appears Cluster 1	Stage Cluster First Appears Cluster 2	Next Stage
1	14	39	.199	0	0	27
2	3	44	.446	0	0	18
3	6	28	.718	0	0	13
4	7	50	.995	0	0	17
5	13	16	1.275	0	0	20

Clustering

In **Stage 1**, case 14 and case 39 are combined into a cluster. The reason is that the distance between these two cases, in the **Coefficients** column, is the smallest distance between any two objects. Note that it is possible that there could be a tie for the smallest distance. The next clustering **Stage** that involves this cluster is **Stage 27**. In **Stage 2**, case 3, and case 44 are combined, and so on.

Here is the end of the `Agglomeration Schedule` table:

46	6	12	103.497	35	40	47
47	2	6	122.113	0	46	48
48	1	2	157.653	45	47	49
49	1	7	240.043	48	42	50
50	1	9	350.000	49	0	0

Typically, you are interested in detecting a point where the cluster analysis combines clusters or objects that are relatively far apart. Admittedly, there is a judgmental element to this. Reading from bottom up:

- Stage **50** – 2 clusters get combined into 1.
- Stage **49** – 3 clusters get combined into 2.
- Stage **48** – 4 clusters get combined into 3.
- Stage **47** – 5 clusters get combined into 4.

And so on. At **Stage 47**, 5 clusters get combined into 4 by joining two items that are a distance apart equal to 122.113. At **Stage 48**, 4 clusters get combined into 3 by joining two items that are a distance apart equal to 157.653. At **Stage 49**, 3 clusters get combined into 2 by joining two items that are a distance apart equal to 240.043. Given that **Coefficients** are becoming large at this point, some numbers of clusters in the 2-4 range could be considered.

Clustering

You can also use `Dendogram` to identify a tentative number of clusters. Here is the **Dendogram**, rendered to fit easily on one page:

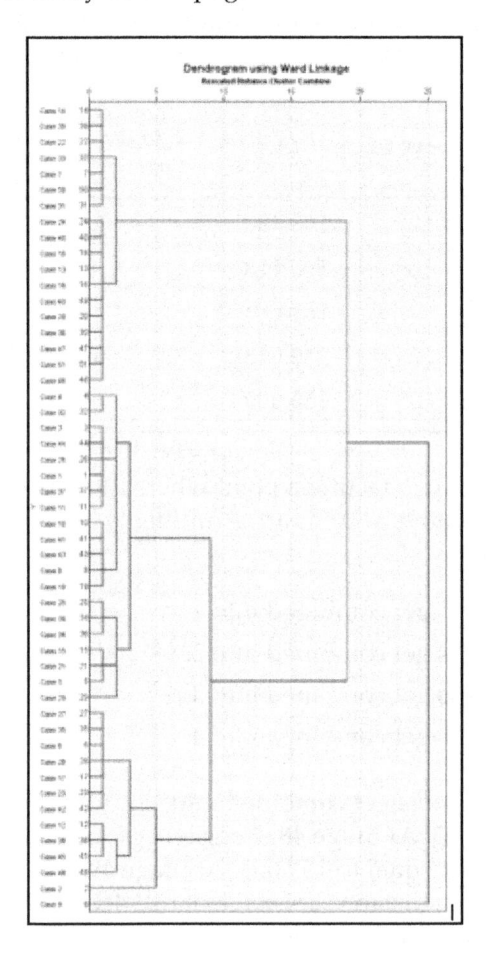

As an agglomerative method, hierarchical cluster analysis combines cases and clusters, which corresponds to reading this chart from left to right. However, it is useful to read the chart from right to left, for this shows how two clusters fold into one, three into two, and so on.

One overall observation we can see is how the bottom object stays out of the cluster solution until the last stage. Therefore, a two-cluster solution would put that object in one cluster and all other objects in the other cluster.

The four-cluster solution consists of that one object in its own cluster and three clusters with similar numbers of objects. To see the clusters, imagine a vertical line dropping from near the number 5 and cutting **Dendogram** at exactly four places. Then, look to the left to see the cases being combined into each cluster at that point. The four-cluster solution would produce three somewhat similarly sized clusters, along with the single-member cluster, while a three-cluster solution would produce a larger, a smaller, and a single-member cluster.

Cluster analysis with four clusters

Given the preceding points, we re-run the cluster analysis and save cluster membership for the 4-cluster solution:

```
DATASET DECLARE D0.9976844462521434.
PROXIMITIES
 MurderandManslaughterRate RevisedRapeRate RobberyRate
AggravatedAssaultRate
 BurglaryRate Larceny_TheftRate MotorVehicleTheftRate
 /MATRIX OUT(D0.9976844462521434)
 /VIEW=CASE
 /MEASURE=SEUCLID
 /PRINT NONE
 /STANDARDIZE=VARIABLE Z.
CLUSTER
 /MATRIX IN(D0.9976844462521434)
 /METHOD WARD
 /PRINT SCHEDULE
 /PLOT DENDROGRAM
 /SAVE CLUSTER(4).
DATASET CLOSE D0.9976844462521434.
```

The SPSS code is very similar to the first run. However, this time you see the CLUSTER /SAVE subcommand, which saves the cluster memberships in a variable named CLU4_1 that is added to the active file.

After running the 4-cluster code, explore the four-cluster solution.

Here is SPSS code for producing summary statistics for the four-cluster solution:

```
MEANS
 TABLES=MurderandManslaughterRate RevisedRapeRate RobberyRate
AggravatedAssaultRate
 BurglaryRate Larceny_TheftRate MotorVehicleTheftRate BY CLU4_1
 /CELLS=MEAN STDDEV COUNT.
```

Clustering

The `MEANS` code produces the following `Report` table:

		MurderandManslaughterRate	RevisedRape Rate	RobberyRate	AggravatedAssaultRate	BurglaryRate	Larceny_Theft Rate	MotorVehicleTheftRate
Ward Method								
1	Mean	5.760	40.760	111.020	288.600	708.165	2090.780	233.400
	Std. Deviation	1.4770	11.0954	32.1737	85.2697	115.8287	277.4513	68.5004
	N	20	20	20	20	20	20	20
2	Mean	3.108	52.592	53.925	216.108	456.925	1932.775	239.750
	Std. Deviation	1.2236	18.7229	23.6420	86.3965	122.5323	347.1273	72.1936
	N	12	12	12	12	12	12	12
3	Mean	2.822	30.439	63.278	153.944	373.283	1477.611	115.539
	Std. Deviation	1.2288	7.3545	38.8684	57.4954	72.7359	139.8032	39.7331
	N	18	18	18	18	18	18	18
4	Mean	15.900	71.600	530.700	626.100	526.000	4082.300	574.100
	Std. Deviation	.	.	.	.	.	.	.
	N	1	1	1	1	1	1	1
Total	Mean	4.298	40.506	88.965	230.635	527.284	1876.239	199.976
	Std. Deviation	2.5185	15.2707	75.2287	110.3125	181.6954	485.9266	98.2804
	N	51	51	51	51	51	51	51

The `Means` table shows cluster sizes of 20, 12, 18, and 1 respectively. The assignment of labels 1, 2, 3, and 4 to the clusters is arbitrary. It turns out that cluster 4 consists of a single object, case 9, that corresponds to DC. Note that DC has relatively high values across all the variables, except for `BurglaryRate`, where its value is lower than the mean `BurglaryRate` value in cluster 1. A single case in a cluster is called a **singleton**. While you might view it as an outlier, there is merit in treating it as its own cluster, since overall its values are so extreme on many of the variables. Recall that in the PCA analysis of these data, DC stood out in the plot of the component scores.

You can focus on the means by re-specifying the `MEANS` program and asking only for means:

```
MEANS
  TABLES=MurderandManslaughterRate RevisedRapeRate RobberyRate
  AggravatedAssaultRate
  BurglaryRate Larceny_TheftRate MotorVehicleTheftRate BY CLU4_1
  /CELLS=MEAN.
```

Clustering

The MEANS syntax resembles the previous code, except that here the /CELLS subcommand specifies only the mean.

Here is the resulting Report table:

Report

Mean

Ward Method	MurderandManslaughterRate	RevisedRape Rate	RobberyRate	AggravatedAssaultRate	BurglaryRate	Larceny_Theft Rate	MotorVehicleTheftRate
1	5.760	40.760	111.020	288.600	708.165	2090.780	233.400
2	3.108	52.592	53.925	216.108	456.925	1932.775	239.750
3	2.822	30.439	63.278	153.944	373.283	1477.611	115.539
4	15.900	71.600	530.700	626.100	526.000	4082.300	574.100
Total	4.298	40.506	88.965	230.635	527.284	1876.239	199.976

The preceding table shows only the means. Each row, except for the **Total**, is a cluster mean profile. You should explore the means for patterns. Note that if there are more variables in the analysis, this table can become very wide, in which case you can use the **Pivot Table Editor** to transpose the rows and columns.

The following table shows colors added by hand in the table editor using **Cell Formats**:

Ward Method	MurderandManslaughterRate	RevisedRape Rate	RobberyRate	AggravatedAssaultRate	BurglaryRate	Larceny_Theft Rate	MotorVehicleTheftRate
1	5.760	40.760	111.020	288.600	708.165	2090.780	233.400
2	3.108	52.592	53.925	216.108	456.925	1932.775	239.750
3	2.822	30.439	63.278	153.944	373.283	1477.611	115.539
4	15.900	71.600	530.700	626.100	526.000	4082.300	574.100

Cluster 4 features a purple backgrounds, highlighting the relatively high means on all variables but BurglaryRate. Recall that cluster 4 consists of DC, and the mean indicates high crime rates on all violent crimes except BurglaryRate, with a high, but not highest, value:

- Cluster 1 has the second highest means in the four blue highlighted cells, with the highest BurglaryRate mean and middle values on RevisedRapeRate and MotorVehicleTheftRate

Clustering

- Cluster 2 has the third highest mean in the four green highlighted cells, along with the lowest `RobberyRate` mean
- Cluster 3 has the lowest mean in the six red highlighted cells, with a fairly low but not lowest `RobberyRate` means

Having characterized the clusters, you can gain further insight by seeing which states fall in which clusters. For example, cluster 3 features states from the northeast and midwest, along with some others.

If you had available other variables measured for each state, you could run a descriptive analysis to see whether the four clusters vary on these variables.

You can gain further insight into the clusters by first standardizing the input variables, and then obtaining the `Means` table.

Here is an SPSS code for producing the standardized variables and their `Means` by cluster:

```
DESCRIPTIVES
  VARIABLES=MurderandManslaughterRate RevisedRapeRate   RobberyRate
AggravatedAssaultRate
  BurglaryRate Larceny_TheftRate MotorVehicleTheftRate
  /SAVE
  /STATISTICS=MEAN STDDEV MIN MAX.
MEANS
  TABLES=ZMurderandManslaughterRate ZRevisedRapeRate   ZRobberyRate
ZAggravatedAssaultRate
  ZBurglaryRate ZLarceny_TheftRate ZMotorVehicleTheftRate BY   CLU4_1
  /CELLS=MEAN.
```

Here is the `Means` table:

Mean Ward Method	Zscore (MurderandManslaughterRate)	Zscore (RevisedRapeRate)	Zscore (RobberyRate)	Zscore (AggravatedAssaultRate)	Zscore (BurglaryRate)	Zscore (Larceny_TheftRate)	Zscore (MotorVehicleTheftRate)
1	.5805000	.0166409	.2931766	.5254591	.9955161	.4415086	.3400833
2	-.4723959	.7914357	-.4657758	-.1316892	-.3872378	.1163463	.4046943
3	-.5860018	-.6592355	-.3414512	-.6952145	-.8475778	-.8203463	-.8591495
4	4.6067842	2.0361934	5.8718986	3.5849494	-.0070685	4.5399053	3.8066942
Total	.0000000	.0000000	.0000000	.0000000	.0000000	.0000000	.0000000

Clustering

The means are now understood in standard units. The values for cluster 4 are relatively extreme on a number of variables.

You might also display mean profiles in a line chart. Here is an SPSS code for the multiple line chart:

```
GGRAPH
 /GRAPHDATASET NAME="graphdataset"
VARIABLES=MEAN(ZMurderandManslaughterRate)
 MEAN(ZRevisedRapeRate) MEAN(ZRobberyRate)  MEAN(ZAggravatedAssaultRate)
MEAN(ZBurglaryRate)
 MEAN(ZLarceny_TheftRate) MEAN(ZMotorVehicleTheftRate) CLU4_1
MISSING=LISTWISE REPORTMISSING=NO
 TRANSFORM=VARSTOCASES(SUMMARY="#SUMMARY"  INDEX="#INDEX")
 /GRAPHSPEC SOURCE=INLINE.
BEGIN GPL
 SOURCE: s=userSource(id("graphdataset"))
 DATA: SUMMARY=col(source(s), name("#SUMMARY"))
 DATA: INDEX=col(source(s), name("#INDEX"), unit.category())
 DATA: CLU4_1=col(source(s), name("CLU4_1"), unit.category())
 GUIDE: axis(dim(2), label("Mean"))
 GUIDE: legend(aesthetic(aesthetic.color.interior), label("Ward Method  ",
 " "))
 SCALE: cat(dim(1), include("0", "1", "2", "3", "4", "5", "6"))
 SCALE: linear(dim(2), include(0))
 ELEMENT: line(position(INDEX*SUMMARY), color.interior(CLU4_1),
missing.wings())
END GPL.
```

The chart is easily constructed in `Chart Builder`. Once built, you can `paste` the syntax and run it.

Here is the multiple lines chart:

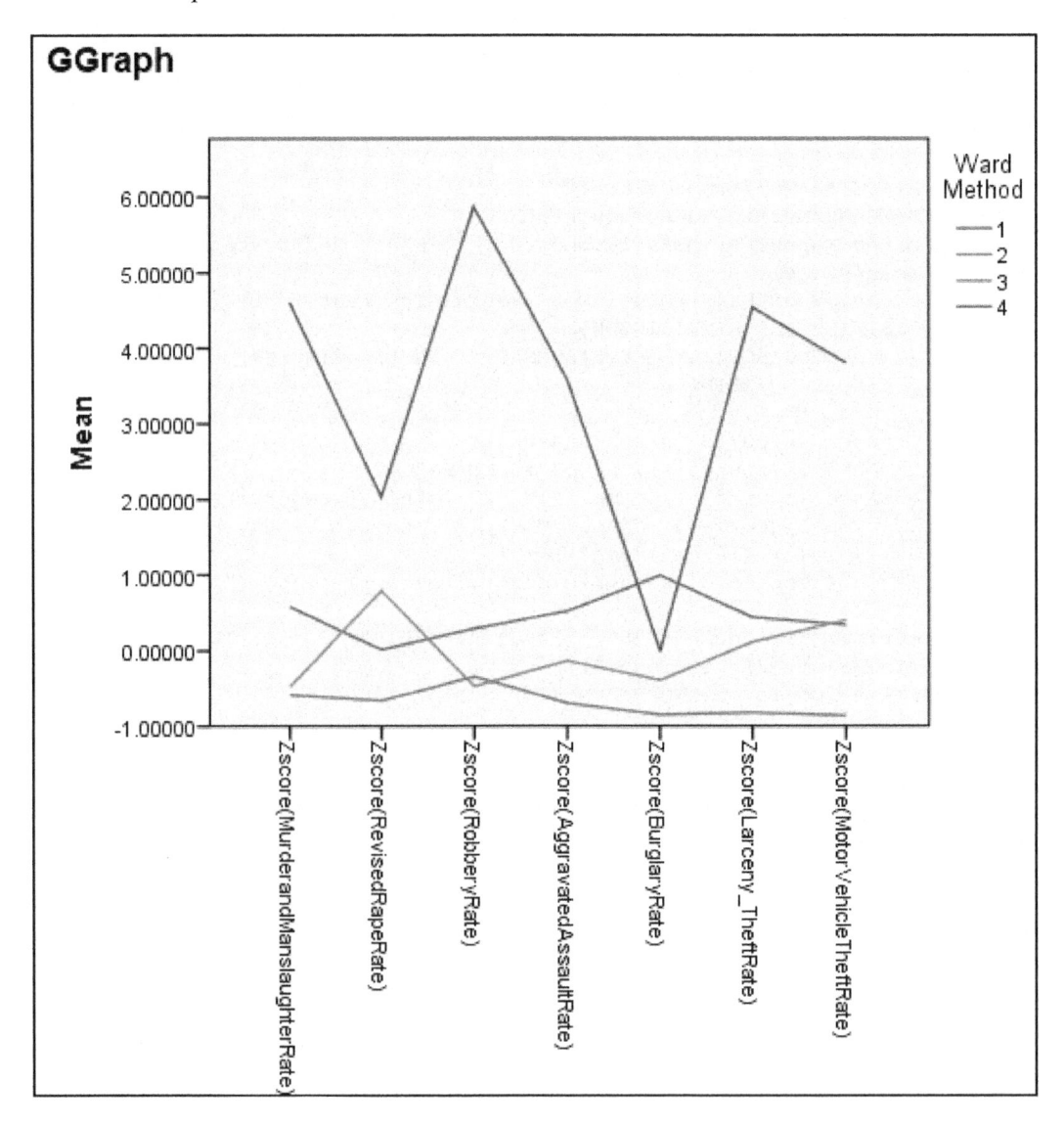

[Figure: GGraph showing Mean vs Zscore variables (MurderandManslaughterRate, RevisedRapeRate, RobberyRate, AggravatedAssaultRate, BurglaryRate, Larceny_TheftRate, MotorVehicleTheftRate) for Ward Method clusters 1, 2, 3, 4]

The multiple lines chart clearly shows how cluster 4 differs from the others, as well as showing the spread of means on each input in a standardized vertical metric.

Finally, you can use scatterplots to gain understanding of clusters.

Clustering

Here is an SPSS code for a bivariate scatterplot of two of the inputs, with the points colored by cluster membership:

```
GGRAPH
 /GRAPHDATASET NAME="graphdataset" VARIABLES=RevisedRapeRate  BurglaryRate
CLU4_1 MISSING=LISTWISE
 REPORTMISSING=NO
 /GRAPHSPEC SOURCE=INLINE.
BEGIN GPL
 SOURCE: s=userSource(id("graphdataset"))
 DATA: RevisedRapeRate=col(source(s), name("RevisedRapeRate"))
 DATA: BurglaryRate=col(source(s), name("BurglaryRate"))
 DATA: CLU4_1=col(source(s), name("CLU4_1"), unit.category())
 GUIDE: axis(dim(1), label("RevisedRapeRate"))
 GUIDE: axis(dim(2), label("BurglaryRate"))
 GUIDE: legend(aesthetic(aesthetic.color.exterior), label("Ward Method   ",
 " "))
 ELEMENT: point(position(RevisedRapeRate*BurglaryRate),
color.exterior(CLU4_1))
END GPL.
```

The chart is easily constructed in `Chart Builder`. Once built, you can `paste` the syntax.

Here is the resulting chart:

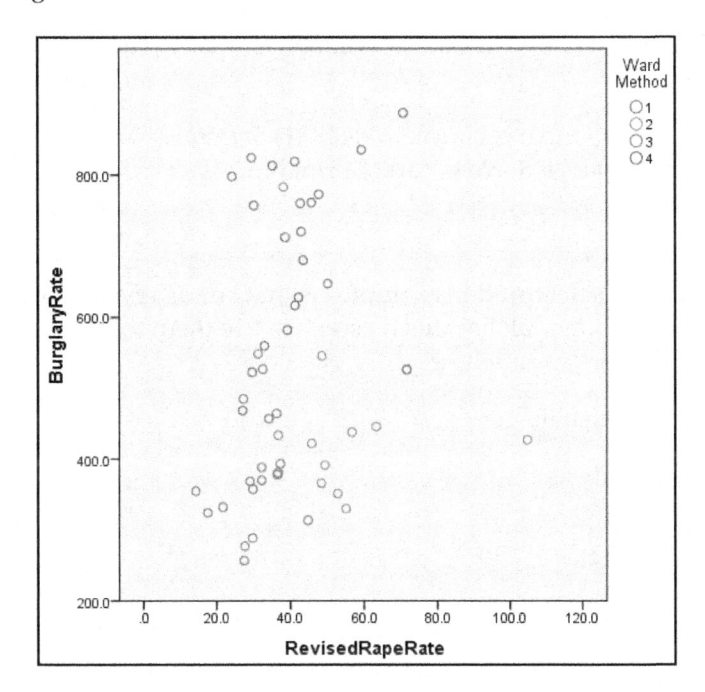

[377]

Clustering

On the pair of variables shown, the different states occupy different parts of the space, and the clusters appear largely separate. The plot reveals one point in cluster 2 with a `RevisedRapeRate` value of over 100--that state turns out to be Alaska.

In sum, we looked at the use of hierarchical cluster analysis as a way to cluster the states based on violent crime rates on seven measures. We decided to employ the z-score transformation on the variables to put them on the same scale.

> There are various methods from which to choose, and we used the Ward's method to cluster the cases. The Ward's method works with squared Euclidean distances, which aligns with its goal in fusing clusters in such a way as to minimize the increase in sum of squares within clusters.

`Schedule` and `Dendogram` are useful aids in choosing the tentative number of clusters. We saved the cluster membership as a variable, and then performed various descriptive analyses to gain understanding of the clusters.

K-means cluster analysis example

The example data includes 272 observations on two variables--eruption time in minutes and waiting time for the next eruption in minutes--for the Old Faithful geyser in Yellowstone National Park, Wyoming, USA. This data is available in many places, including the freeware R program.

> An original source is Hardle, W. (1991) *Smoothing Techniques with Implementation in S*. New York: Springer.

One reason that this data is featured in examples is that charts reveal that the observations on each input are clearly bimodal. For this reason, we use them to illustrate K-means clustering with two clusters specified.

Our analysis proceeds as usual:

- Descriptive analysis
- Cluster analysis
- Cluster profiling

Descriptive analysis

Here is a histogram of eruption:

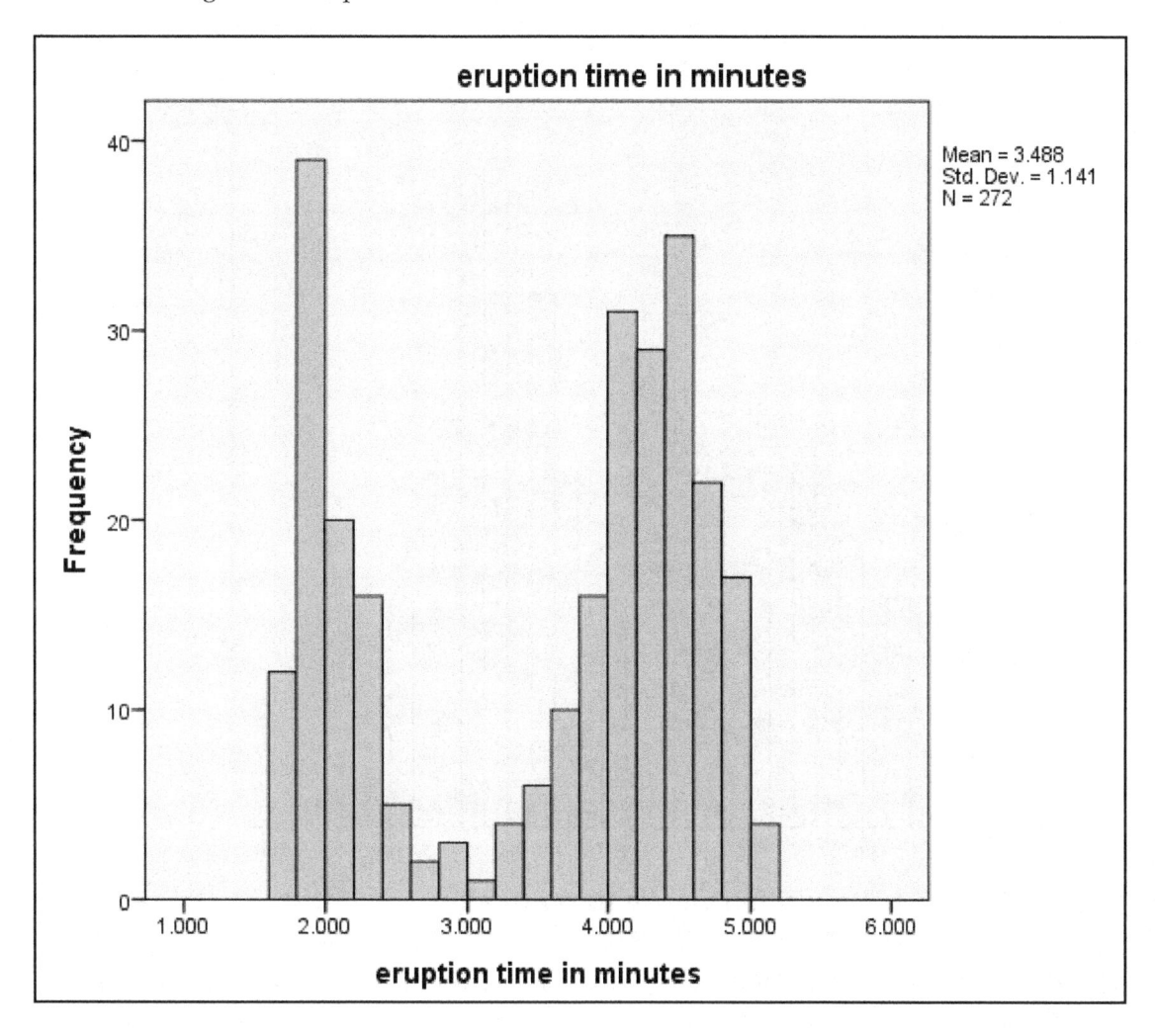

You can clearly see the bimodal nature of the distribution, with one center around 2 and another center around 4.5.

Clustering

Here is a histogram of the **waiting time to next eruption**:

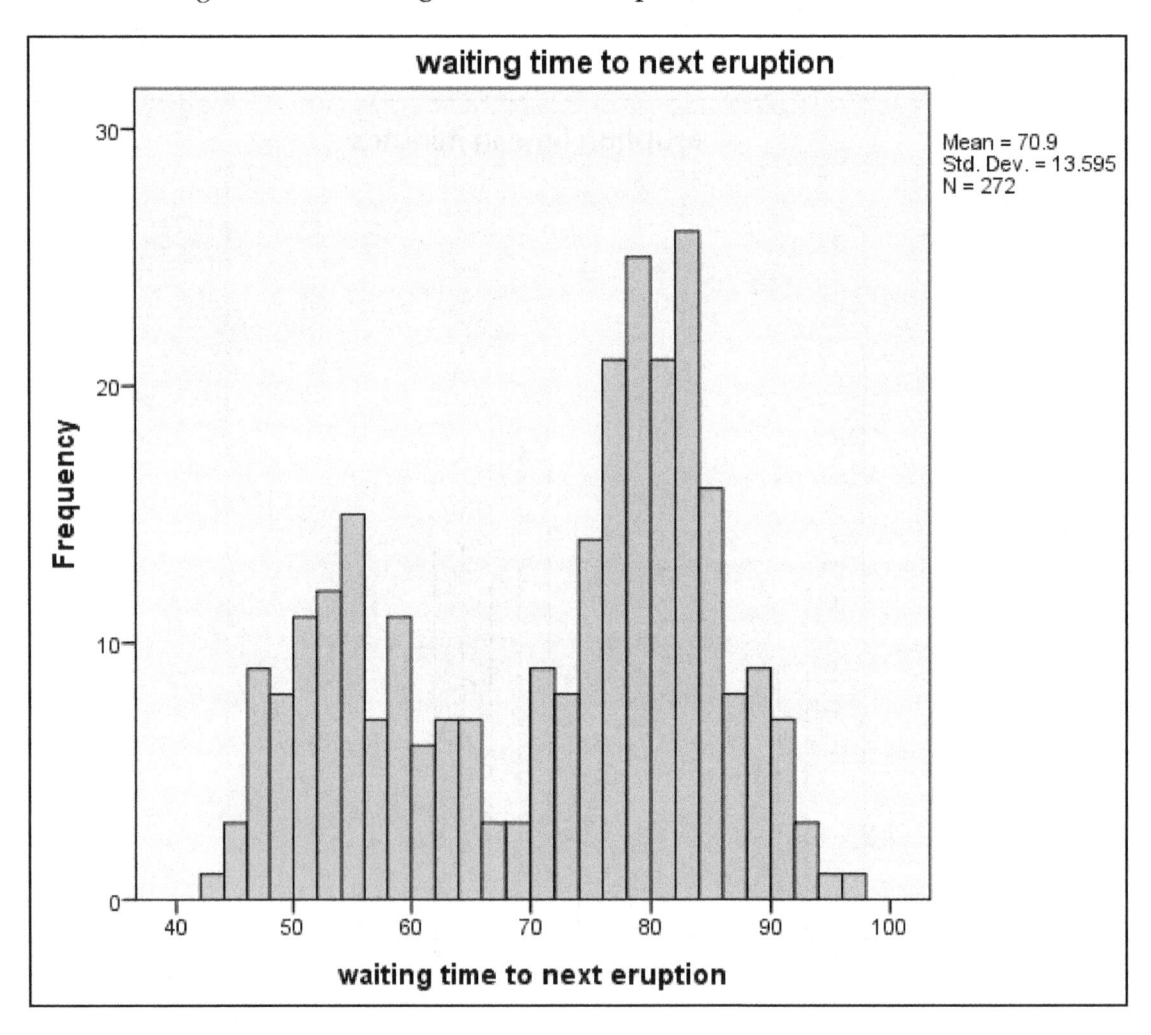

waiting time to next eruption

Mean = 70.9
Std. Dev. = 13.595
N = 272

Again, you can clearly see the bimodal nature of the distribution, with one center in the mid-50s and the other in the low 80s.

You can also look at the two variables jointly, via a scatterplot. Here is the scatterplot:

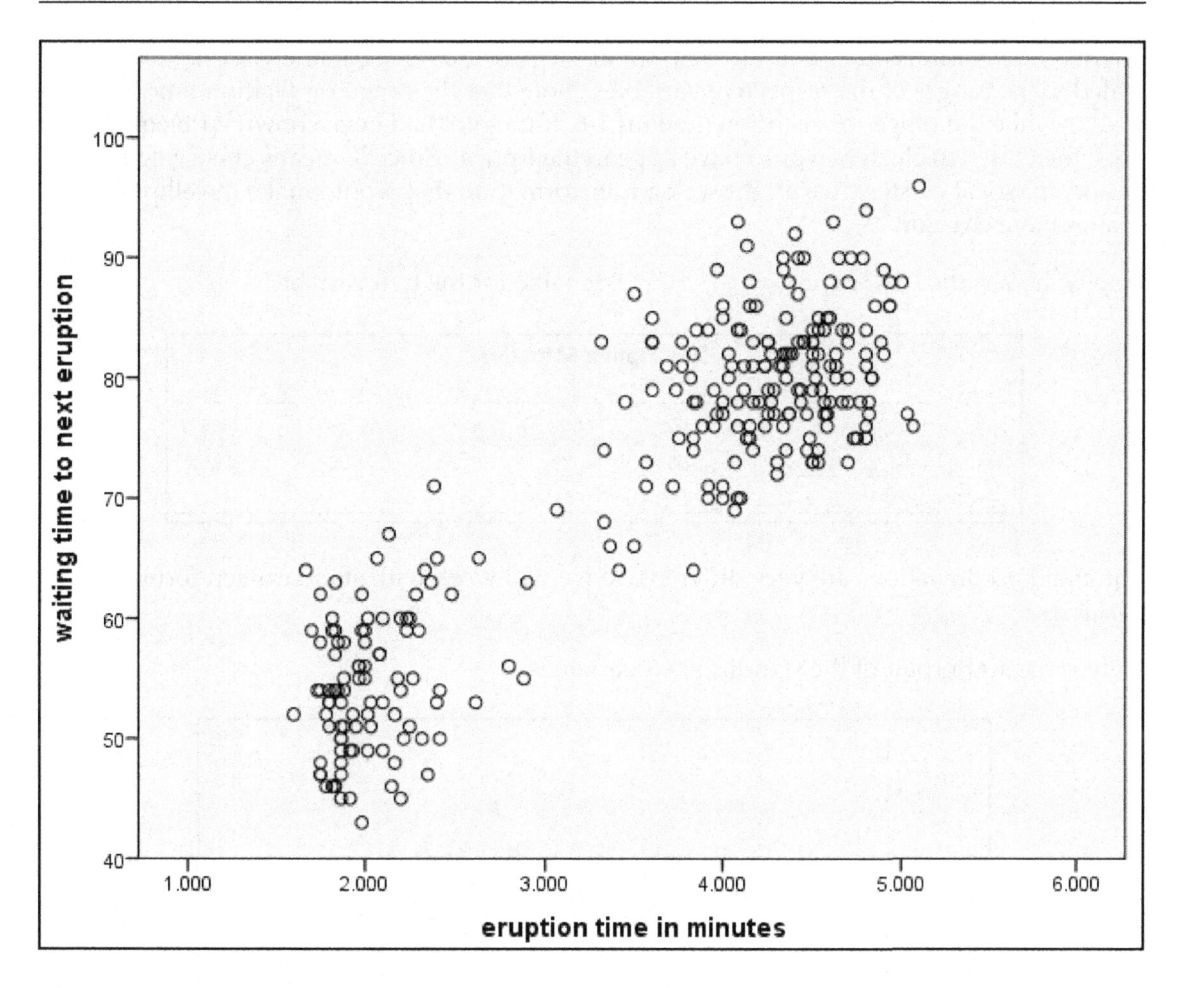

The scatter of points shows a two-cluster structure. In general, shorter eruption times are associated with shorter waiting times between eruptions, while longer eruption times are associated with longer waiting times between eruptions. It seems that over the observation period, the eruption times and waiting times shifted between two centers, although the nature of that shifting is not apparent from the chosen display. In point of fact, while they are interesting questions, we are not addressing the shifting between the two centers, or predicting one variable from the other. Instead, the purpose of the analysis is to cluster the events.

Clustering

There is another important point to note about the previous chart, namely, the axes are scaled to the ranges of the respective variables. Note that the range for waiting time is about 40-100, while the range for eruption is about 1-6. If the plot had been shown with equated axes, then the two clusters would have appeared elliptical. Since K-means clustering tends to find spherical clusters, we might seek a transformation that would make the elliptical shapes more circular.

Finally, here is the `Descriptive Statistics` table for the two variables:

Descriptive Statistics

	N	Minimum	Maximum	Mean	Std. Deviation
eruption time in minutes	272	1.600	5.100	3.48778	1.141371
waiting time to next eruption	272	43	96	70.90	13.595
Valid N (listwise)	272				

The standard deviations are very different, so we will work with standardized forms of the variables.

Here is the scatterplot of the standardized variables:

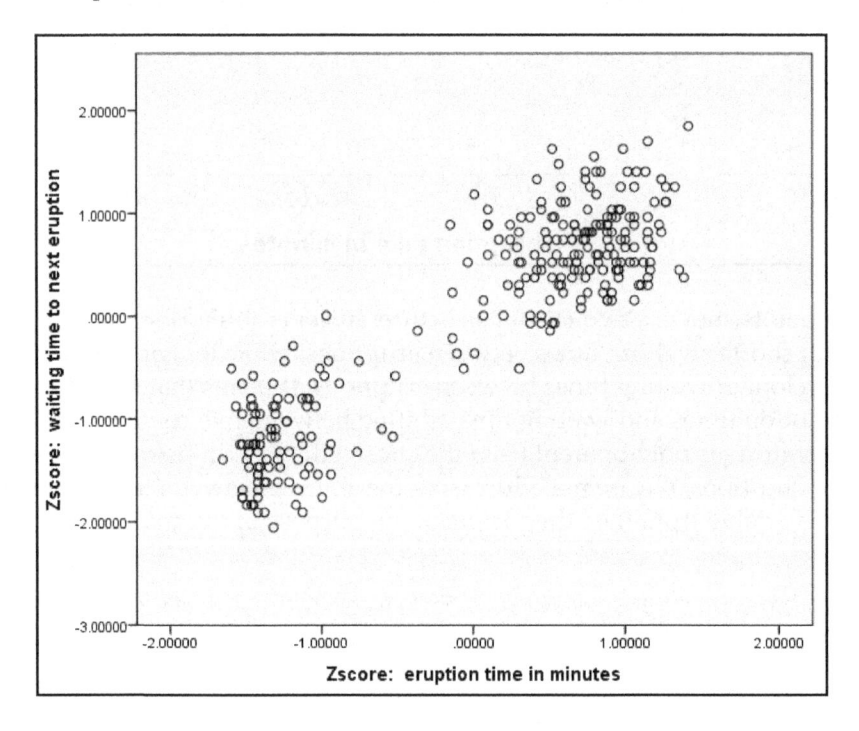

The shapes are very similar to the previous plot, but this time the two variables are in the same metric (standardized). However, note that the axes are not quite equated, that is, a one-unit horizontal distance is not rendered the same as a one-unit vertical distance. Nonetheless, we can see that the two apparent clusters of points are roughly circular/spherical.

K-means cluster analysis of the Old Faithful data

Since charting suggests a two-cluster spherical structure, you could try k-means clustering with k tentatively identified as 2.

Here is SPSS code for k-means analysis of the standardized input variables:

```
QUICK CLUSTER Zeruption Zwaiting
 /MISSING=LISTWISE
 /CRITERIA=CLUSTER(2) MXITER(10) CONVERGE(0)
 /METHOD=KMEANS(NOUPDATE)
 /SAVE CLUSTER
 /PRINT INITIAL ANOVA CLUSTER DISTAN.
```

Key elements of the SPSS code are:

- The input variables are the standardized forms of eruption and waiting
- `/CRITERIA` specifies two clusters, as well as default values for iteration and convergence criteria
- `/SAVE` specifies that cluster membership should be saved in a new variable that will be added to the active file
- `/PRINT` specifies: initial cluster centers, the ANOVA table for the clustering variables, a cluster membership table for each case, and a table of pairwise distances between all final cluster centers

Clustering

Here is the `Initial Cluster Centers` table:

Initial Cluster Centers

	Cluster 1	Cluster 2
Zscore: eruption time in minutes	1.41253	-1.31840
Zscore: waiting time to next eruption	1.84649	-2.05201

By default, SPSS Statistics performs a data pass and finds two well-separated cases. These become the starting centroids for the K-means algorithm. Note that poor choice of initial cluster centers can lead to a poor cluster solution. For this reason, you should inspect both the `Initial Cluster Centers` table and the final solution. Note that poor initial cluster centers can result if you use random starts or grab the first K cases off the top of the file.

Here is the `Iteration History` table:

Iteration History[a]

Iteration	Change in Cluster Centers 1	Change in Cluster Centers 2
1	1.330	.903
2	.022	.045
3	.008	.014
4	.008	.014
5	.000	.000

a. Convergence achieved due to no or small change in cluster centers. The maximum absolute coordinate change for any center is .000. The current iteration is 5. The minimum distance between initial centers is 4.760.

Clustering

By default, the algorithm does ten iterations and stops when there is no change across the iterations. You should check to see that the program actually converged. If not, you could raise the number of iterations. Or, you could be satisfied if the changes between the iterations become very small, although still exceeding zero. In this case, the algorithm stopped after five iterations.

Here is the beginning of the `Cluster Membership` table:

Cluster Membership

Case Number	Cluster	Distance
1	1	.615
2	2	.225
3	1	.955
4	2	.581
5	1	.417

This table shows the cluster membership for each case. You might avoid printing this when the number of records is large. In addition, since you can save the cluster memberships as an added variable, you need not print this table.

Here is the `Final Cluster Centers` table:

Final Cluster Centers

	Cluster 1	Cluster 2
Zscore: eruption time in minutes	.70840	-1.25777
Zscore: waiting time to next eruption	.67550	-1.19936

This shows the cluster centroids, which are in standardized metric because the inputs were standardized.

Clustering

Here is the `Distances between Final Cluster Centers` table:

Distances between Final Cluster Centers		
Cluster	1	2
1		2.717
2	2.717	

In the case of a two-cluster solution, this shows the one and only distance between the two clusters. In general, you are interested in ascertaining between-cluster separation, so it can be useful to know how far apart the clusters are.

Here is the `ANOVA` table:

ANOVA						
	Cluster Mean Square	df	Error Mean Square	df	F	Sig.
Zscore: eruption time in minutes	242.352	1	.106	270	2284.078	.000
Zscore: waiting time to next eruption	220.365	1	.188	270	1175.045	.000

The F tests should be used only for descriptive purposes because the clusters have been chosen to maximize the differences among cases in different clusters. The observed significance levels are not corrected for this and thus cannot be interpreted as tests of the hypothesis that the cluster means are equal.

This table provides the F statistics as a heuristic for understanding the relative importance of the input variables in cluster separation. Note that the comment below the table indicates that the F tests are for descriptive purposes only, since the cases were assigned to clusters in a way that attempted to create between-cluster differences. The F statistics suggest that the standardized eruption times are more important to cluster separation than the standardized waiting times.

Here is the `Number of Cases in each Cluster` table:

Number of Cases in each Cluster		
Cluster	1	174.000
	2	98.000
Valid		272.000
Missing		.000

Assignment of codes 1 and 2 to the clusters is arbitrary. Here, cluster 1 has 174 observations while cluster 2 has 98 observations.

Further cluster profiling

Here is a scatterplot of the observations color-coded by cluster membership:

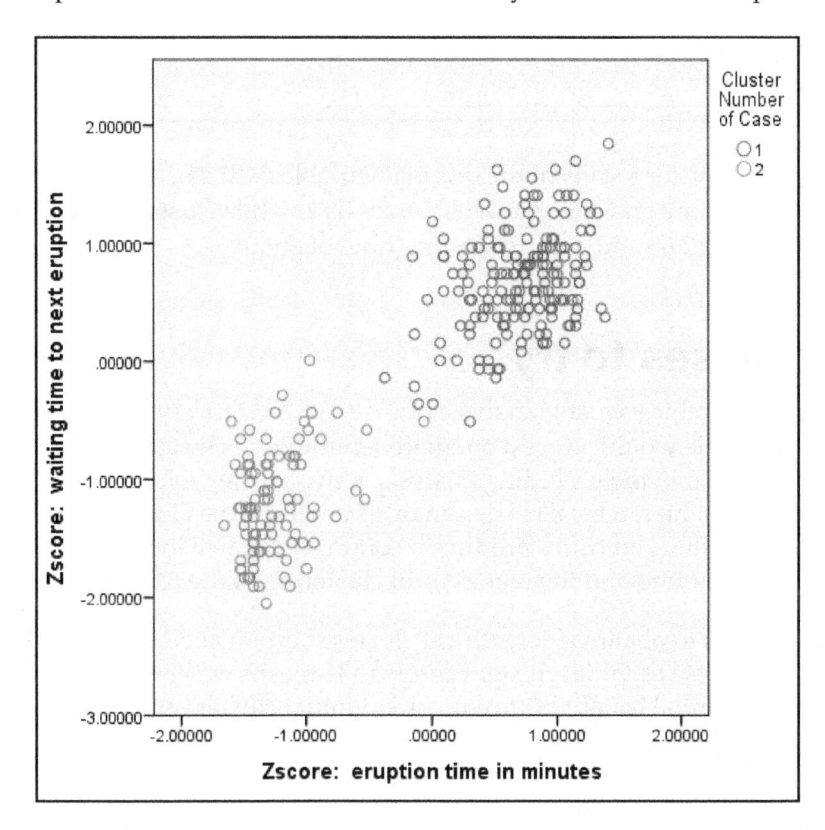

Clustering

Visually, the clusters are well-separated, relatively homogeneous, and roughly spherical.

Here is the `Report` table from the `Means` procedure, featuring the original variables as inputs:

Cluster Number of Case		eruption time in minutes	waiting time to next eruption
1	Mean	4.29633	80.08
	N	174	174
	Std. Deviation	.406609	5.887
2	Mean	2.05220	54.59
	N	98	98
	Std. Deviation	.299806	5.889
Total	Mean	3.48778	70.90
	N	272	272
	Std. Deviation	1.141371	13.595

Report

The table shows the cluster means of the original variables. Cluster 1 has a mean eruption time of about 4.3 and a mean waiting time of about 80.1, while cluster 2 has a mean eruption time of about 2.05 and a mean waiting time of about 54.6.

Other analyses to try

You could run a hierarchical cluster analysis of the `Old Faithful` data. If you do, the agglomeration schedule would suggest a tentative number of clusters. In this instance, given the structure seen in the preceding analysis, a two-cluster solution would be suggested. If you run a hierarchical cluster analysis and save the cluster memberships as a variable added to the file, you could produce a contingency table looking at agreement between k-means clustering and the hierarchical clustering of the `Old Faithful` data.

Another thing to try is to obtain a hierarchical cluster solution and calculate the cluster means. Then, input these as initial cluster centers in K-means clustering. Such a hybrid approach has the potential benefit of proving good initial cluster centers for k-means clustering. See the SPSS documentation on the `QUICK CLUSTER / INITIAL` subcommand.

Twostep cluster analysis example

For this example, we return to the USA states violent crime data example. Recall that `TWOSTEP CLUSTER` offers an automatic method for selecting the number of clusters, as well as a `Likelihood` distance measure. We will run it to show some of the visuals in the model viewer output.

The approach here is to:

1. First run `TWOSTEP CLUSTER` in automatic mode to identify a tentative number of clusters.
2. Then run `TWOSTEP CLUSTER` again with a specified number of clusters.

Here is the SPSS code for the first run:

```
TWOSTEP CLUSTER
 /CONTINUOUS VARIABLES=MurderR RRapeR RobberyR AssaultR  BurglaryR LarcenyR VehicleTheftR
 /DISTANCE Likelihood
 /NUMCLUSTERS AUTO 15 BIC
 /HANDLENOISE 0
 /MEMALLOCATE 64
 /CRITERIA INITHRESHOLD(0) MXBRANCH(8) MXLEVEL(3)
 /VIEWMODEL DISPLAY=YES
 /PRINT IC COUNT SUMMARY.
```

Here are comments on the SPSS code:

- In a step not shown, the variable names were shortened. This makes for a more informative model viewer output.
- `/CONTINUOUS` specifies the continuous variables in the analysis.
- `/DISTANCE` specifies the `Likelihood` distance. `TWOSTEP CLUSTER` assumes that the continuous variables are normally distributed.
- `/NUMCLUSTERS` specifies automatic identification of the number of clusters based on the **Schwarz's Bayesian Criterion (BIC)** criterion, and specifies cluster solutions from 15 down to 1. BIC is an information criterion that rewards a cluster solution for closeness of fit, while penalizing it for complexity. The usual use of BIC is to favor the solution that minimizes the BIC. We will use this rule. `TWOSTEP CLUSTER` uses some other heuristics involving changes across cluster solutions, but there is only ad hoc justification for these, so we will not use them.

Clustering

- `/HANDLENOISE` offers an option to place atypical cases in an outlier cluster. We set the value to 0 here, but this option could be tried with other settings if you feel that you have data with some anomalous observations.
- `/MEMALLOCATE` specifies the maximum amount of memory in megabytes (MB) that the cluster algorithm should use. If the procedure exceeds this maximum, it will use the disk to store information that will not fit in memory. This is a technical parameter that can affect algorithm performance in large-scale problems. Here, the default of 64 suffices for our small problem.
- `/CRITERIA` specifies technical parameters that affect the `TWOSTEP CLUSTER` algorithm. These are described in detail in the `TWOSTEP CLUSTER` documentation, which advises using care if you change them. We run with the default values.
- `/VIEWMODEL` specifies the display of the model viewer output.
- `/PRINT` specifies the display of the `Auto-Clustering` table, descriptive statistics by cluster, and cluster frequencies.

Here is the `Auto-Clustering` table:

Auto-Clustering

Number of Clusters	Schwarz's Bayesian Criterion (BIC)	BIC Change[a]	Ratio of BIC Changes[b]	Ratio of Distance Measures[c]
1	298.982			
2	289.842	-9.140	1.000	1.158
3	289.482	-.360	.039	2.285
4	320.275	30.793	-3.369	2.052
5	363.500	43.224	-4.729	1.274
6	409.267	45.768	-5.008	1.076
7	455.691	46.423	-5.079	1.307
8	504.141	48.450	-5.301	1.183
9	553.610	49.469	-5.413	1.039
10	603.286	49.676	-5.435	1.184
11	653.796	50.510	-5.526	1.059
12	704.558	50.762	-5.554	1.057
13	755.553	50.995	-5.580	1.204
14	807.235	51.682	-5.655	1.181
15	859.433	52.199	-5.711	1.266

a. The changes are from the previous number of clusters in the table.
b. The ratios of changes are relative to the change for the two cluster solution.
c. The ratios of distance measures are based on the current number of clusters against the previous number of clusters.

The BIC measure balances closeness of fit with parameter complexity. Here, as the number of clusters increases beyond three, the complexity due to the increased number of clusters begins to dominate, and leads to an increase in the BIC. Note that the minimum BIC is associated with three clusters. BIC change is the difference in BIC values between the given cluster solution and the next smaller one. Ratio of BIC changes is the ratio of the current BIC change to the BIC change from going from 1 to 2 clusters.

Ratio of distance measures is the ratio of the distance measure for the next smallest model to the distance measure for the current model. The SPSS Statistics documentation documents some heuristics involving these measures, but the heuristics have only an ad hoc justification. We prefer to use the information criterion as intended, that is, favor the model that produces the minimum BIC, or the **Akaike Information Criterion** (**AIC**), if you use that measure instead. However, do not obtain both the BIC and the AIC, but instead stick with one of the measures. In sum, the BIC here favors the three-cluster model.

Here is the follow-up TWOSTEP CLUSTER run:

```
TWOSTEP CLUSTER
  /CONTINUOUS VARIABLES=MurderR RRapeR RobberyR AssaultR  BurglaryR LarcenyR VehicleTheftR
  /DISTANCE Likelihood
  /NUMCLUSTERS FIXED=3
  /HANDLENOISE 0
  /MEMALLOCATE 64
  /CRITERIA INITHRESHOLD(0) MXBRANCH(8) MXLEVEL(3)
  /VIEWMODEL DISPLAY=YES
  /PRINT IC COUNT SUMMARY
  /SAVE VARIABLE=TSC_3clusters.
```

There are two noteworthy changes in the SPSS code:

- /NUMCLUSTERS specifies a three-cluster solution
- /SAVE specifies a variable name for the cluster memberships

Clustering

Here is the `Cluster Distribution` table:

Cluster Distribution

		N	% of Combined	% of Total
Cluster	1	30	58.8%	58.8%
	2	20	39.2%	39.2%
	3	1	2.0%	2.0%
	Combined	51	100.0%	100.0%
Total		51		100.0%

There are three clusters. `TWOSTEP CLUSTER` assigns data codes to cluster by size. Cluster 1 has 30 members, cluster 2 has 20, and cluster 3 has one member.

Here is the `Centroids` table, transposed for readability:

Centroids

		Cluster 1	Cluster 2	Cluster 3	Combined
MurderR	Mean	4.907	2.805	15.900	4.298
	Std. Deviation	1.8649	1.1691	.	2.5185
RRapeR	Mean	44.760	32.570	71.600	40.506
	Std. Deviation	15.6810	9.6230	.	15.2707
RobberyR	Mean	94.023	59.290	530.700	88.965
	Std. Deviation	37.5606	38.7606	.	75.2287
AssaultR	Mean	264.310	160.350	626.100	230.635
	Std. Deviation	93.6082	58.5426	.	110.3125
BurglaryR	Mean	631.667	370.775	526.000	527.284
	Std. Deviation	159.9756	69.4762	.	181.6954
LarcenyR	Mean	2068.463	1477.600	4082.300	1876.239
	Std. Deviation	282.4040	133.7618	.	485.9266
VehicleTheftR	Mean	240.743	120.120	574.100	199.976
	Std. Deviation	67.2643	42.5344	.	98.2804

Cluster 2 has the lowest mean values across all variables, while cluster 3 has the highest values on all variables except `BurglaryR`.

Here is the default Model Viewer output:

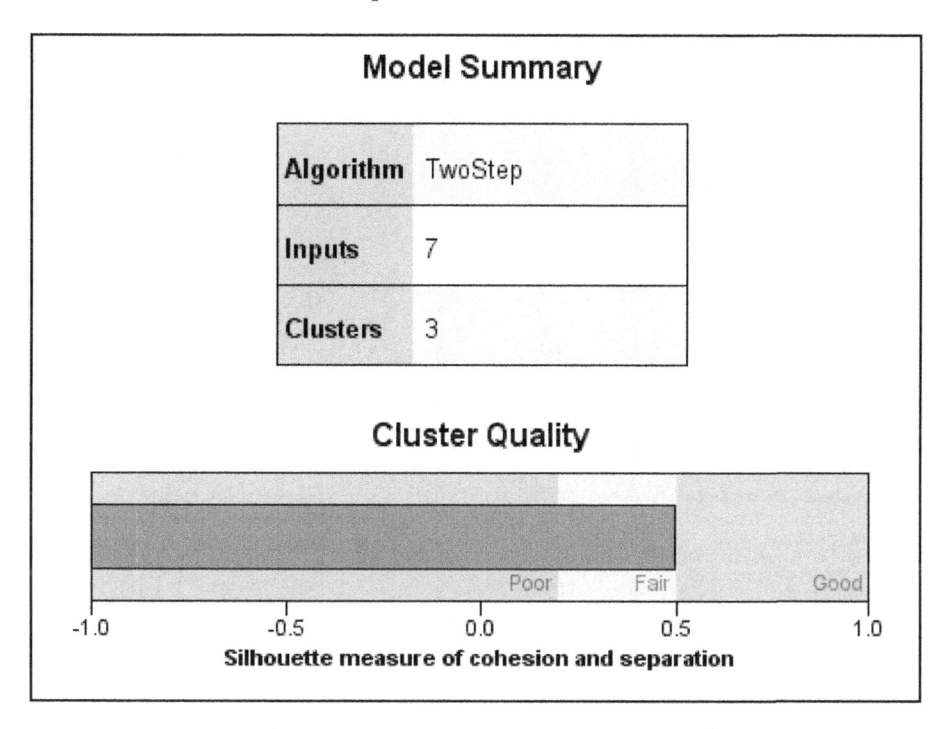

Model Summary

Algorithm	TwoStep
Inputs	7
Clusters	3

Cluster Quality

Silhouette measure of cohesion and separation

The `Model Summary` table gives information on the algorithm, the number of inputs, and the number of clusters. The **Cluster Quality** chart gives a graphical rendering of the silhouette measure. From SPSS Statistics help:

> "The silhouette measure averages, over all records, (B−A) / max(A,B), where A is the record's distance to its cluster center and B is the record's distance to the nearest cluster center that it doesn't belong to. A silhouette coefficient of 1 would mean that all cases are located directly on their cluster centers. A value of −1 would mean all cases are located on the cluster centers of some other cluster. A value of 0 means, on average, cases are equidistant between their own cluster center and the nearest other cluster."

Clustering

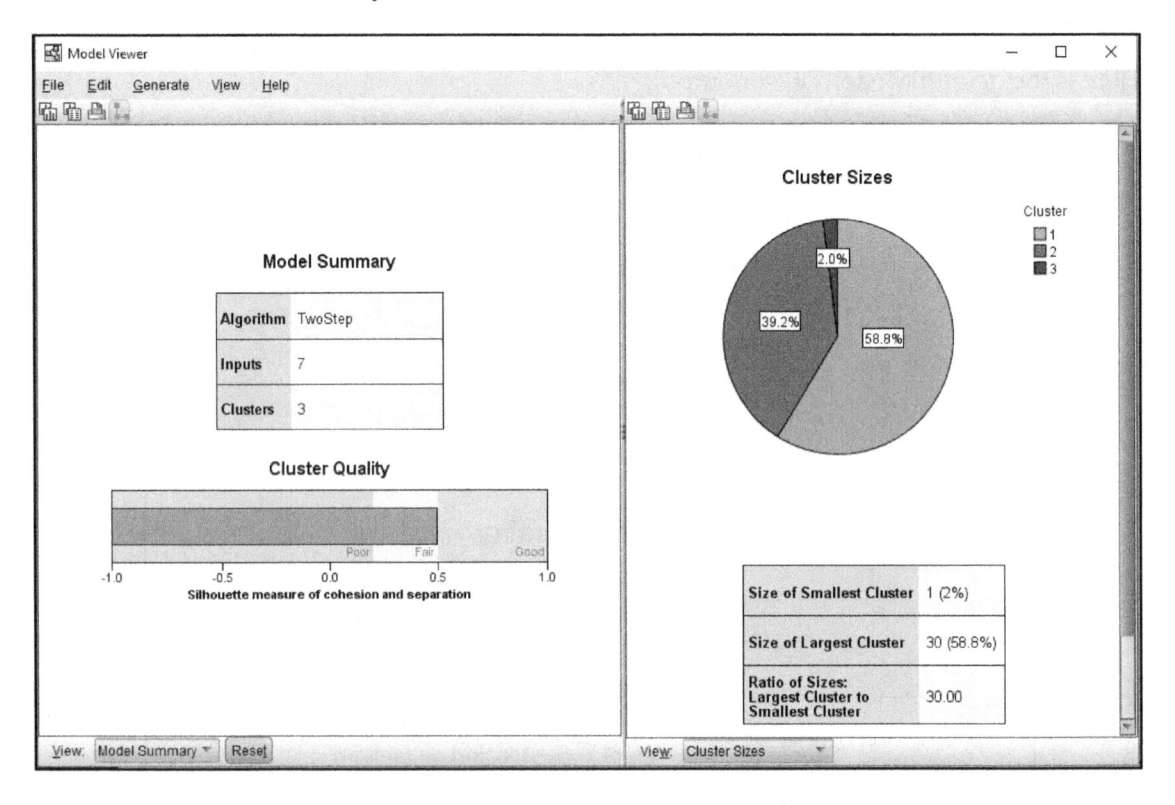

Here is **Model Viewer** after you double-click to activate it:

The screen splits into left and right halves. The left half is **Main View** and the right half is **Auxiliary View**. Both views have a drop bar with multiple selections. **Main View** presents **Model Summary** while **Auxiliary View** presents **Cluster Sizes**.

Here is **Main View** with **Clusters** selected in the drop bar:

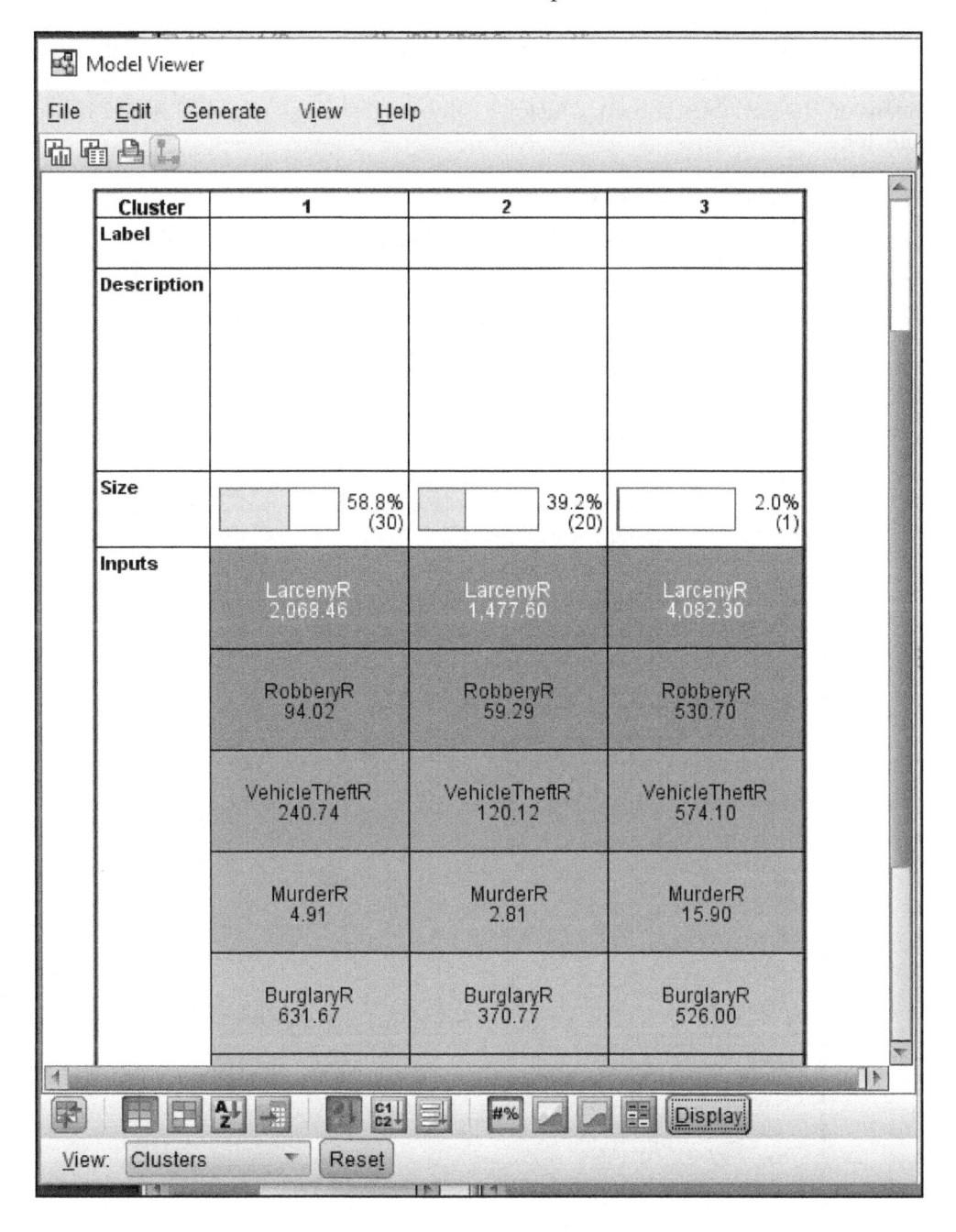

Cluster	1	2	3
Label			
Description			
Size	58.8% (30)	39.2% (20)	2.0% (1)
Inputs	LarcenyR 2,068.46	LarcenyR 1,477.60	LarcenyR 4,082.30
	RobberyR 94.02	RobberyR 59.29	RobberyR 530.70
	VehicleTheftR 240.74	VehicleTheftR 120.12	VehicleTheftR 574.10
	MurderR 4.91	MurderR 2.81	MurderR 15.90
	BurglaryR 631.67	BurglaryR 370.77	BurglaryR 526.00

View: Clusters

[395]

Clustering

Clusters are labeled **1**, **2**, **3** by size, and displayed left to right. Variables are ordered top to bottom by overall importance in driving the clustering. The **Clusters** view displays the means for each variable in each cluster. You should make an effort to compare the means across clusters and try to characterize the clusters. For example, Cluster 3 is a singleton with high means on the variables shown, Cluster 1 is the largest cluster, and Cluster 2 is a low-crime cluster.

Here is the corresponding **Auxiliary View**:

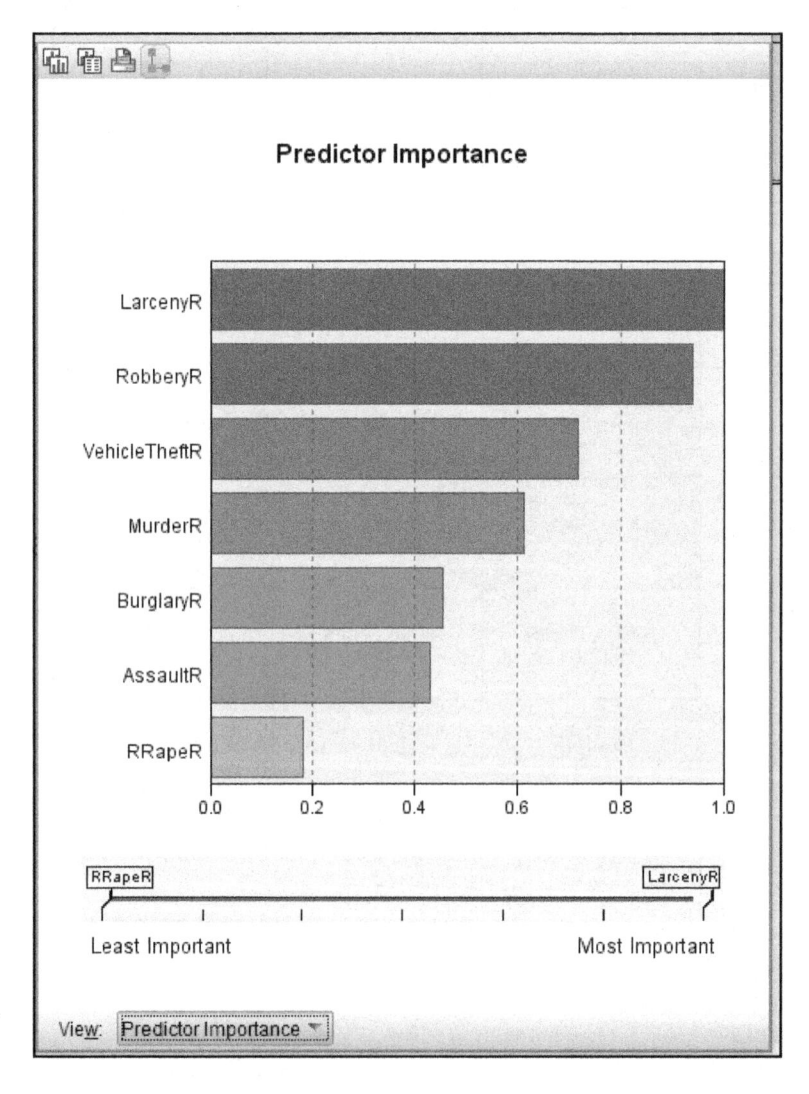

Clustering

SPSS Statistics procedures that offer **Model Viewer** output typically present an intuitive bar chart showing the relative importance of the inputs. Here, the Larceny rate and Robbery rate have the highest importance, meaning that these variables are the most important in determining which cluster an object is in.

You can select one or more cluster columns in the **Clusters** view in **Main View**. When you do so, **Auxiliary View** presents the **Cluster Comparison** view:

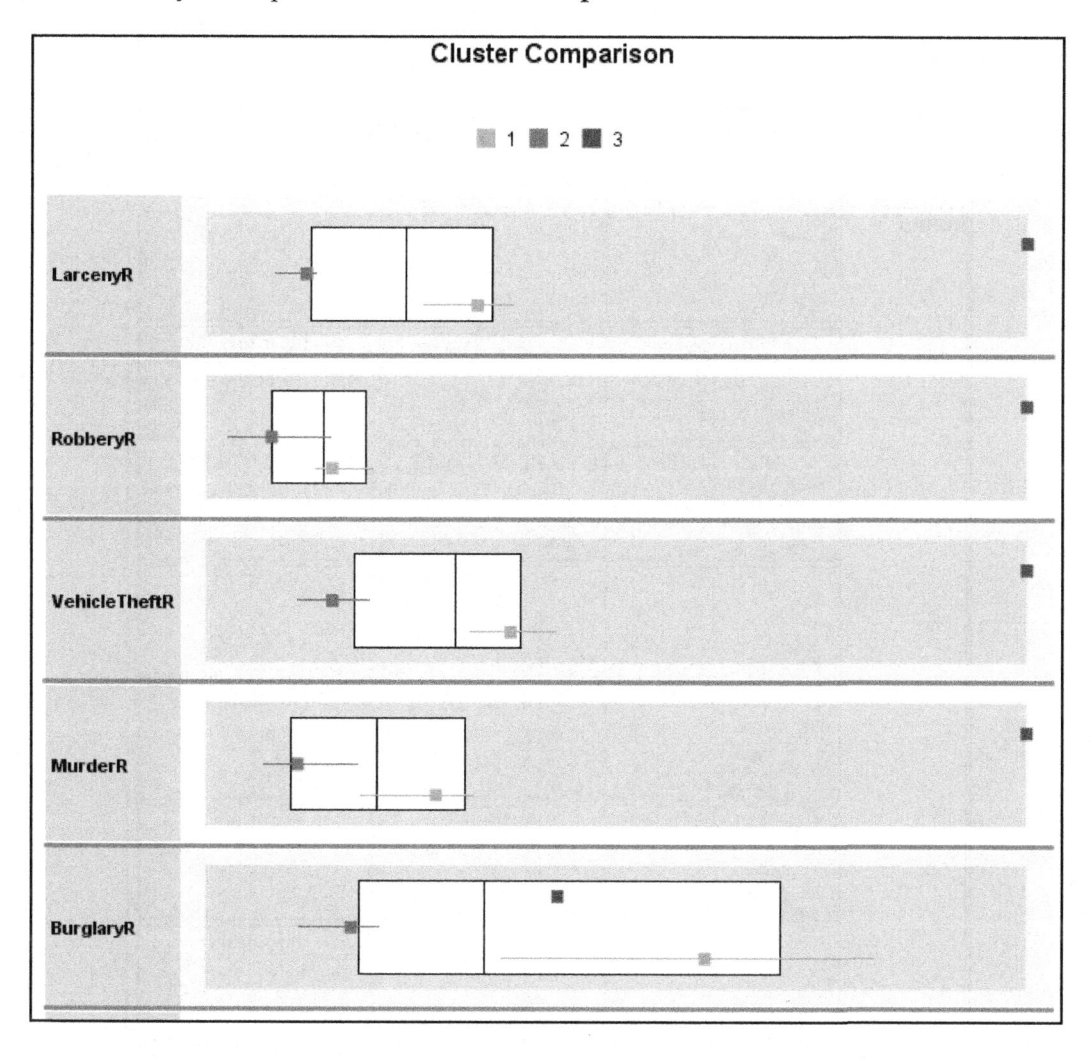

Clustering

The boxplots show the overall distribution of the variable, while the color-coded displays show the cluster centers and spread. Cluster 3 is a single observation, so there is no spread around its center point. Overall, cluster 2 exhibits low means across the shown crime rate variables, while cluster 3 is unusually extreme on many of the measures. This chart could be read in conjunction with the **Predictor Importance** chart, in that variables such as `Larceny Rate` show big spread in the cluster means relative to the overall center of the variable.

Here is the **Clusters** view showing **absolute distributions**:

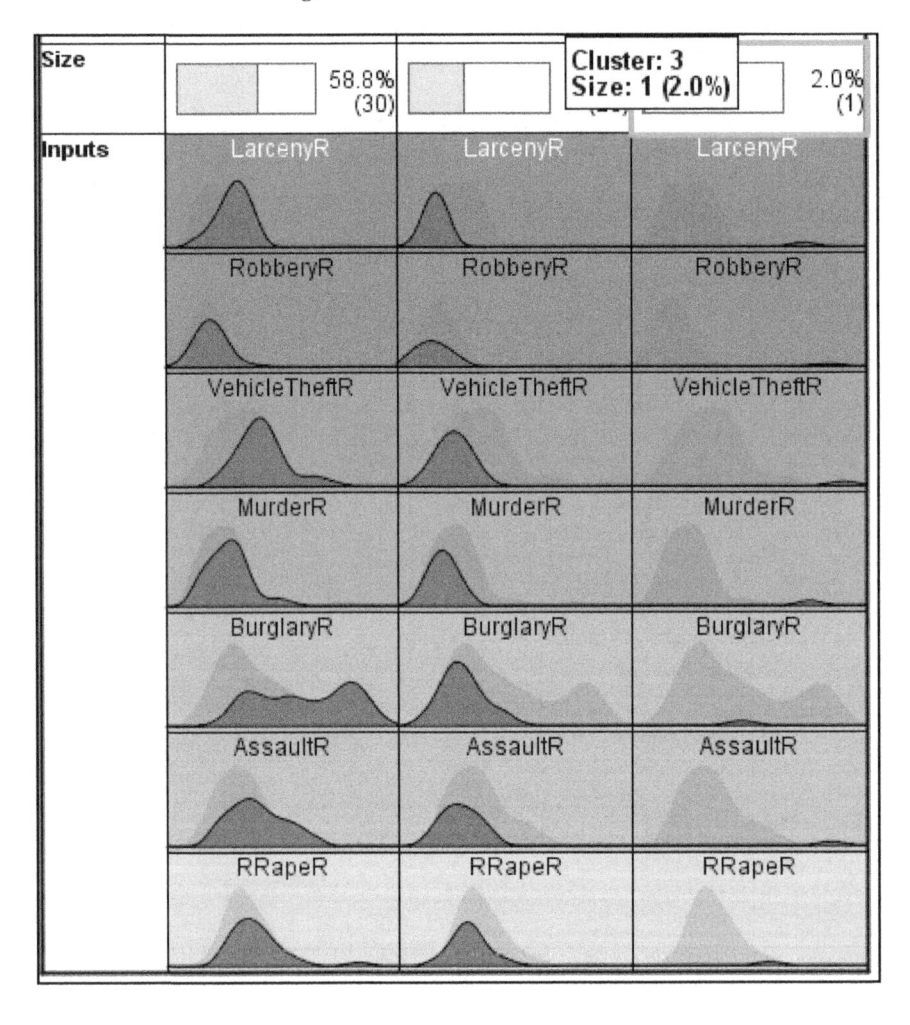

Size	58.8% (30)	Cluster: 3 Size: 1 (2.0%)	2.0% (1)
Inputs	LarcenyR	LarcenyR	LarcenyR
	RobberyR	RobberyR	RobberyR
	VehicleTheftR	VehicleTheftR	VehicleTheftR
	MurderR	MurderR	MurderR
	BurglaryR	BurglaryR	BurglaryR
	AssaultR	AssaultR	AssaultR
	RRapeR	RRapeR	RRapeR

Clustering

The lightly-tinted distributions in the background are the overall distributions of the variables, while the intensely-tinted distributions in the foreground show the within-cluster distributions. Again, cluster 2 centers are smaller and therefore to the left, while cluster 3 is extreme on most measures.

Here is the **Clusters** view showing relative distributions:

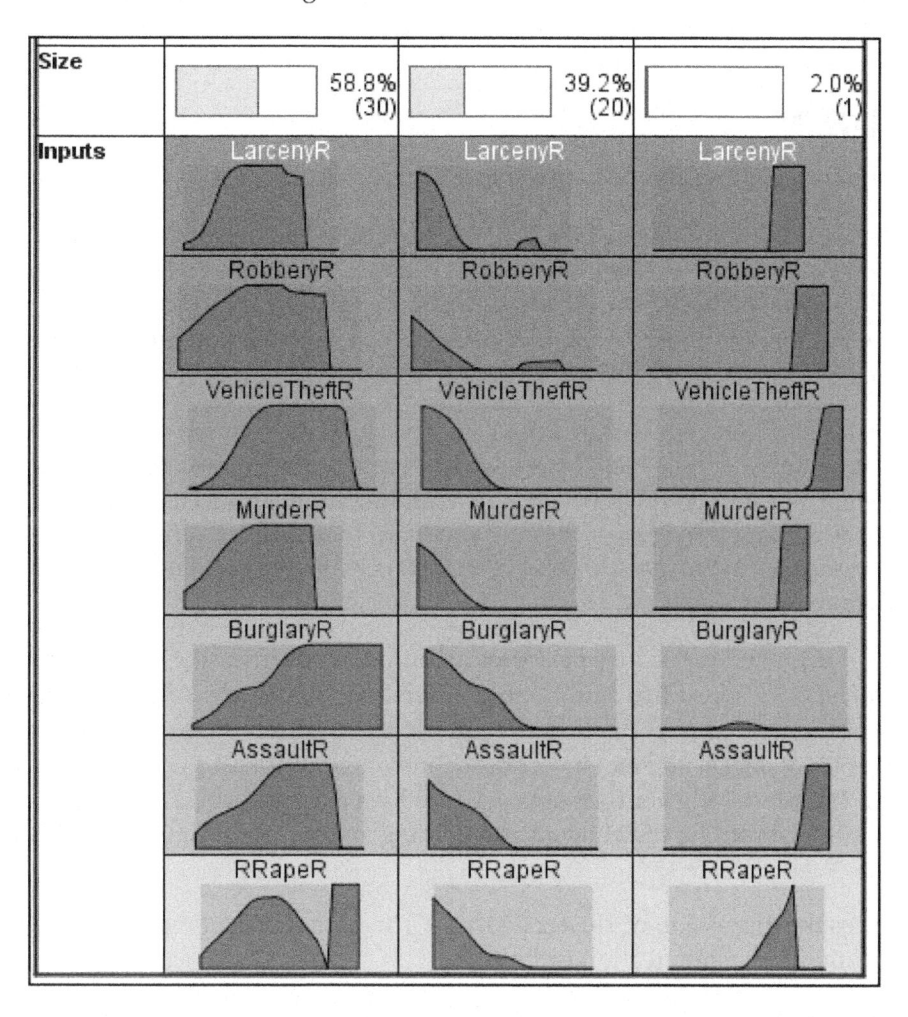

The interpretation is similar. In sum, TWOSTEP CLUSTER with automatic clustering produced a BIC table. If we favor the cluster solution that minimizes the BIC, we get the shown 3-cluster solution. The **Model Viewer** output provides many visualizations that give insight into the cluster solution.

Recall that we also analyzed these data using hierarchical clustering, featuring the Ward's method. In analysis that we leave as an exercise, you can confirm that ward's 3-cluster solution is very similar in its cluster assignment to TWOSTEP CLUSTER with three clusters. In addition, Ward's 4-cluster solution is also very similar in its cluster assignment to TWOSTEP CLUSTER with four clusters. It is up to you to decide which clustering solution best tells the story in the data.

Summary

SPSS Statistics offers three procedures for cluster analysis.

The CLUSTER procedure performs hierarchical clustering. Hierarchical clustering starts with the casewise proximities matrix and combines cases and clusters into clusters using one of the seven clustering methods. Schedule, Dendogram, and icicle plots are aids to identifying the tentative number of clusters. Consider using CLUSTER when you are unsure of the number of clusters at the start and are willing to compute the proximity matrix.

The QUICK CLUSTER procedure performs K-means clustering, which requires specification of an explicit tentative number of clusters. K-means clustering avoids forming the proximities matrix along with all the steps of agglomeration, and so it can be used on files with lots of cases. K-means clustering is not invariant to scaling, and furthermore, can impose a spherical structure on the observed clusters even when the natural clusters in the data are of some other shape.

The TWOSTEP CLUSTER procedure performs agglomerative clustering on two passes of the data. You can specify an explicit number of clusters, or you can use AIC or BIC to aid in identifying a tentative number of clusters. You can use the Euclidean distance or the Likelihood distance, and can incorporate both continuous and categorical inputs into the analysis. The Model Viewer output is activated via a double-click, and provides many useful displays for profiling the clusters and gaining an understanding of the cluster solution.

This concludes the discussion of cluster analysis. The next chapter looks at discriminant analysis, an important classification technique.

16
Discriminant Analysis

Discriminant analysis is a statistical technique used in classification. In general, a **classification** problem features a categorical target variable with two or more known classes and one or more inputs to be used in the classification. Discriminant analysis assumes that the inputs are numeric (scale) variables, although practitioners often employ discriminant analysis when the inputs are a mixture of numeric and categorical variables. To use categorical variables as inputs in SPSS Statistics Discriminant, you must employ dummy variable coding. If your inputs are exclusively categorical, you might consider using logistic regression instead.

A classic example where discriminant analysis could be used is the oft-cited Fisher Iris data example. A botanist approached the great statistician and geneticist R. A Fisher with a classification problem. He had four measurements on 50 individual flowers from each of three species of iris flowers. The task was to come up with a classification scheme such that Fisher could classify a new observation into the correct species with a high degree of accuracy. The approach that Fisher invented was discriminant analysis.

From that beginning, discriminant analysis has become one of the standard statistical approaches to classification in various subject-matter domains, from education to the sciences to auditing of tax returns.

In discriminant analysis, a `discriminant` function is a linear combination of inputs that maximally separates groups. Contingent on the number of classes in the target variable and number of inputs, there could be more than one `discriminant` function. When there is more than one `discriminant` function, the first one accounts for as much between-groups variation as possible; the second one is orthogonal to the first and accounts for as much remaining between-groups variations as possible; and so on.

When using discriminant analysis, goals in the analysis include the following:

- Assessing overall classification accuracy and accuracy by groups
- Assessing the relative importance of the inputs
- In situations where there is more than one `discriminant` function, assessing the relative importance of the functions
- Classifying new observations for which inputs are known but the target class is not known

This chapter will cover the following topics:

- Descriptive discriminant analysis
- Predictive discriminant analysis
- Assumptions underlying discriminant analysis
- Example data
- Statistical and graphical summary of the data
- Discriminant analysis setup--key decisions
- Examining the results
- Scoring new observations

Descriptive discriminant analysis

One purpose of discriminant analysis is description--finding a way to separate and characterize the three species in terms of differences on the classifying variables. In the Iris data, Fisher saw that size matters--members of a certain species tend to have larger values for dimensional measurements on the individual samples such as petal length and width and sepal length and width. In addition, there was another pattern--members of a certain species that otherwise had small dimensional measurements on three of the indicators had relatively large sepal widths. Taking into account both of these patterns, one is able to classify irises with great accuracy as well as understand what characterizes exemplars of each species.

In descriptive discriminant analysis, you would report and focus on summary statistics within groups such as means, standard deviations, and correlations or covariances. You would also characterize differences between the groups in terms of the summary statistics on the classifying variables. Charts would also be useful to illustrate differences between groups. Charts could include grouped histograms or scatterplots with the target variable shown using different colors or marker symbols.

Predictive discriminant analysis

A second purpose of discriminant analysis is prediction--developing equations such that if you plug in the input values for a new observed individual or object, the equations would classify the individual or object into one of the target classes.

In modern predictive analytics, discriminant analysis is one of a large number of techniques that could be used in classification. The reason that so many classification techniques exist is that no method dominates the others across all problems and data. Typically, in a project, you might try a number of approaches and compare and contrast their performance on the data. A statistical method such as discriminant analysis could be one of these methods. In the event that the data meet the assumptions of discriminant analysis, it should perform well. As discriminant analysis is an equation-based method, the prediction model is transparent and relatively easy to understand.

The activity of deploying prediction equations and plugging in input values to get a predicted outcome is called **scoring**. As a practitioner, you wish to find a way to make SPSS Statistics do the work. We will show later in this chapter how to do scoring of new records in SPSS Discriminant.

Assumptions underlying discriminant analysis

When using discriminant analysis, you make the following assumptions:

- Independence of the observations. This rules out correlated data such as multilevel data, repeated measures data, or matched pairs data.
- Multivariate normality within groups. Strictly speaking, the presence of any categorical inputs can make this assumption untenable. Nonetheless, discriminant analysis can be robust to violations of this assumption.
- Homogeneity of covariances across groups. You can assess this assumption using the Box's M test.
- Absence of perfect multicollinearity. A given input cannot be perfectly predicted by a combination of other inputs also in the model.
- The number of cases within each group must be larger than the number of input variables.

Discriminant Analysis

> IBM SPSS Statistics gives you statistical and graphical tools to assess the normality assumption. See Chapter 4 for a way to assess multivariate normality. Box's M test is available as part of the Discriminant procedure.

Example data

The data analyzed in this chapter is the `Wine` dataset found in the UC-Irvine Machine Learning repository. The data is the result of a chemical analysis of wines grown in the same region in Italy but derived from three different cultivars. The analysis determined the quantities of 13 chemical components found in each of the three types of wine. There are 59, 71, and 48 instances respectively in the three classes. The class codes are 1, 2, and 3.

The attributes are as follows:

- Alcohol
- Malic acid
- Ash
- Alcalinity of ash
- Magnesium
- Total phenols
- Flavanoids
- Nonflavanoid phenols
- Proanthocyanins
- Color intensity
- Hue
- OD280/OD315 of diluted wines
- Proline

In the context of classification, the task is to use the 13 attributes to classify each observation into one of the three wine types. Note that all 13 attributes are numeric.

Statistical and graphical summary of the data

There are many exploratory analyses that you can undertake at this point. Here, we show a simple table means as well as a scatterplot matrix that reveals the group structure.

Here are the group means on the attributes:

Report

Mean

	Type 1	Type 2	Type 3	Total
Alcohol	13.7447	12.2787	13.1538	13.0006
Malic_Acid	2.0107	1.9327	3.3338	2.3363
Ash	2.4556	2.2448	2.4371	2.3665
Ash_Alcalinity	17.0373	20.2380	21.4167	19.4949
Magnesium	106.34	94.55	99.31	99.74
Total_Phenols	2.8402	2.2589	1.6787	2.2951
Flavanoids	2.9824	2.0808	.7815	2.0293
Nonflavanoid_Phenols	.2900	.3637	.4475	.3619
Proanthocyanins	1.8993	1.6303	1.1535	1.5909
Color_Intensity	5.5283	3.0866	7.3962	5.0581
Hue	1.0620	1.0563	.6827	.9574
Dilution	3.1578	2.7854	1.6835	2.6117
Proline	1115.71	519.51	629.90	746.89

These statistics are presented for descriptive purposes. You are looking for overt differences in the means across the three types. If an input's means vary across type, then this suggests that the variable might be a useful discriminator. On the other hand, do not make too much of apparent differences as these are single-variable statistics. Discriminant analysis brings all of the inputs into the model at the same time, and therefore you get a sense of a variable's impact in the presence of other variables.

Discriminant Analysis

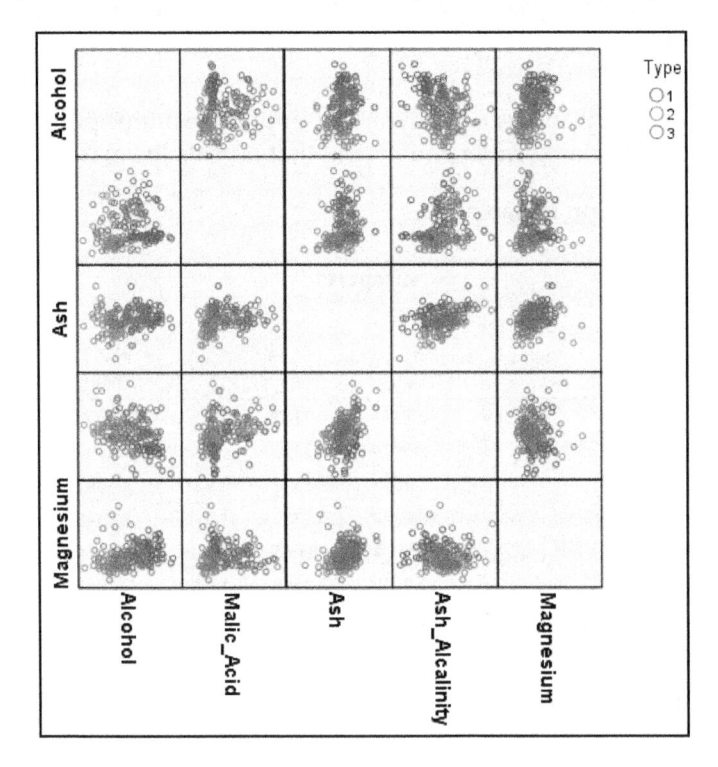

You might also try various charts. Here is a scatterplot matrix showing five of the attributes:

The challenge in producing such a display is that, with 13 discriminating variables, there are 0.5 * 13 * 12 equals 78 pairwise scatterplots. The scatterplot matrix presents every pair in a specified list, but if you specify too many variables, the plot will not show sufficient details. With this in mind, we limited the display to five variables. The plot uses color to overlay wine type. You should look for evidence of group separation--non-overlap of the groups as well as separation of the group centers. For example, the scatterplot of Magnesium versus Alcohol shows that the three Types are in different parts of the plot.

Discriminant analysis setup - key decisions

You can run discriminant either from the menus or via syntax. When running discriminant analysis, you must make several higher-level decisions about the analysis.

Priors

First, do you have any prior information about the relative sizes of the target variable classes in the population? In the absence of any knowledge of target class sizes, you can use equal prior probabilities, which is the default, or prior probabilities can be in the proportions of the target variable class sizes in the data. A third alternative is that you can specify your own target class prior probabilities. The list of probabilities must sum to 1. Prior probabilities are used during classification. For more discussion, see the documentation of the /PRIORS subcommand.

Pooled or separate

Should discriminant analysis use the pooled within-groups covariance matrix or should it use separate within-groups covariance matrices for classification? Technically, linear discriminant analysis uses the pooled within-groups covariance matrix. This is appropriate when your data meets the assumption of homogeneity of covariance matrices across groups.

> **TIP**
> You can use the Box's M test to help assess whether the homogeneity assumption is tenable. In the event that this assumption is untenable, you could use separate covariance matrices for classification. For more discussion, see the documentation of the /CLASSIFY subcommand.

Do not use separate covariance matrices if the homogeneity assumption is satisfied as you are estimating extra parameters unnecessarily.

> In addition, if the homogeneity assumption is not satisfied but the overall sample size is not large, you might consider using the pooled covariance matrix even though the homogeneity assumption is violated, as you have too little data to get good estimates of the separate covariance matrices. As a technical point, if the sample size is not large relative to the number of inputs, you could be computing a lot of covariances imprecisely if you compute separate covariance matrices.

Dimensionality

The dimension of the problem is given by the following comparison:

dimensionality = minimum(g-1,p)

Discriminant Analysis

Here, g is the number of classes in the target variable and p is the number of input variables. Special cases that follow from this are as follows:

- A two-group problem always has only one dimension.
- A one-input problem always has only one dimension.
- A three-group problem with two or more inputs has two dimensions.
- A three- or more group problem with two inputs has two dimensions.
- A four-group problem with three or more inputs has three dimensions. However, you can assess whether the first two dimensions represent most of the information in the discriminant analysis, in which case visualization is easier.

In general, when the dimensionality of the problem is greater than one, you can also perform a step-down evaluation to determine whether you can use fewer than the full number of dimensions. For more discussion, see the documentation of the /FUNCTIONS subcommand.

Syntax for the wine example

Here is a syntax specification for the wine type classification problem:

```
DISCRIMINANT
 /GROUPS=Type(1 3)
 /VARIABLES=Alcohol Malic_Acid Ash Ash_Alcalinity
 Magnesium Total_Phenols Flavanoids Nonflavanoid_Phenols
 Proanthocyanins Color_Intensity Hue Dilution Proline
 /ANALYSIS ALL
 /SAVE=CLASS SCORES PROBS
 /PRIORS SIZE
 /STATISTICS=UNIVF BOXM COEFF RAW TABLE CROSSVALID
 /PLOT=MAP
 /CLASSIFY=NONMISSING POOLED.
```

Highlights of the syntax specification include the following points:

- /GROUPS declares the target variable. The target variable values must be numeric and its codes must be integers. Empty groups are ignored. Cases with values outside the value range or missing are ignored during analysis. Here, the data codes of the target variable are 1,2,3.

- `/VARIABLES` specifies the classifying variables. Coupled with `/ANALYSIS ALL`, the syntax specifies direct entry of the classifying variables. The only thing preventing entry of a classifying variable is the tolerance criterion, which prevents an input from entering if it is too highly correlated with an input already in the discriminating model.
- `/SAVE` creates added fields that contain predicted target class membership, discriminant function scores, and posterior probabilities of group membership in each target class.
- `/PRIORS` indicates that the prior probabilities of group membership are in proportion to the sizes of the target classes.
- `/CLASSIFY POOLED` means that the pooled within-groups covariance matrix is used to classify cases. This is how to specify linear discriminant analysis.

Examining the results

Running the syntax produces a lot of output. Here, we highlight and comment on some of the results.

Here is the **Analysis Case Processing Summary**:

Unweighted Cases		N	Percent
Valid		178	100.0
Excluded	Missing or out-of-range group codes	0	.0
	At least one missing discriminating variable	0	.0
	Both missing or out-of-range group codes and at least one missing discriminating variable	0	.0
	Total	0	.0
Total		178	100.0

Discriminant Analysis

The summary reports on cases missing for various reasons:

- Missing or out-of-range group codes
- At least one missing discriminating variable
- Both missing or out-of-range group codes and at least one missing discriminating variable

In our analysis, the data is complete.

Here are the **Tests of Equality of Group Means**:

Tests of Equality of Group Means					
	Wilks' Lambda	F	df1	df2	Sig.
Alcohol	.393	135.078	2	175	.000
Malic_Acid	.703	36.943	2	175	.000
Ash	.868	13.313	2	175	.000
Ash_Alcalinity	.710	35.772	2	175	.000
Magnesium	.876	12.430	2	175	.000
Total_Phenols	.483	93.733	2	175	.000
Flavanoids	.272	233.926	2	175	.000
Nonflavanoid_Phenols	.760	27.575	2	175	.000
Proanthocyanins	.743	30.271	2	175	.000
Color_Intensity	.420	120.664	2	175	.000
Hue	.463	101.317	2	175	.000
Dilution	.315	189.972	2	175	.000
Proline	.296	207.920	2	175	.000

The standard statistical test for the equality of means for three or more groups is the **F** test for equality of means. The table considers each variable one at a time. Inspection of the table shows that each variable is statistically significant, meaning that the means of each variable differ somewhere across the three wine type. A smaller **Wilks' Lambda** is associated with a larger F. Judging by the magnitudes of the **F** statistics or **Wilks' Lambda**, **Flavanoids** and **Proline** look to be the most important inputs viewed singly. As all predictors are significant one at a time, you could consider entering all variables in the discriminant analysis.

Discriminant Analysis

Here is the `Box's Test of Equality of Covariance Matrices` table:

Box's Test of Equality of Covariance Matrices

Log Determinants

Type	Rank	Log Determinant
1	13	-10.902
2	13	-2.443
3	13	-11.055
Pooled within-groups	13	-3.189

The ranks and natural logarithms of determinants printed are those of the group covariance matrices.

Test Results

Box's M		764.806
F	Approx.	3.748
	df1	182
	df2	67805.689
	Sig.	.000

Tests null hypothesis of equal population covariance matrices.

The **Log Determinants** table presents intermediate results used in the BOXM test. The **Box's M** test tests the null hypothesis that the covariance matrices of the classifying variables are equal across groups. Recall that this assumption is made in linear discriminant analysis, justifying the use of the pooled within-groups covariance matrix.

For the Wine data, the **Box's M** test is statistically significant, so we conclude that the groups differ in their covariance matrices, violating an assumption of linear discriminant analysis. It is known that the **Box's M** test is sensitive to departures from multivariate normality. You can assess this via various statistical and graphical means. In addition, if the sample size is large (not the case here), small deviations from homogeneity can lead to a significant **Box's M**.

Discriminant Analysis

In this example, given the relatively modest overall sample size as well as the small group sizes, it would not be good practice to use separate covariance matrices for classification, so we will proceed with the present analysis that specified that discriminant analysis use the pooled within-groups covariance matrix for classification.

Here is the canonical analysis, which is useful to ascertain the dimensionality of the problem:

Summary of Canonical Discriminant Functions

Eigenvalues

Function	Eigenvalue	% of Variance	Cumulative %	Canonical Correlation
1	9.082[a]	68.7	68.7	.949
2	4.128[a]	31.3	100.0	.897

a. First 2 canonical discriminant functions were used in the analysis.

Wilks' Lambda

Test of Function(s)	Wilks' Lambda	Chi-square	df	Sig.
1 through 2	.019	666.795	26	.000
2	.195	276.282	12	.000

Given a target variable with three classes and a total of 13 inputs, the dimensionality of the analysis is two.

In the `Eigenvalue` table, the **Eigenvalues** reflect the relative discriminating power of the discriminant functions. Typically, the first discriminant function accounts for the most between-groups variance in the target variable categories. The second discriminant function here accounts for the remaining between-groups variance. The percents of variance explained suggest that the first dimension is more important but does not dominate. The **canonical correlations** measure the association between the target classes and the given discriminant function. Here, the correlations are high.

Discriminant Analysis

The `Wilks' Lambda` table performs a step-down analysis. The first row, labeled **1 through 2**, assesses whether there is any discriminatory power at all. The significance level of **0.000** suggests that there is. The statistically significant lambda for this row means that we can reject the null hypothesis that the three groups have the same mean discriminant function scores, and therefore we can conclude that the model is indeed discriminating between the target classes.

The second row, labeled **2**, assesses whether the second discriminant function adds any discriminatory power when discriminant function one is taken into account. The significance level of **.000** suggests that the second discriminant function should be retained.

Here is the `Standardized Canonical Discriminant Function Coefficients` table:

Standardized Canonical Discriminant Function Coefficients

	Function 1	Function 2
Alcohol	.207	.446
Malic_Acid	-.156	.288
Ash	.095	.603
Ash_Alcalinity	-.438	-.414
Magnesium	.029	-.006
Total_Phenols	-.270	-.014
Flavanoids	.871	-.258
Nonflavanoid_Phenols	.163	-.178
Proanthocyanins	-.067	-.152
Color_Intensity	-.537	.383
Hue	.128	-.237
Dilution	.464	.021
Proline	.464	.492

Discriminant Analysis

The **Standardized Canonical Discriminant Function Coefficients** are semi-partial coefficients reflecting the unique contribution of each variable to discriminating the target classes on the indicated discriminant function. Judging by relative magnitudes, **Flavanoids**, **Color_Intensity**, **Dilution**, **Proline**, and **Ash_Alcalinity** are important in function **1**, while **Ash**, **Proline**, **Alcohol**, and **Ash_Alcalinity** are important in function **2**.

Here is the **Structure Matrix**:

Structure Matrix

	Function 1	Function 2
Flavanoids	.542*	-.022
Dilution	.477*	-.160
Total_Phenols	.342*	.045
Hue	.316*	-.245
Ash_Alcalinity	-.198*	-.113
Proanthocyanins	.194*	-.026
Nonflavanoid_Phenols	-.186*	-.013
Malic_Acid	-.184*	.167
Alcohol	.141	.575*
Proline	.356	.545*
Color_Intensity	-.167	.522*
Ash	.006	.192*
Magnesium	.065	.158*

Pooled within-groups correlations between discriminating variables and standardized canonical discriminant functions
Variables ordered by absolute size of correlation within function.

*. Largest absolute correlation between each variable and any discriminant function

Discriminant Analysis

The elements of the **Structure Matrix** are simple correlations between the inputs and discriminant functions. IBM SPSS Statistics sorts the variables and their coefficients in a way that can reveal structure in the inputs. Sizable structure coefficients in the function **1** column include those for **Flavanoids, Dilution, Total_Phenols,** and **Hue**, while sizable structure coefficients in the Function 2 column include those for **Alcohol, Proline,** and **Color_Intensity**.

Here are the (unstandardized) **Canonical Discriminant Function Coefficients**:

Canonical Discriminant Function Coefficients	Function 1	Function 2
Alcohol	.403	.872
Malic_Acid	-.165	.305
Ash	.369	2.346
Ash_Alcalinity	-.155	-.146
Magnesium	.002	.000
Total_Phenols	-.618	-.032
Flavanoids	1.661	-.492
Nonflavanoid_Phenols	1.496	-1.631
Proanthocyanins	-.134	-.307
Color_Intensity	-.355	.253
Hue	.818	-1.516
Dilution	1.158	.051
Proline	.003	.003
(Constant)	-9.231	-14.642

Unstandardized coefficients

The unstandardized discriminant coefficients are the analog to the unstandardized regression coefficients in multiple regression and are used to compute discriminant scores.

Here is the `Functions at Group Centroids` table:

Functions at Group Centroids

Type	Function 1	Function 2
1	3.422	1.692
2	.080	-2.473
3	-4.325	1.578

Unstandardized canonical discriminant functions evaluated at group means

The `Functions at Group Centroids` table presents the mean discriminant scores for each target variable category for each discriminant function.

Here is the `Prior Probabilities for Groups` table:

Prior Probabilities for Groups

		Cases Used in Analysis	
Type	Prior	Unweighted	Weighted
1	.331	59	59.000
2	.399	71	71.000
3	.270	48	48.000
Total	1.000	178	178.000

Recall that the `/PRIORS` subcommand in the preceding syntax specified that prior probabilities should be based on group sizes. These are used in classification.

Here is the table of **Classification Function Coefficients**:

Classification Function Coefficients			
	Type 1	Type 2	Type 3
Alcohol	57.351	52.373	54.127
Malic_Acid	.854	.134	2.099
Ash	39.031	28.029	35.906
Ash_Alcalinity	-.662	.465	.554
Magnesium	.502	.496	.485
Total_Phenols	-3.261	-1.061	1.531
Flavanoids	3.579	.075	-9.235
Nonflavanoid_Phenols	39.626	41.418	28.223
Proanthocyanins	1.243	2.970	2.317
Color_Intensity	-3.988	-3.856	-1.266
Hue	27.600	31.177	21.434
Dilution	22.527	18.445	13.554
Proline	.021	.000	.000
(Constant)	-523.443	-427.199	-453.783

Fisher's linear discriminant functions

There are as many sets of Fisher **Classification Function Coefficients** as there are target classes. You can use these coefficients to score an observation using its input values. Each column represents a weighted combination of the input values for a case. Plug the case's values into each function to obtain a score. Compare the three scores. Assign the observation to the target class associated with the maximum score. You can also use these coefficients to obtain posterior probabilities of group membership in each of the groups for a given set of input values.

Discriminant Analysis

Here is the `Classification Results` table:

Classification Results[a,c]

		Type	Predicted Group Membership 1	2	3	Total
Original	Count	1	59	0	0	59
		2	0	71	0	71
		3	0	0	48	48
	%	1	100.0	.0	.0	100.0
		2	.0	100.0	.0	100.0
		3	.0	.0	100.0	100.0
Cross-validated[b]	Count	1	59	0	0	59
		2	1	69	1	71
		3	0	0	48	48
	%	1	100.0	.0	.0	100.0
		2	1.4	97.2	1.4	100.0
		3	.0	.0	100.0	100.0

a. 100.0% of original grouped cases correctly classified.

b. Cross validation is done only for those cases in the analysis. In cross validation, each case is classified by the functions derived from all cases other than that case.

c. 98.9% of cross-validated grouped cases correctly classified.

Although the classification results table is one of the last tables in the output, many researchers look at it first in order to assess the discriminant analysis. If you specify `/STATISTICS CROSSVALID`, the classification results table is really a two-stacked table.

The `Original` table presents a plug-in cross-classification of the training data, with observed target class membership in the rows and predicted target class membership in the columns. Inspect either the counts or percents. In the `Original` table, you see that the classification is perfect. This is unusual and such a result deserves a closer look. It turns out that the target classes are well-separated in this instance.

Discriminant Analysis

There is a built-in optimism when a model is applied to the data used to build the model. For this reason, you might turn to some form of cross-validation. The **Cross-validated** table presents the results of leave-one-out analysis, where each case is classified by a model that involves all cases but the case in question. In the **Cross-validated** table, there are two errors in the classification out of 178 cases classified.

Recall that the /SAVE subcommand specified the saving of added fields that contain predicted target class membership, discriminant function scores, and posterior probabilities of group membership in each target class.

Here is a figure showing the added fields for a few cases:

Obs	Type	Dis_1	Dis1_1	Dis2_1	Dis1_2	Dis2_2	Dis3_2
1	1	1	4.70024	1.97914	1.00000	.00000	.00000
2	1	1	4.30196	1.17041	1.00000	.00000	.00000
3	1	1	3.42072	1.42910	1.00000	.00000	.00000
4	1	1	4.20575	4.00287	1.00000	.00000	.00000
5	1	1	1.50998	.45122	.92512	.07488	.00000

IBM SPSS Statistics uses default names for the added variables:

- **Dis_1** is the predicted target class. Compare with the observed target class in the **Type** column
- **Dis1_1** is the discriminant score for the first discriminant function
- **Dis2_1** is the discriminant score for the second discriminant function
- **Dis1_2** is the posterior probability that the observation is type 1 given its input values
- **Dis2_2** is the posterior probability that the observation is type 2 given its input values
- **Dis3_2** is the posterior probability that the observation is type 3 given its input values

As an example, consider observation 5. It is a Type 1 wine and is predicted based on its input values to be a Type 1 wine. Its discriminant function score on function *1* is *1.50998* and its discriminant function score on function *2* is *.45122*. Its posterior probability of being in group 1 is *.92512*, which is why it is predicted to be a Type 1 wine.

Here is a plot of all of the individual wines in the discriminant space:

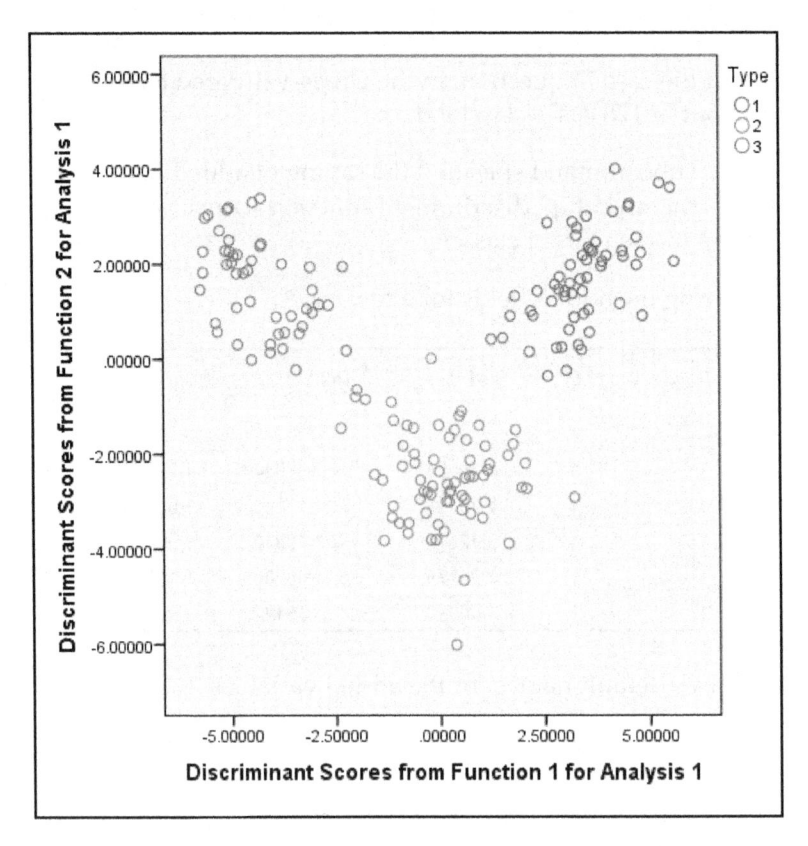

Note that discriminant function 1 does a pretty good job of separating wine Type 3 from 2 and from 1 and Type 2 from Type 1, albeit with some overlap between 3 and 2 and also 2 and 1. Discriminant function 2 provides additional discrimination as group 2 has largely negative scores on discriminant function 2, while the other two groups have largely positive scores on discriminant function 2. Taken together, the groups are well-separated. In another context, involving some other problem and data, discriminant analysis might not separate groups so well.

Discriminant Analysis

Here is a plot of the variables with coordinates given by the standardized canonical discriminant function coefficients:

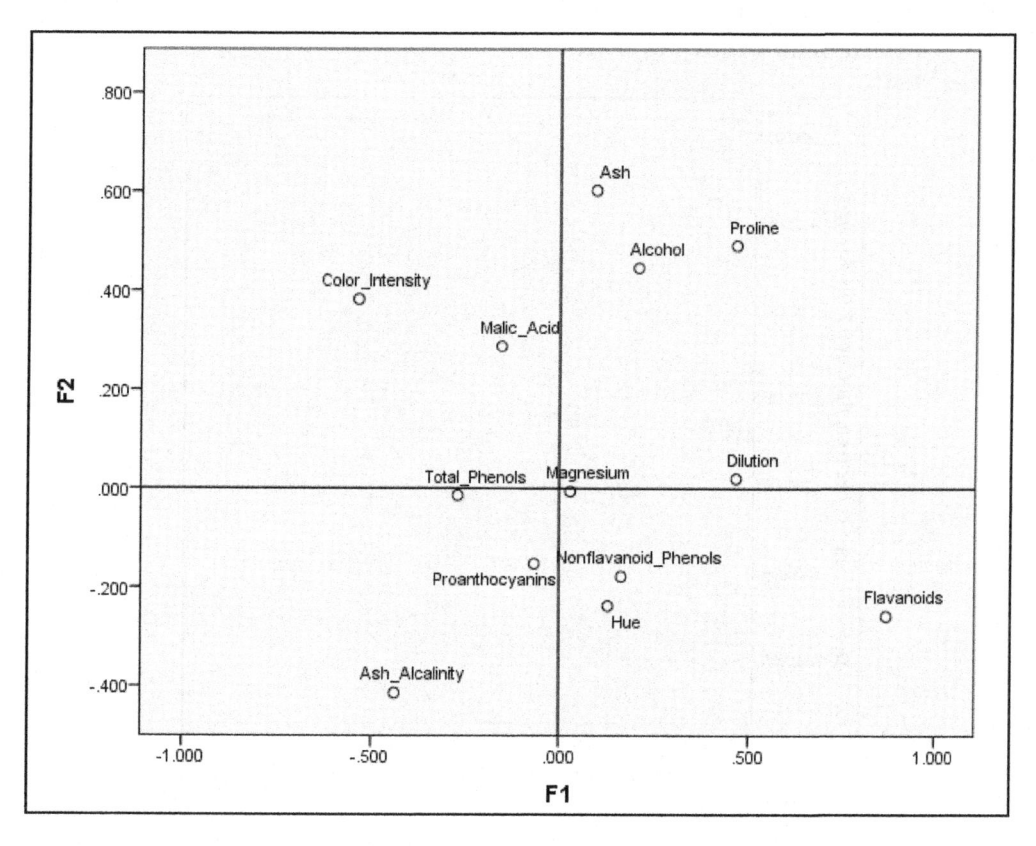

Interpret this plot in the light of the previous plot. Variables such as **Flavanoids**, **Color_Intensity**, **Dilution**, **Proline**, and **Ash_Alcalinity** drive left-right separation along function 1, while variables such as **Ash**, **Proline**, **Alcohol**, and **Ash_Alcalinity** drive top-down separation along function 2.

Here is an example of how to read the two charts together.

Discriminant Analysis

Note the direction of **Color-Intensity** relative to the origin--up and to the left. The most extreme positive value on **Color_Intensity** is a value of 13, and is associated with observation number 159. In the plot of the individual wines, that observation is up and to the left--it is labeled in the following chart:

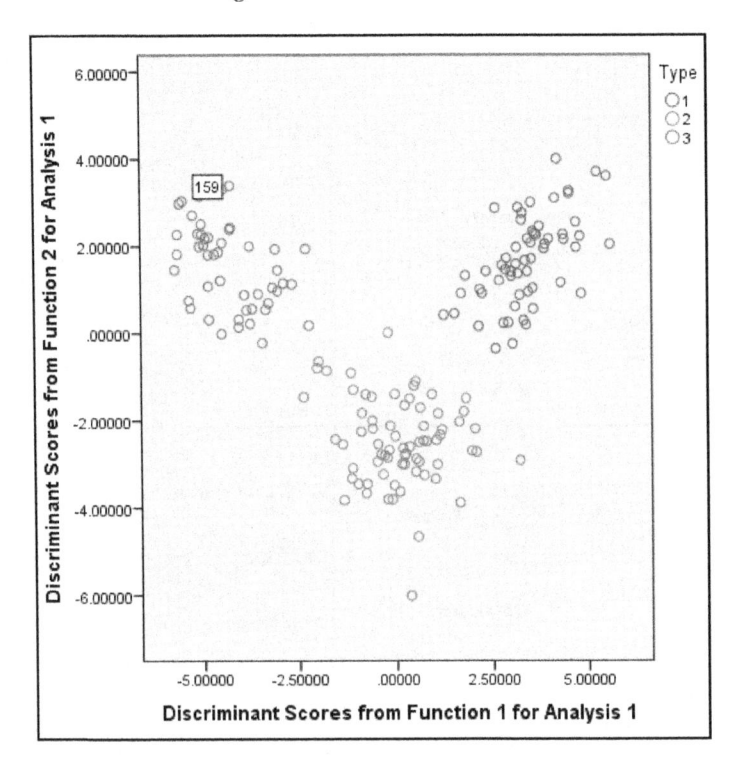

In the preceding chart, the label for observation number 159 is just to the right of the point.

Scoring new observations

After you have developed and evaluated a model based on historical data, you can apply the model to new data in order to make predictions. In predictive analytics, this is called **scoring**. You score cases for which the outcome is not yet known. Your evaluation of the historical data gives you a sense of how the model is likely to perform in the new situation.

Discriminant Analysis

One way to implement scoring is to make use of the classification function coefficients. Here is the syntax in which the **classification function coefficients** are used in `compute`:

```
compute cf1=57.351*alcohol+.854*malic_acid+39.031*ash
  -.662*ash_alcalinity+.502*magnesium-3.261*total_phenols
  +3.579*flavanoids+39.626*nonflavanoid_phenols+1.243*proanthocyanins
  -3.988*color_intensity+27.600*hue+22.527*dilution
  +.021*proline-523.443.
compute cf2=52.373*alcohol+.134*malic_acid+28.029*ash
  +.465*ash_alcalinity+.496*magnesium-1.061*total_phenols
  +.075*flavanoids+41.418*nonflavanoid_phenols+2.970*proanthocyanins
  -3.865*color_intensity+31.177*hue+18.445*dilution
  -.00016*proline-427.199.
compute cf3=54.127*alcohol+2.099*malic_acid+35.906*ash
  +.554*ash_alcalinity+.485*magnesium+1.531*total_phenols
  -9.235*flavanoids+28.223*nonflavanoid_phenols+2.317*proanthocyanins
  -1.266*color_intensity+21.434*hue+13.554*dilution
  -.00045*proline-453.783.
compute pp1=exp(cf1)/( exp(cf1)+exp(cf2)+exp(cf3) ).
compute pp2=exp(cf2)/( exp(cf1)+exp(cf2)+exp(cf3) ).
compute pp3=exp(cf3)/( exp(cf1)+exp(cf2)+exp(cf3) ).
execute.
```

The first three `compute` commands are direct translations of the classification function coefficients into `compute`. The next three `compute` commands compute posterior probabilities of being wine Type 1, 2, or 3, respectively. The observation would be classified into the group for which the posterior probability is the highest.

> **TIP**
> For reasons of space, the coefficients in the `compute` statements are represented to three decimal places. However, for certain problems, you might need more precision than three places in order to obtain accurate classification.

Another way to score new observations is via the `/SELECT` subcommand. As documented, `/SELECT` limits cases used in the analysis phase to those with a specified value for any one variable. To implement scoring, compute a new variable that is equal to 1, say, for cases in the training sample and 0, say, for records to be scored. SPSS Statistics will classify all cases, whether selected or not. If you also specify `/SAVE`, you can obtain predicted group membership and posterior probabilities of group membership for both selected and unselected cases.

Discriminant Analysis

Here is how you might use the syntax for the scoring:

```
DISCRIMINANT
  /GROUPS=Type(1 3)
  /VARIABLES=Alcohol Malic_Acid Ash
  Ash_Alcalinity Magnesium Total_Phenols
  Flavanoids Nonflavanoid_Phenols Proanthocyanins
  Color_Intensity Hue Dilution Proline
  /SELECT Selectvar(1)
  /ANALYSIS ALL
  /SAVE=CLASS SCORES PROBS
  /PRIORS SIZE
  /STATISTICS=UNIVF BOXM COEFF RAW TABLE CROSSVALID
  /PLOT=MAP
  /CLASSIFY=NONMISSING POOLED.
```

The preceding syntax assumes that there is a variable named `Selectvar` that has 1 for observations in the training sample.

Summary

Discriminant analysis is a standard statistical approach to classification. Here are the takeaways from the presentation of discriminant analysis on the Wine data:

- Discriminant analysis makes assumptions of multivariate normality within groups and homogeneity of covariance matrices across groups. You can use both the Discriminant procedure and IBM SPSS Statistics more generally to assess these assumptions.
- As the analyst, you must make decisions regarding prior probabilities, whether to classify based on pooled or separate covariance matrices and what dimensionality represents the data.
- The **classification results** table shows you overall classification accuracy and classification accuracy by class. You should assess accuracy not only on the training data, but also via leave-one-out analysis or cross-validation via the /SELECT subcommand.
- The standardized canonical discriminant function coefficients and structure matrix help you understand what variables drive group separation by dimension.
- The classification function coefficients enable you to classify new observations based on input values. A second approach is the use of /SELECT to score *unselected* cases based on the model that is fit to *selected* cases.

Index

A

ADD FILES
  example of combining cases 166, 167, 168
aggregated file
  matching, to find records 188, 189
aggregated variables
  used, for creating fields 176, 177
aggregation
  data, preparing for 182, 183, 184
  used, for adding fields to file 172, 173, 174, 175
ANOVA procedure 269, 270, 271

B

bar charts
  obtaining, with frequencies 94, 96, 97, 98, 99
Bartlett's test of sphericity 335
basic SPSS session
  executing 17, 18, 19, 20
bivariate 276
boxplot
  about 63
  creating, chart builder used 108, 109
Brown-Forsythe tests 259

C

chart builder
  used, for creating boxplot 108, 109
  used, for creating graphs 103
Chi-square test, with crosstabs
  about 222
  context sensitive help 225
  expected counts 223, 224
classical linear regression model
  assumptions 298
  motor trend example 299
cluster analysis

overview 362, 363
  with four clusters 371, 372, 373, 374, 375, 376, 377, 378
cluster profiling 387, 388
coding issues
  discovering, frequencies used 57, 59
columns
  rows, restructuring to 190, 191
COMPUTE command 143, 145
correlations
  about 273
  partial correlations 291, 292
  Pearson correlations 275, 276
  rank order correlations 289, 290
  versus mean differences 279
  visualizing, with scatterplots 287, 288, 289
crosstab pivot table
  editing 209, 210, 211, 212, 213
crosstab
  Chi-square test, using with 222
  differences, testing in column proportions 205, 207, 208
  interval with nominal association measure 228
  layer variable, adding 214, 215
  layer, adding 217, 220
  nominal measure of association 230
  ordinal measures of association 226

D

data check 24
data overview
  accessing 24
  organizing 24
data restructuring techniques
  patient test data example 192, 193, 194, 195, 196, 197
data

preparing, for aggregation 182, 183, 184
delimited text data files
  reading 28, 29, 30
delimiter 28
descriptive analysis 366
descriptive discriminant analysis 402
descriptive statistics
  for numeric fields 50, 51, 52
descriptives display order
  controlling 54, 55
descriptives
  for standardized scores 75, 76
  missing values 86, 87
discriminant analysis setup
  about 406
  dimensionality 407, 408
  pooled 407
  priors 407
  separate 407
  syntax, for wine example 408, 409
discriminant analysis
  about 401
  assumptions 403
  descriptive discriminant analysis 402
  example data 404
  predictive discriminant analysis 403
  results, examining 409, 410, 411, 413, 414, 415, 416, 417, 418, 419, 420, 421, 422
DO IF command 148, 149
drilling down 113
dummy variable
  creating, RECODE command used 137, 138, 139, 140

E

ELSE IF command 151
Excel files
  reading 25, 26, 27
exploratory data analysis 72
explore procedure
  employing, in SPSS 60, 61
  for boxplot 76, 77, 78, 79
  for extreme values 76, 77
explore
  boxplot 63

leaf plot 62
stem 62
used, for checking subgroup patterns 64, 65, 66, 67

F

factor analysis (FA)
  about 325, 345
  and principal components analysis (PCA), selecting between 326
fields
  creating, aggregated variables used 176, 177
  rescaling, RECODE command used 141
  transforming, in SPSS 136
filter variable
  using 126
filtering 113
frequencies
  about 33, 34
  bar charts, obtaining with 94, 96, 97, 98, 99
  for histogram 72, 73, 74
  for percentile values 72, 73, 74
  histogram, obtaining with 99, 100, 102
  missing values 85, 86
  used, for verifying missing data patterns 59
frequency distribution 57

G

General Social Survey (GSS) data 94
graphical summary
  of data 406
graphs, in SPSS procedures
  about 94
  bar charts 94
  boxplot 108
  histogram 99
  scatterplot 103
graphs
  creating, chart builder used 103

H

Help option, ANOVA
  Dunnet 266
  Scheffe 265
  Tamhane's T2 266

Tukey 265
hierarchical cluster analysis
  descriptive analysis 366
  example 365
  SPSS statistics code 366, 369, 370
histogram
  obtaining, with frequencies 99, 100, 102
homogeneity of variance test
  about 250
  subsets, comparing 251, 252

I

IBM SPSS Statistics files
  reading 32
  saving 30, 31
IF command 146, 147, 148
If condition is satisfied case
  about 116
  combined with Copy 121, 122
  combined with Delete unselected cases 122
  combined, with Filter 117, 118, 119, 120
independent samples t-test 249, 250
influential points 313
interquartile range (IQR) 79
interquartile range value 63

K

K-means cluster analysis example
  about 378
  descriptive analysis 379, 380, 381, 382, 383
  of Old Faithful data 383, 384, 385, 386

L

leaf plot 62
level
  aggregating 178, 180, 181
licensing, SPSS
  available options, confirming 14
listwise correlation matrices
  versus pairwise correlation matrices 281
listwise missing values
  versus pairwise missing values 280

M

Mahalanobis distance 81
maximum likelihood (ML) 327
mean 74
mean differences
  versus correlations 279
means procedure
  about 236, 237, 238
  second variable, adding 239, 240, 241
  strength of nonlinear relationships, testing 244, 245
  test of linearity example 241, 242, 243, 244
measure, variable properties
  nominal 40
  ordinal 40
  scale 40
median 74, 79
menu
  versus syntax 25
missing data 84
missing data patterns
  verifying, frequencies used 59
missing data, concerns
  bias 84
  statistical efficiency 84
missing value patterns 87, 88, 90
missing values command 24
missing values
  in descriptives 86, 87
  in frequencies 85, 86
  replacing 90, 91, 92
motor trend example
  associations between target and predictors, exploring 300
  for classical linear regression model 299
multiple regression
  about 317
  reference link 318
multivariate outliers
  detecting 80, 81, 83, 84

N

Northwind sample database 155, 156

O

observations
  scoring 422, 423, 424
one-to-many merge
  about 164, 165
  Customer table 156, 157
  Customer-Orders relationship 159
  example 156
  Order table 158
  SPSS code 160, 161, 162
one-to-one merge 163
one-way analysis of variance
  about 258
  planned comparisons 260, 261, 262, 264
ordinary least squares regression 298
outliers 72
Output radio buttons 115

P

paired t-test 252
paired t-test split
  by gender 254, 256
pairwise correlation matrices
  versus listwise correlation matrices 281
pairwise missing values
  versus listwise missing values 280
parameters
  setting, within SPSS software 16
partial correlations
  about 291, 292
  second control variable, adding 294
Pearson correlations
  about 275, 276
  testing for significance 278
percentages, in crosstabs 201, 202, 204, 205
post hoc comparisons 265, 266, 267, 268
predictive discriminant analysis 403
principal axis factoring (PAF) 327
principal components analysis (PCA)
  about 325
  and factor analysis (FA), selecting between 326
  FACTOR command 331
  factorability of data, assessing 332
  of crime variables 336
  simple descriptive analysis 330
  SPSS code 331
  two-component solution 340
  violent crime example 328
purchasing power parity (PPP) 278

Q

Q-Q plot approach 83, 84

R

random sample of cases
  selecting 127, 129
rank order correlations 289, 290
RECODE command
  about 137
  example 142
  used, for creating dummy variables 137, 138, 139, 140
  used, for rescaling field 141
reduced correlation matrix 347
rows
  restructuring, to columns 190, 191

S

sample 127
sample data
  obtaining 49
scatterplot
  building 103, 105
  correlations, visualizing with 287, 288, 289
Schwarz's Bayesian Criterion (BIC) 389
scoring 422
second level aggregation
  about 185
  aggregated data, preparing for further usage 185, 187
Select Cases dialog box
  about 113
  filter variable 126
  Temporary command 123, 124
Select cases
  based on case range 124
  based on time range 124
  example 117
  IF condition is satisfied 115

Select radio buttons 114
simple regression model
　casewise diagnostics, interpreting 313
　casewise diagnostics, saving 313
　fitting 304
　interpreting 304
　residual analysis 309
single sample t-test 246, 247, 248
singleton 372
Split File 129, 131
SPSS code
　for one-to-many merge 160, 161, 162
SPSS installation utility 8
SPSS procedure
　ANOVA procedure 269, 270, 271
　homogeneity of variance test 250
　independent samples t-test 249, 250
　means procedure 236, 237, 238
　means, comparing 236
　one-way analysis of variance 257, 258
　paired t-test 254
　single sample t-test 246, 247
SPSS software
　parameters, setting within 16
SPSS Statistics cluster analysis procedures
　CLUSTER 363
　QUICK CLUSTER 364
　TWOSTEP CLUSTER 364
SPSS statistics code
　for hierarchical cluster analysis 366, 369, 370
SPSS Statistics commands
　files, merging 154, 155
SPSS transformation commands
　COMPUTE 143
　DO IF/ELSE IF 148
　IF 146
　pointers 151
　RECODE 137
SPSS
　explore procedure, employing 60, 61
　fields, transforming 136
　launching 15
　licensing 11, 13
　Python, installing for scripting 9, 10
　using 15

standardization 75
statistical summary
　of data 405
stem 62
subgroup patterns
　checking, explore used 64, 65, 66, 67
syntax
　variable properties, adding via 42, 43
　versus menu 25
system-missing value 39

T

table
　pivoting, to enhance correlation matrices 282, 284, 285
Temporary command 123, 124
text file 28
trimmed matrix
　creating 286
Two-tailed test 276
twostep cluster analysis example 389, 390, 391, 392, 393, 395, 396, 397, 398, 399

V

value labels 25
variable properties
　about 25, 34, 35
　adding, to Variable View 41
　adding, via syntax 42, 43
　align 40
　columns 40
　decimals 38
　defining 44, 45, 46
　label 38
　measure 40
　missing 39
　name 36
　role 41
　type 37
　values 38, 39
　width 37
Variance Inflation Factors 334

W
Weight command
    using 132
    weighting 113

Made in United States
North Haven, CT
01 April 2022